THE PLAYS AND
POEMS OF
Philip Massinger

THE PLAYS AND POEMS OF

Philip Massinger

EDITED BY

PHILIP EDWARDS

AND

COLIN GIBSON

VOLUME IV

OXFORD

AT THE CLARENDON PRESS

1976

Oxford University Press, Ely House, London W. 1
GLASGOW NEW YORK TORONTO MELBOURNE WELLINGTON
CAPE TOWN IBADAN NAIROBI DAR ES SALAAM LUSAKA ADDIS ABABA
DELHI BOMBAY CALCUTTA MADRAS KARACHI DACCA
KUALA LUMPUR SINGAPORE HONG KONG TOKYO

ISBN 0 19 811894 5

Printed in Great Britain
at the University Press, Oxford
by Vivian Ridler
Printer to the University

CONTENTS

VOLUME IV

POEMS (*cont.*)

THE CITY MADAM

INTRODUCTION

(a) *Date*

Sir Henry Herbert's production licence of 25 May 1632, establishes the latest date for the composition of *The City Madam*: '*The City Madam*, by Philip Massinger, licensed for the King's Company'.[1] Plays were normally licensed soon after their completion, but in 1885 Fleay asserted that *The City Madam* was a revision by Massinger of a play written by Jonson about 1619.[2] That the comedy is wholly Massinger's work is now accepted without dispute, but several scholars, including Schelling, Ward, Farrier, Kirk and Dunn, have argued for a date of composition about 1625, if not earlier.

Fleay questioned the evidence of Herbert's licence because he had observed that a passage in the Prologue to *The Guardian* states that Massinger was writing for the stage once more after a period of 'two years silence', following the failure of two of his plays.[3] *The Guardian* was licensed on 31 October 1633, so Fleay argued that *The City Madam* must have been written before 1632, and that the two unsuccessful plays must have been *Believe As You List* and *The Unfortunate Piety*, licensed on 6 May and 13 June 1631 respectively. *The Emperor of the East* has also been mentioned in this connexion, for the commendatory verses indicate that it met with a bad public reception; it was licensed on 11 March 1631.

In his 1934 Princeton thesis, Rudolph Kirk attempted to date *The City Madam* by means of its allusions to dress and to fashion;

[1] Adams, *Herbert*, p. 34.

[2] 'On the Chronology of the Plays of Fletcher and Massinger', *Englische Studien*, ix, 12–35; Fleay developed his theory in *A Biographical Chronicle of the English Drama* (*1559–1642*), 1891, i. 225–7.

[3] The Prologue to *The Guardian*, ll. 1–9; there is further discussion of the matter in the General Introduction (vol. i, pp. xli–xlii), and in the introduction to *The Guardian* (below, p. 107).

on the authority of M. C. Linthicum, and with some reservations, he concluded that the play was written about 1625.[1]

There are arguments against all of the earlier datings of *The City Madam*. There may be no contradiction between the date of Herbert's licence and the statement in the *Guardian* prologue; Gifford was the first to suggest that the period of seventeen months between the licensing of *The City Madam* and *The Guardian* might have been near enough to two years for the writer of the prologue,[2] and it has been suggested that *The City Madam* was one of the two stage failures to which the prologue alludes.[3] Further, *The Guardian* was not printed until 1655, and its prologue may have become attached to the play text by mistake, as were several of the prologues published in the Beaumont and Fletcher Folio of 1647. Again, Bentley's doubts about the accuracy with which allusions to fashion can be dated, 'especially when they are dependent, as a number of these are, on a nice discrimination of the social class and sophistication of the characters involved' (iv. 772), are cogent ones. As Kirk himself saw, if the play was written well before 1632, there is the question why it was not licensed on completion; and it is generally accepted that Malone's transcripts of Herbert's licences are our most reliable evidence for the dating of Caroline plays.

The most recent editors of *The City Madam*, Craik and Hoy, with some reservations accept 1632 as the likeliest date of composition, and there is some positive evidence that Massinger's comedy was written after 1629.

At III. i. 22–9, there is a reference to the arrival together of a French and a Venetian ambassador 'after a long Vacation'. As I have shown elsewhere,[4] it is tolerably certain that this passage alludes to the arrival of Chasteauneuf and Soranzo within a few days of each other in July 1629, after a two year's break in diplomatic relations between England and France. Other allusions discussed in the same article, to peaceful and profitable trade with the Indies and with the Barbary States, as well as to the rigors of the contemporary search for the North-West passage,[5] best fit the early 1630s.

[1] *The City-Madam, A Comedy by Philip Massinger*, Princeton Studies in English, 10, pp. 1–6; P. H. Farrier had earlier favoured the same date in his unpublished doctoral edition of the play, Kentucky Wesleyan College, 1929, pp. 20–32.

[2] Gifford, 1805, iv. 120.

[3] The initial reception of the comedy is discussed on pp. 10–11.

[4] 'Massinger's London Merchant and the Date of *The City Madam*', *MLR*, lxv (1970), 737–49.

[5] *The City Madam*, I. i. 1–5; IV. i. 87–91; II. iii. 12–13.

The pretence (in III. ii) that Sir John Frugal has travelled to the Jesuit centre of Louvain—apparently without difficulty—also implies a date of composition close to 1632, for although there had long been an illegal and hazardous route for Catholics to the English colleges in France and the Low Countries,[1] the peace treaties of 1629 and 1630 with France and Spain brought a large measure of official tolerance after a period of intense persecution. The breach between Charles and Parliament in 1629 contributed to the improvement in conditions for Catholics in England, and G. Davies gathers evidence of 'a distinct Catholic revival in the 1630's', in *The Early Stuarts (1603–1660)*, 2nd edn. 1959, 209–10. Without such a change in attitudes, Massinger could hardly have given his comedy its highly unusual Roman Catholic colouring.[2]

To sum up, although the Prologue to *The Guardian* cannot be ignored, it does not provide an irrefutable argument for a date of composition very much in advance of the licensing date of *The City Madam*, and the weight of evidence is for 1632, rather than 1625 or even earlier.

(b) *Sources*

No single literary source for *The City Madam* has ever been found, and it is very likely that the plot structure is largely an original one, drawing on elements in plays by Shakespeare and Jonson, as well as making a fresh use of incidents and characters taken from *A New Way to Pay Old Debts* (1625).

One obvious source for the idea of the Sir John and Luke Frugal narrative is Shakespeare's *Measure for Measure*,[3] though each dramatist works it out in very different ways. In both plays the true character of a subordinate is revealed when he is left with absolute authority by his master, who then returns in disguise to watch his behaviour and prevent any real harm. With Duke Vincentio's words, 'hence shall we see, / If power change purpose, what our seemers be'

[1] See D. Mathews, *The Age of Charles I*, 1951, p. 135, and the note to *The Fatal Dowry*, II. ii. 120–2.

[2] This aspect of *The City Madam* is discussed by Dunn, pp. 186–8.

[3] Noted by T. W. Craik, who gives the fullest account to date of the sources of the comedy in his edition of *The City Madam*, 1964, pp. ix–x. Joe Lee Davis has suggested that Massinger 'borrowed his intrigue from that of Middleton's Quomodo in *Michaelmas Term* and Gullman in *A Mad World, My Masters*' (*The Sons of Ben*, Detroit, 1967, p. 99), but this is too sweeping a claim.

(*Measure for Measure*, I. iii. 53–4), may be compared Sir John Frugal's:

> Outward gloss
> Often deceivs, may it not prove so in him,
> And yet my long acquaintance with his nature
> Renders me doubtful, but that shall not make
> A breach between us: Let us in to dinner,
> And what trust, or imployment you think fit
> Shall be conferred upon him: If he prove
> True gold in the touch, I'le be no mourner for it.
> (I. iii. 152–9)

However, Luke's particular character traits, his obsequiousness and triumphant revenge on his persecutors, as well as the nexus of pride and wealth, derive from the figure of Marrall, in *A New Way to Pay Old Debts*: 'The Ideot; the Patch; the Slaue . . . your Drudge, / Can now anatomize you . . . and leuell with the earth / Your hill of pride' (V. i. 215–21). Other parallels confirm the reworking of material from the earlier play. Luke's 'toughnesse of nature' is expressed in the same language as Overreach's;[1] the scenes in which Luke and Sir John deal with their debtors have a predecessor in Welborne's treatment of his debtors and creditors (IV. ii); Sir John's indignation at the quarrel between Lacy and Plenty parallels Lady Alworth's anger at the quarrelling Overreach and Welborne;[2] and Lady Frugal and her daughters' attitude towards title and rank may be seen as an elaboration of Overreach's ambition for his daughter Margaret (II. i. 74–83). Even the name Frugal had already been used for a wealthy landowner briefly mentioned in *A New Way to Pay Old Debts*, II. i. 28–48.

The central scene for the exhibition of the Frugal women's pride (II. ii) is one of a number of 'proviso' scenes in contemporary plays, the earliest of which is probably Fletcher's in *The Woman's Prize* (1611), II. vi.[3] However, Massinger may well have been prompted to introduce such a scene by the success of Brome's play *The Northern Lass*, first produced in July 1629; it includes a scene (I. vi) in which the City Widow, Mistress Fitchow, reads out a long 'remembrance

[1] Cf. *The City Madam*, V. iii. 30–70 with *A New Way to Pay Old Debts*, IV. i. 111–33; *Volpone*, I. i. 48–51 lies behind both passages.

[2] Cf. *The City Madam*, I. ii. 27 ff. with *A New Way to Pay Old Debts*, V. i. 114 ff.

[3] An incomplete list is given in 'D'Urfé's *L'Astrée* and the 'Proviso' scenes in Dryden's Comedy', K. M. Lynch, *PQ*, iv (1925), 302–8.

for after mariage. *Imprimis*, To haue the whole sway of the house, and all domesticall affaires . . .'.[1]

Stargaze's astrological cant imitates that of Jonson's Norbret, in *The Bloody Brother*, IV. ii, a play which Massinger himself probably revised in the late 1620s.[2] Jonson supplied Massinger with ideas for other parts of *The City Madam*. Luke's ecstatic apostrophe to his newly acquired wealth is modelled on Volpone's address to his riches,[3] and as Craik pointed out, Ramble and Scuffle's flight 'out at the back-door', in III. i, imitates the flight of the rogues in *The Alchemist*, V. iv. 132–6:

> All I can doe
> Is to helpe you ouer the wall, o' the back-side;
> Or lend you a sheet, to saue your veluet gowne, Dol.
> Here will be officers, presently; bethinke you,
> Of some course sodainely to scape the dock.

Much of the abuse hurled in the same scene is borrowed from the opening dialogue of *The Alchemist*, but the main incidents—the women's reluctance to admit the roarers, and the quarrel in which weapons are drawn—are modelled on Doll Tearsheet and the Hostess's encounter with Pistol, in *2 Henry IV*, II. iv.

For the social and topographical detail of *The City Madam* Massinger needed no source other than his own observation and experience of London life; as evidence of his concern to make his portrait of a London merchant as realistic as possible I have traced the career of the prominent merchant Sir William Cockayne, in the article cited on page 2. The introduction of Indians and Indian disguises into the comedy was taken by Fleay to have been prompted by memories of Pocohontas's visit to London in 1616; a more probable and more recent dramatic source is Aurelian Townshend's masque *Tempe Restored*, which was produced at Whitehall on 14 February 1632, and which included an Antimasque of 'Indians and Barbarians, who naturally are bestiall . . . *adoring their Pagode*'.[4]

1 Shirley may have admired the same scene; his comedy *Hyde Park*, licensed within a month of *The City Madam* (on 20 Apr.), also contains a 'proviso' scene (II. iv), as does Marmion's *A Fine Companion* (1632–3).

2 See Bentley, iii. 404–6.

3 *Volpone*, I. i. 1 ff. L. C. Knights, *Drama and Society in the Age of Jonson*, 1962, 225–6, points out other minor borrowings from *Epicœne* and *Sejanus*. There is little to support Gilchrist's idea that Massinger was indebted to the opening lines of Marlowe's *The Jew of Malta* (Dodsley's *Select Collection of Old Plays*, ed. J. P. Collier, viii (1825), 252).

4 *Tempe Restored* (1632), B1r. Bentley, v. 1229–30, prints contemporary accounts of

(c) *Text*

The City Madam was published in 1658, in quarto, for Andrew Pennycuicke, 'one of the Actors'. Twenty-one of the thirty copies of this edition of the play recorded to date in public libraries and institutions have a variant title-page, dated 1659. As he had done with *The Sun's Darling*, issued with title-pages dated 1656 and 1657, Pennycuicke had copies printed with at least five different dedications, in hopes of receiving payment from several patrons.[1] Of the known copies, twenty-five are dedicated 'To the truly Noble and virtuous / Lady *Ann*, Countess of *Oxford*'; two copies (British Museum, Ashley 1127, and University of Chicago) are dedicated 'To the truly Noble / M^r LEE / ESQUIRE'; and one copy each is dedicated 'To the truly Noble / THOMAS FREAKE / ESQUIRE' (Bodleian, Malone Q 23), 'To the truly Noble / RICHARD STEADWEL / ESQUIRE' (Bodleian, Malone Q 57), and 'To the truly Noble / JOHN WRATH / ESQUIRE' (Bodleian, Malone 185 (4)). The dedication to the Countess of Oxford is found on copies dated both 1658 and 1659; the other dedications are found only on copies dated 1658. There are two attendant changes in the text of the dedication: either 'LADY!' or 'SIR!' at line 3, and either 'MADAM' or 'SIR' at line 19. There is insufficient evidence to determine the order in which the dedications were printed; in the present edition, the standard address to Lady Ann replaces the dedication to John Wrath in the copy-text.

From a study of the headpieces and the ornamental initial T found in *The City Madam* (A2^r; B1^r) and in several works printed by Jane Bell, Kirk was able to demonstrate that the play was printed in her shop.[2] A London printer and bookseller, active between 1650–9, she had already printed *The Sun's Darling* for Bird and Pennycuicke. There is no entry of *The City Madam* in the Stationers' Register, probably because Pennycuicke was not a member of the Company and therefore had no rights to protect, but the comedy is named in

this 'sumptuous masque, performed with wonderfully rich decorations before a numerous assembly'; it is tempting to conjecture that some of the Indian costumes found their way on to the stage at Blackfriars.

[1] Other instances of this sharp practice are discussed in 'Some notes on Authors and Patrons in Tudor and Stuart Times', F. P. Wilson, in *Joseph Quincy Adams Memorial Studies*, Washington, 1948, pp. 553–61; for *The Sun's Darling* see *The Dramatic Works of Thomas Dekker*, edited by Fredson Bowers, 1961, iv. 1–9.

[2] Kirk, pp. 8–11. See also Kirk's 'Jane Bell: Printer at the East End of Christ-Church', in *Essays in Dramatic Literature: The Parrott Presentation Volume*, Princeton, 1935, pp. 443–54.

booksellers' catalogues and lists of 1661, 1663, 1670, 1671, and 1700.[1] From now on this edition (whether dated 1658 or 1659 on the title-page) will be referred to as *58*; the title-page is reproduced on page 17.

58 is in quarto, A², B–L⁴ (42 leaves, paged 1–80, commencing with B1ʳ); see Greg, *Bibliography*, no. 788 (ii. 892–3). The contents are: A1ʳ, *title*; A1ᵛ, 'The Actors names.'; A2ʳ, *dedication begins, as detailed above, and ends* (A2ᵛ) *signed* '*Andrew Pennycuicke.*'; B1ʳ, 'THE City-Madam, A COMEDIE.', *text begins*; L4ᵛ, *text ends*, 'FINIS.'. The text is set in roman, 20 lines measuring approximately 79 mm. There is a standard of thirty-eight lines to the page (thirty-nine on E1ʳ, which carries a large amount of prose).

Two skeletons were used in the printing, one for each inner and one for each outer forme. The sets of running titles for B(o) and (i) are exchanged for C (i) and (o), and retain these positions for the remaining sheets, with remarkably little disturbance. The quarto is carefully printed by a competent workman, supplying a text which is generally sound and free from serious corruption. It is reasonably certain that the text was set up by one compositor throughout. In spelling and other characteristics, he strongly resembles the man identified by Hinman as Compositor A, who set up half of the text of *The Sun's Darling*.[2] For instance, there is a consistent preference for medial and final *ie* to *y* (*air*, *eie*, *daies*, *crie*, *toies*), for final *k* or *ck* rather than *que* (*physick*, *musick*, *stoicks*, *Mechanicks*, *cambrick*), and for *-ear* rather than *-eer*. Excluding the accidental shifting of type in the line, five of the twenty-two formes are variant: A (o) and (i), D (o), G (i) and K (o). All but two of the twenty-eight press corrections noted are confined to D (o) and G (i); the multiple dedications account for most of the other variant readings. One manuscript correction has been found on I1ʳ in several copies, dated both 1658 and 1659. At IV. ii. 113, 'Boman' has been altered to 'Roman' by a heavy curved stroke through the lower loop of the B. The likelihood is that this correction was made in the printing house.[3]

[1] Greg, *Bibliography*, ii. 893; iii. 1151, 1187, 1342; iv. 1655.

[2] 'Principles Governing the Use of Variant Spelling as Evidence of Alternate Setting by Two Compositors', C. Hinman, *The Library*, 4th Series, xxi (1941), 78–103.

[3] 'Pen-and-ink Corrections in Books of the Seventeenth Century', A. K. McIlwraith, *RES*, vii (1931), 204–7. Copies known to have this correction are Bodleian, Malone Q 23 and Malone 185 (4); British Museum, Ashley 1128; Worcester College; University of Chicago; a copy with the bookplate of Sir Thomas Hanmer, Bart., formerly in the possession of Dobell.

The printer's manuscript was undoubtedly the prompt copy of *The City Madam.* The evidence for this lies in the number of anticipatory stage directions, of the kind found in the manuscript of *Believe As You List*, which have been printed in the margin of the quarto as the compositor found them.[1] Several scholars have gathered evidence that the prompt book was Massinger's own manuscript of the play, annotated by the book-keeper, again as was the manuscript of *Believe As You List.* A. K. McIlwraith drew attention to the survival of some spellings characteristic of the dramatist in *58*;[2] to his examples, *perfit*, *sinck*, and *trunck*, might be added many more, such as *carkase*, *Divel*, *principall*, *cyndars*, and *morall.* The uncorrected 'Hymas' (I. iii. 131) is an easy misreading of Massinger's idiosyncratic 'Hym as'. W. J. Lawrence noted two stage directions showing traces of the use of points rather than commas in lists of names, as in the manuscript of *Believe As You List*,[3] and Cyrus Hoy, in his edition of *The City Madam*, 1964, p. xx, pointed out that many of the stage directions within the text have the fullness of an author's rather than a book-keeper's directions: '*Enter Star-gaze, Ladie, Anne, Mary, Milliscent, in several postures, with looking-glasses at their girdles.*'; '*Enter Lady, Anne, Mary, in course habit weeping.*' The Latin direction, '*Exeunt omnes preter Luke.*', and the very long and detailed direction at V. iii. 59 confirm the point. Massinger, rather than the stage manager, specified '*Music*', '*wanton Musicke*', '*Sad musicke*'; with such vague requirements, with their insistence on mood, compare the terse, practical annotation '*Cornets flor.*' in the margin at IV. ii. 31.

There are copies of *The City Madam* dated 1658 in the following libraries and institutions: the Bodleian Library (3 copies); the British Museum (2 copies); the University of Chicago; the Henry E. Huntington Library; Princeton University; and Yale University. There are copies dated 1659 in the Bodleian Library; the Boston Public Library; the British Museum (4 copies); Columbia University; the Library of Congress; the Folger Shakespeare Library; Harvard University; the Henry E. Huntington Library; the University of London; the Newberry Library; the University of

[1] Clear instances are found at I. ii. 143, IV. iv. 131, and V. i. 95. In his edition of *The City Madam*, 1964, pp. xxi–xxiv, T. W. Craik has usefully collected and discussed all the book-keeper's annotations.

[2] 'The Printer's Copy for *The City-Madam*', *MLN*, xl (1935), 173–4.

[3] *Those Nut-Cracking Elizabethans*, 1935, pp. 194–205: the instances are *The City Madam*, IV. i. 118 SD., and IV. ii. SD.

Pennsylvania; the National Library of Scotland; the University of Texas; the Alexander Turnbull Library, Wellington; the Victoria and Albert Museum (2 copies); Worcester College, Oxford; and Yale University.

The present text has been set up from a Bodleian copy of the comedy, Malone 185 (4).

The City Madam was printed in the standard collected editions of Coxeter, Mason, Gifford, Coleridge, and Cunningham. For the texts of the stage adaptations titled *The Cure of Pride* and *Riches*, for Phelps's alteration, and for the text of the 1964 revival, see the following section of this introduction. The play was included in the first edition only of Dodsley's *A Select Collection of Old Plays* (viii, 1744), and in the first volume of Arthur Symon's Mermaid selection, 1887. A bowdlerized text appeared in the second volume of *The Plays of Philip Massinger, adapted for Family Reading*, edited by W. Harness for Murray in 1830; an American edition was published by Harper in 1831. Three young scholars edited the play for their doctoral theses: P. H. Farrier (Kentucky Wesleyan College, 1929), A. K. McIlwraith (Oxford, 1931), and Rudolph Kirk (Princeton, 1934). Kirk's thorough work, in particular, has greatly eased the preparation of the present edition. There are also modern editions by R. Chapman and A. Grant, *The City and the Court. Five Seventeenth Century Comedies of London Life*, San Francisco, 1948; by Cyrus Hoy, in the Regents Renaissance Drama series, 1964; and by T. W. Craik, in the New Mermaid series, 1964.

Excerpts and selections from Massinger's comedy were printed in *The British Muse*, edited by T. Hayward, 1738; *The Beauties of the English Drama*, printed for G. Robinson, 1777; *The School of Shakespeare* (volume 3 of Capell's *Notes and Various Readings to Shakespeare*), 1779; Lamb's *Specimens of English Dramatic Poets*, 1808; *The Beauties of Massinger*, printed for John Porter in 1817; *Golden Leaves from the British and American Dramatic Poets*, edited by J. W. S. Hows, New York, 1865; and in *Specimens of the Elizabethan Drama from Lyly to Shirley*, edited by W. H. Williams, 1905.

Wolf Grafen von Baudissin published a German translation of *The City Madam* in *Ben Jonson und seine Schule*, Leipzig, 1836, and M. Horn-Monval records an undated manuscript translation by Joseph de Smet, *La Belle Dame de la cité*, in *Répertoire bibliographique des traductions et adaptations françaises du théâtre étranger*, Paris, 1963, v, no. 275. Brief selections from the play were translated by A. J. F. Mézières, in *Contemporains et successeurs de Shakspeare*, Paris, 1864.

(d) *Stage History*

Massinger's comedy has a satisfying record of productions from 1632 to modern times. The play was first licensed for performance by Sir Henry Herbert on 25 May 1632 (see page 1), and the quarto title-page says that 'it was acted at the private House in *Black Friers* with great applause.' Presumably this is as reliable as the general run of such statements, and it is seconded by the assertion in Pennycuicke's Dedication that '*this Poem was the object of love and Commendations*' (A2r). The text contains a passage mentioning an 'Academie of valour, / Newly erected for the institution / Of elder Brothers, where they are taught the ways, / Though they refuse to seal for a Duellist, / How to decline a challenge' (I. ii. 22–6), which may well be a hit at Jonson's play *The Magnetic Lady*. There young Compass expostulates at length on the nature of honour with his brother Captain Ironside, who is waiting with sword drawn to start a duel; the relative age of the brothers is not mentioned, but Jonson's didactic purpose is unmistakable. Any allusion to *The Magnetic Lady*, which was written by 20 September, and licensed for performance on 12 October 1632, must have been added to the text of *The City Madam* some five months after its first appearance, and constitutes modest evidence that Massinger's comedy met with some success and continued to be performed.[1] Additional evidence that the play remained in the Blackfriars repertoire lies in the fact that the text was withheld from publication until the closing of the theatres, and that when (on 7 August 1641) the King's men secured an order from the Lord Chamberlain protecting sixty of their plays against unauthorized printing, the list included 'The Citty madam'.[2]

Kirk points out that Pennycuicke does not mention a court performance of *The City Madam*, as he was able to do on the title-page of *The Sun's Darling*, and there is a passage in the Prologue to

[1] Jonson's earlier play *The New Inn*, licensed on 19 Jan. 1629, also contains a long harangue against 'all other valour / But what is for the public' (IV. iv. 24–221), but there is no other point of contact with *The City Madam*. The possibility of a connection between *The City Madam* and either of the Jonson plays was first raised in a private communication from Mrs. E. E. Duncan-Jones, Senior Lecturer in English at the University of Birmingham.

[2] The list is printed with a brief discussion in 'Plays of the King's Men in 1641', E. K. Chambers, *Malone Society Collections*, vol. i, parts 3 and 4 (1911), pp. 364–9.

The Guardian which might be taken to imply that Massinger's comedy failed on its first production (see page 1), but on the whole the available evidence suggests that *The City Madam* enjoyed a deserved measure of success at the Blackfriars Theatre.

Two plays written before the publication of *The City Madam* seem to show some indebtedness to it: *Wit in a Constable*, by Henry Glapthorne, and *The City Match*, by Jasper Mayne.[1] The clearest parallels occur in *Wit in a Constable*, II. i, where two scornful city girls, Clare and Grace, haughtily reject their well-born country suitors, and IV. i, where the girls lay down provisos for marriage. The play also contains a character named Holdfast. *The City Match* offers occasional verbal parallels to *The City Madam* (the clearest instances are again found in a scene (V. ii) echoing Massinger's proviso scene), and some correspondences in plot, in that Mayne shows two merchants who test their sons' characters by pretending to go on a voyage and later giving out that they have been drowned. The boys are then watched by their disguised parents. There is a character named Millicent in this comedy, and a scene (V. iii) in which two suitors pretend to be figures in a large picture. For its possible bearing on the staging of the comparable scene in *The City Madam*, it is worth noting that in Mayne's play two footmen carry on 'the Frame of a great Picture. Curtaines drawne.' The suitors are in the frame (before a backdrop ?), and when the curtains are opened they reveal themselves by moving.[2]

The publication of *The City Madam* made the text available to Thomas Thompson, who crudely plagiarized passages for his *The Life of Mother Shipton*, probably written and printed between 1668 and 1671.[3] The chief borrowings are found in I. v (drawn from *The City Madam*, I. iii), and V. v (drawn from *The City Madam*, I. ii and IV. iii). McManaway also found resemblances between the plot of Massinger's comedy and that of Sir John Lacy's *Sir Hercules Buffoon*, which was acted at Dorset Garden in 1684, three years

[1] Both plays were written in or about 1636, but Glapthorne's comedy appears to have been extensively revised in 1639 (Bentley, iv. 496). Kirk, pp. 36–9, presents in detail the evidence for borrowing.

[2] See Craik, pp. xxiii–xxiv, on the staging of the picture business in *The City Madam*, V. iii.

[3] See Kirk, pp. 39–40, and McManaway, *Studies*, pp. 19–23. The statement on the title-page that Thompson's play 'was Acted Nineteen dayes together with great Applause' is apparently the only evidence that it reached the stage; see Nicoll, *History of English Drama*, i. 435.

after its author's death.[1] Kirk found traces of *The City Madam* in Thomas Dilke's *The City Lady* (1697), and Congreve's *The Way of the World* (1700).[2]

In his 1805 edition of Massinger, Gifford stated that *The City Madam* was not revived 'till the year 1771, when the late Mr. Love made some changes in it, and procured it to be acted at Richmond' (iv. 2). In the 1813 edition he added that Waldron had informed him that Love 'played the part of Luke with great success'. No record of such a performance has survived, but Gifford's statement is authoritative and precise, and is both supported by Waldron and accepted by Genest (vi. 261). Love's version of the comedy was never printed, but the Henry E. Huntington Library possesses a manuscript play, *The Cure of Pride*, *Or*, *Every One in their Way* (MS HM 95), which some scholars have taken to be the 1771 playtext.[3] Neither the date of composition nor the author's name is known for certain, and there is no sign of the manuscript's use in the theatre. Social allusions and the language of the text suggest that it was written no later than the first decade of the eighteenth century: Nicoll doubtfully assigns it to the Restoration and proposes a date of 1680, while Schoenbaum, in his revision of Harbage's *Annals of English Drama 975–1700*, 1964, equally doubtfully places it about 1675. The names of nearly all of Massinger's characters are changed, topical allusions are brought up to date, and much of the original verse is broken down into prose. The general outline of the plot remains, though III. i. and IV. iii are cut out, and two new scenes are introduced, one supplying a fuller account of Sir John Frugal's departure, and the other showing Astrolabe (= Stargaze) introducing two pretended Lords as suitors to Julia and Mariana (= Anne and Mary).

In his 1813 edition of Massinger, Gifford again reports Waldron as saying that after 1771 Love 'prevailed on Mr. Garrick to bring the Play forward at Drury Lane' (iv. 2). The context makes it uncertain whether 'the Play' was *The City Madam* or *The Cure of Pride*, and no record of such a performance by Garrick has been found. On 29 April 1783, however, Massinger's comedy was given a single performance at Drury Lane, for Baddeley's benefit. The

[1] McManaway, *Studies*, p. 27; Nicoll, *History of English Drama*, i. 418.

[2] Kirk, pp. 40–2; cf. *The City Madam*, II. ii. 115–26 with *The Way of the World*, IV. i. 225–7, 234–9 (*The Complete Plays of William Congreve*, ed. H. Davis, 1967).

[3] Kirk, pp. 18–27, gives a full description of the play.

cast consisted of Palmer (Luke), Baddeley (Sir John), Parsons (Holdfast), King (Plenty), Aickin (Lord Lacy), Brereton (Lacy's son), Fawcett and Chaplin (old Goldwire and Tradewell), Bannister and Farren (young Goldwire and Tradewell), Wright (Banks), R. Palmer (Ranter), Waldron (Fortune), Wrighten (Penury), Mrs. Hopkins (Lady Frugal), Miss Farren (Mary), Mrs. Brereton (Anne), and Mrs. Wrighten (Milliscent).[1]

In 1810 Sir James Bland Burges wrote a play which he called *Riches*; *or*, *the Wife and Brother*, founded on Massinger's comedy which it replaced in the theatre for more than thirty years. It is a severely bowdlerized version, taking over less than half of the original lines, and omitting all the low-life scenes, as well as the business of Sir John's disguise as an Indian. Mary and Anne become warm-hearted lovers checked by a tyrannical mother, and Luke is made 'a wretched dependent, a dupe, an injured man, who mindful of his sufferings, naturally rejoices at the reverse of fortune, and excites pity for his disappointment.'[2]

The Drury Lane company gave fourteen performances of *Riches* at the Lyceum Theatre between February 3 and December 10, 1810. The original cast included Powell (Sir John), Raymond (Luke), Holland and Wrench (Lacey and his son), Decamp (Heartwell), Vaughan (Invoice), J. Smith (Ledger), Ray (Venture), Miller (Risk), Smith (Penury), Penson (Holdfast), Mrs. Edwin (Lady Traffic), Miss Ray and Mrs. Orger (Maria and Eliza), and Mrs. Scott (Furbish). The manuscript, carrying the licence of the Lord Chamberlain dated 25 January 1810, is among the Larpent collection (Larpent 1609). It is titled *The Mind's Magnet or The School for Arrogance*, but another hand has written in the usual title at the top of the Prologue. There are minor differences from the printed text; the only significant one being that I. ii is severely cut at its beginning and end. *The Monthly Mirror*, xxix (1810), 145–56, printed a long, perceptive, and severe review, in which Burges was said to have 'reduced his *City Madam* to a mere shadow of the original.' The reviewer found Raymond 'unequal to the part of Luke, although his subdued voice in the first scene interested us much for the sufferings of the character.... The whole revival... was better dressed than acted.'[3]

[1] *The London Stage* (*1660–1800*), part 5, ed. C. B. Hogan, Carbondale, Illinois, 1968, i. 545 and 607. A playbill for this performance is in the British Museum.

[2] W. C. Oulton, *History of the Theatres of London*, 1818, i. 191.

[3] For other reviews of the 1810 and 1814 productions of *Riches* see D. J. Rulfs, 'The

Two editions of Burges's play were published in 1810; it appeared in volume 2 of *The Mirror of Taste and Dramatic Censor*, published at New York and Philadelphia in the same year, and was included in the 1817 collected edition of Burges's plays (ii. 295–422).

Macready played the part of Luke in *Riches* at the Theatre Royal, Birmingham, on 29 November 1810, repeating the role there three times. Kirk records more than fifteen later performances, at London, Bath, Dublin, and Newcastle, between 1810 and 1841.

Edmund Kean also attempted the part, beginning with an enormously successful performance at Drury Lane on 25 May 1814.[1] Five more performances were given between 27 May and 3 November, and there were later revivals at Drury Lane on 28 and 29 June 1815, 16, 18 and 27 May, 18 November, and 18 December, 1817, 13 February 1822, and 25 January 1830. The text of *Riches* 'as now performed at the Theatre Royal, London' was printed in *Cumberland's British Theatre*, xxiv (1830), with details of the costumes and stage business used; it was reprinted in *Dicks' Standard Plays*, no. 717 (1886). There were also occasional performances in the provincial theatres, among them three at Bath, on 6 July 1816 and 12 and 24 May 1830. Kean acted the part of Luke on his visit to America in 1821 and 1822.[2]

On 30 October 1844, Samuel Phelps produced a new alteration of *The City Madam* at the Theatre Royal, Sadlers Wells, 'got up in most costly manner'.[3] Sixteen performances followed, with Phelps as Luke, Bennet as Sir John, Marston as Plenty, Mrs. Warner as Lady Frugal, Miss Cooper as Mary, and Miss Levatt as Milliscent. There were later revivals on 29 September 1852, 30, 31 January, and 1 February 1856, and 15 March 1862. The Lord Chamberlain's manuscript of the play-text, with its licence dated 17 October 1844, is now in the British Museum (Add. MSS. 42979). The anonymous

Reception of the Elizabethan Playwrights on the London Stage 1776–1833', *SP*, xlvi (1949), 54–69. See also Kirk, pp. 27–34 and 45–50.

[1] See G. W. Playfair, *Kean*, 1939, pp. 118–19. Hazlitt's review of 'Mr. Kean's Luke', in *The Morning Chronicle*, is reprinted in the *Complete Works*, ed. P. P. Howe, xviii, 1933, 195–6; Keats's review in *The Champion* for 21 Dec. is reprinted in his *Poetical Works*, ed. H. B. Forman, revised edition, New York, 1938–9, v. 227–32. See also D. J. Rulfs, 'The Romantic Writers and Edmund Kean', *MLQ*, xi (1950), 425–37.

[2] *Riches* had already been performed at New York on 16 May 1810, and Odell noted revivals there on 24 Jan. 1819, 29 Sept. 1820, and 20 July 1830. Junius Brutus Booth played the part of Luke at Baltimore in 1831.

[3] *The Theatrical Journal*, v (1844), 350. See Kirk, pp. 34–6 and 50–1; several reviews are printed in *The Life and Life-Work of Samuel Phelps*, W. M. Phelps and J. Forbes-Robertson, 1866, pp. 70–3.

reviser sentimentalized the comedy, making Luke the victim of Goldwire and Tradewell's persuasions to evil. 'The play, as now acted, presents Luke repentant. The turning point is beautifully managed, by making it depend on the affectionate phrasing of "good Luke" addressed to him by the more "tender-hefted" of the City Madam's daughters—the tone at once arresting the current of madness and turning his mind inward on itself.'[1] In keeping with this, the low-life scenes were severely cut, and the parts of Stargaze and of Goldwire and Tradewell's parents were also omitted.

Finally, on 7 April 1964, and for the following month, a highly successful production of Massinger's original play was mounted at the Birmingham Repertory Theatre, directed by John Harrison and designed by Diana Dewes. The cast included Bunny May (Goldwire), Peter Kelly (Tradewell), Rosamund Greenwood (Lady Frugal), Karin Fernald and Angela Pleasence (Anne and Mary), Elspeth Duxbury (Milliscent), Derek Smith (Luke), Frank Ellis (Holdfast), Colin Pinney and Robert Grange (Lord Lacy and his son), Desmond Gill (Plenty), Ralph Nossek (Sir John), Peter Badger, Murray Noble, and Anthony Healey (Hoist, Penury, Fortune), Robert Robinson (Stargaze), Linda Gardner (Shave'em), Monica Stewart (Secret), Norman Jones (Ramble and Goldwire senior), Ian Ralston (Scuffle and Tradewell senior), and William Ingram (Ding'em).

The text of the production was printed in *Plays of the Year* (*1963–4*), edited by J. C. Trewin, 1965, pp. 329–455. The *Times* reviewer said that 'Smith gives a magnetic and controlled performance as Luke, distinguished by a curiously appropriate skimping of gestures and in appearance suggesting a cross between Honoré de Balzac and David Lloyd George . . . Harrison's direction is superb, particularly in the way it makes theatrically impressive what, textually, seem to be absurdities, e.g. the "statues" and the bogus Red Indians. Miss Diana Dewes' permanent set, built on a revolve, allows uninterrupted continuity, and provides evocative seventeenth-century backgrounds for the splendid colouring of her costumes.'[2]

[1] *The Athenaeum*, x (1852), 2.

[2] *The Times*, 10 Apr. 1964, p. 16; other reviews are found in *The Birmingham Post* and *The Guardian* for 9 April, and *The Observer Weekend Review* for 19 Apr. 1964.

THE

City-Madam,

A

COMEDIE.

As it was acted at the private Houſe in *Black Friers* with great applauſe.

Written by *Phillip Maſſinger* Gent.

LONDON
Printed for *Andrew Pennycuicke*, one of the Actors, in the year 1659.

The Actors names.

Lord Lacie.
Sir John Frugal a Merchant.
Sir Maurice Lacie Son to *Lord Lacy.*
Master Plenty a Country Gentleman.
Luke Brother to *Sir John Frugal.*
Old Goldwire } Two Gentlemen.
Old Tradewell }
Young Goldwire } their sons, prentices to *Sir John Frugal.*
Young Tradewell }
Stargaze an Astrologer.
Fortune a decaied Merchant.
Hoyst a decaied gentleman.
Penurie.
Holdfast a Steward.
Ramble, *Scuffle*, two Hectors.
Dingem a Pimpe.
Gettall a Box-keeper.
Lady Frugal.
Anne } her daughters.
Mary }
Milliscent her woman.
Shavem a Wench.
Secret a Baud.
[Porters.]
[Page.]
[Three Serving-men.]
[Musicians.]
[Sheriff.]
[Marshal.]
[Officers.]
[Serjeants.]
[Yeoman.]
[Servants.]
[*Cerberus.*]
[*Charon.*]
[*Orpheus.*]
[Chorus.]

Scene London.

3. *Frugal*] *Gifford*; *Rich 58* 4. *Maurice*] *Gifford*; *John 58* 6. *Frugal*] *Gifford*; *Rich 58* 10. *Frugal*] *Gifford*; *Rich 58* 19. *Frugal*] *Gifford*; *Rich 58* 25–32. Porters . . . Serjeants.] *Gifford*; *not in 58* 33. Yeoman.] *Craik*; *not in 58* 34–37. Servants . . . Chorus.] *Gifford*; *not in 58*

A2r

To the truly Noble and virtuous Lady *Ann*, Countess of *Oxford*.

HONOURED LADY!

In that age when wit and learning were not conquered by injury, and violence; this Poem was the object of love and Commendations, it being composed by an infallible pen, and censured by an unerring Auditory. In this Epistle I shall not need to make an Apologie for Playes in generall by exhibiting their antiquity and utility, in a word they are mirrors or glasses which none but deformed faces, and fouler consciences A2v *fear to look into. The encouragement I had to prefer this dedication to your powerfull protection proceeds from the universall fame of the deceased Author, who (although he composed many) writ none amiss, and this may justly be ranked amongst his best. I have redeemed it from the teeth of time, by committing of it to the press, but more in imploring your Patronage. I wil not slander it with my praises, it is commendations enough to call it* Massingers; *if it may gain your allowance and pardon, I am highly gratified, and desire only to wear the happy title of,*

MADAM,

Your humblest Servant,

Andrew Pennycuicke.

1–2. To . . . *Oxford*] *For the variant dedications see Introduction, p. 6* 3 LADY] SIR *in copies dedicated to Freake, Lee, Steadwel, Wrath* 4 *not*] *Mason*; *out 58* 7. *Apologie*] *Coxeter*; ~: *58* 14. *more in*] *Coxeter*; *in more 58* 15. *Patronage.*] *Coxeter*; ~, *58* 19. MADAM] SIR *in copies dedicated to Freake, Lee, Steadwel, Wrath*

B1r

The City-Madam

A Comedie

[I. i]

Actus primus, Scena prima.

Enter GOLDWIRE, *and* TRADEWELL.

Goldwire. THE Ship is safe in the Pool then?
Tradewell. And makes good,
In her rich fraught, the name shee bears, the *Speedwell*:
My Master will find it, for on my certain knowledg
For every hundred that hee ventured in her
She hath return'd him five.
Goldwire. And it comes timely,
For besides a paiment on the nail for a Mannor
Late purchas'd by my Master, his young daughters
Are ripe for marriage.
B1v *Tradewell.* Who? *Nan*, and *Mall*?
Goldwire. Mistris *Anne* and *Mary*, and with some addition,
Or 'tis more punishable in our house
Then *Scandalum magnatum*.
Tradewell. 'Tis great pitie
Such a Gentleman as my Master, for that title
His being a Citizen, cannot take from him,
Hath no male heir to inherit his estate,
And keep his name alive.
Goldwire. The want of one
Swells my young Mistresses, and their madam mother
With hopes above their birth, and scale. Their dreams are
Of being made Countesses, and they take state
As they were such already. When you went
To the *Indies*, there was some shape and proportion
Of a Merchants house in our family, but since
My Master, to gain precedencie for my Mistris
Above some Elder Merchants Wives, was knighted,

'Tis grown a little Court, in bravery,
Variety of fashions, and those rich ones:
There are few great Ladies going to a Masque
That do out-shine ours in their every-day habits.

Tradewell. 'Tis strange my Master in his wisdom can
Give the reins to such exorbitancie.

Goldwire. He must,
Or there's no peace nor rest for him at home;
I grant his state will bear it, yet hee's censur'd
For his indulgence, and for Sir *John Frugall*
By some styl'd Sir *John Prodigal.*

Tradewell. Is his brother
Master *Luke Frugal* living?

Goldwire. Yes, the more
His misery, poor man.

Tradewell. Still in the Counter?

Goldwire. In a worser place. He was redeemed from the hole,
To live in our house in hell: since his base usage
Consider'd, 'tis no better. My proud Ladie
Admits him to her Table, marry ever
Beneath the Salt, and there he sits the subject
B2r Of her contempt and scorn; and dinner ended,
His courteous Neeces find emploiment for him
Fitting an under-prentice, or a Footman,
And not an Uncle.

Tradewell. I wonder, being a Scholler
Well read, and travel'd, the world yielding means
For men of such desert, he should endure it.

Enter STARGAZE, LADIE, ANNE, MARY, MILLISCENT, *in several postures, with looking-glasses at their girdles.*

Goldwire. He does, with a strange patience; and to us
The servants so familiar, nay humble.
I'le tell you, but I am cut off. Look these
Like a Citizens wife and daughters?

Tradewell. In their habits
They appear other things; but what are the motives

I. i. 29. exorbitancie] *58*; exorbitance *Gifford* 44–6. *rearranged by Gifford*; *58 reads* I . . . travel'd, / The . . . desert, / He . . . it. 46 SD. MARY, MILLISCENT . . . *girdles.*] *58*; MARY . . . *girdles*; MILLICENT. *Craik*

Of this strange preparation?
Goldwire. The young wag-tails
Expect their suitors. The first, the Son and Heir
Of the Lord *Lacie*, who needs my Masters money,
As his daughter does his honour. The second Master *Plenty*,
A rough hew'n gentleman, and newly come
To a great estate, and so all aids of Art
In them's excusable.
Ladie. You have done your parts here:
To your studie, and be curious in the search
Of the Nativities. *Exit* STARGAZE.
Tradewell. Me thinks the mother,
As if she could renew her youth, in care,
Nay curiosity to appear lovely,
Comes not behind her daughters.
Goldwire. Keeps the first place,
And though the Church-book speak her fifty, they
That say she can write thirty, more offend her,
Then if they tax'd her honesty: t'other day
A Tenant of hers, instructed in her humor,
But one she never saw, being brought before her,
For saying onely, Good young Mistris help me
B2v To the speech of your Ladie mother, so far pleas'd her,
That he got his Lease renew'd for't.
Tradewell. How she bristles:
Prethee observe her.
Milliscent. As I hope to see
A Country Knights son and heir walk bare before you
When you are a Countess, as you may be one
When my Master dies, or leavs trading; and I continuing
Your principal woman, take the upper-hand
Of a Squires wife, though a Justice, as I must
By the place you give me, you look now as young
As when you were married.
Ladie. I think I bear my years well.
Milliscent. Why should you talk of years? Time hath not plough'd
One furrow in your face; and were you not known
The mother of my young Ladies, you might passe
For a Virgin of fifteen.

58. parts] *58*; part *Craik*

Tradewell. Here's no grosse flattery:
Will she swallow this?
Goldwire. You see she does, and glibly.
Milliscent. You never can be old; wear but a Masque
Forty years hence, and you will still seem young
In your other parts: What a waste is here! O *Venus*!
That I had been born a King! and here a hand
To be kiss'd ever; Pardon my boldnesse, Madam:
Then, for a leg and foot you will be courted
When a great Grandmother.
Ladie. These indeed, Wench, are not
So subject to decayings as the face,
Their Comliness last's longer.
Milliscent. Ever, ever:
Such a rare Featur'd, and proportion'd *Madam*
London could never boast of.
Ladie. Where are my Shoos?
Milliscent. Those that your Ladyship gave order should
Be made of the Spanish Perfum'd Skins?
Ladie. The same.
B3r *Milliscent.* I sent the prison-bird this morning for em,
But he neglects his duty.
Anne. He is grown
Exceeding carelesse.
Mary. And begins to murmur
At our commands, and sometimes grumbles to us,
He is forsooth our Uncle.
Ladie. He is your slave,
And as such use him.
Anne. Willingly, but hee's grown
Rebellious *Madam.*

Enter LUKE, *with Shooes, Garters and Roses.*

Goldwire. Nay like Hen, like Chicken.
Ladie. I'le humble him.
Goldwire. Here he comes sweating all over,
He shews like a walking fripperie.
Ladie. Very good Sir,
Were you drunk last night, that you could rise no sooner

96–7. order should / Be] *Gifford*[2]; order / Should be *58*

With humble diligence to do what my Daughters,
And woman did command you?
Luke. Drunk, an't please you?
Ladie. Drunk, I said, Sirrah. Dar'st thou in a look
Repine, or grumble? thou unthankful wretch,
Did our charitie redeem thee out of prison,
Thy Patrimonie spent, ragged, and lowsie,
When the Sheriffs basket, and his broken meat
Were your Festivall exceedings, and is this
So soon forgotten?
Luke. I confesse I am
Your Creature *Madam*.
Ladie. And good reason why
You should continue so.
Anne. Who did new cloath you?
Mary. Admitted you to the Dining-room?
Milliscent. Allowed you
A fresh bed in the garret?
Ladie. Or from whom
Receiv'd you spending money?
Luke. I owe all this
B3v To your goodnesse, *Madam*: For it you have my prayers,
The beggars satisfaction; all my studies,
(Forgetting what I was, but with all duty
Remembring what I am) are how to please you.
And if in my long stay I have offended,
I ask your pardon. Though you may consider,
Being forc'd to fetch these from the Old Exchange,
These from the Tower, and these from Westminster,
I could not come much sooner.
Goldwire. Here was a walke
To breath a Foot-man.
Anne. 'Tis a curious Fan.
Mary. These Roses will shew rare; would t'were in fashion
That the Garters might be seen too.
Milliscent. Many Ladyes
That know they have good legs, wish the same with you:
Men that way have th'advantage.

119–20. you / A] *Gifford*; *undivided in 58* 124. with all] *Dodsley*; withall *58*

Luke. I was with
The *Lady*, and delivered her the Sattin
For her Gown, and Velvet for her Petticote;
This night She vows Shee'l pay you.
Goldwire. How I am bound
To your favour Master *Luke.*
Milliscent. As I live, you will
Perfume all rooms you walk in.
Ladie. Get your Furr,
You shall pull 'em on within.
Goldwire. That servile office
Her pride imposes on him. *Exit* LUKE.
Sir John within. *Goldwire. Tradewell.*
Tradewell. My Master calls. We come Sir.
Exeunt GOLDWIRE, TRADEWELL.

Enter HOLDFAST *with Porters.*

Ladie. What have you brought there?
Holdfast. The Cream of the market, provision enough
To serve a garrison. I weep to think on't.
When my Master got his wealth, his family fed
On roots, and livers, and necks of beef on Sundays.
B4r But now I fear it will be spent in poultry.
Butchers meat will not go down.
Ladie. Why, you Rascall,
Is it at your expence? what Cooks have you provided?
Holdfast. The best of the City. They have wrought at my Lord Mayors.
Anne. Fye on em, they smel of Fleet-Lane, and Pie-corner.
Mary. And think the happinesse of mans life consists
In a mighty shoulder of mutton.
Ladie. I'le have none
Shall touch what I shall eat, you grumbling Curr,
But French-men and Italians; they wear Sattin,
And dish no meat but in Silver.
Holdfast. You may want, though,
A dish or two when the service ends.

135–6. *rearranged by Gifford; 58 reads* I . . . *Lady,* / And . . . Sattin 142. *Sir . . . within.*] *Dodsley: in right hand margin 58* 149–50. *rearranged by editor; 58 reads* Why . . . at / Your . . . provided? 153. think] *Dodsley*; thinks *58*

Ladie. Leave prating,
I'le have my will; do you as I command you. *Exeunt.*

[I. ii] *Actus primus, Scena secunda.*

Enter LACIE, *and* PAGE.

Lacie. You were with *Plenty*?
Page. Yes Sir.
Lacie. And what answer
Return'd the clown?
Page. Clown Sir! he is transform'd,
And grown a gallant of the last edition;
More rich then gaudie in his habit, yet
The freedom, and the bluntnesse of his language
Continues with him. When I told him that
You gave him Caution, as he lov'd the peace,
And safety of his life, he should forbear
To passe the *Merchants* threshold, untill you
Of his two Daughters had made choice of her
Whom you design'd to honour as your wife,
B4v He smil'd in scorn.
Lacie. In scorn?
Page. His words confirm'd it,
They were few, but to this purpose; Tell your Master,
Though his Lordship in reversion were now his,
It cannot awe me. I was born a Free-man,
And will not yeeld in the way of affection
Precedence to him. I will visit em,
Though he sate Porter to deny my entrance.
When I meet him next I'le say more to his face.
Deliver thou this, then gave me a piece
To help my memorie, and so we parted.
Lacie. Where got he this spirit?
Page. At the Academie of valour,
Newly erected for the institution
Of elder Brothers, where they are taught the ways,
Though they refuse to seal for a Duellist,

I. ii. 18. my] *58*; me *Gifford* 20. thou] *58*; thou him *conj. Craik*

How to decline a challenge. He himself
Can best resolve you.

Enter PLENTY *and three Serving-men.*

Lacie. You Sir!
Plenty. What with me Sir?
How big you look! I will not loose a hat
To a hairs breadth; move your Bever, I'le move mine,
Or if you desire to prove your sword, mine hangs
As near my right hand, and will as soon out, though I keep
Not a Fencer to breath me; walke into Moor-fields,
I dare look on your Toledo. Do not shew
A foolish valour in the streets, to make
Work for shop-keepers, and their clubs, 'tis scurvie,
And the women will laugh at us.
Lacie. You presume
On the protection of your Hinds.
Plenty. I scorn it:
Though I keep men I fight not with their fingers,
Nor make it my Religion to follow
The gallants fashion, to have my family
Consisting in a Foot-man, and a Page,
C1r And those two sometimes hungrie. I can feed these,
And cloath 'em too, my gay Sir.
Lacie. What a fine man
Hath your Taylor made you!
Plenty. 'Tis quite contrary,
I have made my Taylor, for my cloaths are pai'd for
Assoon as put on, a sin your man of title
Is seldom guiltie of, but Heaven forgive it.
I have other faults too very incident
To a plain Gentleman. I eat my Venison
With my neighbours in the Countrie, and present not
My phesants, partridges, and growse to the userer,
Nor ever yet paid brokage to his scrivener.
I flatter not my mercers wife, nor feast her
With the first cherries, or pescods, to prepare me
Credit with her husband, when I com to London.

31–2. keep / Not a] *58*; keep not / A *Gifford* 44. you!] *Dodsley*; ~? *58*
55. husband, . . . London.] *58*; husband. . . . London, *McIlwraith*

The wooll of my sheep, or a score or two of fat oxen
In Smithfield, give me money for my expences.
I can make my wife a jointure of such lands too,
As are not encombred, no annuity
Or statute lying on 'em. This I can do
And it please your future honour, and why therefore
You should forbid my being a suiter with you
My dulnesse apprehends not.
Page. This is bitter.
Lacie. I have heard you Sir, and in my patience shewn
To much of the stoicks. But to parley further,
Or answer your grosse jeers would write me coward.
This onely, thy great grandfather was a Butcher,
And his son a Grasier, thy sire Constable
Of the hundred, and thou the first of your dunghill,
Created gentleman. Now you may come on Sir,
You, and your thrashers.
Plenty. Stir not on your lives.
This for the grasier, this for the butcher. *They fight.*
Lacie. So Sir.
Page. I'le not stand idle, draw! my little rapier
C1v Against your bumb blades. I'le one by one despatch you.
Then house this instrument of death, and horrour.

Enter SIR JOHN, LUKE, GOLDWIRE, TRADEWELL.

Sir John. Beat down their weapons. My gate ruffians hall:
What insolence is this?
Luke. Noble Sir *Maurice*,
Worshipfull Master *Plenty*.
Sir John. I blush for you,
Men of your qualitie expose your fame
To every vulgar censure. This at midnight
After a drunken supper in a Tavern,
(No civill man abroad to censure it)
Had shewen poor in you, but in the day, and view
Of all that pass by, monstrous!

60. statute] *Dodsley*; statue *58* 65. stoicks] *58*; stoick's *Dodsley*; stoick *Coxeter*
68–70. *rearranged by Coxeter*; *58 reads* And ... Grasier, / Thy ... gentleman / Now ... Sir, 72. grasier] *Dodsley*; grasiers *58* 73. draw!] *conj. Waldron*; draw *58*
80. censure.] *58*; ~! *Dodsley*

Plenty. Very well Sir;
You look'd for this defence.
Lacie. 'Tis thy protection,
But it will deceive thee.
Sir John. Hold, if you proceed thus
I must make use of the next Justices power,
And leave perswasion. And in plain terms tell you

Enter LADIE, ANNE, MARY, *and* MILLISCENT.

Neither your birth, Sir *Maurice*, nor your wealth,
Shall priviledg this riot. See whom you have drawn
To be spectators of it? can you imagine
It can stand with the credit of my daughters,
To be the argument of your swords? 'ith street too?
Nay ere you do salute, or I give way
To any private conference, shake hands
In sign of peace. He that draws back parts with
My good opinion. This is as it should be.
Make your approaches, and if their affection
Can sympathize with yours, they shall not come
On my credit beggars to you. I will hear
What you reply within.
Lacie. May I have the honor
To support you *Lady*?
Plenty. I know not what's supporting,
C2r But by this fair hand, glove and all, I love you.
Exeunt omnes preter LUKE.

To him enter HOYST, PENURIE, FORTUNE.

Luke. You are come with all advantage. I wil help you
To the speech of my Brother.
Fortune. Have you mov'd him for us?
Luke. With the best of my endeavours, and I hope
You'l find him tractable.
Penurie. Heaven grant he prove so.
Hoyst. Howe're I'le speak my mind.

Enter LORD LACIE.

Luke. Do so Master *Hoyst*.

85. look'd] *Mason*; look 58

Go in. I'le pay my duty to this Lord,
And then I am wholly yours.
[*Exeunt* HOYST, PENURIE, FORTUNE.]
Heaven bless your honor.
Lord. Your hand Master *Luke*, the world's much chang'd with you
Within these few months; then you were the gallant:
No meeting at the Horse-race, Cocking, Hunting,
Shooting, or Bowling, at which Master *Luke*
Was not a principal gamester, and companion
For the Nobility.
Luke. I have paid dear
For those follies, my good Lord, and 'tis but justice
That such as soar above their pitch, and will not
Be warn'd by my example, should like me
Share in the miseries that wait upon't.
Your Honor in your charitie may do well
Not to upbraid me with those weaknesses
Too late repented.
Lord. I nor do, nor will;
And you shall find I'le lend a helping hand
To raise your fortunes: How deals your brother with you?
Luke. Beyond my merit, I thank his goodnesse for't.
I am a Freeman, all my debts discharg'd,
Nor does one Creditor undone by me
Curse my loose riots. I have meat and cloaths,
Time to ask heaven remission for what's past;
Cares of the world by me are laid aside,
C2v My present poverty's a blessing to me;
And though I have been long, I dare not say
I ever liv'd till now.
Lord. You bear it well;
Yet as you wish I should receive for truth
What you deliver, with that truth acquaint me
With your brothers inclination. I have heard
In the acquisition of his wealth, he weighs not
Whose ruines he builds upon.
Luke. In that report
Wrongs him, my Lord. He is a Citizen,
And would increase his heap, and will not lose

110 SD. *Exeunt* . . . FORTUNE.] *Gifford*; *not in 58*

What the Law gives him. Such as are worldly wise
Pursue that tract, or they will ne're wear skarlet.
But if your Honor please to know his temper,
You are come opportunely. I can bring you
Where you unseen shall see, and hear his carriage
Towards some poor men, whose making or undoing
Depend upon his pleasure.

A Table, Count book, Standish, Chair and stools set out.

Lord. To my wish,
I know no object that could more content me. *Exeunt.*

[I. iii] *Actus primus, Scena tertia.*

Enter SIR JOHN, HOYST, FORTUNE, PENURIE, GOLDWIRE.

Sir John. What would you have me do? reach me a chair.
When I lent my moneys I appear'd an Angel;
But now I would call in mine own, a Divel.
Hoyst. Were you the Divels damme, you must stay till I have it.
For as I am a Gentleman,

Enter LUKE *placing the* LORD LACIE.

Luke. There you may hear all.
Hoyst. I pawn'd you my land for the tenth part of the value.
Now, cause I am a Gamester, and keep Ordinaries,
And a Liverie punk, or so, and trade not with
C3r The money-mongers wives, not one will be bound for me:
'Tis a hard case, you must give me longer day
Or I shall grow very angry.
Sir John. Fret, and spare not.
I know no obligation lies upon me
With my honey to feed Drones. But to the purpose,
How much owes *Penurie*?
Goldwire. Two hundred pounds:
His Bond three times since forfeited.
Sir John. Is it su'd?
Goldwire. Yes Sir, and execution out against him.
Sir John. For bodie and goods?
Goldwire. For both, Sir.
Sir John. See it serv'd.

143. tract] *58*; track *Gifford*

Penurie. I am undone; my wife and family
Must starve for want of bread.
Sir John. More Infidel thou
In not providing better to support 'em.
What's *Fortunes* debt?
Goldwire. A thousand, Sir.
Sir John. An estate
For a good man. You were the glorious Trader,
Embrac'd all bargains; the main venturer
In every Ship that launch'd forth; kept your wife
As a Ladie, she had her Coach, her choice
Of Summer-houses, built with other mens moneys
Took up at Interest, the certain road
To Ludgate in a Citizen. Pray you acquaint me
How were my thousand pounds imploy'd?
Fortune. Insult not
On my calamity, though being a debtor,
And a slave to him that lends, I must endure it.
Yet hear me speak thus much in my defence;
Losses at sea, and those Sir, great, and many,
By storms, and tempests, not domestical riots
In soothing my wives humor, or mine own,
Have brought me to this low ebb.
Sir John. Suppose this true;
C3v What is't to me? I must, and will have my money,
Or I'le protest you first, and that done have
The Statute made for Bankrupts serv'd upon you.
Fortune. 'Tis in your power, but not in mine to shun it.
Luke. Not as a brother, Sir, but with such dutie
As I should use unto my Father, since
Your charitie is my parent, give me leave
To speak my thoughts.
Sir John. What would you say?
Luke. No word, Sir,
I hope shall give offence; nor let it relish
Of flattery, though I proclaim aloud:
I glory in the bravery of your mind,
To which your wealths a servant. Not that riches
Is or should be contemn'd, it being a blessing

I. iii. 25. Coach] *58*; Caroch *Gifford*

Deriv'd from heaven, and by your industry
Pull'd down upon you; but in this, dear Sir,
You have many equals: Such a mans possessions
Extend as far as yours, a second hath
His bags as full; a third in credit flies
As high in the popular voice: but the distinction
And noble difference by which you are
Divided from 'em, is, that you are styl'd
Gentle in your abundance, good in plentie,
And that you feel compassion in your bowels
Of others miseries (I have found it, Sir,
Heaven keep me thankful for't) while they are curs'd
As rigid and inexorable.

Sir John. I delight not
To hear this spoke to my face.

Luke. That shall not grieve you,
Your affability, and mildnesse cloath'd
In the garments of your debtors breath
Shall every where, though you strive to conceal it
Be seen, and wondred at, and in the act
With a prodigall hand rewarded. Whereas such
As are born only for themselvs, and live so,
Though prosperous in worldly understandings,
C4r Are but like beasts of rapine, that by odds
Of strength, usurp, and tyrannize o're others
Brought under their subjection.

Lord. A rare fellow!
I am strangely taken with him.

Luke. Can you think Sir,
In your unquestion'd wisdome, I beseech you,
The goods of this poor man sold at an out-crie,
His wife turn'd out of doors, his children forc'd
To beg their bread: this gentleman's estate
By wrong extorted can advantage you?

Hoyst. If it thrive with him hang me, as it will damn him
If he be not converted.

Luke. You are too violent.
Or that the ruine of this once brave Merchant
(For such he was esteem'd though now decay'd)

65. debtors] *58*; thankful debtors' *Gifford* 70. worldly] *Dodsley*; wordly *58*

Will raise your reputation with good men?
But you may urge, pray you pardon me, my zeal
Makes mee thus bold and vehement, in this
You satisfie your anger, and revenge
For being defeated. Suppose this, it will not
Repair your losse, and there was never yet
But shame, and scandall in a victorie
When the rebells unto reason, passions, fought it.
Then for revenge, by great souls it was ever
Contemn'd, though offered; entertain'd by none
But cowards, base, and abject spirits, strangers
To morall honestie, and never yet
Acquainted with religion.
Lord. Our divines
Cannot speak more effectually.
Sir John. Shall I be
Talk'd out of my money?
Luke. No, Sir, but intreated
To do your self a benefit, and preserve
What you possesse intire.
Sir John. How my good brother?
Luke. By making these your beads-men. When they eat,
C4v Their thanks next heaven, will be paid to your mercy.
When your Ships are at Sea, their prayers will swell
The Sails with prosperous winds, and guard 'em from
Tempests, and pirates: keep your ware-houses
From fire, or quench 'em with their tears.
Sir John. No more.
Luke. Write you a good man in the peoples hearts,
Follow you every-where.
Sir John. If this could be.
Luke. It must or our devotions are but words,
I see a gentle promise in your eie,
Make it a blessed act, and poor me, rich
In being the instrument.
Sir John. You shall prevail.
Give 'em longer day. But do you hear, no talk of't.
Should this arrive at twelve on the Exchange
I shall be laught at for my foolish pity

91. reason] *Dodsley*; reasons *58*

Which mony men hate deadly. Take your own time
But see you break not. Carrie 'em to the Cellar,
Drink a health, and thank your Orator.
Penurie. On our knees Sir.
Fortune. Honest Master *Luke*!
Hoyst. I blesse the Counter where
You learn'd this Retorick.
Luke. No more of that friends.
Exeunt LUKE, HOYST, FORTUNE, PENURIE.
Sir John. My honorable Lord!
Lord. I have seen and heard all,
Excuse my manners, and wish heartily
You were all of a peece. Your charity to your debtors
I do commend, but where you should expresse
Your pietie to the height, I must boldly tell you
You shew your self an Athiest.
Sir John. Make me know
My error, and for what I am thus censur'd,
And I will purge my self, or else confesse
A guiltie cause.
Lord. It is your harsh demeanour
To your poor brother.
D1r *Sir John.* Is that all?
Lord. 'Tis more
Then can admit defence. You keep Hym as
A Parasite to your table, subject to
The scorn of your proud wife: an underling
To his own Neeces. And can I with mine honor
Mix my blood with his, that is not sensible
Of his brothers miseries?
Sir John. Pray you take me with you,
And let mee yeeld my reasons why I am
No opener handed to him. I was born
His elder brother, yet my fathers fondnesse
To him the younger robb'd me of my birth-right:
He had a fair estate, which his loose riots
Soon brought to nothing. Wants grew heavy on him
And when layd up for debt, of all forsaken,
And in his own hopes lost, I did redeem him.

131. Hym as] *editor*; Hymas *58*[1]; him as *58*[2]

Lord. You could not do lesse.
Sir John. Was I bound to it my Lord?
What I possesse, I may with justice call
The harvest of my industry. Would you have me,
Neglecting mine own family, to give up
My estate to his disposure?
Lord. I would have you,
What's pass'd forgot, to use him as a brother;
A brother of fair parts, of a clear soul,
Religious, good, and honest.
Sir John. Outward gloss
Often deceivs, may it not prove so in him,
And yet my long acquaintance with his nature
Renders me doubtful, but that shall not make
A breach between us: Let us in to dinner,
And what trust, or imployment you think fit
Shall be conferred upon him: If he prove
True gold in the touch, I'le be no mourner for it.
Lord. If counterfeit, I'le never trust my judgment. *Exeunt.*

1ᵛ
. i]

Actus secundus, Scena prima.

Enter LUKE, HOLDFAST, GOLDWIRE, TRADEWELL.

Holdfast. THE like was never seen.
Luke. Why in this rage man?
Holdfast. Men may talk of Country-Christmases, and Court-gluttonie,
Their thirty pound butter'd eggs, their Pies of Carps tongues,
Their Pheasants drench'd with Ambergreece, the carkases
Of three fat Weathers bruised for gravie to
Make sauce for a single Peacock, yet their feasts
Were fasts compar'd with the Cities.
Tradewell. What deer dainty
Was it thou murmur'st at?
Holdfast. Did you not observe it?
There were three sucking piggs serv'd up in a dish,
Took from the sow as soon as farrowed,

II. i. 2. Country-Christmases] *58*; Country-Christmass *Dodsley* 3. pound] *58*; pound for *Dodsley*

A fortnight fed with dates, and muskadine,
That stood my Master in twenty marks a piece,
Besides the puddings in their bellies made
Of I know not what. I dare swear the cook that dress'd it
Was the Devill, disguis'd like a Dutch-man.
Goldwire. Yet all this
Will not make you fat, fellow-*Holdfast.*
Holdfast. I am rather
Starv'd to look on't. But here's the mischief, though
The dishes were rais'd one upon another
As woodmongers do billets, for the first,
The second, and third course, and most of the shopps
Of the best confectioners in *London* ransack'd
To furnish out a banquet, yet my Lady
Call'd me penurious rascall, and cri'd out,
There was nothing worth the eating.
Goldwire. You must have patience,
D2[r] This is not done often.
Holdfast. 'Tis not fit it should,
Three such dinners more would break an Alderman,
And make him give up his cloak. I am resolv'd
To have no hand in't. I'le make up my accompts
And since my Master longs to be undone,
The great Fiend be his Steward, I will pray,
And blesse my self from him. *Exit* HOLDFAST.
Goldwire. The wretch shews in this
An honest care.
Luke. Out on him, with the fortune
Of a slave, he has the mind of one. However
She bears me hard, I like my Ladies humor,
And my brothers sufferage to it. They are now
Busie on all hands; one side eager for
Large portions, the other arguing strictly
For jointures, and securitie; but this
Being above our scale, no way concerns us.
How dul you look! in the mean time how intend you
To spend the hours?
Goldwire. We well know how we would,
But dare not serve our wills.
Tradewell. Being prentices,

We are bound to attendance.
Luke. Have you almost serv'd out
The term of your Indentures, yet make conscience
By starts to use your liberty? Hast thou traded
In the other world, expos'd unto all dangers,
To make thy Master rich, yet dar'st not take
Some portion of the profit for thy pleasure?
Or wilt thou being keeper of the Cash,
Like an Ass that carries dainties, feed on Thistles?
Are you gentlemen born, yet have no gallant tincture
Of gentry in you? You are no Mechanicks,
Nor serve some needy shop-keeper, who surveighs
His every-day-takings. You have in your keeping,
A masse of wealth, from which you may take boldly,
And no way be discover'd. He's no rich man
D2v That knows all he possesses, and leavs nothing
For his servants to make prey of. I blush for you,
Blush at your poverty of spirit, you
The brave sparks of the City!
Goldwire. Master *Luke*,
I wonder you should urge this, having felt
What miserie follows riot.
Tradewell. And the penance
You indur'd for't in the Counter.
Luke. You are fools,
The case is not the same. I spent mine own money,
And my stock being smal, no mervail 'twas soon wasted.
But you without the least doubt or suspicion,
If cautelous, may make bold with your Masters.
As for example; when his Ships come home,
And you take your receipts, as 'tis the fashion,
For fifty bales of Silk you may write forty,
Or for so many pieces of Cloth of Bodkin,
Tissue, Gold, Silver, Velvets, Sattins, Taffaties,
A piece of each deducted from the grosse
Will never be miss'd, a dash of a pen will do it.
Tradewell. I, but our fathers bonds that lye in pawn
For our honesties must pay for't.
Luke. A meer bugbear
Invented to fright children. As I live

Were I the master of my brothers fortunes,
I should glory in such servants. Did'st thou know
What ravishing lechery it is to enter
An Ordinarie, *cap a pe*, trim'd like a Gallant,
(For which in truncks conceal'd be ever furnish'd)
The reverence, respect, the crouches, cringes,
The musical chime of Gold in your cram'd pockets,
Commands from the attendants, and poor Porters?
Tradewell. Oh rare!
Luke. Then sitting at the Table with
The braveries of the kingdom, you shall hear
Occurrents from all corners of the world,
The plots, the Counsels, the designs of Princes,
D3r And freely censure 'em; the City wits
Cri'd up, or decri'd, as their passions lead 'em;
Judgment having nought to do there.
Tradewell. Admirable!
Luke. My Lord no sooner shal rise out of his chair,
The gameing Lord I mean, but you may boldly
By the priviledge of a gamester fill his room,
For in play you are all fellows; have your knife
Assoon in the Pheasant; drink your health as freely,
And striking in a luckie hand or two,
Buy out your time.
Tradewell. This may be: but suppose
We should be known.
Luke. Have mony and good cloaths
And you may passe invisible. Or if
You love a Madam-punck, and your wide nostrill
Be taken with the sent of cambrick smocks
Wrought, and perfum'd—
Goldwire. There, there, Master *Luke*,
There lyes my road of happiness.
Luke. Injoy it,
And pleasures stol'n being sweetest, apprehend
The raptures of being hurried in a Coach
To Brainford, Stanes, or Barnet.
Goldwire. 'Tis inchanting,
I have prov'd it.
Luke. Hast thou?

Goldwire. Yes, in all these places,
I have had my several Pagans billeted
For my own tooth, and after ten pound suppers
The curtains drawn, my Fidlers playing all night
The shaking of the sheets, which I have danc'd
Again, and again with my Cockatrice. Master *Luke*,
You shall be of my counsel, and we two sworn brothers,
And therefore I'le be open. I am out now
Six hundred in the Cash, yet if on a sudden
I should be call'd to account, I have a trick
How to evade it, and make up the sum.
D3v *Tradewell.* Is't possible?
Luke. You can instruct your Tutor.
How? how? good Tom.
Goldwire. Why look you. We cash-keepers
Hold correspondence, supply one another
On all occasions. I can borrow for a week
Two hundred pounds of one, as much of a second,
A third lays down the rest, and when they want,
As my Masters monies come in, I do repay it,
Ka me, ka thee.
Luke. An excellent knot! 'tis pity
It e're should be unloos'd; for me it shall not,
You are shew'n the way friend *Tradewell*, you may make use on't,
Or freeze in the ware-house, and keep company
With the Cator *Holdfast*.
Tradewell. No, I am converted.
A Barbican Broker will furnish me with out side,
And then a crash at the Ordinarie.
Goldwire. I am for
The Lady you saw this morning, who indeed is
My proper recreation.
Luke. Go to Tom,
What did you make me?
Goldwire. I'le do as much for you,
Imploy me when you please.
Luke. If you are enquired for,
I will excuse you both.
Tradewell. Kind Master *Luke*!

120. instruct] *Mason*; intrust *58*

Goldwire. Wee'l break my Master to make you!
Luke. You know
I cannot love money, go boyes.—When time serves [*Aside.*]
It shall appear, I have another end in't. *Exeunt.*

[II. ii] *Enter* LORD, SIR JOHN, LACIE, PLENTY, LADIE, ANNE, MARY, MILLISCENT.

Sir John. Ten thousand pounds a piece I'le make their portions,
And after my decease it shall be double,
D4r Provided you assure them for their jointures
Eight hundred pounds *per annum*, and intail
A thousand more upon the heirs male,
Begotten on their bodies.
Lord. Sir, you bind us
To very strict conditions.
Plenty. You my Lord
May do as you please: but to me it seems strange,
We should conclude of portions, and of jointures,
Before our hearts are settled.
Ladie. You say right, *A chair set out.*
There are counsels of more moment, and importance
On the making up of marriages to be
Consider'd duly, then the portion, or the jointures,
In which a mothers care must be exacted,
And I by speciall priviledge may challenge
A casting voice.
Lord. How's this?
Ladie. Even so my Lord,
In these affairs I govern.
Lord. Give you way to't?
Sir John. I must my Lord.
Ladie. 'Tis fit he should, and shall:
You may consult of somthing else, this Province
Is wholly mine.
Lacie. By the City custom Madam?
Ladie. Yes my young Sir, and both must look my daughters
Will hold it by my Copie.
Plenty. Brave i'faith.

139–40 you! . . . I] *McIlwraith*; you; / You know. / *Luke.* I *58*; you; / You know—/ *Luke.* I *Gifford* 140 SD. *Aside.*] *editor*; *not in 58* II. ii. *Scene division Coxeter*; *undivided 58*

Sir John. Give her leave to talk, we have the power to do;
And now touching the businesse we last talk'd of,
In private if you please.

Lord. 'Tis well remembred,
You shall take your own way Madam. *Exeunt* LORD *and* SIR JOHN.

Lacie. What strange lecture
Will she read unto us?

Ladie. Such as wisedom warrants
From the Superiour bodies. Is *Stargaze* ready
D4v With his several Schemes?

Milliscent. Yes Madam, and attends
Your pleasure.

Lacie. *Stargaze*, Ladie: What is he?

Ladie. Call him in. *Exit* MILLISCENT.
You shall first know him, then admire him
For a man of many parts, and those parts rare ones.
Hee's every thing indeed, parcel Physician,
And as such prescribes my diet, and foretells
My dreams when I eat Potato's; parcel Poet,
And sings Encomiums to my virtues sweetly;
My Antecedent, or my Gentleman Usher;
And as the starrs move, with that due proportion
He walks before me; but an absolute Master
In the Calculation of Nativities;
Guided by that ne're-erring science, call'd,
Judicial Astrologie.

Plenty. *Stargaze*! sure
I have a penny Almanack about me
Inscrib'd to you, as to his Patroness,
In his name publish'd.

Ladie. Keep it as a jewel.
Some States-men that I will not name, are wholly
Governed by his predictions, for they serve
For any latitude in Christendome,
Aswell as our own climate.

Enter MILLISCENT, *and* STARGAZE, *with two Schemes.*

Lacie. I believe so.

Plenty. Must we couple by the Almanack?

31 SD. *Exit* MILLISCENT.] *Gifford*; *follows* pleasure (l. 30) *58* 49. *Lacie*.] *Dodsley*; *Lady 58*

Ladie. Be silent,
And ere we do articulate, much more
Grow to a full conclusion, instruct us
Whether this day and hour, by the planets, promise
Happie success in marriage.

Stargaze. *In omni*
Parte, et toto.

Plenty. Good learn'd Sir, in English.
And since it is resolved we must be Coxcombs,
Make us so in our own language.

E1r *Stargaze.* You are pleasant:
Thus in our vulgar tongue then.

Ladie. Pray you observe him.

Stargaze. *Venus* in the West-angle, the house of marriage the seventh house, in Trine of *Mars*, in Conjunction of *Luna*, and *Mars* Almuthen, or Lord of the Horoscope.

Plenty. Hoy day!

Ladie. The Angels language, I am ravish'd! forward.

Stargaze. *Mars* as I said Lord of the Horoscope, or geniture, in mutual reception of each other, shee in her Exaltation, and he in his Triplicitie trine, and face, assure a fortunate combination to *Hymen*, excellent prosperous and happie.

Ladie. Kneel, and give thanks. *The Women kneel.*

Lacie. For what we understand not.

Plenty. And have as little faith in't.

Ladie. Be incredulous,
To me 'tis Oracle.

Stargaze. Now for the sovereigntie of my future Ladies, your daughters after they are married.

Plenty. Wearing the breeches you mean.

Ladie. Touch that point home,
It is a principal one, and with London Ladies
Of main consideration.

Stargaze. This is infallible: *Saturn* out of all dignities in his detriment and fall, combust: and *Venus* in the South-angle elevated above him, Ladie of both their Nativities; in her essential, and accidental dignities; occidental from the Sun, oriental from the Angle of the East, in Cazimi of the Sun, in her joy, and free from the malevolent beams of infortunes; in a sign commanding, and *Mars*

57. our own] 58^2; own 58^1 69. incredulous] *Mason*; credulous *58*

in a constellation obeying, she fortunate, and he dejected, the disposers of marriage in the Radix of the native in feminine figures, argue, foretel, and declare rule, preheminence and absolute soveraignity in women.

Lacie. Is't possible!

Stargaze. 'Tis drawn, I assure you, from the Aphorismes of the old Chaldeans; *Zoroastes* the first and greatest Magician, *Mercurius Trismegistus*, the later *Ptolomy*, and the everlasting Prognosticator, old *Erra Pater*.

Ladie. Are you yet satisfi'd?
E1v *Plenty*. In what?
Ladie. That you
Are bound to obey your Wives, it being so
Determin'd by the starrs, against whose influence
There is no opposition.
Plenty. Since I must
Be married by the Almanack, as I may be,
'Twere requisite the services and duties
Which, as you say, I must pay to my wife,
Were set down in the Calender.
Lacie. With the date
Of my Apprenticeship.
Ladie. Make your demands;
I'le sit as Moderatrix, if they presse you
With over hard conditions.
Lacie. Mine hath the Van,
I stand your charge, sweet.
Stargaze. Silence.
Anne. I require first
(And that since 'tis in fashion with kind husbands,
In civil manners you must grant) my will
In all things whatsoever, and that will
To be obey'd, not argu'd.
Ladie. And good reason.
Plenty. A gentle *Imprimis*.
Lacie. This in grosse contains all;
But your special *Items*, Lady.
Anne. When I am one

84. rule] *Gifford*; preheminence, rule *58*

(And you are honour'd to be styl'd my husband)
To urge my having my Page, my Gentleman-Usher;
My Woman sworn to my secrets; my Caroch
Drawn by six Flanders Mares; my Coachman, Grooms,
Postilian, and Footmen.
Lacie. Is there ought else
To be demanded?
Anne. Yes Sir, mine own Doctor;
French, and Italian Cooks; Musicians, Songsters,
And a Chaplain that must preach to please my fancie;
E2r A friend at Court to place me at a Mask;
The private Box took up at a new Play
For me, and my retinue; a fresh habit,
(Of a fashion never seen before) to draw
The Gallants eies that sit on the Stage upon me;
Some decay'd Ladie for my Parasite,
To flatter me, and rail at other Madams;
And there ends my ambition.
Lacie. Your desires
Are modest, I confess.
Anne. These toies subscrib'd to,
And you continuing an obedient Husband
Upon all fit occasions, you shall find me
A most indulgent Wife.
Ladie. You have said, give place
And hear your younger Sister.
Plenty. If shee speak
Her language, may the great Fiend booted and spurr'd,
With a Sithe at his girdle, as the Scotchman saies,
Ride headlong down her throat.
Lacie. Curse not the Judg
Before you hear the sentence.
Mary. In some part
My Sister hath spoke well for the Citie pleasures,
But I am for the Countries, and must say
Under correction in her demands
She was too modest.
Lacie. How like you this Exordium?
Plenty. Too modest, with a mischief!

114–15. Doctor; / French] *Coxeter*; *undivided 58*

Mary. Yes, too modest:
I know my value, and prize it to the worth;
My youth, my beauty.
Plenty. How your glasse deceives you!
Mary. The greatnesse of the portion I bring with me,
And the Sea of happinesse that from me flows to you.
Lacie. She bears up close.
Mary. And can you in your wisedom,
Or rusticall simplicity imagine,
E2^{v} You have met some innocent Country girle, that never
Look'd further then her fathers farm, nor knew more
Then the price of corn in the Market; or at what rate
Beef went a stone? that would surveigh your dayrie,
And bring in mutton out of Cheese, and butter?
That could give directions at what time of the Moon
To cut her Cocks, for Capons against Christmas,
Or when to raise up Goslings?
Plenty. These are arts
Would not mis-become you, though you should put in
Obedience and duty.
Mary. Yes, and patience,
To sit like a fool at home, and eye your thrashers;
Then make provision for your flavering Hounds,
When you come drunk from an Ale-house after hunting,
With your Clowns and Comrades as if all were yours,
You the Lord Paramount, and I the drudge;
The case Sir, must be otherwise.
Plenty. How, I beseech you?
Mary. Marry thus. I will not like my Sister challenge
What's usefull, or superfluous from my Husband,
That's base all o're. Mine shall receive from me,
What I think fit. I'le have the State convey'd
Into my hands; and he put to his pension,
Which the wise virago's of our climate practise.
I will receive your rents.
Plenty. You shall be hang'd first.
Mary. Make sale, or purchase. Nay I'le have my neighbours
Instructed, when a passenger shall ask,
Whose house is this? though you stand by, to answer,

170. by,] *Dodsley*; ~‸ *58*

The Lady *Plenties*. Or who owes this manner?
The Lady *Plenty*. Whose sheep are these? whose oxen?
The Lady *Plenties*.
Plenty. A plentifull Pox upon you.
Mary. And when I have children, if it be enquir'd
By a stranger whose they are, they shall still eccho
My Lady *Plenties*! the Husband never thought on.
Plenty. In their begetting I think so.
E3r *Mary*. Since you'l marry
In the City for our wealth, in justice, we
Must have the Countries Soveraignty.
Plenty. And we nothing.
Mary. A Nagg of forty shillings, a couple of Spaniels,
With a Spar-Hawk is sufficient, and these too,
As you shall behave your self, during my pleasure,
I will not greatly stand on. I have said Sir,
Now if you like me, so.
Ladie. At my intreaty,
The Articles shall be easier.
Plenty. Shall they i'faith?
Like Bitch, like Whelps.
Lacie. Use fair words.
Plenty. I cannot;
I have read of a house of pride, and now I have found one;
A whirle winde overturn it.
Lacie. On these terms,
Wil your minxship be a Lady?
Plenty. A Lady in a morris,
I'le wedd a Pedlers punck first.
Lacie. Tinkers trull,
A begger without a smock.
Plenty. Let Mounsieur Almanack,
Since he is so cunning with his Jacob's Staffe,
Find you out a Husband in a bowling Ally.
Lacie. The general pimp to a Brothel.
Plenty. Though that now,
All the loose desires of man were rak'd up in me,
And no means but thy Maiden-head left to quench 'em,
I would turn Cynders, or the next Sow-gelder,
On my life should libb me, rather then imbrace thee.

Anne. Wooing do you call this?
Mary. A Bear-baiting rather.
Plenty. Were you worried, you deserve it, and I hope
I shall live to see it.
Lacie. I'le not rail, nor curse you,
Only this; you are pretty peates, and your great portions
E3v Adds much unto your handsomenesse, but as
You would command your Husbands you are beggers,
Deform'd, and uglie.
Ladie. Hear me.
Plenty. Not a word more.
Exeunt LACIE *and* PLENTY.
Anne. I ever thought 'twould come to this.
Mary. Wee may
Lead Apes in Hell for Husbands, if you bind us
T' articulate thus with our sutors. *Both speak weeping.*
Stargaze. Now the Clowd breaks,
And the Storm will fall on me.
Ladie. You rascal, jugler. *She breaks his head, and beats him.*
Stargaze. Dear Madam.
Ladie. Hold you intelligence with the Starrs,
And thus deceive me?
Stargaze. My art cannot erre,
If it does I'le burn my Astrolabe. In mine own Starr
I did fore see this broken head, and beating;
And now your Ladyship sees, as I do feel it,
It could not be avoided.
Ladie. Did you?
Stargaze. Madam,
Have patience but a week, and if you finde not
All my predictions true touching your daughters,
And a change of fortune to your self, a rare one,
Turn me out of doors. These are not the men, the Planets
Appointed for their Husbands, there will come
Gallants of another metall.
Milliscent. Once more trust him.
Anne, *Mary*. Do, Lady mother.
Ladie. I am vex'd, look to it;

203. Adds] *58*; Add *Dodsley*

Turn o're your books, if once again you fool me,
You shall graze elswhere: Come Girles.
Stargaze. I am glad I scap'd thus.
Exeunt.

E4[r]
[II. iii]

Actus secundus, Scena tertia.

Enter LORD, *and* SIR JOHN.

Lord. The plot shews very likely.
Sir John. I repose
My principal trust in your Lordship; 'twill prepare
The physick I intend to minister
To my Wife, and Daughters.
Lord. I will do my parts
To set it off to the life.

Enter LACIE *and* PLENTY.

Sir John. It may produce
A Scene of no vulgar mirth. Here come the Suitors;
When we understand how they relish my Wife's humors,
The rest is feasible.
Lord. Their looks are cloudie.
Sir John. How sits the wind? Are you ready to launch forth
Into this sea of marriage?
Plenty. Call it rather
A Whirle-pool of afflictions.
Lacie. If you please
To injoin me to it, I will undertake
To find the North-passage to the *Indies* sooner,
Then plough with your proud Heifer.
Plenty. I will make
A Voiage to Hell first.
Sir John. How, Sir?
Plenty. And court *Proserpine*
In the sight of *Pluto*, his three-headed Porter
Cerberus standing by, and all the furies,
With their whips to scourge me for't, then say, I *Jeffrey*

224 SD. *Exeunt.*] *Gifford*; *follows* Girles *58* II. iii. 4. parts] *58*; part *Dodsley*

Take your *Mary* for my Wife.
Lord. Why what's the matter?
Lacie. The matter is, the mother, with your pardon,
E4v I cannot but speak so much, is a most insufferable,
Proud, insolent Ladie.
Plenty. And the daughters worse.
The Damm in years had th'advantage to be wicked,
But they were so in her belly.
Lacie. I must tell you,
With reverence to your wealth, I do begin
To think you of the same leaven.
Plenty. Take my counsel;
'Tis safer for your credit to professe
Your self a Cuckold, and upon record,
Then say they are your Daughters.
Sir John. You go too far Sir.
Lacie. They have so Articl'd with us.
Plenty. And will not take us
For their Husbands, but their slaves, and so aforehand
They do profess they'l use us.
Sir John. Leave this heat:
Though they are mine I must tell you, the perverseness
Of their manners (which they did not take from me,
But from their mother) qualified, they deserve
Your equalls.
Lacie. True, but what's bred in the bone
Admits no hope of cure.
Plenty. Though Saints, and Angels
Were their Physitians.
Sir John. You conclude too fast.
Plenty. God bowy you, I'le travail three years, but I'le bury
This shame that lives upon me.
Lacie. With your licence,
I'le keep him company.
Lord. Who shall furnish you,
For your expences?
Plenty. He shall not need your help,
My purse is his, we were rivals, but now friends,
And will live and die so.

19. your] *58*; you *Coxeter* 22. daughters] *Dodsley*; daughter's *58*

Lacie. Ere we go I'le pay
My duty as a son.
F1r *Plenty.* And till then leave you.
Exeunt LACIE *and* PLENTY.
Lord. They are strangely mov'd.
Sir John. What's wealth, accompanied
With disobedience in a wife and children?
My heart will break.
Lord. Be comforted, and hope better;
Wee'l ride abroad, the fresh air and discourse,
May yield us new inventions.
Sir John. You are noble,
And shall in all things, as you please command me. *Exeunt.*

[III. i]

Actus tertius, Scena prima.

Enter SHAVEM *and* SECRET.

Secret. DEAD doings, Daughter.
Shavem. Doings! sufferings mother:
Men have forgot what doing is;
And such as have to pay for what they do,
Are impotent, or Eunuchs.
Secret. You have a friend yet, *Musick come down.*
And a striker too, I take it.
Shavem. *Goldwire* is so,
And comes to me by stealth, and as he can steal,
Maintains me in cloaths, I grant; but alas Dame, what's one friend?
I would have a hundred; for every hour, and use
And change of humour I am in, a fresh one.
'Tis a flock of Sheep that makes a lean Wolf fat,
And not a single Lambkin. I am starv'd,
Starv'd in my pleasures. I know not what a Coach is,
To hurrie me to the Burse, or old Exchange,
The Neathouse for Musk-mellons, and the Gardens
Where we traffick for Asparagus, are to me

III. i. 2. Men] *58*; For poor men *Gifford* 5–7. *rearranged by editor*; *Goldwire* ... so, / And ... me / In ... friend? *58*; *Goldwire* ... comes / To ... me / In ... friend? *Gifford.* 8. hundred;] *Dodsley*; ~‸ *58* 9. in,] *Dodsley*; ~‸ *58*

In the other world.
Secret. There are other places Ladie,
Where you might find customers.
F1v *Shavem.* You would have me foot it
To the Dancing of the Ropes, sit a whole afternoon there
In expectation of Nuts and Pippins;
Gape round about me, and yet not find a Chapman
That in courtesie will bid a chop of mutton,
Or a pint of Drum-wine for me.
Secret. You are so impatient.
But I can tell you news will comfort you,
And the whole Sister hood.
Shavem. What's that?
Secret. I am told
Two Embassadours are come over. A French Monsieur,
And a Venetian, one of the Clarissimi,
A hot-rein'd Marmosite. Their followers,
For their Countries honor, after a long Vacation,
Will make a full term with us.
Shavem. They indeed are
Our certain and best customers: Who knocks there? *Knock within.*
Within Ramble. Open the door.
Secret. What are you?
Within Ramble. *Ramble.*
Within Scuffle. *Scuffle.*
Within Ramble. Your constant visitants.
Shavem. Let 'em not in.
I know em, swaggering, suburbian roarers,
Six-penny truckers.
Within Ramble. Down go all your windows,
And your neighbours too shall suffer.
Within Scuffle. Force the doors.
Secret. They are out-laws, mistrisse *Shavem*, and there is
No remedie against em. What should you fear?
They are but men, lying at your close ward,
You have foyl'd their betters.
Shavem. Out you Baud. You care not
Upon what desperate service you imploy me,
Nor with whom, so you have your fee.

22. Drum-wine] *58*; stum-wine *Dodsley*; strum-wine *Coxeter*

Secret. Sweet ladie-bird
Sing in a milder key.

F2r *Enter* RAMBLE *and* SCUFFLE.

Scuffle. Are you grown proud?
Ramble. I knew you a wastcotier in the garden allies,
And would come to a saylors whistle.
Secret. Good Sir *Ramble*,
Use her not roughly. Shee is very tender.
Ramble. Rank and rotten, is she not?

She draws her knife. RAMBLE *his sword.*

Shavem. Your spittle rogueships
Shall not make me so.
Secret. As you are a man, Squire *Scuffle*,
Step in between em. A weapon of that length
Was ne're drawn in my house.
Shavem. Let him come on,
I'le scoure it in your guts, you dog.
Ramble. You brach,
Are you turn'd mankind? You forgot I gave you,
When wee last join'd issue, twenty pound.
Shavem. O're night,
And kickt it out of me in the morning. I was then
A novice, but I know to make my game now.
Fetch the Constable.

Enter GOLDWIRE *like a Justice of Peace*, DINGEM *like a Constable, the Musicians like watch men.*

Secret. Ah me. Here's one unsent for,
And a Justice of Peace too.
Shavem. I'le hang you both you rascalls,
I can but ride. You for the purse you cut
In Powl's at a sermon. I have smoak'd you. And you for the bacon
You took on the high way from the poor market woman
As she road from Rumford.
Ramble. Mistris *Shavem*.
Scuffle. Mistris *Secret*,
On our knees we beg your pardon.
Ramble. Set a ransom on us.

42. Sing in] *Gifford*; Sing *58* 52–60. When . . . *Secret*,] *58*; *for rearrangements by Coxeter*, *Gifford and Hoy see Commentary* 61. *Ramble.*] *Coxeter*; *Scuffle. 58*

Secret. We cannot stand trifling. If you mean to save them,
Shut them out at the back-door.
Shavem. First for punishment
F2v They shall leave their cloaks behind em, and in sign
I am their soveraign, and they my vassalls,
For homage kiss my Shoo-sole rogues, and vanish.
Exeunt RAMBLE *and* SCUFFLE.
Goldwire. My brave virago. The coasts clear. Strike up.
GOLDWIRE, *and the rest discovered.*
Shavem. My *Goldwire* made a Justice.
Secret. And your scout
Turn'd Constable, and the Musicians watch-men.
Goldwire. We come not to fright you, but to make you merry.
A light Lavolto. *They dance.*
Shavem. I am tir'd. No more.
This was your device?
Dingem. Wholly his own. He is
No pig sconce Mistris.
Secret. He has an excellent head-peece.
Goldwire. Fie no, not I: your jeering gallants say
We Citizens have no wit.
Dingem. He dyes that says so.
This was a master-piece.
Goldwire. A trifling stratagem,
Not worth the talking of.
Shavem. I must kiss thee for it
Again, and again.
Dingem. Make much of her. Did you know
What suiters she had since she saw you?
Goldwire. I'the way of marriage?
Dingem. Yes Sir, for marriage, and the other thing too.
The commoditie is the same. An Irish Lord offer'd her
Five pound a week.
Secret. And a cashier'd Captain, half
Of his entertainment.
Dingem. And a new made Courtier
The next suit he could beg.
Goldwire. And did my sweet one
Refuse all this for me?
Shavem. Weep not for joy,

'Tis true. Let others talk of Lords, and Commanders,
And country heirs for their servants; but give mee
My gallant prentice. He parts with his mony
F3r So civilly, and demurely; keeps no account
Of his expences, and comes ever furnish'd.
I know thou hast brought money to make up
My gown and petticoat, with th'appurtenances.
Goldwire. I have it here Duck, thou shalt want for nothing.
Shavem. Let the chamber be perfum'd, and get you Sirrah
His cap, and pantables ready.
Goldwire. There's for thee,
And thee. That for a banquet.
Secret. And a cawdle
Again you rise?
Goldwire. There.
Shavem. Usher us up in state.
Goldwire. You will be constant?
Shavem. Thou art the whole world to me.
Exeunt, wanton Musick plaid before 'em.

[III. ii] *Actus tertius, Scena secunda.*

Enter LUKE.

Within Anne. Where is this Uncle?
Within Ladie. Call this Beadsman-brother:
He hath forgot attendance.
Within Mary. Seek him out:
Idlenesse spoils him.
Luke. I deserve much more
Then their scorn can load me with, and 'tis but justice,
That I should live the families drudge, design'd
To all the sordid offices their pride
Imposes on me; since if now I sate
A Judge in mine own cause, I should conclude
I am not worth their pitie: such as want

98 SD. *Exeunt, wanton*] *Dodsley*; *Exeunt wanton, 58*; *Exeunt wantonly Coxeter* III. ii. 1. Beadsman-brother] *Dodsley*; Beadsman, brother *58* 1–2. Beadsman-brother: / He] *Coxeter*; *undivided 58* 2–4. *rearranged by Gifford*; *58 reads* Call . . . attendance. / Seek . . . him. / I . . . justice,

Discourse, and judgment, and through weaknesse fall,
May merit man's compassion; but I
That knew profusenesse of expence the parent
Of wretched poverty, her fatal daughter,
To riot out mine own, to live upon
F3v The alms of others! steering on a rock
I might have shun'd: O heaven! 'tis not fit
I should look upward, much lesse hope for mercy.

Enter LADIE, ANNE, MARY, STARGAZE, *and* MILLISCENT.

Ladie. What are you devising, Sir?
Anne. My Uncle is much given
To his devotion.
Mary. And takes time to mumble
A *Pater noster* to himself.
Ladie. Know you where
Your brother is? It better would become you
(Your means of life depending wholly on him)
To give your attendance.
Luke. In my will I do:
But since he rode forth yesterday with Lord *Lacie*,
I have not seen him.
Ladie. And why went not you
By his stirrup? how do you look! were his eies clos'd,
You'd be glad of such imploiment.
Luke. 'Twas his pleasure
I should wait your commands, and those I am ever
Most ready to receive.
Ladie. I know you can speak well,
But say and do.

Enter LORD LACIE *with a Will.*

Luke. Here comes my Lord.
Ladie. Further off:
You are no companion for him, and his businesse
Aims not at you, as I take it.
Luke. Can I live
In this base condition? *Aside.*
Ladie. I hop'd, my Lord,
You had brought Master *Frugall* with you, for I must ask

18–19. given / To] *Gifford*; *undivided 58* 32–3. live / In] *Gifford*; *undivided 58*

An account of him from you.
Lord. I can give it, Ladie;
But with the best discretion of a woman,
And a strong fortifi'd patience, I desire you
To give it hearing.
Luke. My heart beats.
F4r *Ladie.* My Lord, you much amaze me.
Lord. I shall astonish you. The noble Merchant,
Who living was for his integritie
And upright dealing (a rare miracle
In a rich Citizen) Londons best honour;
Is—I am loth to speak it.
Luke. Wondrous strange!
Ladie. I do suppose the worst, not dead I hope?
Lord. Your supposition's true, your hopes are false.
Hee's dead.
Ladie. Ay mee.
Anne. My Father.
Mary. My kind Father.
Luke. Now they insult not.
Lord. Pray hear me out.
Hee's dead. Dead to the world, and you. And now
Lives onely to himself.
Luke. What Riddle's this?
Ladie. Act not the torturer in my afflictions;
But make me understand the summe of all
That I must undergo.
Lord. In few words take it;
He is retir'd into a Monastery,
Where he resolves to end his daies.
Luke. More strange.
Lord. I saw him take poste for Dover, and the wind
Sitting so fair, by this hee's safe at Calice,
And ere long will be at Lovain.
Ladie. Could I guesse
What were the motives that induc'd him to it,
'Twere some allay to my sorrows.
Lord. I'le instruct you,
And chide you into that knowledg: 'twas your pride
Above your rank, and stubborn disobedience

Of these your daughters, in their milk suck'd from you:
At home the harshnesse of his entertainment,
You wilfully forgetting that your all
Was borrowed from him; and to hear abroad
The imputations dispers'd upon you,
F4v And justly too, I fear, that drew him to
This strict retirement: And thus much said for him,
I am my self to accuse you.
Ladie. I confesse
A guilty cause to him, but in a thought,
My Lord, I ne're wrong'd you.
Lord. In fact you have;
The insolent disgrace you put upon
My onely Son, and Master *Plenty*; men, that lov'd
Your daughters in a noble way, to wash off
The scandal, put a resolution in 'em
For three years travel.
Ladie. I am much griev'd for it.
Lord. One thing I had forgot; your rigor to
His decaied brother, in which your flatteries,
Or sorceries, made him a coagent with you,
Wrought not the least impression.
Luke. Humph! this sounds well.
Ladie. 'Tis now past help: after these storms, my Lord,
A little calme, if you please.
Lord. If what I have told you
Shew'd like a storm, what now I must deliver
Will prove a raging tempest. His whole estate
In lands and leases, debts and present moneys,
With all the movables he stood posses'd of,
With the best advice which he could get for gold
From his learned counsel, by this formall Will
Is pass'd o're to his brother. With it take
The key of his counting house. Not a groat left you,
Which you can call your own.
Ladie. Undone for ever.
Anne, *Mary*. What will become of us?
Luke. Humph!
Lord. The Scenes chang'd,
And he that was your slave, by fate appointed

Your governour; you kneel to me in vain,
I cannot help you, I discharge the trust
Impos'd upon me. This humilitie
G1r From him may gain remission, and perhaps
Forgetfulnesse of your barbarous usage to him.
Ladie. Am I come to this?
Lord. Enjoy your own, good Sir,
But use it with due reverence. I once heard you
Speak most divinely in the opposition
Of a revengefull humor; to these shew it,
And such who then depended on the mercy
Of your brother wholly now at your devotion,
And make good the opinion I held of you;
Of which I am most confident.
Luke. Pray you rise,
And rise with this assurance, I am still,
As I was of late, your creature; and if rais'd
In any thing, 'tis in my power to serve you,
My will is still the same. O my Lord!
This heap of wealth which you possesse me of,
Which to a worldly man had been a blessing,
And to the messenger might with justice challenge
A kind of adoration, is to me
A curse, I cannot thank you for; and much lesse
Rejoyce in that tranquility of mind,
My brothers vows must purchase. I have made
A dear exchange with him. He now enjoyes
My peace, and poverty, the trouble of
His wealth confer'd on me, and that a burthen
Too heavy for my weak shouldiers.
Lord. Honest soul,
With what feeling he receivs it.
Ladie. You shall have
My best assistance, if you please to use it
To help you to suport it.
Luke. By no means,
The waight shall rather sinck me, then you part
With one short minute from those lawfull pleasures
Which you were born to in your care to aid me.
You shall have all abundance. In my nature

I was ever liberall, my Lord you know it,
G1v Kind, affable. And now me thinks I see
Before my face the Jubile of joy,
When it is assur'd, my brother lives in me,
His debtors in full cups crown'd to my health,
With Pæans to my praise will celebrate.
For they well know 'tis far from me to take
The forfeiture of a Bond. Nay I shall blush,
The interest never paid after three years,
When I demand my principall. And his servants
Who from a slavish fear pai'd their obedience
By him exacted; now when they are mine
Will grow familiar friends, and as such use me,
Being certain of the mildnesse of my temper,
Which my change of fortune, frequent in most men
Hath not the power to alter.
Lord. Yet take heed Sir
You ruine it not with too much lenity,
What his fit severity rais'd.
Ladie. And we fall from
That height we have maintain'd.
Luke. I'le build it higher,
To admiration higher. With disdain
I look upon these habits, no way suiting
The wife, and daughters of a knighted Citizen
Bless'd with abundance.
Lord. There Sir, I joyn with you;
A fit decorum must be kept, the Court
Distinguished from the City.
Luke. With your favour
I know what you would say, but give me leave
In this to be your advocate. You are wide,
Wide the whole region in what I purpose.
Since all the titles, honours, long descents
Borrow their gloss from wealth, the rich with reason
May challenge their prerogatives. And it shall be
My glory, nay a triumph to revive
In the pomp that these shall shine, the memory

139. their] *Mason*; her *58* 145. ruine it] *58*; ruine *Dodsley* 156. Wide the] *58*[2]; The *58*[1] 158. the] *58*[2]; ye'r *58*[1]; your *conj. editor*

Of the Roman matrons, who kep't captive Queens
G2r To be their hand-maids. And when you appear
Like *Juno* in full majesty, and my Neeces
Like *Iris*, *Hebe*, or what deities else
Old Poets fancie; your cram'd ward-robes richer
Then various natures, and draw down the envy
Of our western world upon you, onely hold me
Your vigilant *Hermes* with aeriall wings,
My caducevs my strong zeal to serve you,
Press'd to fetch in all rarities may delight you,
And I am made immortall.
Lord. A strange frensie.
Luke. Off with these rags, and then to bed. There dream
Of future greatnesse, which when you awake
I'le make a certain truth: but I must be
A doer, not a promiser. The performance
Requiring hast, I kisse your hands, and leave you. *Exit* LUKE.
Lord. Are we all turn'd statues: have his strange words charm'd us?
What muse you on Lady?
Ladie. Do not trouble me.
Lord. Sleep you too, young ones?
Anne. Swift wing'd time till now
Was never tedious to me. Would 'twere night.
Mary. Nay morning rather.
Lord. Can you ground your faith
On such impossibilities? have you so soon
Forgot your good Husband?
Ladie. Hee was a vanitie
I must no more remember.
Lord. Excellent!
You your kind Father?
Anne. Such an Uncle never
Was read of in Storie!
Lord. Not one word in answer
Of my demands?
Mary. You are but a Lord, and know
My thoughts soar higher.
Lord. Admirable! I will leave you

166. cram'd] *58*[2]; examin'd *58*[1]   172. And I] *Dodsley*; And *58*

To your Castles in the Air.—When I relate this [*Aside.*]
G2v It will exceed belief, but he must know it. *Exit* LORD.
Stargaze. Now I may boldly speak: May it please you Madam,
To look upon your Vassal; I foresaw this,
The Starrs assur'd it.
Ladie. I begin to feel
My self another woman.
Stargaze. Now you shall find
All my predictions true, and nobler matches
Prepar'd for my young Ladies.
Milliscent. Princely Husbands.
Anne. I'le go no lesse.
Mary. Not a word more,
Provide my night-rayl.
Milliscent. What shall we be to morrow. *Exeunt.*

. iii] *Actus tertius, Scena tertia.*

Enter LUKE *with a key.*

Luke. 'Twas no phantastick object, but a truth,
A reall truth. Nor dream; I did not slumber,
And could wake ever with a brooding eye
To gaze upon't! It did indure the touch,
I saw, and felt it. Yet what I beheld
And handl'd oft, did so transcend beleefe
(My wonder, and astonishment pass'd ore)
I faintly could give credit to my senses.
Thou dumb magician that without a charm
Did'st make my entrance easie, to possesse
What wise men wish, and toyl for. *Hermes* Moly;
Sybilla's golden bough; the great Elixar,
Imagin'd onely by the Alchymist
Compar'd with thee are shadows, thou the substance
And guardian of felicity. No marvail,
My brother made thy place of rest his bosome,
Thou being the keeper of his heart, a mistris

190 SD. *Aside.*] *Gifford*[2]; *not in 58* 198. Not] *58*; Nor I. Not *conj. Craik*
III. iii. 2. truth. Nor dream;] *after Gifford*: truth. Nor dream *58*; truth, no dream. *Dodsley*

To be hugg'd ever. In by corners of
G3r This sacred room, silver in bags heap'd up
Like billets saw'd, and ready for the fire,
Unworthy to hold fellowship with bright gold
That flow'd about the room, conceal'd it self.
There needs no artificiall light, the splendor
Makes a perpetuall day there, night and darknesse
By that still burning lamp for ever banish'd.
But when guided by that, my eyes had made
Discovery of the caskets, and they open'd,
Each sparkling diamond from it self shot forth
A pyramid of flames, and in the roof
Fix'd it a glorious Star, and made the place
Heavens abstract, or Epitome. Rubies, Saphires,
And ropes of Orient pearl, these seen, I could not
But look on with contempt. And yet I found
What weak credulity could have no faith in,
A treasure far exceeding these. Here lay
A mannor bound fast in a skin of parchment,
The wax continuing hard, the acres melting.
Here a sure deed of gift for a market town,
If not redeem'd this day, which is not in
The unthrifts power. There being scarce one shire
In *Wales* or *England*, where my moneys are not
Lent out at usurie, the certain hook
To draw in more. I am sublim'd! grosse earth
Supports me not. I walk on ayr! who's there?
Thievs, raise the street, thievs!

Enter LORD; SIR JOHN, LACIE, *and* PLENTY, *as Indians.*

Lord. What strange passion's this?
Have you your eies? do you know me?
Luke. You, my Lord!
I do: but this retinue, in these shapes too,
May well excuse my fears. When 'tis your pleasure
That I should wait upon you, give me leave
To do it at your own house, for I must tell you,
Things as they now are with me, well consider'd,
I do not like such visitants.

30. Fix'd] *Mason*; Fix *58*   45 SD. LORD;] *Dodsley*; *Lord*, *58*

Lord. Yesterday
G3v When you had nothing, praise your poverty for't,
You could have sung secure before a thief;
But now you are grown rich, doubts and suspitions,
And needless fears possess you. Thank a good brother,
But let not this exalt you.
Luke. A good brother:
Good in his conscience, I confesse, and wise,
In giving o're the world. But his estate
Which your Lordship may conceive great, no way answers
The general opinion. Alas,
With a great charge, I am left a poor man by him.
Lord. A poor man, say you?
Luke. Poor, compar'd with what
'Tis thought I do possesse. Some little land,
Fair houshold furniture; a few good debts,
But empty bags I find: yet I will be
A faithful Steward to his wife and daughters,
And to the utmost of my power obey
His will in all things.
Lord. I'le not argue with you
Of his estate, but bind you to performance
Of his last request, which is for testimony
Of his religious charitie, that you would
Receive these Indians, lately sent him from
Virginia, into your house; and labour
At any rate with the best of your endeavours,
Assisted by the aids of our Divines,
To make 'm Christians.
Luke. Call you this, my Lord,
Religious charitie? to send Infidells,
Like hungrie Locusts, to devour the bread
Should feed his family. I neither can,
Nor will consent to't.
Lord. Do not slight it, 'tis
With him a businesse of such consequence,
That should he onely hear 'tis not embrac'd,
And chearfully, in this his conscience aiming
At the saving of three souls, 'twill draw him o're
G4r To see it himself accomplish'd.

Luke. Heaven forbid
I should divert him from his holy purpose
To worldly cares again. I rather will
Sustain the burthen, and with the converted
Feast the converters, who I know will prove
The greater feeders.

Sir John. Oh, ha, enewah Chrish bully leika.

Plenty. Enaula.

Lacie. Harrico botikia bonnery.

Luke. Ha! In this heathen language,
How is it possible our Doctors should
Hold conference with 'em? or I use the means
For their conversion?

Lord. That shall be no hinderance
To your good purposes. They have liv'd long
In the English Colonie, and speak our language
As their own Dialect; the businesse does concern you:
Mine own designs command me hence. Continue,
As in your poverty you were, a pious
And honest man. *Exit.*

Luke. That is, interpreted,
A slave, and begger.

Sir John. You conceive it right,
There being no religion, nor virtue
But in abundance, and no vice but want.
All deities serve *Plutus.*

Luke. Oracle.

Sir John. Temples rais'd to our selvs in the increase
Of wealth, and reputation, speak a wiseman;
But sacrifice to an imagin'd power,
Of which we have no sense, but in belief,
A superstitious fool.

Luke. True worldly wisdom.

Sir John. All knowledge else is folly.

Lacie. Now we are yours,
Be confident your better Angel is
Enter'd your house.

G4v *Plenty.* There being nothing in
The compasse of your wishes, but shall end
In their fruition to the full.

Sir John. As yet,
You do not know us, but when you understand
The wonders we can do, and what the ends were
That brought us hither, you will entertain us
With more respect.
Luke. There's somthing whispers to me, [*Aside.*]
These are no common men;—my house is yours,
Enjoy it freely: onely grant me this,
Not to be seen abroad till I have heard
More of your sacred principles. Pray enter.
You are learn'd Europians, and wee worse
Then ignorant Americans.
Sir John. You shall find it. *Exeunt.*

. i] ## *Actus quartus, Scena prima.*

Enter DINGEM, GETTALL, *and* HOLDFAST.

Dingem. NOT speak with him? with fear survey me better,
Thou figure of famine.
Gettall. Comming, as we do,
From his quondam patrons, his dear Ingles now,
The brave spark *Tradewell.*
Dingem. And the man of men
In the service of a woman, gallant *Goldwire.*

Enter LUKE.

Holdfast. I know 'em for his prentices without
These flourishes. Here are rude fellows Sir.
Dingem. Not yours, you rascall?
Holdfast. No, Don pimp: you may seek 'em
In Bridewell, or the hole, here are none of your comrogues.
Luke. One of 'em looks as he would cut my throat:
Your businesse, friends?
I1r *Holdfast.* I'le fetch a constable,
Let him answer him in the Stocks.
Dingem. Stir and thou dar'st.
Fright me with Bridewell and the Stocks? they are flea-bitings
I am familiar with.

122 SD. *Aside.*] *Gifford*[2]*: not in 58*

Luke. Pray you put up.
And sirrah hold your peace.
Dingem. Thy words a law,
And I obey. Live scrape-shoo, and be thankfull.
Thou man of muck, and money, for as such
I now salute thee. The Suburbian gamsters
Have heard thy fortunes, and I am in person
Sent to congratulate.
Gettall. The news hath reach'd
The ordinaries, and all the gamsters are
Ambitious to shake the golden golls
Of worshipfull Master *Luke*. I come from *Tradewell*
Your fine facetious factor.
Dingem. I from *Goldwire*.
He and his *Hellen* have prepar'd a banquet
With the appurtenances to entertain thee,
For I must whisper in thine ear, thou art
To be her *Paris*; but bring mony with thee
To quit old scores.
Gettall. Blind chance hath frown'd upon
Brave *Tradewell*. Hee's blown up, but not without
Hope of recovery, so you supply him
With a good round sum. In my house I can assure you
There's half a million stirring.
Luke. What hath he lost?
Gettall. Three hundred.
Luke. A trifle.
Gettall. Make it up a thousand,
And I will fit him with such tools as shall
Bring in a miriad.
Luke. They know me well,
Nor need you use such circumstances for 'em.
What's mine is theirs. They are my friends, not servants;
H1v But in their care to enrich me, and these courses
The speeding means. Your name, I pray you?
Gettall. *Gettall*;
I have been many years an Ordinary-keeper,
My Box my poor Revenue.
Luke. Your name suits well
With your profession. Bid him bear up, he shall not

Sit long on pennilesse-bench.

Gettall. There spake an Angel.

Luke. You know Mistris *Shave'm*?

Gettall. The Pontifical Punk?

Luke. The same. Let him meet me there some two hours hence,
And tell *Tom Goldwire* I will then be with him,
Furnish'd beyond his hopes, and let your Mistris
Appear in her best trim.

Dingem. She will make thee young,
Old *Æson.* She is ever furnish'd with
Medæas Drugs, Restoratives. I flie
To keep 'em sober till thy worship come,
They will be drunk with joy else.

Gettall. I'le run with you.

Exeunt DINGEM *and* GETTALL.

Holdfast. You will not do as you say, I hope.

Luke. Inquire not,
I shall do what becoms me—to the door. *Knocking.*
New Visitants: What are they?

Holdfast. A whole batch, Sir,
Almost of the same leaven: your needy Debtors,
Penury, *Fortune*, *Hoyst.*

Luke. They come to gratulate
The fortune fall'n upon me.

Holdfast. Rather, Sir,
Like the others, to prey on you.

Luke. I am simple,
They know my good nature. But let 'em in however.

Holdfast. All will come to ruine, I see beggery
Already knocking at the door. You may enter—
But use a conscience, and do not work upon
I2r A tender-hearted Gentleman too much,
'Twill shew like charitie in you.

Enter FORTUNE, PENURIE *and* HOYST.

Luke. Welcome Friends:
I know your hearts, and wishes; you are glad
You have chang'd your Creditor.

Penurie. I weep for joy
To look upon his Worships face.

Fortune. His Worships?
I see Lord Major written on his forehead;
The Cap of Maintenance, and Citie Sword
Born up in state before him.
Hoyst. Hospitals,
And a third Burse erected by his Honour.
Penurie. The Citie Poet on the Pageant-day
Preferring him before *Gresham.*
Hoyst. All the Conduits
Spouting Canary Sack.
Fortune. Not a prisoner left,
Under ten pounds.
Penurie. We his poor Beads-men feasting
Our neighbours on his bounty.
Luke. May I make good
Your prophecies, gentle friends, as I'le indeavour
To the utmost of my power.
Holdfast. Yes, for one year,
And break the next.
Luke. You are ever prating, Sirrha:
Your present businesse, friends?
Fortune. Were your brother present,
Mine had been of some consequence; but now
The power lies in your Worships hand, 'tis little,
And will I know, as soon as ask'd, be granted.
Luke. 'Tis very probable.
Fortune. The kind forbearance
Of my great debt, by your means, heav'n be prais'd for't,
Hath rais'd my sunk estate. I have two Ships,
Which I long since gave lost, above my hopes
H2v Return'd from *Barbary*, and richly fraighted.
Luke. Where are they?
Fortune. Near *Gravesend.*
Luke. I am truly glad of't.
Fortune. I find your worships charity, and dare swear so.
Now may I have your licence, as I know
With willingnesse I shall, to make the best
Of the commodities, though you have execution,
And after judgment against all that's mine,

IV. i. 87. heav'n be] *Dodsley*; heav'n *58* 89. gave] *58*; gave for *Gifford*[2]

As my poor body, I shall be enabl'd
To make payment of my debts to all the world,
And leave my self a competence.
Luke. You much wrong me,
If you onely doubt it. Yours Master *Hoyst*?
Hoyst. 'Tis the surrendring back the morgage of
My lands, and on good tearms, but three daies patience;
By an Uncles death I have means left to redeem it,
And cancell all the forfeited Bonds I seal'd too
In my riots to the Merchant, for I am
Resolv'd to leave off play, and turn good husband.
Luke. A good intent, and to be cherish'd in you.
Yours *Penury*?
Penurie. My state stands as it did, Sir;
What I ow'd I ow, but can pay nothing to you.
Yet if you please to trust me with ten pounds more,
I can buy a commoditie of a Sayler
Will make me a freeman. There Sir is his name;
And the parcels I am to deal for. *Gives him a paper.*
Luke. You are all so reasonable
In your demands, that I must freely grant 'em.
Some three hours hence meet me on the Exchange,
You shall be amply satisfi'd.
Penurie. Heaven preserve you.
Fortune. Happie were *London* if within her walls
She had many such rich men.
Luke. No more, now leave me;
Exeunt FORTUNE, HOYST, *and* PENURIE.
H3r I am full of various thoughts. Be carefull *Holdfast*,
I have much to do.
Holdfast. And I something to say
Would you give me hearing.
Luke. At my better leasure.
'Till my return, look well unto the Indians.
In the mean time do you as this directs you. *Exeunt.*

104. too] *58*; to *Mason*

[IV. ii]

Actus quartus, Scena secunda.

Enter GOLDWIRE, TRADEWELL, SHAVEM, SECRET, GETTALL, *and* DINGEM.

Goldwire. All that is mine is theirs. Those were his words?
Dingem. I am authenticall.
Tradewell. And that I should not
Sit long on pennilesse bench?
Gettall. But suddainly start up
A gamster at the height, and cry at all.
Shavem. And did he seem to have an inclination
To toy with me?
Dingem. He wish'd you would put on
Your best habiliments, for he resolv'd
To make a joviall day on't.
Goldwire. Hug him close wench,
And thou may'st eat gold, and amber. I wel know him
For a most insatiate drabber. He hath given,
Before he spent his own estate, which was
Nothing to the huge masse hee's now possess'd of,
A hundred pound a leap.
Shavem. Hell take my Doctor,
He should have brought me some fresh oyl of Talk,
These Ceruses are common.
Secret. Troth sweet Lady,
The colours are well laid on.
Goldwire. And thick enough,
H3v I find that on my lips.
Shavem. Do you so, Jack sauce?
I'le keep 'em further of.
Goldwire. But be assur'd first
Of a new mainteiner ere you cashire the old one.
But bind him fast by thy sorceries, and thou shalt
Be my revenue; the whole colledge study
The reparation of thy ruin'd face;
Thou shalt have thy proper and bald-headed Coach-man;
Thy Tailor, and Embroiderer shall kneel

IV. ii. 17. I find] *Dodsley*; find *58*

To thee their Idoll. Cheap-side and the Exchange
Shall court thy custome, and thou shalt forget
There ever was a Saint Martins. Thy procurer
Shall be sheath'd in Velvet, and a reverend Vail
Passe her for a grave Matron. Have an eie to the door,
And let lowd musick when this Monarch enters
Proclaim his entertainment.
Dingem. That's my office. *Cornets florish.*
The Consort's ready.

Enter LUKE.

Tradewell. And the god of pleasure,
Master *Luke* our *Comus* enters.
Goldwire. Set your face in order,
I will prepare him. Live I to see this day,
And to acknowledge you my royal master?
Tradewell. Let the iron Chests flie open, and the gold
Rusty for want of use appear again.
Gettall. Make my ordinary flourish.
Shavem. Welcom, Sir,
To your own Palace. *Musick.*
Goldwire. Kisse your *Cleopatra*,
And shew your self in your magnificent bounties
A second *Anthony*.
Dingem. All the Nine Worthies.
Secret. Variety of pleasures wait on you.
And a strong back.
Luke. Give me leave to breath, I pray you.
I am astonish'd! all this preparation
I4r For me? and this choice modest beauty wrought
To feed my appetite?
All. We are all your creatures.
Luke. A house well furnish'd.
Goldwire. At your own cost, Sir,
Glad I the Instrument. I prophecied
You should possesse what now you do, and therefore
Prepar'd it for your pleasure. There's no ragg
This *Venus* wears, but on my knowledge was
Deriv'd from your brothers Cash. The Lease of the house
And Furniture, cost near a thousand, Sir.

Shavem. But now you are master both of it and me,
I hope you'l build elswhere.
Luke. And see you plac'd
Fair one to your desert. As I live, friend *Tradewell*,
I hardly knew you, your cloaths so wel become you.
What is your losse? speak truth.
Tradewell. Three hundred, Sir.
Gettall. But on a new supply he shall recover
The summe told twenty times o're.
Shavem. There is a banket,
And after that a soft Couch that attends you.
Luke. I couple not in the day-light. Expectation
Heightens the pleasure of the night, my sweet one
Your musick's harsh, discharge it: I have provided
A better Consort, and you shall frollick it
In another place. *Cease musick*.
Goldwire. But have you brought gold, and store Sir?
Tradewell. I long to ware the Caster.
Goldwire. I to appear
In a fresh habit.
Shavem. My Mercer and my Silkman
Waited me two hours since.
Luke. I am no Porter
To carrie so much gold as will supply
Your vaste desires, but I have ta'ne order for you,

H4v *Enter* SHERIFF, MARSHAL, *and Officers*.

You shall have what is fitting, and they come here
Will see it perform'd. Do your offices: You have
My Lord Chief Justices Warrant for't.
Sheriff. Seize 'em all.
Shavem. The Citie-Marshal!
Goldwire. And the Sheriff. I know him.
Secret. We are betray'd.
Dingem. Undone.
Gettall. Dear Master *Luke*.
Goldwire. You cannot be so cruel: your perswasion
Chid us into these courses, oft repeating,
Shew your selvs City-sparks, and hang up mony.

54. me,] *Dodsley*; ~. *58* 67. ware] *Gifford*[2]; wear *58*

Luke. True, when it was my brothers I contemn'd it,
But now it is mine own, the case is alter'd.
Tradewell. Will you prove your self a divel? tempt us to mischief,
And then discover it?
Luke. Argue that hereafter.
In the mean time, Master *Goldwire*, you that made
Your ten pound suppers; kep't your puncks at livery
In *Brainford*, *Stanes*, and *Barnet*; and this in *London*.
Held correspondence with your fellow-cashers,
Ka me, ka thee; And knew in your accompts
To cheat my brother, if you can, evade me.
If there be law in London your fathers Bonds
Shall answer for what you are out.
Goldwire. You often told us
It was a bug-bear.
Luke. Such a one as shall fright 'em
Out of their estates to make me satisfaction,
To the utmost scruple. And for you Madam,
My *Cleopatra*, by your own confession
Your house, and all your movables are mine;
Nor shall you, nor your Matron need to trouble
Your Mercer, or your Silkman; a blew gown,
And a whip to boot, as I will handle it
Will serve the turn in Bridewell, and these soft hands,
When they are inur'd to beating hemp, be scour'd
I1r In your penitent tears, and quite forget
Powders, and bitter almonds.
Shavem, *Secret*, *Dingem*. Will you shew no mercy?
Luke. I am inexorable.
Gettall. I'le make bold
To take my leave, the gamsters stay my comming.
Luke. We must not part so, gentle Master *Gettal*.
Your box, your certain in-com, must pay back
Three hundred as I take it, or you lie by it.
There's half a million stirring in your house,
This a poor trifle. Master Shriefe, and Master Marshall
On your perills do your offices.
Goldwire. Dost thou crie now

89. can, . . . me.] *Mason*; can . . . me, *58* 102–3. forget / Powders, and] *58*; forget their powders, / And *Gifford*

Like a maudlin gamster after loss? I'le suffer
Like a Roman, and now in my miserie,
In scorn of all thy wealth, to thy teeth tell thee
Thou wer't my pander.
Luke. Shall I hear this from
My prentice?
Marshal. Stop his mouth.
Sheriff. Away with 'em.
Exeunt SHERIFF, MARSHAL, *and the rest.*
Luke. A prosperous omen in my entrance to
My alter'd nature. These house-thievs remov'd,
And what was lost, beyond my hopes recover'd,
Will add unto my heap. Increase of wealth
Is the rich mans ambition, and mine
Shall know no bounds. The valiant Macedon
Having in his conceit subdu'd one world,
Lamented that there were no more to conquer:
In my way he shall be my great example.
And when my private house in cram'd abundance
Shall prove the chamber of the City poor,
And Genoways banquers shall look pale with envy
When I am mention'd, I shall grieve there is
No more to be exhausted in one Kingdome.
Religion, conscience, charity, farewell.
To me you are words onely, and no more,
All humane happinesse consists in store. *Exit.*

I1v

[IV. iii] *Actus quartus, Scena tertia.*

Enter SERJEANTS, [*Yeoman*,] FORTUNE, HOYST, PENURIE.

Fortune. At Master *Lukes* suite? the action twenty thousand?
1 *Serjeant*. With two or three executions, which shall grind you
To powder when we have you in the Counter.
Fortune. Thou dost belie him varlet. He, good gentleman,
Will weep when he hears how we are us'd.
1 *Serjeant*. Yes milstones.
Penurie. He promis'd to lend me ten pound for a bargain,

113. Roman] *MS correction in several copies, Gifford*[1]; Boman *58* IV. iii. SD. *Yeoman*,] *Craik*; *not in 58* 2–3. grind you / To] *Gifford*; grind / You to *58*

He will not do it this way.
2 Serjeant. I have warrant
For what I have done. You are a poor fellow,
And there being little to be got by you,
In charity, as I am an officer,
I would not have seen you, but upon compulsion,
And for mine own security.
3 Serjeant. You are a gallant,
And I'le do you a courtesie; provided
That you have mony. For a piece an hour
I'le keep you in the house, till you send for bail.
2 Serjeant. In the mean time yeoman run to the other Counter,
And search if there be ought else out against him.
3 Serjeant. That done, haste to his creditors. Hee's a prize,
And as we are City pirates by our oaths,
We must make the best on't. [*Exit Yeoman.*]
Hoyst. Do your worst, I care not.
I'le be remov'd to the Fleet, and drink and drabbe there
In spite of your teeth. I now repent I ever
Intended to be honest.

Enter LUKE.

3 Serjeant. Here he comes,
You had best tell so.
Fortune. Worshipfull Sir,
I2r You come in time to free us from these ban-dogs;
I know you gave no way to't.
Penurie. Or if you did,
'Twas but to try our patience.
Hoyst. I must tell you
I do not like such trialls.
Luke. Are you Serjeants
Acquainted with the danger of a rescue,
Yet stand here prating in the street? The Counter
Is a safer place to parly in.
Fortune. Are you in earnest?
Luke. Yes faith, I will be satisfi'd to a token,
Or build upon't you rott there.
Fortune. Can a gentleman,

13. I'le] *Mason*; I *58* 20 SD. *Exit Yeoman.*] *Craik*; *not in 58* 24. tell] *58*; tell him *Dodsley*

Of your soft and silken temper, speak such language?
Penurie. So honest, so religious?
Hoyst. That preach'd
So much of charity for us to your brother?
Luke. Yes when I was in poverty it shew'd well,
But I inherite with his state, his minde,
And rougher nature. I grant, then I talk'd
For some ends to my self conceal'd, of pitie,
The poor mans orisons; and such like nothing.
But what I thought you all shall feel, and with rigor.
Kind Master *Luke* saies it. Who paies for your attendance?
Do you wait gratis?
Fortune. Hear us speak.
Luke. While I,
Like the Adder stop mine ears. Or did I listen,
Though you spake with the tongues of Angels to me
I am not to be alter'd.
Fortune. Let me make the best
Of my shippes, and their fraight.
Penurie. Lend me the ten pounds you promis'd.
Hoyst. A day or two's patience to redeem my morgage,
And you shall be satisfi'd.
Fortune. To the utmost farthing.
Luke. I'le shew some mercie; which is, that I will not
I2v Torture you with false hopes, but make you know
What you shall trust to. Your Ships to my use
Are seized on. I have got into my hands
Your bargain from the Sailor, 'twas a good one
For such a petty summ. I will likewise take
The extremity of your Morgage, and the forfeit
Of your several Bonds; the use, and principle
Shall not serve. Think of the basket, wretches,
And a Coal-sack for a winding-sheet.
Fortune. Broker.
Hoyst. Iew.
Fortune. Imposter.
Hoyst. Cut-throat.
Fortune. Hypocrite.

41. nothing] *58*; nothings *Mason* 55. bargain] *Dodsley*; bargains *58* 61. Imposter] *Dodsley*; Impos er *58*

Luke. Do, rayle on.
Move mountaines with your breath, it shakes not me.
Penurie. On my knees I beg compassion. My wife and children
Shall hourly pray for your worship.
Fortune. Mine betake thee
To the Devil thy tutor.
Penurie. Look upon my tears.
Hoyst. My rage.
Fortune. My wrongs.
Luke. They are all a like to me.
Intreats, curses, prayers, or imprecations.
Doe your duties Serjants, I am else where look'd for. *Exit* LUKE.
3 *Serjeant.* This your kind creditor?
2 *Serjeant.* A vast villan rather.
Penurie. See, see, the Serjeants pitie us. Yet hee's marble.
Hoyst. Buried alive!
Fortune. There's no meanes to avoid it. *Exeunt.*

I3r
iv]

Actus quartus, Scena quarta.

Enter HOLDFAST, STARGAZE, *and* MILLISCENT.

Stargaze. Not waite upon my Lady?
Holdfast. Nor come at her,
You finde it not in your Alminack.
Milliscent. Nor I have licence
To bring her breakfast?
Holdfast. My new master hath
Decreed this for a fasting day. She hath feasted long
And after a carnivale Lent ever follows.
Milliscent. Give me the key of her ward-robe. You'l repent this:
I must know what Gown shee'l wear.
Holdfast. You are mistaken,
Dame president of the sweet meates. Shee and her daughters
Are turn'd Philosophers, and must carry all
Their wealth about em. They have cloaths lai'd in their chamber,
If they please to put em on, and without help too,
Or they may walk naked. You look Master *Stargaze*

67. Intreats] *58*; Intreaties *Gifford* 68 SD. *Exit* LUKE.] *Dodsley*; *follows* imprecations. (l. 67) *58*

As you had seen a strange comet, and had now foretold
The end of the world, and on what day. And you,
As the wasps had broke into the galley-pots,
And eaten up your Apricocks.
  Within Ladie.   *Stargaze. Milliscent.*
  Milliscent. My Ladyes voice.
  Holdfast.   Stir not, you are confin'd here.
Your Ladiship may approach them if you please,
But they are bound in this circle.
  Within Ladie.   Mine own bees
Rebell against me! When my kind brother knows this
I will be so reveng'd.
  Holdfast.   The world's well alterd.
Hee's your kind brother now. But yesterday
Your slave and jesting-stock.

I3v *Enter* LADIE, ANNE, MARY, *in course habit, weeping.*

  Milliscent.   What witch hath transform'd you?
  Stargaze. Is this the glorious shape your cheating brother
Promis'd you should appear in?
  Milliscent.   My young Ladies
In buffin gowns, and green aprons! tear 'em off,
Rather shew all then be seen thus.
  Holdfast.   'Tis more comly
I wis then their other whim-whams.
  Milliscent.   A french hood too;
Now 'tis out of fashion, a fools cap would shew better.
  Ladie. We are fool'd indeed; by whose command are we us'd thus?

Enter LUKE.

  Holdfast. Here he comes that can best resolve you.
  Ladie.   O good brother!
Do you thus preserve your protestation to me?
Can Queens envy this habit? or did *Juno*
E're feast in such a shape?
  Anne.   You talk'd of *Hebe*,
Of *Iris*, and I know not what; but were they
Dres'd as we are, they were sure some Chandlers daughters
Bleaching linnen in Moor-fields.

IV. iv. 16. *Stargaze*] *Dodsley*; Stargazer *58* 20. me!] *Mason*; ~. *58*; ~? *Dodsley*. 36. are, they] *Mason*; are; They *58*; are? They *Dodsley*

Mary. Or Exchange-wenches,
Comming from eating pudding-pies on a Sunday
At *Pemlico*, or *Islington*.
Luke. Save you Sister.
I now dare style you so: you were before
Too glorious to be look'd on; now you appear
Like a City Matron, and my pretty Neeces
Such things as were born, and bred there. Why should you ape
The fashions of Court-Ladies? whose high titles
And pedegrees of long descent, give warrant
For their superfluous braverie? 'twas monstrous:
Till now you ne're look'd lovely.
Ladie. Is this spoken
In scorn?
Luke. Fie, no, with judgment. I make good
I4r My promise, and now shew you like your selvs,
In your own naturall shapes, and stand resolv'd
You shall continue so.
Ladie. It is confess'd Sir—
Luke. Sir! Sirrah. Use your old phrase, I can bear it.
Ladie. That if you please forgotten. We acknowledge
We have deserv'd ill from you, yet despair not,
Though we are at your disposure, youll maintain us
Like your brothers wife, and daughters.
Luke. 'Tis my purpose.
Ladie. And not make us ridiculous.
Luke. Admir'd rather,
As fair examples for our proud City dames,
And their proud brood to imitate. Do not frown;
If you do, I laugh, and glory that I have
The power in you to scourge a generall vice,
And rise up a new Satyrist: but hear gently,
And in a gentle phrase I'le reprehend
Your late disguis'd deformity, and cry up
This decency, and neatnesse, with th'advantage
You shall receive by't.
Ladie. We are bound to hear you.
Luke. With a soul inclin'd to learn. Your father was
An honest Country farmer. Good-man Humble,

54. not,] *Dodsley*; ~; *58*

By his neighbours ne're call'd master. Did your pride
Descend from him? but let that passe: your fortune,
Or rather your husbands industry, advanc'd you
To the rank of a Merchants wife. He made a Knight,
And your sweet mistris-ship Ladyfi'd, you wore
Sattin on solemn days, a chain of gold,
A Velvet hood, rich borders, and somtimes
A dainty Miniver cap, a silver pin
Headed with a pearl worth three-pence, and thus far
You were priviledg'd, and no man envi'd it,
It being for the Cities honour, that
There should be a distinction between
The Wife of a Patritian, and Plebean.
Milliscent. Pray you leave preaching, or choose some other text;
I4v Your Rhetorick is too moving, for it makes
Your auditory weep.
Luke. Peace, chattering Mag-pie,
I'le treat of you anon: but when the height
And dignity of *Londons* blessings grew
Contemptible, and the name Lady Maioress
Became a by-word, and you scorn'd the means
By which you were rais'd, (my brothers fond indulgence
Giving the reigns too't) and no object pleas'd you
But the glittering pomp, and bravery of the Court:
What a strange, nay monstrous Metamorphosis follow'd!
No English workman then could please your fancy;
The French, and Tuscan dresse your whole discourse;
This Baud to prodigality entertain'd
To buz into your ears, what shape this Countesse
Appear'd in the last mask; and how it drew
The young Lords eyes upon her; and this usher
Succeeded in the eldest prentices place
To walk before you.
Ladie. Pray you end.
Holdfast. Proceed Sir,
I could fast almost a prentiship to hear you.
You touch 'em so to the quick.
Luke. Then as I said,
The reverend hood cast off, your borrow'd hair
Powder'd, and curl'd, was by your dressers art

Form'd like a Coronet, hang'd with diamonds,
And the richest Orient pearl: Your Carkanets
That did adorn your neck of equall value:
Your Hungerland bands, and Spanish quellio ruffes:
Great Lords and Ladies feasted to survey
Embroider'd petticoats: and sicknesse fain'd
That your night rayls of forty pounds a piece
Might be seen with envy of the visitants;
Rich pantables in ostentation shown,
And roses worth a family; you were serv'd in plate;
Stir'd not a foot without your Coach. And going
To Church not for devotion, but to shew
Your pomp, you were tickl'd when the beggars cry'd
K1r Heaven save your honour, this idolatrie
Paid to a painted room.
Holdfast. Nay, you have reason
To blubber all of you.
Luke. And when you lay
In child-bed, at the Christning of this minx,
I well remember it, as you had been
An absolute princess, since they have no more,
Three severall chambers hung. The first with Arras,
And that for waiters; the second Crimson Sattin
For the meaner sort of guests; the third of Skarlet,
Of the rich Tirian dy; a Canopie
To cover the brats cradle: you in state
Like *Pompie's Julia.*
Ladie. No more I pray you.
Luke. Of this be sure you shall not. I'le cut off
What ever is exorbitant in you,
Or in your Daughters, and reduce you to
Your naturall forms, and habits: not in revenge
Of your base usage of me, but to fright
Others by your example. 'Tis decree'd
You shall serve one another, for I will
Allow no waiter to you. Out of doors
With these useless drones.
Holdfast. Will you pack?

131. *marginal SD. in 58: Whil'st the / Act Plays, / the Foot- / step, little / Table, and / Arras hung / up for the / Musicians.*

Milliscent. Not till I have
My truncks along with me.
Luke. Not a rag, you came
Hither without a box.
Stargaze. You'l shew to me
I hope Sir more compassion.
Holdfast. 'Troth I'le be
Thus far a suitor for him. He hath printed
An Almanack for this year at his own charge,
Let him have th' impression with him to set up with.
Luke. For once I'le be intreated: let it be
Thrown to him out of the window.
Stargaze. O cursed Stars
K1v That raign'd at my nativity! how have you cheated
Your poor observer!
Anne. Must we part in tears?
Mary. Farewell, good *Milliscent.*
Ladie. I am sick, and meet with
A rough Physician. O my pride! and scorn!
How justly am I punish'd!
Mary. Now we suffer
For our stubbornnesse and disobedience
To our good father.
Anne. And the base conditions,
We impos'd upon our Suitors.
Luke. Get you in,
And Catterwall in a corner.
Ladie. There's no contending.

LADIE, ANNE, MARY, *go off at one door*;
STARGAZE *and* MILLISCENT *at the other.*

Luke. How lik'st thou my carriage, *Holdfast*?
Holdfast. Well in some part,
But it rellishes I know not how, a little
Of too much tyranny.
Luke. Thou art a fool:
Hee's cruel to himself, that dares not be
Severe to those that us'd him cruelly. *Exeunt.*

Whil'st the Act plays, the Footstep, little Table, and Arras hung up for the Musicians.

160 SD. *Whil'st . . . Musicians.*] *editor: at l. 131 in 58*

V. i]

Actus quintus, Scena prima.

Enter LUKE, SIR JOHN, LACIE *and* PLENTY.

Luke. YOU care not then, as it seems, to be converted
To our religion.
Sir John. We know no such word,
Nor power but the Divel, and him we serve for fear,
Not love.
Luke. I am glad that charge is sav'd.
Sir John. We put
That trick upon your brother, to have means
To come to the Citie. Now to you wee'l discover
K2r The close design that brought us, with assurance
If you lend your aids to furnish us with that
Which in the Colonie was not to be purchas'd,
No merchant ever made such a return
For his most pretious venture, as you shall
Receive from us; far, far, above your hopes,
Or fancie to imagine.

Musicians come down to make ready for the song at Aras.

Luke. It must be
Some strange commoditie, and of a dear value,
(Such an opinion is planted in me,
You will deal fairly) that I would not hazard.
Give me the name of 't.
Lacie. I fear you will make
Some scruple in your conscience to grant it.
Luke. Conscience! No, no; so it may be done with safety,
And without danger of the Law.
Plenty. For that
You shall sleep securely. Nor shall it diminish,
But add unto your heap such an increase,
As what you now possess shall appear an Atome
To the mountain it brings with it.
Luke. Do not rack me
With expectation.
Sir John. Thus then in a word:
The Divel. Why start you at his name? if you
Desire to wallow in wealth and worldly honors,

You must make haste to be familiar with him.
This Divel, whose Priest I am, and by him made
A deep Magician (for I can do wonders)
Appear'd to me in *Virginia*, and commanded
With many stripes (for that's his cruel custome)
I should provide on pain of his fierce wrath
Against the next great sacrifice, at which
We groveling on our faces, fall before him,
Two Christian Virgins, that with their pure blood
Might dy his horrid Altars, and a third
(In his hate to such embraces as are lawful)
Married, and with your cerimonious rites,
K2v As an oblation unto *Hecate*,
And wanton Lust her favorite.
Luke. A divellish custom:
And yet why should it startle me? there are
Enough of the Sex fit for this use; but Virgins,
And such a Matron as you speak of, hardly
To be wrought to it.
Plenty. A Mine of Gold for a fee
Waits him that undertakes it and performs it.
Lacie. Know you no distressed Widow, or poor Maids,
Whose want of dower, though well born, makes 'em weary
Of their own Country?
Sir John. Such as had rather be
Miserable in another world, then where
They have surfeited in felicity?
Luke. Give me leave,
I would not loose this purchase.—A grave Matron! [*Aside.*]
And two pure virgins. Umph! I think my Sister
Though proud was ever honest; and my Neeces
Untainted yet. Why should not they be shipp'd
For this employment? they are burdensome to me,
And eat too much. And if they stay in *London*,
They will find friends that to my losse will force me
To composition. 'Twere a Master-piece
If this could be effected. They were ever

V. i. 43. for this] *58*[1]; fort his *58*[2] 47–9. *rearranged by Gifford*; *58 reads* Know . . . poor / Maids . . . born, / Makes . . . Country? / Such . . . be 52 SD. *Aside.* *Gifford*; *not in 58*

Ambitious of title. Should I urge
Matching with these they shall live *Indian* Queens,
It may do much. But what shall I feel here,
Knowing to what they are design'd? They absent,
The thought of them will leave me. It shall be so.—
I'le furnish you, and to indear the service
In mine own family, and my blood too.

Sir John. Make this good, and your house shall not contain
The gold wee'l send you.

Luke. You have seen my Sister,
And my two Neeces?

Sir John. Yes Sir.

Luke. These perswaded
K3r How happily they shall live, and in what pomp
When they are in your kingdoms, for you must
Work 'em a beliefe that you are Kings.

Plenty. We are so.

Luke. I'le put it in practice instantly. Study you
For moving language. Sister, Neeces.

Enter LADIE, ANNE, MARY.

How
Stil mourning? dry your eyes, and clear these clouds
That do obscure your beauties. Did you believe
My personated reprehension, though
It shew'd like a rough anger, could be serious?
Forget the fright I put you in. My ends
In humbling you was, to set off the height
Of honour, principle honor, which my studies
When you least expect it shall confer upon you.
Still you seem doubtfull: be not wanting to
Your selvs, nor let the strangenesse of the means,
With the shadow of some danger, render you
Incredulous.

Ladie. Our usage hath been such,
As we can faintly hope that your intents,
And language are the same.

68–70. *rearranged by Gifford*; *58 reads* Make . . . not / Contain . . . you. / You . . . Neeces? / Yes Sir. 73. Work 'em] *58*; Work in 'em *Dodsley* 80. ends] *58*; end *Mason*

Luke. I'le change those hopes
To certainties.
Sir John. With what art he winds about them! [*Aside.*]
Luke. What wil you say? or what thanks shall I look for?
If now I raise you to such eminence, as
The wife, and daughters of a Citizen
Never arriv'd at. Many for their wealth (I grant)
Have written Ladies of honor, and some few *The Banquet*
Have higher titles, and that's the farthest rise *ready. One*
You can in England hope for. What think you *Chair, and*
If I should mark you out a way to live *Wine.*
Queens in another climate?
Anne. Wee desire
A competence.
Mary. And prefer our Countries smoke
Before outlandish fire.
K3v *Ladie.* But should we listen
To such impossibilities, 'tis not in
The power of man to make it good.
Luke. I'le doo't.
Nor is this seat of majesty far remov'd.
It is but to *Virginia.*
Ladie. How, *Virginia*!
High Heaven forbid. Remember Sir, I beseech you,
What creatures are shipp'd thither.
Anne. Condemn'd wretches,
Forfeited to the law.
Mary. Strumpets and Bauds,
For the abomination of their life,
Spew'd out of their own Country.
Luke. Your false fears
Abuse my noble purposes. Such indeed
Are sent as slaves to labour there, but you
To absolute soveraignty. Observe these men,
With reverence observe them. They are Kings,
Kings of such spacious territories, and dominions
As our great *Brittain* measur'd, will appear
A garden too't.
Lacie. You shall be ador'd there

90. *Aside.*] *Gifford*[2]*: not in 58*

As Goddesses.
Sir John. Your litters made of gold
Supported by your vassalls, proud to bear
The burthen on their shoulders.
Plenty. Pomp, and ease,
With delicates that Europe never knew,
Like Pages shall wait on you.
Luke. If you have minds
To entertain the greatnesse offer'd to you,
With outstretched arms, and willing hands embrace it.
But this refus'd, imagine what can make you
Most miserable here, and rest assur'd,
In storms it falls upon you: take em in,
And use your best perswasion. If that fail,
I'le send em aboard in a dry fat.
K4r *Exeunt* LACIE, PLENTY, LADIE, ANNE, MARY.
Sir John. Be not mov'd Sir.
Wee'l work 'em to your will: yet ere we part,
Your worldly cares defer'd, a little mirth
Would not misbecome us.
Luke. You say well. And now
It coms into my memory, this is my birth-day,
Which with solennity I would observe,
But that it would ask cost.
Sir John. That shall not grieve you.
By my art I will prepare you such a feast,
As *Persia* in her height of pomp, and riot
Did never equall: and ravishing Musick
As the *Italian* Princes seldome heard
At their greatest entertainments. Name your guests.
Luke. I must have none.
Sir John. Not the City Senate?
Luke. No.
Nor yet poor neighbours. The first would argue me
Of foolish ostentation, and the latter
Of too much hospitality, a virtue
Grown obsolete, and uselesse. I will sit
Alone, and surfet in my store, while others

129 SD. *Exeunt* . . . MARY.] *Gifford*; *follows* Sir. *58* 143. ostentation, and] *Gifford*; ostentation, *58* 144. hospitality, a] *Gifford*; hospitality, and a *58*

With envy pine at it. My Genius pamper'd
With the thought of what I am, and what they suffer
I have mark'd out to miserie.
Sir John. You shall;
And somthing I will add, you yet conceive not,
Nor will I be slow-pac'd.
Luke. I have one businesse,
And that dispatch'd I am free.
Sir John. About it Sir,
Leave the rest to me.
Luke. Till now I ne're lov'd magick. *Exeunt.*

K4v

[V. ii]

Actus quintus, Scena secunda.

Enter LORD, OLD GOLDWIRE, *and* OLD TRADEWELL.

Lord. Believe me, gentlemen! I never was
So cozen'd in a fellow. He disguis'd
Hypocrisie in such a cunning shape
Of reall goodnesse, that I would have sworn
This divell a Saint. Master *Goldwire*, and Master *Tradewell*,
What do you mean to do? put on.
Old Goldwire. With your Lordships favour.
Lord. I'le have it so.
Old Tradewell. Your will, my Lord, excuses
The rudenesse of our manners.
Lord. You have receiv'd
Penitent letters from your sons I doubt not?
Old Tradewell. They are our onely sons.
Old Goldwire. And as we are fathers,
Remembering the errours of our youth,
We would pardon slips in them.
Old Tradewell. And pay for 'em
In a moderate way.
Old Goldwire. In which we hope your Lordship
Will be our mediator.
Lord. All my power,
You freely shall command.

Enter LUKE.

'Tis he! you are wel met.
And to my wish. And wondrous brave; your habit
Speaks you a Merchant royall.
Luke. What I wear,
I take not upon trust.
Lord. Your betters may,
And blush not for't.
Luke. If you have nought else with me
But to argue that, I will make bold to leave you.
Lord. You are very peremptory, pray you stay. I once held you
An upright honest man.
Luke. I am honester now
L1r By a hundred thousand pound, I thank my stars for't,
Upon the Exchange, and if your late opinion
Be alter'd, who can help it? good my Lord
To the point. I have other businesse then to talk
Of honesty, and opinions.
Lord. Yet you may
Do well, if you please, to shew the one, and merit
The other from good men, in a case that now
Is offer'd to you.
Luke. What is't? I am troubl'd.
Lord. Here are two gentlemen, the fathers of
Your brothers prentices.
Luke. Mine, my Lord, I take it.
Lord. Master *Goldwire*, and Master *Tradewell.*
Luke. They are welcome, if
They come prepar'd to satisfie the damage
I have sustain'd by their sons.
Old Goldwire. We are, so you please
To use a conscience.
Old Tradewell. Which we hope you will do,
For your own worships sake.
Luke. Conscience, my friends,
And wealth are not always neighbours. Should I part

V. ii. 15–22. *rearranged after Gifford*[2]; *58 reads* You . . . met. / And . . . brave, / Your . . . royall. / What . . . trust. / Your . . . for't. / If . . . me / But . . . you. / You . . . stay. / I . . . man. 33–4. welcome, if / They] *58*; welcome, / If they *Kirk*

With what the law gives me, I should suffer mainly
In my reputation. For it would convince me
Of indiscretion. Nor will you I hope move me
To do my self such prejudice.

Lord. No moderation?

Luke. They cannot look for't, and preserve in me
A thriving Citizens credit. Your bonds lie
For your sons truth, and they shall answer all
They have run out. The masters never prosper'd
Since gentlemens sons grew prentices. When we look
To have our business done at home, they are
Abroad in the Tenis-court, or in partridge-alley,
In *Lambeth* Marsh, or a cheating Ordinary
Where I found your sons. I have your Bonds, look too't.
L1v A thousand pounds apiece, and that will hardly
Repair my losses.

Lord. Thou dar'st not shew thy self
Such a divel.

Luke. Good words.

Lord. Such a cut-throat. I have heard of
The usage of your brothers wife, and daughters.
You shall find you are not lawlesse, and that your moneys
Cannot justifie your villanies.

Luke. I indure this.
And good my Lord, now you talk in time of moneys,
Pay in what you owe me. And give me leav to wonder
Your wisedome should have leisure to consider
The businesse of these gentlemen, or my carriage
To my Sister, or my Neeces, being your self
So much in my danger.

Lord. In thy danger?

Luke. Mine.
I find in my counting house a Mannor pawn'd,
Pawn'd, my good Lord, Lacie-Mannour, and that Mannour
From which you have the title of a Lord,
And it please your good Lordship. You are a noble man
Pray you pay in my moneys. The interest
Will eat faster in't, then *Aqua fortis* in iron. PLENTY *ready to speak within.*

43–4. in me / A] *Gifford*; in / Me a *58* 56–7. your moneys / Cannot] *Gifford*; your / Moneys cannot *58*

Now though you bear me hard, I love your Lordship.
I grant your person to be priviledg'd
From all arrests. Yet there lives a foolish creature
Call'd an Under-sheriffe, who being well paid, will serve
An extent on Lords, or Lowns land. Pay it in,
I would be loth your name should sink. Or that
Your hopefull son, when he returns from travel,
Should find you my lord without land. You are angry
For my good counsell. Look you to your Bonds: had I known
Of your comming, believe it I would have had Serjeants ready:
Lord how you fret! but that a Tavern's near
You should taste a cup of Muscadine in my house,
To wash down sorrow, but there it will do better,
I know you'l drink a health to me. *Exit* LUKE.

.2r *Lord.* To thy damnation.
Was there ever such a villain! Heaven forgive me
For speaking so unchristianly, though he deservs it.

Old Goldwire. We are undone.

Old Tradewell. Our families quite ruin'd.

Lord. Take courage gentlemen. Comfort may appear,
And punishment overtake him, when he least expects it. *Exeunt.*

iii] *Actus quintus, Scena ultima.*

Enter SIR JOHN, *and* HOLDFAST.

Sir John. Be silent on your life.

Holdfast. I am or'ejoy'd.

Sir John. Are the pictures plac'd as I directed?

Holdfast. Yes Sir.

Sir John. And the musicians ready?

Holdfast. All is done
As you comanded.

Sir John. Make haste, and be carefull, *At the door.*
You know your cue, and postures.

Plenty within. We are perfit.

Sir John. 'Tis well: the rest are come too?

Holdfast. And dispos'd of
To your own wish.

V. iii. 4 SD. *At . . . door.*] *Coxeter*; *follows* comanded. *58*

Sir John. Set forth the table. So.

Enter Servants with a [chair, a table, and] rich Banquet.

A perfit Banquet. At the upper end,
His chair in state, he shall feast like a Prince.
Holdfast. And rise like a Dutch hang-man.

Enter LUKE.

Sir John. Not a word more.
How like you the preparation? fill your room,
And taste the cates, then in your thought consider
A rich man, that lives wisely to himself,
In his full height of glory.
L2v *Luke.* I can brook
No rivall in this happinesse. How sweetly
These dainties, when unpay'd for, please my palate!
Some wine. *Joves* Nectar. Brightnesse to the star
That govern'd at my birth. Shoot down thy influence,
And with a perpetuity of being
Continue this felicity, not gain'd
By vows to Saints above, and much lesse purchas'd
By thriving industry; nor fal'n upon me
As a reward to piety, and religion,
Or service for my Country. I owe all this
To my dissimulation, and the shape
I wore of goodnesse. Let my brother number
His beads devoutly, and believe his alms
To beggars, his compassion to his debters,
Will wing his better part, disrob'd of flesh,
To sore above the firmament. I am well,
And so I surfet here in all abundance;
Though stil'd a cormorant, a cut-throat, Jew,
And prosecuted with the fatal curses
Of widdows, undone Orphans, and what else
Such as maligne my state can load me with,
I will not envie it. You promis'd musick?
Sir John. And you shall hear the strength and power of it,

7. SD. *chair . . . and*] *editor*; *marginal SD. in 58*: *A table, and / rich Ban- / quet.*
14. glory.] *58*; glory— *Craik* 22. By] *Dodsley*; By the *58* 24–5. all this / To] *58*; all / This to *Gifford* 25. my dissimulation] *Craik*; dissimulation *58*
37–8. *rearranged by Gifford*; *58 reads* And . . . power / Of . . . good,

The spirit of *Orpheus* rais'd to make it good,
And in those ravishing strains with which he mov'd
Charon and *Cerberus* to give him way
To fetch from hell his lost *Euridice*.
Appear swifter then thought.

Musick. At one door CERBERUS, *at the other,* CHARON, ORPHEUS, *Chorus.*

Luke. 'Tis wondrous strange.
Sir John. Does not the object and the accent take you?
Luke. A pretty fable. [*Exeunt* CERBERUS *and the rest.*]
But that musick should
Alter in fiends their nature, is to me
Impossible. Since in my self I find
What I have once decreed, shall know no change.

PLENTY *and* LACIE *ready behind.*

Sir John. You are constant to your purposes, yet I think
3r That I could stagger you.
Luke. How?
Sir John. Should I present
Your servants, debters, and the rest that suffer
By your fit severity, I presume the sight
Would move you to compassion.
Luke. Not a mote.
The musick that your *Orpheus* made, was harsh
To the delight I should receive in hearing
Their cries, and groans. If it be in your power
I would now see 'em.
Sir John. Spirits in their shapes
Shal shew them as they are. But if it should move you?
Luke. If it do may I ne're find pity.
Sir John. Be your own judge.
Appear as I commanded.

Sad musick. Enter GOLDWIRE, *and* TRADEWELL *as from prison.* FORTUNE, HOYST, PENURIE *following after them.* SHAVEM *in a blew gown,* SECRET, DINGEM, OLD TRADEWELL, *and* OLD GOLDWIRE *with Serjeants as arrested. They all kneel to* LUKE, *heaving up their hands for mercy.* STARGAZE *with a pack of Alminacks,* MILLISCENT.

44 SD. *Exeunt . . . rest.*] *after Gifford*; *not in 58* 45. fiends] *Dodsley*; friends *58*
59 SD. *Serjeants as arrested.*] *Craik*; *Serjeants. As erected 58*; *Serjeants. As directed Dodsley*

Luke. Ha, ha, ha!
This move me to compassion? or raise
One sign of seeming pity in my face?
You are deceiv'd: it rather renders me
More flinty, and obdurate. A South wind
Shall sooner soften marble, and the rain
That slides down gently from his flaggy wings
O'reflow the Alps: then knees, or tears, or groans
Shall wrest compunction from me. 'Tis my glory
That they are wretched, and by me made so,
It sets my happinesse off. I could not triumph
If these were not my captives. Ha! my tarriers
As it appears have seiz'd on these old foxes,
As I gave order. New addition to
L3v My Scene of mirth. Ha, ha! They now grow tedious,
Let 'em be remov'd. Some other object, if
Your art can shew it.
Sir John. You shall perceive 'tis boundlesse.
Yet one thing reall if you please?
Luke. What is it?
Sir John. Your Neeces ere they put to Sea, crave humbly
Though absent in their bodys, they may take leave
Of their late suitors statues.

Enter LADIE, ANNE, *and* MARY.

Luke. There they hang,
In things indifferent I am tractable.
Sir John. There pay your vows, you have liberty.
Anne. O sweet figure
Of my abused *Lacie*! when remov'd
Into another world, I'le daily pay
A sacrifice of sighs, to thy remembrance;
And with a shower of tears strive to wash of
The stain of that contempt, my foolish pride,
And insolence threw upon thee.
Mary. I had been
Too happie, if I had injoy'd the substance,
But far unworthy of it, now I fall
Thus prostrate to thy statue.

80. indifferent] *Dodsley*; different *58* 89. fall] *Mason*; shall *58*

Ladie. My kind husband,
Blessed in my misery, from the monastery
To which my disobedience confin'd thee,
With thy souls eye, which distance cannot hinder,
Look on my penitence. O that I could
Call back time past, thy holy vow dispens'd,
With what humility would I observe
My long neglected duty.
Sir John. Does not this move you?
Luke. Yes as they do the statues, and her sorrow
My absent brother. If by your magick art
You can give life to these, or bring him hither
To witnesse her repentance, I may have
Perchance some feeling of it.
4r *Sir John.* For your sport
You shall see a Master-piece. Here's nothing but
A superficies, colours, and no substance.
Sit still, and to your wonder, and amazement
I'le give these Organs. This the sacrifice
To make the great work perfect.

Enter LACIE *and* PLENTY.

Luke. Prodigious.
Sir John. Nay they have life, and motion. Descend.
And for your absent brother, this wash'd off,
Against your will you shall know him.

Enter LORD *and the rest.*

Luke. I am lost.
Guilt strikes me dumb.
Sir John. You have seen my Lord the pageant.
Lord. I have, and am ravish'd with it.
Sir John. What think you now
Of this clear soul? this honest pious man?
Have I stripp'd him bare? Or will your Lordship have
A farther triall of him? 'tis not in
A wolf to change his nature.
Lord. I long since
Confess'd my errour.

115–17. *rearranged by Gifford*; *58 reads* A . . . nature. / I . . . errour. / Look . . . you,

Sir John. Look up, I forgive you,
And seal your pardons thus.
Ladie. I am too full
Of joy to speak it.
Anne. I am another creature,
Not what I was.
Mary. I vow to shew my self
When I am married, an humble wife,
Not a commanding mistris.
Plenty. On those terms
I gladly thus embrace you.
Lacie. Welcome to
My bosome. As the one half of my self,
I'le love you, and cherish you.
Goldwire. Mercy.
Tradewell and the rest. Good Sir mercy.
L4v *Sir John.* This day is sacred to it. All shall find me
As far as lawfull pity can give way too't,
Indulgent to your wishes, though with losse
Unto my self. My kind, and honest brother,
Looking into your self, have you seen the Gorgon?
What a golden dream you have had in the possession
Of my estate! but here's a revocation
That wakes you out of it. Monster in nature,
Revengefull, avaritious Atheist,
Transcending all example. But I shall bee
A sharer in thy crimes, should I repeat 'em.
What wilt thou do? Turn hypocrite again,
With hope dissimulation can aid thee?
Or that one eye will shed a tear in sign
Of sorrow for thee? I have warrant to
Make bold with mine own, pray you uncase. This key too
I must make bold with. Hide thy self in some desart,
Where good men ner'e may find thee: or in justice
Pack to *Virginia*, and repent. Not for
Those horrid ends to which thou did'st design these.
Luke. I care not where I go, what's done, with words
Cannot be undone. *Exit* LUKE.
Ladie. Yet Sir, shew some mercy;
Because his cruelty to me, and mine,

Did good upon us.
Sir John. Of that at better leisure,
As his penitencie shall work me. Make you good
Your promis'd reformation, and instruct
Our City dames, whom wealth makes proud, to move
In their own spheres, and willingly to confesse
In their habits, manners, and their highest port,
A distance 'twixt the City, and the Court. *Exeunt omnes.*

FINIS.

151. instruct] *Dodsley*; mistrust *58*

THREE NEW
PLAYES

VIZ.

The { Bashful Lover, Guardian, Very Woman. }

As they have been often Acted at the Private-House in *Black-Friers*, by His late MAJESTIES Servants, with great Applause.

WRITTEN BY
PHILIP MASSENGER, Gent.

Never Printed before.

LONDON,
Printed for *Humphrey Moseley*, and are to be sold at his Shop at the Sign of the *Prince's Arms* in St. *Pauls* Church-yard. 1655.

THREE NEW PLAYES

INTRODUCTION

The Bashful Lover, *The Guardian*, and *A Very Woman* were published together by Humphrey Moseley in 1655 as *Three New Playes . . . . Written By Philip Massenger, Gent.* They had been among the many plays entered in the Stationers' Register on 9 September 1653 by Moseley, and there each title was unnaturally yoked to an alternative title which must in fact belong to a quite different (but no longer extant) play.[1]

September. y^{e}. 9th: 1653.

. . . .

M^{r}. Mosely. Entred also for his Copies the severall Playes following.

. . . .

Alexius the Chast Gallant or.
The Bashfull Lover.
A Very Woman, or ye Womans Plot.
. . . .
The Citie honest man, or ye Guardian.[2]
} by Phill: Massinger.

'The Bashfull Lovers' and 'The Gardian' were given as single titles when Moseley re-entered a number of his plays in the Register on 29 June 1660 (see vol. i, p. xxv). Since he had already published them, the entry was unnecessary.

Why Moseley selected the three plays out of the many manuscripts of Massinger which he possessed (perhaps as many as twenty-two) it is impossible to say; the 1655 volume forms part of a series of little collections which he had begun with new plays of Shirley and Brome. All three plays belong to the later period of Massinger's dramatic career. The Thomason copy of *Three New Playes* in the British Museum carries the purchase date, 'June. 14'.

[1] The problems of the entry are discussed in the General Introduction, vol. i, pp. xxiii–xxvi.

[2] Register E 285–6; Greg, *Bibliography*, i. 61; Eyre, i. 428–9.

The printer of the volume has been identified as Thomas Newcombe.[1] There is an engraved portrait of Massinger by Thomas Cross, who spent his life producing poor-quality portraits for book-publishers.[2] It is the only portrait of Massinger, and though it appeared fifteen years after its subject's death Cross probably had some likeness in front of him to work on. The portrait is reproduced as the frontispiece of this edition, and the general title-page on page 101.

Three New Playes is printed in octavo, π^2 A^2 B–S^8 T^6 (146 leaves). The three plays are separately paged. See Greg, *Bibliography*, iii. 1091–2.[3] The contents are: $\pi 1^r$, *blank*; $\pi 1^v$, *portrait*; $\pi 2^r$, *general title*; $\pi 2^v$, *blank*; A1^r, *title*, 'THE BASHFUL LOVER . . .'; A1^v, *blank*; A2^r, 'PROLOGUE.'; A2^v, '*Dramatis Personæ*.'; B1^r, 'THE Bashful Lover.', *text begins*; G3^v, *text ends*, '*FINIS*.'; G4^r, 'EPILOGUE.'; G4^v, *blank*; G5^r, *title*, 'THE GUARDIAN . . .'; G5^v, *blank*; G6^r, 'PROLOGUE.'; G6^v, '*Dramatis Personæ*.'; G7^r, 'THE GUARDIAN.', *text begins*; N3^v, *text ends*; N4^r, 'I. SONG.'; N4^v, 'II. SONG.'; N5^r, 'EPILOGUE.' . . . 'FINIS'; N5^v, *blank*; N6^r, *title*, 'A Very Woman . . .'; N6^v, *blank*; N7^r, 'PROLOGUE.'; N7^v, *names of the characters*; N8^r, 'A Very Woman.', *text begins*; T6^r, *text ends*; T6^v, 'EPILOGUE.' . . . 'FINIS'. The text is in roman, 20 lines measuring approximately 79 mm. There are normally 36 lines to a page, but 34 on B6^v, C4^v, C8^v; 35 on C5^r, O5^v, P7^r; 37 on I6^v, K8^v, O8^v; 38 on E8^r, F2^v, F6^v, F7^r. A new act is begun on a new page on 8 out of 12 occasions. Only act-divisions are marked, although each new act-heading misleadingly adds 'Scæn. 1.'

Spellings and style of composition are not sufficiently varied to differentiate between compositors, except in one respect, the use of roman and italic type in entries. There are three types, 'Enter *Name*', '*Enter* Name', and '*Enter Name*'. Although all three types are once found on a single page (F8^r), entries of one style are normally

[1] See Greg, *Bibliography*, iii. 1091–2; and C. W. Miller, 'Thomas Newcomb: A Restoration Printer's Ornament Stock', *Studies in Bibliography*, Virginia, iii (1950–1), 155–70. The large rose ornament at the head of the first page of text in each of the three plays is found on the title-page of Cox's *Actæon and Diana*, 1655, 'Printed at *London* by *T. Newcomb*.' and on the title-page of Davenant's *Works*, 1673, 'Printed by T. N.'; the factotum on B1^r also appears on A2^r of Ford's *The Queen*, 1653, 'Printed by T. N.'

[2] See *DNB*, and Corbett and Norton, *Engraving in England in the Sixteenth and Seventeenth Centuries*, part iii, 1964, pp. 277, 295–6.

[3] Greg makes the slight error of saying that signature M2 is misprinted as M. In fact the 2, though faint, is clearly visible in some copies.

bunched together. For example, in sheet P and the first half of Q (*A Very Woman*), we find '*Enter Name*' throughout, changing in the second half of sheet Q to 'Enter *Name*', while in *The Guardian*, '*Enter Name*' is found in the first half of sheet I, changing to 'Enter *Name*' in the second half of the sheet and throughout sheet K. Unfortunately, entries are not sufficiently numerous to provide anything like the evidence needed to establish a sequence of shifts or stints, but the data so far as it goes indicates that the copy for *Three New Playes* was not cast off, but set continuously.[1] However, at the very end of the volume, in the last few pages of sheet S and in sheet T, '*Enter Name*' and 'Enter *Name*' alternate by formes, indicating that once the end was in sight, the remaining copy was cast off.

The Bashful Lover and *The Guardian* share a peculiarity which makes it likely that the copy for those two plays was a transcript of Massinger's manuscript made by a single scribe. The text of *A Very Woman* indicates a different (and complicated) type of copy, the problems of which are discussed in the introduction to that play. The peculiarity is that whenever (as so frequently happens in Massinger) a new speaker completes a line of verse begun by the previous speaker, the text prints the remaining half line on the same line as the one following, thus producing an inordinately long line which often the compositor has to run over. For example, *The Guardian*, III. vi. 115–119 should have been printed as follows:

> Almost made up?
> *Jol.* What shall we do?
> *Calyp.* Betray him;
> I'll instantly raise the Watch.
> *Jol.* And so make me
> For ever infamous.
> *Calyp.* The Gentleman,
> The rarest Gentleman is at the door,
> Shall he lose his labour? since that you must perish,

But this is how it appears:

> Almost made up?
> *Jol.* What shall we do?
> *Calyp.* Betray him; I'll instantly raise the Watch.

[1] A contrary view is expressed by C. A. M. Parssinen in her unpublished edition of *The Guardian* (Brandeis University dissertation, 1971), p. xxxv.

> *Jol.* And so make me for ever infamous.
> *Calyp.* The Gentleman, the rarest Gentleman is
> at the door,
> Shall he lose his labour? since that you must perish,

This peculiarity can hardly be the fault of Newcombe's printing-house because only two of the three plays are so affected and because the only motive for altering the lines, the saving of space, does not apply, since the need to take over the ends of excessively long lines defeats the purpose, and in any case it is clear from the appearance of the book that there was no pressure to save space. On a written page, on the other hand, a scribe might well have found that he achieved a significant saving of space by combining half-lines with their successors; the practice is very frequent in the scribal transcript of *The Parliament of Love.*

The first two texts are again distinguished from *A Very Woman* by a feature which can be attributed to a single scribe. In entries, there is a habit of enclosing additional information, particularly about properties, within round brackets. In *The Bashful Lover*, for example, we find, '*Enter* Manfroy (*with a Letter.*)'; in *The Guardian*, '*Enter Mirtilla* (with Letter and Jewel.)'; but in *A Very Woman*, '*Enter Don John with a Letter in his hand.*'

Further consideration of the transcripts and their relation to Massinger's autograph and to the playhouse will be found in the introductions to the individual plays.

There are copies of *Three New Playes* in the following libraries and institutions: Bodleian Library; British Museum (2 copies); Chapin Library, Williamstown; University of Columbia, Butler Library; Library of Congress; Cornell University; Folger Shakespeare Library (2 copies); Harvard College Library; Huntington Library; University of Illinois; University of London; Pierpont Morgan Library; Newberry Library; Pforzheimer Collection; Princeton University; University of Texas; Victoria and Albert Museum (2 copies); Worcester College, Oxford; Yale University.

The three plays now follow in the presumed order of composition, and not in the order in which they are printed in *Three New Playes.* Square brackets surrounding original stage-directions have been silently removed to avoid confusion with editorial additions (see vol. i, p. lxxii).

THE GUARDIAN

INTRODUCTION

(a) *Date*

Malone found two references to *The Guardian* in the now-missing Office-book of Sir Henry Herbert, Master of the Revels; the first is to the licensing of the play on 31 October 1633, '*The Guardian*, by Philip Massinger, licensed for the King's Company', and the second is to a court performance on 12 January 1634, '*The Guardian*, a play of Mr. Messengers, was acted at court on Sunday the 12 January, 1633 [i.e. 1633–4], by the Kings players, and well likte.'[1] The only other indication of date is the baffling but unavoidable inference from the play's Prologue that it was written after 'two years silence' following the failure of two plays (lines 1–9). By the end of October 1633, two years had not elapsed since *The City Madam* was licensed for performance on 25 May 1632, and there is no evidence that that play was a failure. There is some discussion of the problem in the General Introduction (vol. i, p. xli) and in the introduction to *The City Madam* (above, pp. 1–2); in the end there seems no way of squaring *The Guardian's* Prologue with what we know of the dates and fates of Massinger's plays between 1631 and 1633 (*The Emperor of the East*, *Believe As You List*, *The Unfortunate Piety*, *The City Madam*, and *The Guardian*). There can, however, be no challenge to the strong external evidence provided by Malone from Herbert dating *The Guardian* in the late autumn of 1633.

(b) *Source*

The main source of *The Guardian* is the *Comus* of Erycus Puteanus (Hendrik van den Putten or Henri Dupuy), the Flemish scholar: *Eryci Puteani Comus, sive Phagesiposia Cimmeria. Somnium.* This prose-fantasy, which is supposed to have influenced Milton, was

[1] Adams, *Herbert*, pp. 35, 54.

published at Louvain in 1608, reprinted in 1611, and published in Oxford in 1634. Massinger must have used one of the Louvain editions. A portion of the work was translated into English in 1668 by 'P. M.' (curiously enough) as *The Cimmerian Matron*, and Gerard Langbaine saw the resemblance to the incident in which Severino finds his wife Iolante in a compromising situation but in the dark slits the confidante's nose, for he said of *The Guardian* in his *Momus Triumphans* (1688, p. 16), '*Plot from the* Cimmerian Matron, 8°.' In 1797, Richard Hole pointed out in his *Remarks on the Arabian Nights' Entertainments* (pp. 229–33) that Massinger had got not only the nose-cutting plot but also the play's main story of Caliste, Caldoro, and Adorio from the original of *The Cimmerian Matron*, namely Puteanus's *Comus*. Strangely, Gifford mentioned Hole's book in a very off-hand way in the course of his discussion of some of the versions of the very ancient and widespread tale of the adulteress who had her nose slit and then was miraculously 'cured'. He did not indicate that Hole had found anything more than the story of the nose. Arthur Symons went so far as to look up Hole but came away with a garbled summary. For some reason, Koeppel in 1897 missed the signposts to Hole completely and thus led G. E. Bentley to report that 'no comprehensive source for the play has been found' (iv. 790).

In discussing the history of the nose-slitting story, Hole mentions Massinger's use of it in *The Guardian* and concludes that the *Comus* must have been Massinger's source because of 'the agreement of the principal plot in his comedy, in its most material incidents, with another tale in the same performance. The character of the Guardian, the adventures of Caldoro and Caliste, of Adorio and Myrtilla, are to be traced in the COMUS of Puteanus; with this difference that Massinger has adopted Calyste for Myrtilla, and substituted Myrtilla for Circe.' In a footnote, Hole adds that Massinger's characterization of Durazzo is an attempt to 'fill up and expand . . . this remarkable phrase "vir mitissimae severitatis" [a man of most mild strictness]'.

Puteanus's story of the Cimmerian matron may be told briefly since Massinger does not follow its details very closely, and the story is in its various forms widely known. (Koeppel pointed out that an English version had appeared in *Westward for Smelts* in 1620.) A wife has fallen in love with a soldier and her suspicious husband pretends to go away on a journey. The wife arranges through an old procuress for the soldier to visit her. She prepares a little banquet (this detail Massinger takes over) and awaits her lover. The husband returns, is outraged, strips his wife naked, ties her to a post outside, and goes to bed. The procuress arrives and the wife persuades her to change places with her while she goes to meet her lover in the garden. As they embrace, the husband is woken by an ominous dream; he rushes out, goes to the pillar and in fury cuts off the nose of the old woman, who has kept silence for fear of betraying her employer. The wife returns, sends the procuress to a doctor and resumes her place at the pillar. In a loud voice she beseeches heaven to prove her innocence by restoring her nose. The husband comes out and is deeply penitent when he sees the miracle of a perfectly sound nose.

The second story in Puteanus is of Chaerestratus, a rich and talented young man [= Caldoro], who is helplessly in love with the very beautiful Myrtilla [= Caliste]. But the latter loves Hylaeus [= Adorio], who is not in love with her. Chaerestratus's misery makes Paneutus [= Durazzo] entice him with stories of rural delights to retire with him to the country. A quarrel with her mother leads Myrtilla to propose the idea of flight with Hylaeus. Her maid Circe [= Massinger's Mirtilla] pleads with Hylaeus, and offers him a necklace of great price in which the rape of Proserpine is elaborately worked [cf. I. ii. 127–9 and II. iii. 115–17]. (At this interview, Circe herself falls in love with Hylaeus.) Hylaeus accepts the proposal and, having arranged for a sumptuous banquet and for one of the city gates to be left open, he goes at night on horseback to Myrtilla's house. But Myrtilla cannot get free of her mother, so Hylaeus moves off for a while. Finally, Myrtilla is ready, having promised Circe, in answer to her pleading to come too, that she will send for her that very same night.

At this very moment, Chaerestratus, unable any longer to endure his absence from his loved one, returns on horseback to the city through the open gate and salutes the well-known threshold with a sigh. Myrtilla hears the noise of the horse, rushes out and is swept away by her astonished worshipper at a gallop through the open city gate. Arrived at a convenient sward, he dismounts, and Myrtilla almost collapses on finding that her rescuer is not Hylaeus. But Chaerestratus pleads so earnestly that she is much moved, and she consents to his love. He draws her down on the grass, overcomes her modesty with a multitude of kisses and wins the spoils of Venus.

When Hylaeus returns to the house, Myrtilla's flight has been discovered; Circe rushes out of the house to escape the mother's fury and is joyfully carried away by Hylaeus, who only discovers his mistake when they reach his house. He hears about the horseman galloping through the open gate and decides to pursue. When he comes on Myrtilla asleep in the arms of a young man, he is about to kill him and abduct her when his friends, finding that it is Chaerestratus, persuade him to wait for him to wake and explain. As they rest, they all fall asleep. Chaerestratus and Myrtilla waken up, and having taken Myrtilla's jewels from Hylaeus's hat, they speed away and eventually reach Cimmeria. Hylaeus decides to make the best of a bad job and makes do with Myrtilla, though it doesn't turn out well.

It will be seen that Massinger has incorporated a very great deal of this story within his play, though he could not allow Caliste and Caldoro to unite themselves as Chaerestratus and Myrtilla do. The chief interest, however, is in Massinger's ingenuity in uniting Puteanus's two separate stories into one by turning Caliste's mother into the Cimmerian matron, and in his virtuosity in combining two stories of nocturnal complications into a single comedy of errors in the dark, thus illustrating that power to twist two stories into a single spiral which so took Coleridge's admiration.

Massinger's most significant changes and additions to Puteanus's two stories are as follows: (i) the expansion of the role of the guardian, who hardly appears in the *Comus*; (ii) the addition of the early and contumelious relations between Adorio and Caldoro; (iii) changing the object of the wife's adulterous affection from a mere soldier into her disguised brother-in-law (and of course removing from *him* any desire for *her*); (iv) the whole idea of the husband as a banished man leading a Robin Hood life; (v) the preposterous discovery that the maidservant, Mirtilla, is in fact of noble birth. Items (iii), (iv) and (v) are so much the stuff of tragicomedy and romance that it is hardly necessary to look for sources.

(c) *Text*

The entry of *The Guardian* in the Stationers' Register in 1653 by Humphrey Moseley and its publication in 1655 as the second play in the volume *Three New Playes* are described above (pp. 103–6) and in the General Introduction (vol. i, pp. xxiii–xxv). It is argued that the printer's copy for *The Bashful Lover* and *The Guardian* was a transcript by a single scribe. In the case of *The Guardian*, the transcript was presumably from Massinger's manuscript, though the successive intervention of scribe and compositor has ironed out most of the characteristics of Massinger's hand. But spellings such as 'ghess' (frequently), 'ghest', 'nooze', 'coursely', 'noyse', probably derive from the autograph. The speech-heading '1 *Wom.*' for Mirtilla at V. ii. 11 must be a relic of the author's manuscript. As in *The Bashful Lover*, all intermediate scene divisions have been omitted.

The stage-directions for *The Guardian* are detailed and full. If they are all Massinger's, he was intent on indicating just what was to happen on the stage; e.g.,

A noyse within, as the fall of a Horse,—then
Enter Durazzo, Caldoro, Caliste,
Servant. (IV. i)

Enter Severino (*throwing open the doors violently*)
having a knife. (III. vi. 142)

We are told that Mirtilla is to enter in III. ii wearing the gown that Caliste wore on her first appearance, that the King throws down *three* bags of gold (V. iv. 110), that Severino and Iolante are to wear 'Oaken-leav'd garlands'. The concern for detail, especially as regards properties, raises the question of whether the transcript had been prepared, or had been added to, for stage use. At II. ii we have '*Enter Calypso, and Jolante* (with a Purse and a Jewel)'; the purse and jewel are not necessary for the entry, but are required 35 lines later. The first direction in III. vi appears like this:

Enter *Jolante* (*with a rich banquet, and tapers*)
(*in a chair, behind a curtain.*)

The second parenthesis could indicate a stage-keeper's addition to an author's direction (see the introduction to *The Maid of Honour*). We have such particularity as 'two servants', 'six banditi'. On the other hand, directions for music are vague and sometimes inadequate. The transcript was evidently not the prompt-copy, and the stage-directions are basically Massinger's, but it is arguable that the transcript was made for the playhouse.

The 1655 text will be referred to as 55. The metrical misdivision is so extensive that the list of corrections is given separately at the end of the play as an appendix, instead of being included in the textual footnotes.

The text of the present edition has been prepared from the Huntington Library copy, photocopies of which have been checked against the editor's copy of *Three New Playes*.

The Guardian was first re-edited in 1744 for volume viii of Dodsley's *Select Collection of Old Plays*; this edition is referred to as *Dodsley* in the textual notes. Thereafter it appeared in the standard collected editions and also in volume ii of Symons's Mermaid selection, 1889. Carol A. M. Parssinen prepared an edition for the degree of Ph.D. at Brandeis University in 1971 (unpublished).

(d) *Stage History*

The Guardian was originally acted by the King's company at Blackfriars, having been licensed on 31 October 1633. It was performed at court on 12 January (Adams, *Herbert*, p. 54). *The Guardian* is in the long list of plays belonging to the King's men which the Lord Chamberlain protected from publication on 7 August 1641 (Bentley, i. 65–6). In records of Restoration productions, it is not always possible to distinguish the play from Cowley's play of the same name, even though the latter was altered to *Cutter of Coleman Street*. 'The Guardian' which Wood saw given by the 'yong loyall scholars of Oxford' on 19 July 1660, 'to spite the Presbyterians', must have been Cowley's play.[1] McManaway and Bentley agree that *The Guardian* in the list of the older plays allotted to Killigrew in 1669 is almost certainly Massinger's. (See Nicoll, *A History of Restoration Drama*, pp. 315–16.) *Love Lost in the Dark; or The Drunken Couple*, a miserable farce acted at Newmarket in 1680, was made up of bits collected from *Three New Playes*, most coming from *The Guardian*. Langbaine had observed the plunder but Genest (x. 146) was the first to give details; McManaway (*Studies*, pp. 23–5) gives fuller information. *The Guardian* was also plundered by Aphra Behn, who borrowed a good deal from Durazzo and others in creating *The City-Heiress*, 1682. Langbaine reported the similarities in *Momus Triumphans*, p. 2, and *An Account of the English Dramatick Poets*, p. 19.[2] Garrick's *The Guardian* of 1759 (Larpent MS. 153) has nothing to do with Massinger.

[1] Clark, *Life and Times of Anthony Wood*, i. 322.

[2] See also Montague Summers in Aphra Behn, *Works*, 1905, vol. ii, p. 197, and McManaway, *Studies*, p. 26.

THE
GUARDIAN,
A
COMICAL-HISTORY.

As it hath been often acted at the Private-House in *Black-Friars*, by his late MAIESTIES Servants, with great Applause.

Written by

PHILIP MASSENGER, **Gent.**

LONDON,
Printed for *Humphrey Moseley*, and are to be sold at his shop at the sign of the *Prince's Arms* in St. *Pauls* Church-yard. 1655.

G6r

PROLOGUE.

After twice putting forth to Sea, his Fame
Shipwrack'd in either, and his once known Name
In two years silence buried, perhaps lost
I'the general opinion; at our cost
(*A zealous sacrifice to* Neptune *made*
For good success in his uncertain trade)
Our Author weighs up anchors, and once more
Forsaking the security of the shore,
Resolves to prove his fortune: What 'twill be,
Is not in him, or us to prophesie;
You only can assure us. Yet he pray'd
This little in his absence might be said,
Designing me his Orator. He submits
To the grave censure of those abler Wits
His weakness; nor dares he profess that when
The Critiques laugh, he'l laugh at them agen.
(*Strange self-love in a writer!*) *He would know*
His errors as you find 'em, and bestow
His future studies to reform from this
What in another might be judg'd amiss.
And yet despair not, Gentlemen; though he fear
His strengths to please, we hope that you shall hear
Some things so writ, as you may truly say
He hath not quite forgot to make a Play,
As 'tis with malice rumour'd. His intents
Are fair; and though he want the complements
Of wide-mouth'd Promisers, who still engage
(*Before their Works are brought upon the Stage*)
Their parasites to proclaim 'em: This last birth
Deliver'd without noise, may yield such mirth,
As ballanc'd equally, will cry down the boast
Of arrogance, and regain his credit lost.

G6v

Dramatis Personæ

Alphonso, King of *Naples*.
Generall of *Milain*.
Severino, a Nobleman banished.
Monteclaro, his Brother in law, disguised [under the name of *Laval*].
Durazzo, the Guardian.
Caldoro, his Ward, in love with *Caliste*.
Adorio, Beloved by *Caliste*.
Camillo
Lentulo } Neapolitan Gentlemen.
Donato
Cario, Servant to *Adorio*.
Claudio, Servant to *Severino*.
Captains.
Servants.
Bandetti.

Iolante, Wife to *Severino*.
Caliste, her Daughter.
Mirtilla, *Caliste*'s Maid.
Calypso, the Confident of *Iolante*.

5. under . . . *Laval*] *Gifford*; *not in 55* 18, 21. *Iolante*] *Gifford*; *Jolantre 55*
21. *Calypso*] *editor*; *Calipso 55*

The Guardian

G7r

Act. 1. Scæn. 1.

I. i]

Enter DURAZZO, CAMILLO, LENTULO, *and* DONATO; *two Servants.*

Durazzo. TELL me of his expences? Which of you
Stands bound for a gazet? he spends his own;
And you impertinent Fools, or Knaves, make choice
Of either title, which your Signiorships please,
To meddle in't.
Camillo. Your age gives priviledge
To this harsh language.
Durazzo. My age! do not use
That word agen; if you do, I shall grow young,
And swinge you soundly: I would have you know,
G7v Though I write fifty odd, I do not carry
An Almanack in my bones to predeclare
What weather we shall have; nor do I kneel
In adoration at the Spring and Fall
Before my Doctor, for a dose or two
Of his Restoratives, which are things I take it
You are familiar with.
Camillo. This is from the purpose.
Durazzo. I cannot cut a caper, or groan like you
When I have done, nor run away so nimbly
Out of the field. But bring me to a Fence-school,
And crack a blade or two for exercise,
Ride a barb'd horse, or take a leap after me
Following my hounds or hawks, (and by your leave
At a gamesom Mistress) and you shall confess
I am in the *May* of my abilities,
And you in your *December.*
Lentulo. We are glad you bear
Your years so well.

Durazzo. My years! No more of years;
If you do, at your peril.
Camillo. We desire not
To prove your valour.
Durazzo. 'Tis your safest course.
Camillo. But as friends to your fame and reputation,
Come to instruct you: Your too much indulgence
To the exorbitant waste of young *Caldoro*,
Your Nephew and your Ward, hath rendred you
But a bad report among wise men in *Naples*.
Durazzo. Wise men? in your opinion; but to me
That understand my self and them, they are
Hide-bounded mony-mongers: they would have me
Train up my Ward a hopeful youth, to keep
A Merchants book, or at the plough, and clothe him
In Canvas or course Cotton; while I fell
His Woods, grant Leases; which he must make good
When he comes to age, or be compell'd to marry
G8r With a cast whore and three bastards: Let him know
No more then how to cypher well, or do
His tricks by the square root; grant him no pleasure
But Coyts and Nine-pins; suffer him to converse
With none but Clowns and Coblers; as the *Turk* says,
Poverty, old age, and aches of all seasons
Light on such heathenish Guardians!
Donato. You do worse
To the ruine of his state, under your favour,
In feeding his loose riots.
Durazzo. Riots! what riots?
He wears rich clothes, I do so; keeps horses; games, and wenches;
'Tis not amiss, so it be done with decorum:
In an Heir 'tis ten times more excusable
Then to be over-thrifty. Is there ought else
That you can charge him with?
Camillo. With what we grieve for,
And you will not approve.
Durazzo. Out with it, man.
Camillo. His rash endeavour, without your consent,
To match himself into a Family

I. i. 45. Coblers;] *Mason*; ~, *55* says,] *Mason*; ~: *55* 50. horses;] *editor*; ~, *55*

Not gracious with the times.
Durazzo. 'Tis still the better;
By this means he shall scape Court-visitants,
And not be eaten out of house and home
In a Summer-progress. But does he mean to marry?
Camillo. Yes sir, to marry.
Durazzo. In a beardless chin
'Tis ten times worse then wenching. Family! whose family?
Camillo. Signior *Severino's*.
Durazzo. How? not he that kill'd
The brother of his wife (as it is rumour'd)
Then fled upon it; since proscrib'd, and chosen
G8v Captain of the *Banditi*; the Kings pardon
On no suit to be granted?
Lentulo. The same, sir.
Durazzo. This touches near: How is his love return'd
By the Saint he worships?
Donato. She affects him not,
But dotes upon another.
Durazzo. Worse and worse.
Camillo. You know him, young *Adorio*.
Durazzo. A brave Gentleman!
What proof of this?
Lentulo. I dogg'd him to the Church;
Where he, not for devotion, as I ghess,
But to make his approaches to his Mistress,
Is often seen.
Camillo. And would you stand conceal'd
Among these trees, for he must pass this green,
The Mattins ended, as she returns home,
You may observe the passages.
Durazzo. I thank you;
This torrent must be stopt.

Enter ADORIO, CALISTE, MIRTILLA, CALDORO (*muffel'd.*)

Donato. They come.
Camillo. Stand close.
Caliste. I know I wrong my modesty.
Adorio. And wrong me,
In being so importunate for that

I neither can nor must grant.
Caliste. A hard sentence!
And to increase my misery, by you
Whom fond affection hath made my Judge,
Pronounc'd without compassion. Alas sir,
Did I approach you with unchaste desires,
A sullid reputation; were deform'd,
As it may be I am, though many affirm
I am something more then handsom.—
Durazzo. I dare swear it.
H1r *Caliste.* Or if I were no Gentlewoman, but bred coursely,
You might with some pretence of reason slight
What you should sue for.
Durazzo. Were he not an Eunuch,
He would, and sue agen; I am sure I should.
Pray look in my collar, a flea troubles me:
Hey-day! there are a legion of young *Cupids*
At barley-break in my breeches.
Caliste. Hear me sir;
Though you continue, nay increase your scorn,
Only vouchsafe to let me understand
What my defects are; of which once convinc'd,
I will hereafter silence my harsh plea,
And spare your further trouble.
Adorio. I'll tell you,
And bluntly, as my usual manner is,
Though I were a Woman-hater, which I am not,
But love the sex, for my ends; take me with you:
If in my thought I found one taint or blemish
In the whole fabrick of your outward features,
I would give my self the lye. You are a Virgin
Possess'd of all your mother could wish in you:
Your father *Severino's* dire disaster
In killing of your Uncle, which I grieve for,
In no part taking from you. I repeat it;
A noble Virgin, for whose grace and favours
Th' *Italian* Princes might contend as Rivals;
Yet unto me, a thing far, far beneath you,

102. I'll] *55*; I will *Gifford* 115. me,] *Gifford, after Dodsley*; ~‸ *55* you,] *Gifford*; ~. *55*

A noted Libertine I profess my self:
In your mind there does appear one fault so gross,
Nay, I might say unpardonable at your years,
If justly you consider it, that I cannot
As you desire, affect you.
Caliste. Make me know it,
I'le soon reform it.
H1v *Adorio.* Would you would keep your word.
Caliste. Put me to the test.
Adorio. I will. You are too honest,
And like your mother, too strict and religious,
And talk too soon of marriage: I shall break,
If at that rate I purchase you. Can I part with
My uncurb'd liberty, and on my neck
Wear such a heavy yoke? hazard my fortunes,
With all th'expected joys my life can yield me,
For one commodity before I prove it?
Venus forbid on both sides; let crook'd hams,
Bald heads, declining shoulders, furrow'd cheeks
Be aw'd by ceremonies: If you love me
I' the way young people should, I'll flie to meet it,
And we'll meet merrily.
Caliste. 'Tis strange such a man
Can use such language.
Adorio. In my tongue my heart
Speaks freely, fair one! Think upon't, a close friend
Or private Mistress, is Court-rhetorick;
A Wife, meer rustick Solecism. So good morrow.
ADORIO *offers to go, is staid by* CALDORO.
Camillo. How like you this?
Durazzo. A well-bred Gentleman!
I am now thinking if ere in the dark,
Or drunk I met his mother? He must have
Some drops of my blood in him; for at his years
I was much of his religion.
Camillo. Out upon you!
Donato. The Colts tooth still in your mouth?
Durazzo. What means this whispering?
Adorio. You may perceive I seek not to displant you,
Where you desire to grow: For further thanks,

'Tis needless complement.

Caldoro. There are some natures
Which blush to owe a benefit, if not
Receiv'd in corners; holding it an impairing
H2r To their own worth, should they acknowledge it.
I am made of other clay, and therefore must
Trench so far on your leisure, as to win you
To lend a patient ear, while I profess
Before my glory, though your scorn, *Caliste*,
How much I am your servant.

Adorio. My designs
Are not so urgent, but they can dispence
With so much time.

Camillo. Pray you now observe your Nephew.

Durazzo. How he looks! like a School-boy that had plaid the Truant,
And went to be breech'd.

Caldoro. Madam!

Caliste. A new affliction:
Your suit offends as much as his repulse,
It being not to be granted.

Mirtilla. Hear him Madam,
His sorrow is not personated; he deserves
Your pitty, not contempt.

Durazzo. He has made the Maid his;
And as the Master of the Art of Love
Wisely affirms, it is a kind of passage
To the Mistress favour.

Caldoro. I come not to urge
My merit to deserve you, since you are,
Weigh'd truly to your worth, above all value:
Much less to argue you of want of judgment
For following one that with wing'd feet flies from you;
While I, at all parts (without boast) his equal,
In vain pursue you; bringing those flames with me,
Those lawful flames, (for Madam know, with other
I never shall approach you) which *Adorio*
In scorn of *Hymen* and religious rites
With atheistical impudence contemns,
H2v And in his loose attempt to undermine

The fortress of your honor, seeks to ruine
All holy Altars by clear mindes erected
To Virgin-honor.
Durazzo. My Nephew is an ass,
What a devil hath he to do with Virgin-honor,
Altars, or lawful flames? when he should tell her
They are superstitious nothings, and speak to the purpose,
Of the delight to meet in the old dance
Between a pair of sheets; my Grandame call'd it
The peopling of the world.
Caliste. How, gentle sir?
To vindicate my honor, that is needless;
I dare not fear the worst aspersion malice
Can throw upon it.
Caldoro. Your sweet patience, Lady,
And more then dove-like innocence renders you
Insensible of an injury, for which
I deeply suffer. Can you undergo
The scorn of being refus'd? I must confess
It makes for my ends; for had he embrac'd
Your gracious offers tender'd him, I had been
In my own hopes forsaken; and if yet
There can breathe any air of comfort in me,
To his contempt I owe it: but his ill
No more shall make way for my good intents,
Then vertue powerful in her self, can need
The aids of vice.
Adorio. You take that licence, sir,
Which yet I never granted.
Caldoro. I'll force more,
Nor will I for mine own ends undertake it,
(As I will make apparent) but to do
A justice to your sex, with mine own wrong
And irrecoverable loss. To thee I turn,
Thou goatish Ribaud, in whom lust is grown
H3r Defensible, the last descent to hell,
Which gapes wide for thee: Look upon this Lady,
And on her fame, (if it were possible
Fairer then she is) and if base desires
And beastly appetite will give thee leave,

Consider how she sought thee, how this Lady
In a noble way desir'd thee: Was she fashion'd
In an inimitable mould, (which nature broke,
The great work perfected) to be made a slave
To thy libidinous twines, and when commanded,
To be us'd as physick after drunken surfets?
Mankind should rise against thee: What even now
I heard with horror, shew'd like blasphemy,
And as such I will punish it.

He strikes ADORIO, *the rest make in, they all draw.*

Caliste. Murder!

Mirtilla. Help!

Durazzo. After a whining Prologue, who would have look'd for
Such a rough Catastrophe? Nay, come on, fear nothing:
Never till now my Nephew. And do you hear sir,
(And yet I love thee too) if you take the wench now
I'll have it posted first, then chronicled,
Thou wert beaten to't.

Adorio. You think you have shewn
A memorable masterpiece of valor
In doing this in publick; and it may
Perhaps deserve her shoo-string for a favor:
Wear it without my envy; but expect
For this affront, when time serves, I shall call you
To a strict accompt.

Exeunt [ADORIO, CAMILLO, LENTULO, DONATO].

Durazzo. Hook on, follow him Harpies,
You may feed upon this business for a moneth,
If you manage it handsomly: when two heirs quarrel,
The sword-men of the City shortly after
Appear in Plush, for their grave consultations
In taking up the difference; some I know
H3v Make a set living on't. Nay, let him go,
Thou art master of the field; enjoy thy fortune
With moderation: For a flying foe,
Discreet and provident Conquerors build up
A bridge of gold. To thy mistress, boy! if I were
I'thy shirt, how I could nick it!

233 SD. *Exeunt* [ADORIO . . . DONATO].] *editor*; *Exeunt.* 55; *Exit. Gifford* (*with Exeunt for the others at l.* 235)

Caldoro. You stand, Madam,
As you were rooted, and I more then fear
My passion hath offended: I perceive
The roses frighted from your cheeks, and paleness
T'usurp their room; yet you may please to ascribe it
To my excess of love, and boundless ardor
To do you right; for my self I have done nothing:
I will not curse my stars, howere assur'd
To me you are lost for ever: For suppose
Adorio slain, and by my hand, my life
Is forfeited to the law; which I contemn,
So with a tear or two you would remember
I was your martyr, and died in your service.
Caliste. Alas, you weep! and in my just compassion
Of what you suffer, I were more then marble,
Should I not keep you company: You have sought
My favours nobly, and I am justly punish'd
In wild *Adorio's* contempt and scorn,
For my ingratitude, it is no better,
To your deservings: Yet such is my fate,
Though I would, I cannot help it. O *Caldoro*!
In our misplac'd affection I prove
Too soon, and with dear bought experience, *Cupid*
Is blind indeed, and hath mistook his arrows.
If it be possible, learn to forget:
And yet that punishment is too light; to hate
A thankless Virgin: practise it; and may
Your due consideration that I am so,
In your imagination disperse
H4r Lothsom deformity upon this face
That hath bewitch'd you. More I cannot say,
But that I truly pitty you, and wish you
A better choice, which in my prayers (*Caldoro*)
I ever will remember. *Exeunt* CALISTE, MIRTILLA.
Durazzo. 'Tis a sweet rogue:
Why how now? thunderstruck?
Caldoro. I am not so happy:
Oh that I were but master of my self,
You soon should see me nothing.
Durazzo. What would you do?

Caldoro. With one stab give a fatal period
To my woes and life together.
Durazzo. For a Woman!
Better the kind were lost, and generation
Maintain'd a new way.
Caldoro. Pray you sir forbear
This profane language.
Durazzo. Pray you be a man,
And whimper not like a girl: All shall be well,
As I live it shall; this is no Hectique feaver,
But a Love-sick ague easie to be cur'd,
And I'll be your Physitian, so you subscribe
To my directions. First you must change
This City whorish air, for 'tis infected,
And my potions will not work here, I must have you
To my Country-villa: Rise before the sun,
Then make a breakfast of the morning-dew
Serv'd up by nature on some grassie hill;
You'll find it Nectar, and far more cordial
Then Cullises, Cock-broth, or your distillations
Of a hundred crowns a quart.
Caldoro. You talk of nothing.
Durazzo. This tane as a preparative to strengthen
Your queasie stomack, vault into your saddle;
With all this flesh I can do it without a stirrup:
My hounds uncoupled, and my huntsmen ready,
You shal hear such musick from their tunable mouths
H4v That you will say the Viol, Harp, Theorbo,
Nere made such ravishing harmony, from the groves
And neighboring Woods, with frequent iterations,
Enamor'd of the cry, a thousand eccho's
Repeating it.
Caldoro. What's this to me?
Durazzo. It shall be,
And you give thanks for't. In the afternoon
(For we will have variety of delights)
We'll to the field agen, no game shall rise
But we'll be ready for't; if a Hare, my Greyhounds
Shall make a course; for the Pye or Jay, a Sparhawk
Flies from the Fist; the Crow so near pursu'd,

Shall be compell'd to seek protection under
Our Horses bellies; a Hearn put from her siege,
And a Pistol shot off in her breech, shall mount
So high, that to your view she'll seem to soar
Above the middle Region of the Air.
A cast of Haggard Falcons, by me man'd,
Eying the prey at first, appear as if
They did turn tayl, but with their laboring wings
Getting above her, with a thought their pinions
Cleaving the purer Element, make in,
And by turns binde with her; the frighted Fowl,
Lying at her defence upon her back,
With her dreadful Beak, a while defers her death,
But by degrees forc'd down, we part the fray
And feast upon her.
Caldoro. This cannot be, I grant,
But pretty pastime—
Durazzo. Pretty pastime, Nephew!
'Tis royal sport, then for an Evening flight
A Tercel gentle, which I call, my Masters,
As he were sent a Messenger to the Moon,
In such a place flies, as he seems to say,
See me, or see me not; the Partridge sprung,
He makes his stoop; but wanting breath, is forc'd
H5r To cancellier, then with such speed, as if
He carried Lightning in his Wings, he strikes
The trembling Bird; who even in death appears
Proud to be made his quarry.
Caldoro. Yet all this,
Is nothing to *Caliste*.
Durazzo. Thou shalt finde
Twenty *Calistes* there, for every night
A fresh, and lusty one; I'll give thee a Ticket,
In which my name, *Durazzo's* name subscrib'd,
My Tenants Nutbrown daughters, wholsom Girls,
At midnight shall contend to do thee service.
I have bred them up to't; should their Fathers murmure,
Their Leases are void; for that is a main point
In my Indentures: And when we make our progress

332. call,] *Gifford*; ~‸ 55

There is no entertainment perfect, if
This last dish be not offer'd.
Caldoro. You make me smile.
Durazzo. I'll make thee laugh outright. My horses, knaves!
'Tis but six short hours riding: yet ere night
Thou shalt be an alter'd man.
Caldoro. I wish I may, sir. *Exeunt.*

[I. ii] *Enter* IOLANTE, CALISTE, CALYPSO, MIRTILLA.

Iolante. I had spies upon you Minion; the relation
Of your behaviour was at home before you:
My daughter to hold parley, from the Church too,
With noted Libertines? her fame and favours
The quarrel of their swords?
Caliste. 'Twas not in me
To help it, Madam.
Iolante. No? how have I liv'd?
My neighbour knows my manners have been such,
That I presume I may affirm, and boldly,
In no particular action of my life
I can be justly censur'd.
H5v *Calypso.* Censur'd, Madam?
What Lord or Lady lives, worthy to sit
A competent Judge on you?
Caliste. Yet black detraction
Will find faults where they are not.
Calypso. Her foul mouth
Is stopp'd, you being the object: Give me leave
To speak my thoughts, yet still under correction;
And if my young Lady and her woman hear
With reverence they may be edifi'd.
You are my gracious Patroness and supportress,
And I your poor observer, nay your creature
Fed by your bounties; and but that I know
Your Honor detests flattery, I might say
(And with an emphasis) You are the Lady
Admir'd and envied at, far, far above
All imitation of the best of women

I. ii. 16. hear] *Dodsley*; here, *55*

That are or ever shall be. This is truth:
I dare not be obsequious; and 'twould ill
Become my gravity, and wisdom glean'd
From your oraculous Ladiship, to act
The part of a she-parasite.
Iolante. If you do,
I never shall acknowledge you.
Caliste. Admirable!
This is no flattery.
Mirtilla. Do not interrupt her:
'Tis such a pleasing itch to your Lady-mother,
That she may peradventure forget us,
To feed on her own praises.
Iolante. I am not
So far in debt to age, but if I would
Listen to mens bewitching sorceries,
I could be courted.
Calypso. Rest secure of that;
All the Braveries of the City run mad for you,
And yet your vertue's such, not one attempts you.
Iolante. I keep no mankind servant in my house,
In fear my chastity may be suspected:
6r How is that voic'd in *Naples*?
Calypso. With loud applause,
I assure your Honor.
Iolante. It confirms I can
Command my sensual appetites.
Calypso. As vassals
To your more then masculine reason that commands 'em:
Your palace stil'd a Nunnery of pureness,
In which not one lascivious thought dares enter,
Your clear soul standing Sentinel.
Mirtilla. Well said, Eccho.
Iolante. Yet I have tasted those delights which women
So greedily long for, know their titillations;
And when with danger of his head thy father
Comes to give comfort to my widowed sheets,
As soon as his desires are satisfied,
I can with ease forget 'em.
Calypso. Observe that,

It being indeed remarkable: 'tis nothing
For a simple Maid that never had her hand
In the hony-pot of pleasure, to forbear it;
But such as have lick'd there, and lick'd there often,
And felt the sweetness of't.—
Mirtilla. How her mouth runs over
With rank imagination!
Calypso. If such can,
As I urg'd before, the kickshaw being offer'd,
Refuse to take it, like my matchless Madam,
They may be Sainted.
Iolante. I'll lose no more breath
In fruitless reprehension; look to't,
I'll have thee wear this habit of my mind,
As of my body.
Calypso. Seek no other president:
In all the books of *Amadis de Gaul*,
The *Palmerins*, and that true Spanish story
The Mirror of Knighthood, which I have read often,
H6v Read feelingly, nay more, I do believe in't,
My Lady has no parallel.
Iolante. Do not provoke me.
If from this minute, thou ere stir abroad,
Write Letter or receive one, or presume
To look upon a man, though from a Window,
I'll chain thee like a slave in some dark corner,
Prescribe thy daily labor: Which omitted,
Expect the usage of a Fury from me,
Not an indulgent Mothers. Come *Calypso*.
Calypso. Your Ladiships injunctions are so easie,
That I dare pawn my credit, my yong Lady
And her woman shall obey 'em. *Exeunt* IOLANTE, CALYPSO.
Mirtilla. You shall fry first
For a rotten peece of dry Touchwood, and give fire
To the great Fiends Nostrils, when he smokes Tobacco.
Note the injustice Madam; they would have us
Being yong and hungry, keep a perpetual Lent,
And the whole yeer to them a Carnivale.
Easie injunctions, with a mischief to you:

70. in't,] *Mason*; ~‸ *55* 76. Prescribe] *Dodsley*; Proscribe *55*

Suffer this, and suffer all.
Caliste. Not stir abroad!
The use and pleasure of our eyes deny'd us?
Mirtilla. Insufferable.
Caliste. Nor write, nor yet receive
An amorous Letter!
Mirtilla. Not to be endured.
Caliste. Nor look upon a man out of a Windore.
Mirtilla. Flat tyranny, insupportable tyranny
To a Lady of your Blood.
Caliste. She is my Mother,
And how should I decline it?
Mirtilla. Run away from't,
Take any course.
Caliste. But without means *Mirtilla*,
How shall we live?
Mirtilla. What a question's that; as if
A bucksom Lady could want maintenance
H7r In any place in the World, where there are Men,
Wine, Meat, or Money stirring.
Caliste. Be you more modest,
Or seek some other Mistress: Rather then
In a thought or dream, I will consent to ought
That may take from my honor, I'll endure
More then my Mother can impose upon me.
Mirtilla. I grant your honor is a specious dressing,
But without conversation of men,
A kinde of nothing; I will not perswade you
To disobedience: Yet my Confessor told me
(And he you know is held a learned Clerk)
When Parents do enjoyn unnatural things,
Wise Children may evade 'em. She may as well
Command when you are hungry, not to eat,
Or drink, or sleep; and yet all these are easie
Compar'd with the not seeing of a man,
As I perswade no farther; but to you
There is no such necessity, you have means
To shun your Mothers rigor.

95. should I] *Dodsley*; I should *55* 115. As] *55*; But *Dodsley* farther;] *Gifford*; ~, *55* but] *55*; As *Dodsley* 116. necessity,] *editor*; ~; *55*

Caliste. Lawful means?
Mirtilla. Lawful, and pleasing too, I will not urge
Caldoro's loyal love, you being averse to't,
Make tryal of *Adorio*.
Caliste. And give up
My honor to his lust.
Mirtilla. There's no such thing
Intended, Madam; in few words write to him
What slavish hours you spend under your Mother,
That you desire not present marriage from him,
But as a noble Gentleman to redeem you
From the tyranny you suffer. With your Letter
Present him some rich Jewel; you have one,
In which the Rape of *Proserpine*, in little,
Is to the life express'd. I'll be the Messenger
With any hazard, and at my return,
Yeeld you a good accompt of't.
H7v *Caliste.* 'Tis a business
To be consider'd of.
Mirtilla. Consideration,
When the converse of your Lover is in question,
Is of no moment: If she would allow you
A Dancer in the morning to well breathe you,
A Songster in the afternoon, a Servant
To air you in the evening; give you leave
To see the Theater twice a week, to mark
How the old Actors decay, the young sprout up,
A fitting observation, you might bear it;
But not to see, or talk, or touch a man,
Abominable!
Caliste. Do not my blushes speak
How willingly I would assent?
Mirtilla. Sweet Lady,
Do somthing to deserve 'em, and blush after. *Exeunt.*

I. i]

Act. 2. Scæn. 1.

Enter IOLANTE, CALYPSO.

Iolante. AND are these *French-men*, as you say, such Gallants?
Calypso. Gallant and active; their free breeding knows not
The *Spanish* and *Italian* preciseness
Practis'd among us. What we call immodest,
With them is stil'd bold Courtship: they dare fight
Under a Velvet-Ensign at fourteen.
Iolante. A Petticoat you mean.
Calypso. You are i' the right;
Let a Mistress wear it under an armor of proof,
They are not to be beaten off.
H8r *Iolante*. You are merry Neighbor.
Calypso. I fool to make you so; pray you observe 'em,
They are the forwardest Monsieurs, born Physitians
For the malady of yong Wenches, and ne'er miss;
I ow my life to one of 'em; when I was
A raw yong thing, not worth the ground I trod on,
And long'd to dip my Bread in Tar, my Lips
As blue as Salt-water, he came up roundly to me,
And cur'd me in an instant, *Venus* be prais'd for't.

Enter ALPHONSO, GENERAL, MONTECLARO [*disguised*], *Attendants, and* CAPTAIN.

Iolante. They come, leave prating.
Calypso. I am dumb, an't like your honor.
Alphonso. We will not break the league confirm'd between us,
And your great Master; the passage of his Army
Through all our Territories, lies open to him;
Onely we grieve that your design for *Rome*
Commands such haste, as it denies us means
To entertain you, as your worth deserves,
And we would gladly tender.
General. Royal *Alphonso*,
The King my Master, your confederate,
Will pay the debt he ows, in Fact, which I

II. i. 10. so;] *Gifford*; ~, *55* 'em,] *Gifford*; ~. *55* 17 SD. MONTECLARO [*disguised*]] *editor*; *Monteclaro 55*; Laval *Gifford*

Want words t'express; I must remove to night,
And yet, that your intended favors may not
Be lost, I leave this Gentleman behinde me,
To whom you may vouchsafe 'em; I dare say
Without Repentance. I forbear to give
Your Majesty his character; in *France*
He was a President for Arts and Arms
Without a rival, and may prove in *Naples*
Worthy the imitation. ALPHONSO *receives* MONTECLARO.
H8v *Calypso.* Is he not Madam
A Monsieur in print? What a garb was there! O rare!
Then how he wears his clothes, and the fashion of 'em.
A main assurance that he is within
All excellent: By this, wise Ladies ever
Make their conjectures.
Iolante. Peace, I have observ'd him
From head to foot.
Calypso. Eye him agen, all over.
Monteclaro. It cannot royal Sir, but argue me
Of much presumption, if not impudence,
To be a suitor to your Majesty,
Before I have deserv'd a gratious grant,
By some employment prosperously atchiev'd.
But pardon gracious Sir: when I left *France*
I made a vow to a bosom Friend of mine
(Which my Lord General, if he please, can witness)
With such humility as well becomes
A poor Petitioner, to desire a Boon
From your magnificence. *He delivers a Petition.*
Calypso. With what punctual form
He does deliver it.
Iolante. I have eyes; no more.
Alphonso. For *Severino's* pardon, you must excuse me,
I dare not pardon murther.
Monteclaro. His fact Sir,
Ever submitting to your abler judgment,
Merits a fairer name: He was provok'd,
As by unanswerable proofs it is confirm'd,

36. the] *Dodsley*; thy *55*

By *Monteclaro's* rashness; who repining
That *Severino*, without his consent,
Had married *Iolante* his sole sister
(It being conceal'd almost for thirteen years)
I1r Though the Gentleman, at all parts, was his equal,
First challeng'd him, and that declin'd, he gave him
A blow in publick.
General. Not to be endur'd,
But by a slave.
Monteclaro. This, great Sir, justly weigh'd,
You may a little, if you please, take from
The rigor of your Justice, and express
An act of mercy.
Iolante. I can hear no more,
This opens an old wound, and makes a new one.
Would it were cicatriz'd, waite me.
Calypso. As your shadow.
Exeunt IOLANTE, CALYPSO.
Alphonso. We grant you these are glorious pretences,
Revenge appearing in the shape of valor,
Which wise Kings must distinguish. The defence
Of Reputation, now made a Bawd
To murther; every trifle falsly stil'd
An injury, and not to be determin'd
But by a bloody Duel; though this vice
Hath taken root and growth beyond the Mountains
(As *France*, and in strange fashions her Ape
England can deerly witness, with the loss
Of more brave spirits, then would have stood the shock
Of the *Turks* army) while *Alphonso* lives
It shall not here be planted: Move me no further
In this. In what else suiting you to ask,
And me to give, expect a gratious answer;
How ever, welcome to our Court. Lord General,
I'll bring you out of the Ports, and then betake you
To your good fortune.
General. Your Grace overwhelms me. *Exeunt.*

88. ever,] *Mason*; ~‸ 55, *McIlwraith* Court.] *Mason*; ~, 55, *McIlwraith*

I1v

[II. ii] *Enter* CALYPSO, *and* IOLANTE (*with a Purse and a Jewel.*)

Calypso. You are bound to favor him: Mark you how he pleaded
For my Lords pardon.
Iolante. That's indeed a tye;
But I have a stronger on me.
Calypso. Say you love
His person, be not asham'd of't; he's a man,
For whose embraces though *Endimion*
Lay sleeping by, *Cinthia* would leave her orb,
And exchange kisses with him.
Iolante. Do not Fan
A fire that burns already to hot in me,
I am in my honor sick, sick to the death,
Never to be recovered.
Calypso. What a coyl's here
For loving a man? It is no Africk wonder,
If like *Pasiphae* you doted on a Bull,
Indeed 'twere monstrous: but in this you have
A thousand thousand presidents to excuse you.
A Sea-mans wife may ask relief of her Neighbor
When her husbands bound to the Indies, and not blam'd for't;
And many more besides of higher calling,
Though I forbear to name 'em. You have a husband,
But as the case stands with my Lord, he is
A kinde of no husband; and your Ladiship
As free as a widow can be. I confess
If Ladies should seek change, that have their husbands
At Boord and Bed, to pay their marriage duties,
The surest bond of concord, 'twere a fault,
Indeed it were: But for your honor that
Do lie alone so often, Body of me,
I am zealous in your cause; let me take breath.

I2r

Iolante. I apprehend what thou wouldst say: I want all
As means to quench the spurious fire that burns here.
Calypso. Want means while I your Creature live? I dare not
Be so unthankful.
Iolante. Wilt thou undertake it?
And as an earnest of much more to come
Receive this Jewel, and Purse cramn'd full of Crowns.

How dearly I am forc'd to buy dishonor.
Calypso. I would do it *gratis*, but 'twould ill become
My breeding to refuse your honors bounty,
Nay, say no more, all Rhetorick in this
Is comprehended; let me alone to work him,
He shall be yours; that's poor, he is already
At your devotion. I will not boast
My faculties this way, but suppose he were
Coy as *Adonis*, or *Hippolitus*,
And your desires more hot then *Citherea's*,
Or wanton *Phedras*, I will bring him chain'd
To your embraces, glorying in his Fetters.
I have said it.
Iolante. Go and prosper, and imagine
A salary beyond thy hopes.
Calypso. Sleep you
Secure on either ear, the burthens yours
To entertain him, mine to bring him hither. *Exeunt.*

iii] *Enter* ADORIO, CAMILLO, LENTULO, DONATO.

Donato. Your wrong's beyond a challenge, and you deal
To fairly with him, if you take that way
To right your self.
Lentulo. The least that you can do
I'th' terms of honor is, when next you meet him
[2v To give him the bastinado.
Camillo. And that done,
Draw out his Sword to cut your own throat. No,
Be rul'd by me, shew your self an *Italian*,
And having received one injury, do not put off
Your Hat for a second; there are fellows that
For a few crowns will make him sure, and so
With your revenge, you prevent future mischief.
Adorio. I thank you Gentlemen for your studied care
In what concerns my honor; but in that
I'll steer mine own course, yet that you may know
You are still my Cabinet Counsellers, my bosom
Lies open to you. I begin to feel
A weariness, nay, satiety of looseness,

And something tells me here, I should repent
My harshness to *Caliste*.

Enter CARIO (*in haste.*)

Camillo. When you please,
You may remove that scruple.
Adorio. I shall think on't.
Cario. Sir, Sir, are you ready?
Adorio. To do what? I am sure
'Tis not yet dinner time.
Cario. True; but I usher
Such an unexpected dainty bit for breakfast,
As yet I never cook'd! 'tis not Potargo,
Fride Frogs, Potato's Marrow'd, Cavear,
Carps Tongues, the Pith of an English Chine of Beef,
Nor our Italian delicate Oyl'd Mushrooms,
And yet a drawer on too; and if you shew not
An appetite, and a strong one, I'll not say
To eat it, but devour it, without grace too,
I3r For it will not stay a Preface, I am sham'd,
And all my past provocatives will be jeer'd at.
Adorio. Art thou in thy wits? what new found rarity
Hast thou discover'd?
Cario. No such matter Sir;
It grows in our own Country.
Donato. Serve it up,
I feel a kinde of stomach.
Camillo. I could feed too.
Cario. Not a bit upon a march; there's other Lettice
For your course Lips; this is peculiar onely
For my Masters palate, I would give my whole years wages
With all my vails, and fees due to the Kitchin,
But to be his Carver.
Adorio. Leave your fooling Sirrah,
And bring in your dainty.
Cario. 'Twill bring in it self,
It has life and spirit in it, and for proof,
Behold: Now fall to boldly, my life on't
It comes to be tasted.

Enter MIRTILLA (*with Letter and Jewel.*)

Camillo. Ha! *Calistes* Woman.
Lentulo. A handsom one by *Venus.*
Adorio. Pray you forbear,
You are welcome fair one.
Donato. How that blush becomes her.
Adorio. Aim your designs at me?
Mirtilla. I'm trusted Sir
With a business of near consequence, which I would
To your private ear deliver.
Cario. I told you so.
3v Give her audience on your Couch, it is fit state
To a she Ambassador.
Adorio. Pray you Gentlemen
For a while dispose of your selves, I'll strait attend you.
[*Exeunt* CAMILLO, LENTULO, DONATO.]
Cario. Dispatch her first for your honor, the quickly doing,
You know what follows.
Adorio. Will you please to vanish— *Exit* CARIO.
Now pretty one, your pleasure; you shall finde me
Ready to serve you, if you'll put me to
My Oath, I'll take it on this Book.
Mirtilla. O Sir,
The favor is too great, and far above
My poor ambition, I must kiss your hand
In sign of humble thankfulness.
Adorio. So modest.
Mirtilla. It well becomes a Maid, Sir; spare those blessings
For my noble Mistress, upon whom with Justice,
And with your good allowance, I might adde
With a due gratitude, you may confer 'em,
But this will better speak her chast desires *Delivers the Letter.*
Then I can fancy what they are, much less
With moving language to their fair deserts
Aptly express 'em. Pray you read, but with
Compassion, I beseech you: if you finde
The Paper blur'd with tears faln from her eyes,
While she endeavor'd to set down that truth

II. iii. 48. I'm] *Dodsley*; I'em *55* 53 SD. *Exeunt* . . . DONATO.] *Gifford*; *Exit. 55*

Her Soul did dictate to her, it must challenge
A gratious answer.
Adorio. O the powerful charms!
By that fair hand writ down here; not like those
Which dreadfully pronounc'd by *Circe*, chang'd
Ulysses followers into Beasts; these have
An opposite working, I already feel
I4[r] But reading 'em, their saving operations,
And all those sensual, loose, and base desires
Which have too long usurped, and tyranniz'd
Over my Reason, of themselves fall of;
Most happy Metamorphosis! in which
The film of Error that did blinde my Judgment
And seduc'd Understanding, is remov'd.
What Sacrifice of Thanks can I return
Her pious Charity, that not alone
Redeems me from the worst of slavery,
The tyranny of my beastly appetites,
To which, I long obsequiously have bow'd,
But addes a matchless favor to receive
A benefit from me, nay, puts her Goodness
In my protection?
Mirtilla. Transform'd? it is *Aside.*
A blessed Metamorphosis, and works
I know not how on me.
Adorio. My joys are boundless,
Curb'd with no limits; for her sake, *Mirtilla*,
Instruct me how I presently may seal
To those strong bonds of loyal love, and service,
Which never shall be cancell'd.
Mirtilla. She'll become
Your debter Sir, if you vouchsafe to answer
Her pure affection.
Adorio. Answer it *Mirtilla*!
With more then adoration I kneel to it.
Tell her I'll rather die a thousand deaths,
Then fail with punctuality to perform
All her commands.
Mirtilla. (I am lost on this assurance,
Which if 'twere made to me, I should have faith in't, *Aside.*

As in an Oracle. Ah me!) She presents you
This Jewel, her dead Grandsirs gift, in which,
4v As by a true *Egyptian* Herogliphick,
(For so I think she call'd it) you may be
Instructed what her suit is, you should do,
And she with joy will suffer.
Adorio. Heaven be pleas'd
To qualifie this excess of happiness
With some disaster, or I shall expire
With a surfeit of Felicity. With what art
The cunning Lapidary hath here express'd
The rape of *Proserpine*; I apprehend
Her purpose, and obey it, yet not as
A helping Friend, but a Husband; I will meet
Her chast desires with lawful heat, and warm
Our *Hymenæal* sheets with such delights
As leave no sting behinde 'em.
Mirtilla. I despair then. *Aside.*
Adorio. At the time appointed, say wench, I'll attend her,
And guard her from the fury of her Mother,
And all that dare disturb her.
Mirtilla. You speak well,
And I believe you.
Adorio. Would you ought else?
Mirtilla. I would carry
Some love sign to her; and now I think on't,
The kinde salute you offer'd at my entrance,
Hold it not impudence that I desire it,
I'll faithfully deliver it.
Adorio. O a kiss,
You must excuse me, I was then mine own,
Now wholly hers. The touch of other Lips
I do abjure for ever; but there's Gold
To binde thee still my advocate. *Exit.*
Mirtilla. Not a kiss?
I was coy when it was offered, and now justly
When I beg one am deni'd, what scortching fires
5r My loose hopes kindle in me! Shall I be
False to my Ladies trust? and from a servant
Rise up her rival? His words have bewitch'd me,

And something I must do, but what? 'tis yet
An embrion, and how to give it form
Alas I know not, pardon me, *Caliste*,
I am nearest to my self, and time will teach me
To perfect that which yet is undetermined. *Exit.*

[II. iv] *Enter* CLAUDIO *and* SEVERINO.

Claudio. You are Master of your self, yet if I may
As a tri'd Friend in my love and affection,
And a servant in my duty speak my thoughts,
Without offence? i' th' way of counsel to you,
I could alleage, and truly, that your purpose
For *Naples* cover'd with a thin disguise
Is full of danger.
Severino. Danger *Claudio*?
'Tis here, and every where our forc'd companion,
The rising and the setting Sun, beholds us
Inviron'd with it; our whole life a journey
Ending in certain ruine.
Claudio. Yet we should not,
Howev'r besieg'd, deliver up our Fort
Of life, till it be forc'd.
Severino. 'Tis so indeed
By wisest men concluded, which we should
Obey as Christians; but when I consider
How different the progress of our actions
Are from Religion, nay, Morality,
I cannot finde in Reason, why we should
Be scrupulous that way onely, or like Meteors
Blaze forth prodigious terrors, till our stuff
Be utterly consum'd, which once put out,
I5v Would bring security unto our selves,
And safety unto those we prey upon.
O *Claudio*! since by this fatal hand
The brother of my wife, bold *Monteclaro*,
Was left dead in the field, and I proscrib'd
After my flight, by the justice of the King,
My being hath been but a living death
With a continued torture.

Claudio. Yet in that
You do delude their bloody violence
That do pursue your life.
Severino. While I by rapines
Live terrible to others as my self,
What one hour can we challenge as our own
(Unhappy as we are) yielding a beam
Of comfort to us? Quiet night that brings
Rest to the labourer, is the Outlaws day,
In which he rises early to do wrong,
And when his work is ended, dares not sleep:
Our time is spent in watches to intrap
Such as would shun us, and to hide our selves
From the Ministers of Justice, that would bring us
To the correction of the Law. O *Claudio*,
Is this a life to be preserv'd? and at
So dear a rate? But why hold I discourse
On this sad subject? since it is a burthen
We are mark'd to bear, and not to be shook off
But with our humane frailty. In the change
Of dangers there is some delight, and therefore
I am resolv'd for *Naples*.
Claudio. May you meet there
All comforts that so fair and chaste a wife
(As fame proclaims her without parallel)
Can yield to ease your sorrows.
Severino. I much thank you;
Yet you may spare those wishes, which with joy
I6r I have prov'd certainties, and from their want
Her excellencies take lustre.
Claudio. Ere you go yet,
Some charge unto your Squires not to flie out
Beyond their bounds, were not impertinent:
For though that with a look you can command 'em,
In your absence they'll be headstrong.
Severino. 'Tis well thought on,
I'll touch my horn, they know my call. *Blows his horn.*
Claudio. And will,
As soon as heard, make in to't from all quarters,
As the flock to the shepherds whistle.

Enter six BANDITI.

1. What's your will?

2. Hail Soveraign of these Woods.

3. We lay our lives
At your Highness feet.

4. And will confess no King,
Nor Laws, but what come from your mouth; and those
We gladly will subscribe to.

Severino. Make this good
In my absence to my substitute, to whom
Pay all obedience as to my self:
The breach of this in one particular
I will severely punish; on your lives
Remember upon whom with our allowance
You may securely prey, with such as are
Exempted from your fury.

Claudio. 'Twere not amiss,
If you please, to help their memory; besides,
Here are some newly initiated.

Severino. To these
Read you the Articles: I must be gone;
Claudio, farewell.

16v *Claudio.* May your return be speedy. *Exit* SEVERINO.

1. Silence; out with your Table-books.

2. And observe.

Claudio. The Cormorant that lives in expectation
Of a long wish'd for dearth, and smiling grindes
The faces of the poor, you may make spoil of;
Even theft to such is Justice.

3. He's in my Tables.

Claudio. The grand Incloser of the Commons, for
His private profit, or delight, with all
His Herds that graze upon't are lawful prize.

4. And we will bring 'em in, although the devil
Stood roaring by, to guard 'em.

Claudio. If a Usurer,
Greedy at his own price, to make a purchase,
Taking advantage upon Bond, or Morgage,

II. iv. 84. with all] *Dodsley*; withal *55*

From a Prodigal, pass through our Territories,
I' the way of custom, or of tribute to us,
You may ease him of his burthen.
2. Wholsome doctrine.
Claudio. Builders of Iron Mills, that grub up Forests,
With Timber Trees for shipping.
1. May we not
Have a touch at Lawyers?
Claudio. By no means; they may
To soon have a gripe at us; they are angry Hornets,
Not to be jested with.
3. This is not so well.
Claudio. The owners of dark shops that vent their wares
With Perjuries; cheating Vintners not contented
With half in half in their reckonings, yet cry out
When they finde their ghests want coyn, 'tis late, and Bed-time;
These ransack at your pleasures.
3. How shall we know 'em?
Claudio. If they walk on foot by their Rat-colour'd stockings,
17r And shining shooes. If Horsmen by short Boots,
And riding furniture of several Counties.
2. Not one of the List escapes us.
Claudio. But for Schollars,
Whose wealth lies in their heads, and not their pockets,
Soldiers that have bled in their Countries service,
The Rent-rack'd Farmer, needy Market folks,
The sweaty Laborer, Carriers that transport
The goods of other men, are priviledg'd;
But above all, let none presume to offer
Violence to women, for our King hath sworn,
Who that way's a Delinquent, without mercy
Hangs for't by Marshal law.
Omnes. Long live *Severino.*
And perish all such cullions as repine
At his new Monarchy.
Claudio. About your business,
That he may finde at his return good cause
To praise your care and discipline.
Omnes. We'll not fail Sir. *Exeunt.*

[II. v] *Enter* MONTECLARO *and* CALYPSO.

Monteclaro. Thou art sure mistaken, 'tis not possible
That I can be the man thou art employ'd too.
Calypso. Not you the man? you are the man of men,
And such another in my Ladies eye,
Never to be discover'd.
Monteclaro. A meer stranger
Newly arriv'd?
Calypso. Still the more probable,
Since Ladies, as you know, affect strange dainties,
And brought far to 'em. This is not an age
In which Saints live, but women, knowing women,
That understand their *summum bonum* is
Variety of pleasures in the touch,
Deriv'd from several Nations; and if men
Would be wise by their example—
Monteclaro. As most are.
'Tis a coupling age!
I7v *Calypso.* Why sir, do Gallants travel?
Answer that question; but at their return
With wonder to the hearers, to discourse of
The garb and difference in foreign Females,
As the lusty Girle of *France*, the sober *German*,
The plump *Dutch* Fro, the stately Dame of *Spain*,
The *Roman* Libertine, and spriteful *Tuscan*,
The merry *Greek*, *Venetian* Courtesan,
The *English* fair Companion, that learns something
From every Nation, and will flie at all.
I say again the difference betwixt these
And their own Country Gamesters.
Monteclaro. Aptly urg'd.
Some make that their main end; but may I ask
Without offence to your gravity, by what title
Your Lady that invites me to her favors,
Is known in the City?
Calypso. If you were a true born Monsieur,
You would do the business first, and ask that after.
If you onely truck with her title, I shall hardly
Deserve thanks for my travel; she is Sir

No single Duccat trader, nor a Beldam
So frozen up, that a Fever cannot thaw her;
No Lioness by her breath.
Monteclaro. Leave these impertinencies,
And come to the matter.
Calypso. Would you would be as forward
When you draw for the upshot, she is Sir a Lady,
A rich, fair, well-complexioned, and what is
Not frequent among *Venus* Votaries,
Upon my credit, which good men have trusted;
A sound and wholesom Lady, and her name is
Madona Iolante.
Monteclaro. *Iolante.*
I have heard of her, for chastity, and beauty,
The wonder of the age.
18ʳ *Calypso.* Pray you not too much
Of chastity; fair, and free I do subscribe too,
And so you'll finde her.
Monteclaro. Come y'are a base Creature,
And covering your foul ends with her fair name,
Give me just reason, to suspect you have
A plot upon my life.
Calypso. A plot! Very fine!
Nay, 'tis a dangerous one, pray you beware of't,
'Tis cunningly contriv'd, I plot to bring you
Afoot with the travel of some forty paces,
To those delights, which a man not made of Snow,
Would ride a thousand miles for. You shall be
Receiv'd at a Postern door, if you be not cautious,
By one whose touch would make old *Nestor* yong,
And cure his *Hernia*! A terrible plot!
A kiss then ravished from you by such Lips
As flow with *Nectar*, a juicy palm more pretious
Then the fam'd *Sibilla*'s Bough to guide you safe
Through Mists of perfumes to a glorious room,
Where *Jove* might feast his *Juno*, a dire plot,
A Banquet I'll not mention, that is common;
But I must not forget, to make the plot

II. v. 36. you would] *Mason*; you woo'd *55*; you'd *Gifford* 64. forget,] *Mason*; ~‸ *55*

More horrid to you, the retiring bower
So furnish'd, as might force the *Persians* envy,
The Silver bathing Tub, the Cambrick rubbers,
Th'embroider'd Quilt, a Bed of Gossamire,
And Damask Roses, a meer Powder plot
To blow you up; and last, a Bed-fellow,
To whose rare entertainment all these are
But foils, and settings off.
Monteclaro. No more, her breath
Would warm an Euenuch.
Calypso. I knew I should heat you;
Now he begins to glow.
Monteclaro. I am flesh and blood,
18v And I were not man, if I should not run the hazard,
Had I no other ends in't; I have consider'd
Your motion, Matron.
Calypso. My plot Sir on your life,
For which, I am deservedly suspected
For a base and dangerous woman. Fare you well Sir,
I'll be bold to take my leave.
Monteclaro. I will along too.
Come pardon my suspition, I confess
My Error; and eying you better, I perceive
There's nothing that is ill that can flow from you.
I am serious, and for proof of it I'll purchase
Your good opinion.
Calypso. I am gently natur'd,
And can forget a greater wrong upon
Such terms of satisfaction.
Monteclaro. What's the hour?
Calypso. Twelve.
Monteclaro. I'll not miss a minute.
Calypso. I shall finde you
At your lodging?
Monteclaro. Certainly, return my service,
And for me kiss your Ladies hands.
Calypso. At twelve,
I'll be your convoy.
Monteclaro. I desire no better. *Exeunt.*

65. you, the] *Gifford*; you. The *55*

II. i]

Act. 3. Scœn. 1.

Enter DURAZZO, CALDORO, *Servant.*

Durazzo. WALK the Horses down the Hill, I have a little
To speak in private.
K1r *Caldoro.* Good Sir, no more anger.
Durazzo. Love do you call it? Madness, wilful Madness;
And since I cannot cure it, I would have you
Exactly mad. You are a lover already,
Be a drunkard too, and after turn small Poet,
And then you are mad *Katexikene*, the Madman.
Caldoro. Such as are safe on shore, may smile at tempests,
But I that am embarqu'd, and every minute
Expect a shipwrack, rellish not your mirthe;
To me it is unseasonable.
Durazzo. Pleasing Viands,
Are made sharp by sick palats. I affect
A handsom Mistress in my grey Beard, as well
As any Boy of you all; and on good terms
Will venture as far i' th' fire, so she be willing
To entertain me; but ere I would dote
As you do, where there is no flattering hope
Ever t'enjoy her, I would forswear Wine,
And kill this letcherous Itch with drinking Water,
Or live like a Carthusian on Poor-John,
Then bathe my self, night by night, in marble dew,
And use no Soap but Camphir-Balls.
Caldoro. You may
(And I must suffer it) like a rough Surgeon,
Apply these burning costicks to my wounds
Already gangreen'd, when soft unguents would
Better express an Uncle, with some feeling
Of his Nephews torments.
Durazzo. I shall melt, and cannot
Hold out if he whimper. O that this yong fellow,
Who on my knowledge is able to beat a man,
Should be baffel'd by this blinde imagin'd Boy,
Or fear his Bird-bolts.
Caldoro. Y'have put your self already

K1[v] To too much trouble in bringing me thus far:
Now if you please, with your good wishes leave me
To my hard fortunes.
Durazzo. I'll forsake my self first.
Leave thee? I cannot, will not; thou shalt have
No cause to be weary of my company,
For I'll be useful, and ere I see thee perish,
Dispensing with my dignity and candor,
I will do something for thee, though it savour
Of the old Squire of *Troy*. As we ride, we will
Consult of the means: Bear up.
Caldoro. I cannot sink,
Having your noble aids to buoy me up;
There was never such a Guardian.
Durazzo. How's this?
Stale complements to me? when my work's done,
Commend th'artificer, and then be thankful. *Exeunt.*

[III. ii] *Enter* CALISTE (*richly habited*) *and* MIRTILLA (*in her first gown.*)

Caliste. How doest thou like my gown?
Mirtilla. 'Tis rich and Courtlike.
Caliste. The dressings too are suitable?
Mirtilla. I must say so,
Or you might blame my want of care.
Caliste. My mother
Little dreams of my intended flight, or that
These are my nuptial ornaments.
Mirtilla. I hope so.
Caliste. How dully thou repliest! thou dost not envy
Adorio's noble change, or the good fortune
That it brings to me?
Mirtilla. My endeavours that way
Can answer for me.
Caliste. True, you have discharged
K2[r] A faithful Servants duty, and it is
By me rewarded like a liberal Mistress:
I speak it not to upbraid you with my bounties,
Though they deserve more thanks and ceremony

III. i. 43. such] *Coxeter*; such such *55*

Then you have yet express'd.
Mirtilla. The miseries
Which from your happiness I am sure to suffer,
Restrain my forward tongue; and gentle Madam,
Excuse my weakness, though I do appear
A little daunted with the heavy burthen
I am to undergo: when you are safe,
My dangers like to roaring torrents will
Gush in upon me; yet I would endure
Your mothers cruelty; but how to bear
Your absence, in the very thought confounds me:
Since we were children, I have lov'd and serv'd you;
I willingly learn'd to obey, as you
Grew up to knowledg, that you might command me;
And now to be divorc'd from all my comforts,
Can this be borne with patience?
Caliste. The necessity
Of my strange fate commands it; but I vow
By my *Adorio's* love, I pitty thee.
Mirtilla. Pitty me, Madam! a cold charity;
You must do more, and help me.
Caliste. Ha! what said you?
I must? is this fit language for a servant?
Mirtilla. For one that would continue your poor servant,
And cannot live that day in which she is
Deni'd to be so: Can *Mirtilla* sit
Mourning alone, imagining those pleasures
Which you this blessed Hymeneal night
Enjoy in the embraces of your Lord,
And my Lord too in being yours, (already
As such I love and honor him.) Shall a stranger
Sew you in a sheet to guard that maidenhead
2v You must pretend to keep, (and 'twill become you.)
Shall another do those bridal offices
Which time will not permit me to remember,
And I pine here with envy? Pardon me,
I must and will be pardon'd, for my passions
Are in extreams, and use some speedy means
That I may go along with you, and share

III. ii. 31. *Mirtilla.*] *Coxeter; Cal.* 55

In those delights, but with becoming distance;
Or by his life, which as a Saint you swear by,
I will discover all.
Caliste. Thou canst not be
So treacherous and cruel, in destroying
The building thou hast rais'd.
Mirtilla. Pray you do not tempt me,
For 'tis resolv'd.
Caliste. I know not what to think of't.
In the discovery of my secrets to her,
I have made my slave my Mistress, I must sooth her,
There's no evasion else. Prethee *Mirtilla*,
Be not so violent, I am strangely taken
With thy affection to me, 'twas my purpose
To have thee sent for.
Mirtilla. When?
Caliste. This very night,
And I vow deeply I shall be no sooner
In the desir'd possession of my Lord,
But by some of his servants I will have thee
Convey'd unto us.
Mirtilla. Should you break?
Caliste. I dare not:
Come, clear thy looks, for instantly we'll prepare
For our departure.
Mirtilla. Pray you forgive my boldness,
Growing from my excess of zeal to serve you.
Caliste. I thank thee for't.
Mirtilla. You'll keep your word?
K3r *Caliste.* Still doubtful?
Mirtilla. 'Twas this I aim'd at, and leave the rest to Fortune.
Exeunt.

[III. iii] *Enter* ADORIO, CAMILLO, LENTULO, DONATO, CARIO, *Servants.*

Adorio. Haste you unto my *Villa*, and take all
Provision along with you, and for use,
And ornament, the shortness of the time
Can furnish you; let my best Plate be set out,

III. iii. 2. you,] *Gifford*; ~; *55*

And costliest Hangings, and if't be possible
With a merry dance to entertain the Bride,
Provide an Epithalamium.
Cario. Trust me
For belly timber, and for a song I have
A Paper blurrer; who on all occasions,
For all times, and all seasons, hath such trinckets
Ready i' th' deck. It is but altering
The names, and they will serve for any Bride,
Or Bridegroom in the Kingdom.
Adorio. But for the dance?
Cario. I will make one my self, and foot it finely,
And summoning your Tenants at my Dresser,
Which is indeed my Drum, make a rare choice
Of th'able youth, such as shall sweat sufficiently,
And smell too, but not of Amber, which you know is
The grace of the Country-hall.
Adorio. About it *Cario*,
And look you be careful.
Cario. For mine own credit Sir. *Exit.*
Adorio. Now noble friends confirm your loves, and think not
Of the penalty of the Law, that does forbid
The stealing away an Heir. I will secure you,
And pay the breach of't.
K3v *Camillo.* Tell us what we shall do,
We'll talk of that hereafter.
Adorio. Pray you be carefull
To keep the West-gate of the City open,
That our passage may be free, and bribe the Watch
With any sum; this is all.
Donato. A dangerous business.
Camillo. I'll make the Constable, Watch, and Porter drunk,
Under a Crown.
Lentulo. And then you may pass while they snore,
Though you had done a murther.
Camillo. Get but your Mistress,
And leave the rest to us.
Adorio. You much engage me,
But I forget my self.
Camillo. Pray you in what, Sir?

Adorio. Yielding too much to my affection,
Though lawful now, my wounded reputation
And honor suffer: The disgrace in taking
A blow in publike from *Caldoro*, branded
With the infamous mark of Coward, in delaying
To right my self, upon my cheek grows fresher,
That's first to be consider'd.
Camillo. If you dare
Trust my opinion, (yet I have had
Some practice and experience in duels)
You are too tender that way: Can you answer
The debt you owe your honor, till you meet
Your Enemy from whom you may exact it?
Hath he not left the City, and in fear
Conceal'd himself, for ought I can imagine?
What would you more?
Adorio. I should do.
Camillo. Never think on't
Till fitter time and place invite you to it.
I have read *Caranza*, and find not in his Grammar
K4r Of Quarrels, that the injur'd man is bound
To seek for reparation at an hour;
But may, and without loss, till he hath setled
More serious occasions that import him,
For a day or two defer it.
Adorio. You'll subscribe
Your hand to this?
Camillo. And justifie't with my life,
Presume upon't.
Adorio. On then, you shall overrule me. *Exeunt.*

[III. iv] *Enter* IOLANTE *and* CALYPSO.

Iolante. I'll give thee a golden tongue, and have it hung up
Ore thy tomb for a monument.
Calypso. I am not prepar'd yet
To leave the world; there are many good pranks
I must dispatch in this kind before I die:
And I had rather, if your Honor please,
Have the crowns in my purse.

Iolante. Take that.
Calypso. Magnificent Lady!
May you live long, and every Moon love change,
That I may have fresh imployment. You know what
Remains to be done.
Iolante. Yes, yes, I will command
My daughter and *Mirtilla* to their chamber.
Calypso. And lock 'em up: Such liquorish Kitlings are not
To be trusted with our cream. Ere I go, I'll help you
To set forth the banquet, and place the candi'd Eringo's
Where he may be sure to taste 'em. Then undress you,
For these things are cumbersom, when you should be active:
4v A thin night mantle to hide part of your Smock,
With your Pearl embroider'd Pantophles on your Feet,
And then you are arm'd for service; nay, no trifling,
We are alone, and you know 'tis a point of folly
To be coy to eat, when meat is set before you. *Exeunt.*

v] *Enter* ADORIO, *and* SERVANT.

Adorio. 'Tis eleven by my Watch, the hour appointed.
Listen at the door; hear'st thou any stirring?
Servant. No Sir, all's silent here.
Adorio. Some cursed business keeps
Her mother up. I'll walk a little circle,
And shew where you shall wait us with the horses,
And then return. This short delay afflicts me,
And I presume, to her it is not pleasing. *Exeunt.*

Enter DURAZZO, CALDORO.

Durazzo. What's now to be done? prethee let's to Bed, I am sleepy.
And here's my hand on't, without more ado,
By fair or foul play, we'll have her to morrow
In thy possession.
Caldoro. Good Sir give me leave
To taste a little comfort in beholding
The place by her sweet presence sanctifi'd:
She may perhaps to take air, ope the Casement,

III. v. 8. sleepy] *Coxeter*; sleep *55*; asleep *Dodsley*

And looking out, a new Star to be gaz'd on
By me with adoration, bless these eyes,
Ne'er happy but when she is made the Object.
Durazzo. Is not here fine fooling?
K5r *Caldoro.* Thou great Queen of Love,
Or real or imagin'd, be propitious
To me thy faithful Votary; and I vow
T'erect a statue to thee, equal to
Thy picture by *Apelles* skilful hand
Left as the great example of his art;
And on thy thigh I'll hang a golden *Cupid*,
His torches flaming, and his quiver full,
For further honour.
Durazzo. End this waking dream,
And let's away.

Enter CALISTE *and* MIRTILLA.

Caliste. *Mirtilla*!
Caldoro. 'Tis her voice.
Caliste. You heard the horses footing?
Mirtilla. Certainly.
Caliste. Speak low: my Lord *Adorio*?
Caldoro. I am dumb.
Durazzo. The darkness friends us too; most honour'd Madam,
Adorio your servant.
Caliste. As you are so,
I do command your silence till we are
Further remov'd; and let this kiss assure you
(I thank the sable night that hides my blushes)
I am wholly yours.
Durazzo. Forward you micher.
Mirtilla. Madam,
Think on *Mirtilla*. *Goes in.*
Durazzo. I'll not now enquire
The mysterie of this, but bless kind Fortune
Favoring us beyond our hopes: yet now I think on't,
I had ever a lucky hand in such smock night-work. *Exeunt.*

27. *Caliste. Mirtilla*!] *Dodsley; Mirtilla!* 55 (*as spoken by Durazzo*) 30. friends] *Dodsley*; friend 55

5v *Enter* ADORIO *and* SERVANT.

Adorio. This slowness does amaze me; she's not alter'd
In her late resolution?
(*Within*) *Iolante*. Get you to bed,
And stir not on your life, till I command you.
Adorio. Her mothers voice! listen.
Servant. Here comes the daughter.

Enter MIRTILLA.

Mirtilla. Whither shall I flie for succor?
Adorio. To these arms,
Your castle of defence, impregnable,
And not to be blown up. How your heart beats!
Take comfort, dear *Caliste*, you are now
In his protection that will nere forsake you,
Adorio: Your chang'd *Adorio* swears
By your best self, an oath he dares not break,
He loves you, loves you in a noble way,
His constancie firm as the poles of heaven.
I will urge no reply, silence becomes you,
And I'll defer the musick of your voice
Till we are in a place of safety.
Mirtilla. O blest error! *Exeunt*.

Enter SEVERINO.

Severino. 'Tis midnight: how my fears of certain death
Being surpris'd, combat with my strong hopes
Rais'd on my chaste wifes goodness! I am grown
A stranger in this City, and no wonder,
I have too long been so unto my self:
Grant me a little truce, my troubled soul,
I hear some footing, ha?

Enter MONTECLARO *and* CALYPSO.

Calypso. That is the house,
6r And there's the key; you'll find my Lady ready
To entertain you: 'tis not fit I should
Stand gaping by while you bill: I have brought you on,

48–9. you, / *Adorio*:] 55; you: / *Adorio, Gifford*

Ch rge home, and come off with honor. *Exit.*

Severino. It makes this way.

Monteclaro. I am much troubled, and know not what to think
Of this design.

Severino. It still comes on.

Monteclaro. The Watch!
I am betraid.

Severino. Should I now appear fearful,
It would discover me; there is no retiring,
My confidence must protect me, I'll appear
As if I walk'd the round. Stand.

Monteclaro. I am lost.

Severino. The word?

Monteclaro. Pray you forbear; I am a stranger,
And missing this dark stormy night my way
To my lodging, you shall do a courteous office
To guide me to't.

Severino. Do you think I stand here for
A page or a porter?

Monteclaro. Good sir grow not so high,
I can justifie my being abroad; I am
No pilfering vagabond, and what you are
Stands yet in supposition; and I charge you
If you are an Officer, bring me before your Captain;
For if you do assault me, though not in fear
Of what you can do alone, I will cry murther
And raise the streets.

Severino. Before my Captain, ha?
And bring my head to the block. Would we were parted,
I have greater cause to fear the Watch then he.

Monteclaro. Will you do your duty?

Severino. I must close with him:
Truth sir, whatere you are, (yet by your language
I ghess you a Gentleman) I'll not use the rigor
K6v Of my place upon you; only quit this street,
For your stay here will be dangerous, and good night.

Monteclaro. The like to you sir; I'll grope out my way
As well as I can. O damn'd Bawd! Fare you well sir.

Exit MONTECLARO.

Severino. I am glad he's gone; there is a secret passage

Unknown to my wife, through which this key will guide me
To her desired imbraces, which must be,
My presence being beyond her hopes, most welcom. *Exit.*

vi] *Enter* IOLANTE (*with a rich banquet*, *and tapers*) (*in a chair*, *behind a curtain.*)

Iolante. I am full of perplexed thoughts: Imperious Blood,
Thou only art a tyrant; Judgment, Reason,
To whatsoever thy Edicts proclaim,
With vassal fear subscribe against themselves.
I am yet safe in the port, and see before me,
If I put off, a rough tempestuous sea,
The raging winds of infamy from all quarters
Assuring my destruction; yet my lust
Swelling the wanton sails, (my understanding
Stow'd under hatches) like a desperate Pilot
Commands me to urge on: My pride, my pride,
Self-love, and over-value of my self
Are justly punish'd: I that did deny
My daughters youth allow'd and lawful pleasures,
And would not suffer in her those desires
She suck'd in with my milk, now in my waning
Am scorcht and burnt up with libidinous fire
That must consume my fame; yet still I throw
More fuel on it.

Enter SEVERINO.

Severino. 'Tis her voice, poor Turtle;
7r She's now at her devotions praying for
Her banished Mate: alas, that for my guilt
Her innocence should suffer! But I do
Commit a second sin in my deferring
The extasie of joy that will transport her
Beyond herself, when she flies to my lips,
And seals my welcom. *Iolante*! [*Draws the curtain.*]
Iolante. Ha?
Good Angels guard me.
Severino. What do I behold?

III. vi. 26 SD. *Draws the curtain.*] *Gifford*; *not in* 55

Some sudden flash of lightning strike me blind,
Or cleave the center of the earth, that I
May living find a sepulchre to swallow
Me and my shame together.

Iolante. Guilt and horror
Confound me in one instant; thus surpris'd,
The subtlety of all Wantons, though abstracted,
Can shew no seeming colour of excuse
To plead in my defence.

Severino. Is this her mourning?
O killing object! the imprison'd vapours
Of rage and sorrow make an earthquake in me:
This little world, like to a tottering tower,
Not to be underpropp'd; yet in my fall
I'll crush thee with my ruines. *Draws a poniard, she kneels.*

Iolante. Good sir, hold:
For, my defence unheard, you wrong your justice,
If you proceed to execution,
And will too late repent it.

Severino. Thy defence?
To move it, adds (could it receive addition)
Ugliness to the loathsom leprosie
That in thy being a Strumpet hath already
Infected every vein, and spreads it self
Over this carrion, which would poison Vulturs
And dogs, should they devour it. Yet to stamp
The seal of Reprobation on thy soul,
K7v I'll hear thy impudent lyes borrow'd from hell
And prompted by the Devil thy tutor, Whore,
Then send thee to him. Speak.

Iolante. Your Gorgon looks
Turn me to stone, and a dead palsie seises
My silenc'd tongue.

Severino. O fate, that the disease
Were general in women; what a calm
Should wretched men enjoy! Speak, and be brief,
Or thou shalt suddenly feel me.

Iolante. Be appeas'd sir,
Until I have deliver'd reasons for
This solemn preparation.

Severino. On, I hear thee.
Iolante. With patience ask your memory; 'twill instruct you,
This very day of the moneth 17 years since
You married me.
Severino. Grant it, what canst thou urge
From this?
Iolante. That day since your proscription sir,
In the remembrance of it annually,
The garments of my sorrow laid aside,
I have with pomp observ'd.
Severino. Alone!
Iolante. The thoughts
Of my felicity then, my misery now,
Were the invited guests; Imagination
Teaching me to believe that you were present
And a partner in it.
Severino. Rare! this real banquet
To feast your fancie: Fiend, could Fancie drink off
These flagons to my health? or th'idol Thought
Like *Baal* devour these delicates? the room
Perfum'd to take his nostrils? this loose habit
Which *Messalina* would not wear, put on
To fire his lustful eyes? Wretch, am I grown
So weak in thy opinion, that it can
3r Flatter credulity that these gross tricks
May be foisted on me? Where's my daughter? where
The Bawd your woman? answer me, *Caliste*,
Mirtilla! they are dispos'd of, if not murther'd,
To make all sure; and yet methinks your neighbour,
Your whistle, agent, parasite *Calypso*,
Should be within call, when you hem to usher in
The close Adulterer.
Iolante. What will you do?
Severino. Not kill thee, do not hope it, I am not
So near to reconcilement. Ha! this scarf
Th'intended favor to your Stallion, now
Is useful: do not strive; thus bound expect
All studied tortures, my assurance, not
My jealousie thou art false, can pour upon thee.

85. within call,] *Dodsley*; within: Call *55*

In darkness howl thy mischiefs; and if rankness
Of thy imagination can conjure
The Ribaud, glut thy self with him:
I will cry aim, and in another room
Determine of my vengeance. Oh my heart-strings!
Exit (*with tapers.*)

Iolante. Most miserable woman! and yet sitting
A Judge in mine own cause upon my self,
I could not mitigate the heavy doom
My incens'd husband must pronounce upon me.
In my intents I am guilty, and for them
Must suffer the same punishment, as if
I had in fact offended.

CALYPSO *speaks at the door.*

Calypso. Bore my eyes out
If you prove me faulty: I'll but tell my Lady
What caus'd your stay, and instantly present you.
How's this? no lights? what new device? will she play
At Blindman-buff? Madam?

K8v *Iolante.* Upon thy life
Speak in a lower key.

Calypso. The mysterie
Of this sweet Lady; where are you?

Iolante. Here fast bound.

Calypso. By whom?

Iolante. I'll whisper that into thine ear,
And then farewell for ever.

Calypso. How? my Lord?
I am in a fever: Horns upon horns grow on him.
Could he pick no hour but this to break a bargain
Almost made up?

Iolante. What shall we do?

Calypso. Betray him;
I'll instantly raise the Watch.

Iolante. And so make me
For ever infamous.

Calypso. The Gentleman,
The rarest Gentleman is at the door,
Shall he lose his labour? since that you must perish,

'Twill shew a womans spleen in you to fall
Deservedly: give him his answer, Madam.
I have on the sudden in my head a strange whimsie,
But I will first unbind you.
Iolante. Now what follows?
Calypso. I will supply your place; and bound, give me
Your mantle, take my night-gown, send away
The Gentleman satisfied. I know my Lord
Wants power to hurt you: I perhaps may get
A kiss by the bargain, and all this may prove
But some neat love-trick: If he should grow furious
And question me, I am resolv'd to put on
An obstinate silence. Pray you dispatch the Gentleman,
His courage may cool.
Iolante. I'll speak with him; but if
To any base or lustful end, may mercy
At my last gasp forsake me. *Exit.*
Calypso. I was too rash,
And have done what I wish undone: say he should kill me,
1r I have run my head in a fine nooze, and I smell
The pickle I am in: 'las how I shudder
Still more and more! would I were a she-*Priapus*,
Stuck up in a garden to fright away the Crows,
So I were out of the house; she's at her pleasure
Whatere she said, and I must endure the torture.
He comes; I cannot pray, my fear will kill me.

Enter SEVERINO (*throwing open the doors violently*) *having a knife.*

Severino. It is a deed of darkness, and I need
No light to guide me: there is something tels me
I am too slow pac'd in my wreak, and trifle
In my revenge. All hush'd? no sigh nor groan
To witness her compunction? can guilt sleep,
And innocence be open-ey'd? Even now
Perhaps she dreams of the Adulterer,
And in her fancie hugs him: Wake thou strumpet;
And instantly give up unto my vengeance
The villain that defiles my bed; discover
Both what and where he is, and suddenly,

That I may bind you face to face, then sew you
Into one sack, and from some steep rock hurl you
Into the sea together: Do not play with
The lightning of my rage; break stubborn silence,
And answer my demands, will it not be?
I'll talk no longer; thus I mark thee for
A common strumpet.
Calypso. Oh!
Severino. Thus stab these arms
That have stretch'd out themselves to grasp a stranger.
Calypso. Oh!
Severino. This is but an induction; I'll draw
The curtains of the Tragedy hereafter:
Howl on, 'tis musick to me. *Exit* SEVERINO.
L1v *Calypso.* He is gone,
A kiss and love-tricks; he hath villainous teeth,
May sublim'd Mercury draw 'em. If all dealers
In my profession were paid thus, there would be
A dearth of Cuckolds. Oh my nose! I had one,
My arms, my arms! I dare not cry for fear:
Cursed desire of gold, how art thou punish'd!

Enter IOLANTE.

Iolante. Till now I never truly knew my self,
Nor by all principles and lectures read
In Chastities cold school was so instructed
As by her contrary. How base and deform'd
Loose appetite is! as in a few short minutes
This stranger hath, and feelingly, deliver'd.
Oh that I could recall my bad intentions,
And be as I was yesterday untainted
In my desires, as I am still in fact
(I thank his temperance); I could look undanted
Upon my husbands rage, and smile at it,
So strong the guards, and sure defences are
Of armed Innocence; but I will endure
The penance of my sin, the onely means,
Is left to purge it. The day breaks. *Calypso.*
Calypso. Here Madam, here.
Iolante. Hath my Lord visited thee?

Calypso. Hell take such visits; these stab'd arms, and loss
Of my nose, you left fast on, may give you a rellish
What a night I have had of't, and what you had suffered,
Had I not supplied your place.
Iolante. I truly grieve for't;
Did not my husband speak to thee?
Calypso. Yes, I heard him
.2r And felt him, *ecce signum*, with a mischief,
But he knew not me; like a true bred Spartan Fox
With silence I endured it, he could not get
One syllable from me.
Iolante. Something may be fashion'd
From this: invention help me, I must be sudden,
Thou art free, exchange, quick, quick, now binde me sure,
And leave me to my fortune.
Calypso. Pray you consider,
The loss of my nose; had I been but carted for you,
Though wash'd with Mire and Chamber-ly, I had
Examples to excuse me; but my nose,
My nose dear Lady.
Iolante. Get off, I'll send to thee. *Exit* [CALYPSO].
If so, it may take; if it fail, I must
Suffer what ever follows.

Enter SEVERINO (*with a Taper.*)

Severino. I have searched
In every corner of the house, yet finde not
My daughter, nor her Maid, nor any print
Of a mans footing, which this wet night would
Be easily discern'd, the ground being soft,
At his coming in or going out.
Iolante. 'Tis he,
And I am within hearing; Heaven forgive this feigning,
I being forc'd to't to preserve my life,
To be better spent hereafter.
Severino. I begin
To stagger, and my love if it knew how,

193. Fox] *55*; Boy *Mason* 196. this: invention help] *Mason*; this invention: Help *55* 202 SD. *Exit* [CALYPSO].] *Gifford*; *Exit. 55* (*opposite* Lady.) 210. And I am within] *55*; And I'm within *Coxeter*; And within *Gifford*

Her piety heretofore, and fame remembred,
Would plead in her excuse.
L2v *Iolante.* You blessed Guardians
Of matrimonial faith, and just revengers
Of such as do in fact offend against
Your sacred rites and ceremonies; by all titles
And holy attributes you do vouchsafe
To be invok'd, look down with saving pitty
Upon my matchless sufferings.
Severino. At her devotions,
Affliction makes her repent.
Iolante. Look down
Upon a wretched woman; and as I
Have kept the knot of wedlock, in the Temple
By the Priest fasten'd firm, (though in loose wishes
I yield I have offended) to strike blind
The eyes of Jealousie that see a crime
I never yet committed, and to free me
From the unjust suspition of my Lord,
Restore my martyr'd face and wounded arms
To their late strength and beauty.
Severino. Does she hope
To be cur'd by miracle?
Iolante. This minute I
Perceive with joy my orisons heard and granted:
You ministers of mercy, who unseen,
And by a supernatural means have done
This work of heavenly charity, be ever
Canoniz'd for't.
Severino. I did not dream, I heard her,
And I have eyes too, they cannot deceive me.
If I have no belief in their assurance,
I must turn sceptick. Ha? this is the hand?
And this the fatal instrument? these drops
Of blood, that gush'd forth from her face and arms,
Still fresh upon the floor: This is something more
Then wonder or amazement, I profess
I am astonish'd.
Iolante. Be incredulous still,
L3r And go on in your barbarous rage, led to it

By your false guide Suspition, have no faith
In my so long try'd loyalty, nor believe
That which you see; and for your satisfaction,
My doubted innocence cleared by miracle,
Proceed, these Veins have now new blood, if you
Resolve to let it out.

Severino. I would not be fool'd
With easiness of belief, and faintly give *Aside.*
Credit to this strange wonder! 'tis now thought on;
In a fitter place and time, I'll sound this further. *Unties her.*
How can I expiate my sin? or hope,
Though now I write my self thy slave, the service
Of my whole life can win thee to pronounce
Despair'd of pardon? shall I kneel? that's poor,
Thy mercy must urge more in my defence,
Then I can fancy; wilt thou have revenge?
My heart lies open to thee.

Iolante. This is needless
To me, who in the duty of a wife,
Know I must suffer.

Severino. Thou art made up of goodness,
And from my confidence that I am alone
The object of thy pleasures, until death
Divorce us, we will know no separation.
Without inquiring why (as sure thou wilt not,
Such is thy meek obedience) thy Jewels
And choicest ornaments pack'd up, thou shalt
Along with me; and as a Queen be honor'd
By such as stile me Soveraign; already
My banishment is repeal'd, thou being present:
The Neapolitan Court a place of exile
When thou art absent; my stay here is mortal,
Of which thou art to sensible, I perceive it.
Come dearest *Iolante*, with this breath
3v All jealousie is blown away.

Iolante. Be constant. *Exeunt.*

256. expiate] *Dodsley*; expect *55* 272. as] *Dodsley*; a *55*

[IV. i]

Act. 4. Scœn. 1.

A noyse within, as the fall of a Horse,—then
Enter DURAZZO, CALDORO, CALISTE, SERVANT.

Durazzo. HELL take the stumbling Jade.
Caldoro. Heaven help the Lady.
Servant. The Horse hath broke his neck.
Durazzo. Would thine were crack'd too
So the Lady had no harm. Give her fresh air,
'Tis but a swoun.
Caldoro. 'Tis more, she's dead.
Durazzo. Examine
Her limbs if they be whole: not too high, not too high
You Ferrit, this is no Cunniborough for you.
How do you finde her?
Caldoro. No breath of comfort sir, too cruel fate!
Had I still pin'd away, and lingred under
The modesty of just and honest hopes
After a long consumption, sleep and death,
To me had been the same, but now as 'twere
Possess'd of all my wishes, in a moment
To have 'em ravished from me? suffer shipwrack
In view of the Port? and like a half starv'd begger,
No sooner in compassion cloath'd, but coffin'd?
Malevolent destinies, too cunning in
L4r Wretched *Caldoro's* tortures. O *Caliste*,
If thy immortal part hath not already
Left this fair pallace, let a beam of light
Dawn from thine eye, in this Cimmerian darkness,
To guide my shaking hand to touch the anchor
Of hope in thy recovery.
Caliste. Oh.
Durazzo. She lives,
Disturb her not, she is no right bred woman
If she die with one fall; some of my acquaintance
Have took a thousand merrily, and are still
Excellent wrestlers at the close hug.
Caldoro. Good Sir.
Durazzo. Prethee be not angry, I should speak thus if

My Mother were in her place.
Caldoro. But had you heard
The musick of the language which she us'd
To me, believ'd *Adorio*, as she rode
Behinde me; little thinking that she did
Embrace *Caldoro*.
Caliste. Ah *Adorio*!
Durazzo. Leave talking, I conceive it.
Caliste. Are you safe?
Caldoro. And rais'd like you from death to life to hear you.
Caliste. Hear my defence then, ere I take my vail off,
A simple maids defence, which looking on you,
I faintly could deliver; willingly
I am become your prize, and therefore use
Your victory nobly; Heavens bright eye, the Sun,
Draws up the grossest vapors, and I hope
I ne'er shall prove an envious cloud to darken
The splendor of your merits. I could urge
With what disdain, nay scorn, I have declin'd
The shadows of insinuating pleasures
4v Tender'd by all men else, you onely being
The object of my hopes: That cruel Prince
To whom the Olive branch of Peace is offer'd,
Is not a conqueror, but a bloody tyrant,
If he refuse it; nor should you wish a triumph,
Because *Caliste*'s humble; I have said
And now expect your sentence.
Durazzo. What a throng
Of Clients would be in the Court of Love,
Were there many such she Advocates: Art thou dumb?
Canst thou say nothing for thy self?
Caldoro. Dear Lady
Open your eyes, and look upon the man,
The man you have elected for your Judge,
Kneeling to you for mercy.
Caliste. I should know
This voice, and something more then fear I am
Deceiv'd, but now I look upon his face,
I am assur'd I am wretched.
Durazzo. Why good Lady?

Hold her up, she'll fall agen, before her time else,
The youth's a well timbred youth, look on his making;
His Hair curl'd naturally, he's whole chested too,
And will do his work as well, and go through stitch with't,
As any *Adorio* in the world; my state on't,
A Chicken of the right kinde; and if he prove not
A Cock of the Game, cuckold him first, and after
Make a Capon of him.

Caliste. I'll cry out a Rape,
If thou unhand me not; would I had died
In my late trance, and never liv'd to know
I am betray'd.

Durazzo. To a yong and active husband,
L5r Call you that trechery? there are a shole of
Yong wenches i' th' City, would vow a pilgrimage
Beyond *Jerusalem*, to be so cheated.
To her agen you milk-sop, violent storms
Are soon blown over.

Caliste. How could'st thou *Caldoro*
With such a frontless impudence, arm thy hopes
So far, as to believe I might consent
To this leud practise? have I not often told thee,
Howere I pitied thy misplaced affection,
I could not answer it? and that there was
A strong antipathy between our Passions,
Not to be reconcil'd?

Caldoro. Vouchsafe to hear me
With an impartial ear, and it will take from
The rigor of your censure. Man was mark'd
A friend in his Creation to himself,
And may with fit ambition conceive
The greatest blessings, and the highest honors
Appointed for him, if he can atchieve 'em
The right and noble way: I grant you were
The end of my design, but still pursu'd
With a becoming modesty, Heaven at length
Being pleas'd, and not my arts, to further it.

Durazzo. Now he comes to her: On boy.

Caldoro. I have serv'd you

IV. i. 80. thee,] *Dodsley*; ~‸ *55* 81. Howere] *Dodsley*; How, ere *55*

With a religious zeal, and borne the burthen
Of your neglect (if I may call it so)
Beyond the patience of a man. To prove this,
I have seen those eyes with pleasant glances play
Upon *Adorio's*, like *Phœbe's* shine
Guilding a Chrystal River, and your Lip
Rise up in civil courtship to meet his,
While I bit mine with envy: Yet these favors
(How ere my passions rag'd) could not provoke me
To one act of rebellion against
5v My loyalty to you; the soveraign
To whom I ow obedience.
Caliste. My blushes
Confess this for a truth.
Durazzo. A flag of truce is
Hung out in this acknowledgment.
Caldoro. I could adde,
But that you may interpret what I speak,
The malice of a rival, rather then
My due respect to your deserts, how faintly
Adorio hath return'd thanks to the bounty
Of your affection, ascribing it
As a tribute to his worth, and not in you
An act of mercy: Could he else, invited
(As by your words I understood) to take you
To his protection, grosly neglect
So gratious an offer? or give power
To fate it self to cross him? O dear Madam,
We are all the Balls of time, toss'd to and fro,
From the Plough unto the Throne, and back agen;
Under the swinge of destinie mankinde suffers,
And it appears by an unchang'd decree
You were appointed mine; wise nature always
Aiming at due proportion; and if so,
I may believe with confidence, Heaven in pity
Of my sincere affection, and long patience,
Directed you by a most blessed error
To your vow'd servants bosom.
Durazzo. By my holidame

98. man. To prove this,] *Dodsley*; man, to prove this. *55*

Tickling-Philosophy.
Caliste. I am Sir, too weak
To argue with you; but my Stars have better
(I hope) provided for me.
Caldoro. If there be
Disparity between us, 'tis in your
Compassion to level it.
Durazzo. Give fire
To the Mine, and blow her up.
Caliste. I am sensible
L6r Of what you have endured, but on the sudden,
With my unusual travel, and late bruise,
I am exceeding weary; in yon grove,
While I repose my self, be you my guard:
My spirits with some little rest reviv'd,
We will consider further: For my part
You shall receive modest and gentle answers
To your demands, though short perhaps to make you
Full satisfaction.
Caldoro. I am exalted
In the employment, sleep secure, I'll be
Your vigilant Sentinel.
Caliste. But I command you,
And as you hope for future grace obey me,
Presume not with one stoln kiss to disturb
The quiet of my slumbers; let your temperance
And not your lust, watch over me.
Caldoro. My desires
Are frozen, till your pitty shall dissolve 'em.
Durazzo. Frozen! think not of Frost fool in the Dog-days,
Remember the old adage, and make use of't,
Occasion's bald behinde.
Caliste. Is this your Uncle?
Caldoro. And Guardian, Madam; at your better leisure,
When I have deserv'd it, you may give him thanks
For his many favours to me.
Caliste. He appears
A pleasant Gentleman. *Exeunt* CALDORO *and* CALISTE.
Durazzo. You should find me so,
But that I do hate incest. I grow heavy;

Sirra provide fresh horses; I'll seek out
Some hollow tree, and dream till you return,
Which I charge you to hasten.
Servant. With all care sir. *Exeunt.*

L6[v]

. ii] *Enter* CARIO *and Country men, (for the Dance and Song.)*

Cario. Let your eyes be rivetted to my heels, and miss not
A hairs breadth of my footing; our Dance has
A most melodious note, and I command you
To have ears like hares this night for my Lords honor,
And something for my Worship: your reward is
To be drunk blind like Moles in the Wine-cellar,
And though you ne'r see after, 'tis the better,
You were born for this nights service: And do you hear,
Wire-string and Cats-guts men, and strong-breath'd Hoboys,
For the credit of your calling, have not your Instruments
To tune, when you should strike up; but twang it perfectly,
As you would read your Neckverse; and you Warbler
Keep your Wind-pipe moist, that you may not spit and hem,
When you should make division. How I sweat!
Authority is troublesom.—They are come, [*A horn within.*]
I know it by the Cornet that I plac'd
On the hill to give me notice: Marshal your selves
I'the Rear, the Van is yours. Now chant it spritely.

Enter ADORIO, MIRTILLA, CAMILLO, LENTULO, DONATO.

Song

Between JUNO *and* HYMEN.

JUNO *to the Bride.*

Enter a Maid, but made a Bride,
Be bold, and freely taste
The Marriage Banquet ne'er deny'd
To such as sit down chaste.
Though he unloose thy Virgin Zone,
Presum'd against thy will,
Those Joys reserv'd to him alone,
Thou art a Virgin still.

IV. ii. 15 SD. *A horn within.*] *Gifford: not in* 55 18–42. *Song. . . Urn.*] *Printed as* I. SONG. *at end of play in* 55 (N4[r]); [*Song*] 55

HYMEN *to the Bridegroom.*

Hail Bridegroom, hail! thy choice thus made,
As thou wouldst have her true
Thou must give o'r thy wanton trade,
And bid loose fires adieu:
That Husband who would have his Wife
To him continue chaste,
In her embraces spends his life,
And makes abroad no waste.

HYMEN *and* JUNO.

Sport then like Turtles, and bring forth
Such pledges as may be
Assurance of the Fathers worth,
And Mothers purity.
Juno *doth bless the Nuptial Bed,*
Thus Hymens *Torches burn.*
Live long, and may, when both are dead,
Your Ashes fill one Urn.

Adorio. A well-penn'd Ditty.
Camillo. Not ill sung.
Adorio. What follows?
Cario. Use your eyes; if ever, now your masterpiece!

Dance

Adorio. 'Tis well perform'd, take that, but not from me,
'Tis your new Ladies bounty, thank her for't,
L7ʳ All that I have is hers.
Cario. I must have three shares
For my pains and properties, the rest shall be
Divided equally. *Exeunt* CARIO *et Rustici.*
Mirtilla. My real fears
Begin, and soon my painted comforts vanish
In my discovery.
Adorio. Welcome to your own:
You have (a wonder in a woman) kept
Three long hours silence; and the greater, holding
Your own choice in your arms, a blessing for which

I will be thankfull to you, nay unmask
And let mine eye and ears together feast,
Too long by you kept empty: Oh you want
Your womans help, I'll do her office for you. *Puls off her mask.*
Mirtilla!
Camillo. It is she, and wears the habit
In which *Caliste* three days since appeared
As she came from the Temple.
Lentulo. All this trouble
For a poor Waiting-maid?
Donato. We are grossly gull'd.
Adorio. Thou child of impudence, answer me, and truly,
Or though the tongues of Angels pleaded mercy,
Tortures shall force it from thee.
Mirtilla. Innocence
Is free and open breasted; of what crime
Stand I accus'd, my Lord?
Adorio. What crime? no language
Can speak it to the height, I shall become
Discourse for fools, and drunkards. How was this
Contriv'd? who help'd thee in the plot? discover.
Were not *Caliste's* aydes in't?
Mirtilla. No on my life;
Nor am I faulty.
Adorio. No: what maygame's this?
Didst thou treat with me for thy Mistriss favors,
To make sale of thine own?
L7v *Mirtilla*. With her and you
I have dealt faithfully: you had her Letter
With the Jewel I presented; she receiv'd
Your courteous answer, and prepar'd herself
To be remov'd by you: And howsoever
You take delight to hear what you have done,
From my simplicity, and make my weakness
The subject of your mirth, as it suits well
With my condition, I know you have her
In your possession.
Adorio. How! has she left
Her mothers house?
Mirtilla. You drive this nail too far;

Indeed she deeply vow'd at her departure
To send some of your Lordships servants for me,
(Though you were pleas'd to take the pains your self)
That I might still be near her, as a shadow
To follow her the substance.
Adorio. She is gone then?
Mirtilla. This is too much; but good my Lord forgive me,
I come a Virgin hither to attend
My noble Mistress, though I must confess
I look with sore eyes upon her good fortune,
And wish it were mine own.
Adorio. Then as it seems
You do yourself affect me?
Mirtilla. Should she hear me,
And in her sudden fury kill me for't,
I durst not, Sir, deny it; since you are
A man so form'd, that not poor I alone,
But all our sex like me I think stand bound
To be enamour'd of you.
Adorio. O my fate!
How justly am I punish'd! in thee punish'd
For my defended wantonness! I that scorn'd
The Mistress when she sought me, now I would
L8r Upon my knees receive her, am become
A prey unto her Bondwoman,
My honor too neglected for this purchase.
Art thou one of those
Ambitious Serving-women, who contemning
Th'embraces of their Equals, aim to be
The wrong way Ladifi'd by a Lord? was there
No forward Page or Footman in the City
To do the feat, that in thy lust I am chosen
To be the executioner? dar'st thou hope
I can descend so low?
Mirtilla. Great Lords sometimes
For change leave calvert Sammon, and eat Sprats,
In modesty I dare speak no more.
Camillo. If 'twere
A Fish-day, though you like it not, I could say
I have a stomach, and would content my self

With this pretty Whiting-mop.
Adorio. Discover yet
How thou cam'st to my hands.
Mirtilla. My Lady gone,
Fear of her mothers rage, she being found absent,
Mov'd me to flie; and quitting of the house,
You were pleas'd unask'd to comfort me, I us'd
No sorceries to bewitch you; then vouchsaf'd
(Thanks ever to the darkness of the night)
To hug me in your arms, and I had wrong'd
My breeding near the Court, had I refus'd it.
Adorio. This is still more bitter; canst thou ghess to whom
Thy Lady did commit herself?
Mirtilla. They were
Horsemen, as you are.
Adorio. In the name of wonder,
How could they pass the Port, where you expected
My coming?
Camillo. Now I think upon't, there came
Three mounted by, and behind one a woman
8v Embracing fast the man that rode before her.
Lentulo. I knew the men, but she was vail'd.
Adorio. What were they?
Lentulo. The first the Lord *Durazzo*, and the second
Your rival yong *Caldoro*; it was he
That carried the wench behinde him.
Donato. The last a servant
That spur'd fast after 'em.
Adorio. Worse and worse! 'twas she!
Too much assurance of her love undid me;
Why did you not stay 'em?
Donato. We had no such commission.
Camillo. Or say we had? who durst lay fingers on
The angry old Ruffian?
Lentulo. For my part I had rather
Take a baited Bull by the Horns.
Adorio. You are sure friends
For a man to build on.
Camillo. They are not far off,
Their horses appeared spent too; lets take fresh ones

And coast the Countrey, ten to one we finde 'em.
Adorio. I will not eat nor sleep, until I have 'em.
Moppet you shall along too.
Mirtilla. So you please,
I may keep my place behinde you; I'll sit fast,
And ride with you all the world over.
Camillo. A good Girle. *Exeunt.*

[IV. iii] *Enter* MONTECLARO *and* CALYPSO.

Monteclaro. Her husband *Severino*?
Calypso. You may see
His handy-work by my flat face; no bridge
Left to support my Organ, if I had one.
The comfort is I am now secure from the Grincomes,
I can loose nothing that way.
Monteclaro. Doest thou not know
What became of the Lady?
M1r *Calypso.* A nose was enough to part with
I think, in the service; I durst stay no longer,
But I am full assur'd the house is empty,
Neither poor Lady, daughter, servant left there:
I only ghess he hath forc'd 'em to go with him
To the dangerous Forrest where he lives like a King
Among the *Banditi*, and how there he hath us'd them,
Is more then to be fear'd.
Monteclaro. I have plaid the fool,
And kept my self too long conceal'd, sans question
With the danger of her life. Leave me—The King!

Enter ALPHONSO *and* CAPTAIN.

Calypso. The Surgeon must be paid.
Monteclaro. Take that.
Calypso. I thank you,
I have got enough by my trade, and I will build
An Hospital only for noseless Bawds,
'Twill speak my charity, and be my self
The Governess of the Sisterhood. *Exit.*
Alphonso. I may

IV. iii. 3. Organ, if I had one.] *Mason*; Organ. If I had one, *55*

Forget this in your vigilance hereafter;
But as I am a King, if you provoke me
The second time with negligence of this kind,
You shall deeply smart for't.
Monteclaro. The King's mov'd.
Alphonso. To suffer
A murtherer by us proscrib'd, at his pleasure
To pass and repass through our guards?
Captain. Your pardon
For this, my gracious Lord, binds me to be
More circumspect hereafter.
Alphonso. Look you be so:
Monsieur *Laval*, you were a suiter to me
For *Severino's* pardon.
M1v *Monteclaro.* I was so, my good Lord.
Alphonso. You might have met him here to have thank'd you for't,
As now I understand.
Monteclaro. So it is rumour'd;
And hearing in the City of his boldness,
(I would not say contempt of your Decrees)
As then I pleaded mercy, (under pardon)
I now as much admire the slowness of
Your justice (though it force you to some trouble)
In fetching him in.
Alphonso. I have consider'd it.
Monteclaro. He hath of late, as 'tis suspected, done
An outrage on his wife, forgetting nature
To his own daughter, in whom sir I have
Some nearer interest then I stand bound to
In my humanity, which I gladly would
Make known unto your Highness.
Alphonso. Go along,
You shall have opportunity as we walk:
See you what I committed to your charge,
In readiness, and without noise.
Captain. I shall sir. *Exeunt.*

M2r [V. i]

Act. 5. Scæn. 1.

Enter CLAUDIO, *and all the* BANDITI (*making a guard*), SEVERINO *and* IOLANTE (*with Oaken-leav'd garlands*) *and Singers.*

Song.

Entertainment of the Forests Queen.

Welcome, thrice welcome to this shady Green,
Our long wish'd Cinthia, *the Forests Queen,*
The Trees begin to bud, the glad Birds sing,
In Winter chang'd by her into the Spring.
We know no night,
Perpetual light
Dawns from your eye.
You being near,
We cannot fear,
Though death stood by.
From you our Swords take edge, our Hearts grow bold.
From you in Fee, their lives your Liegemen hold.
These Groves your Kingdom, and our Law your will;
Smile, and we spare; but if you frown, we kill.
Bless then the hour
That gives the power
In which you may,
At Bed and Board
Embrace your Lord
Both night and day.
Welcome, thrice welcome to this shady Green,
Our long wish'd Cinthia, *the Forests Queen.*

Severino. HERE, as a Queen, share in my soveraignty:
The iron toils pitch'd by the Law to take
The forfeiture of my life, I have broke through,
And secure in the guards of these few subjects
Smile at *Alphonso's* fury, though I grieve for
The fatal cause in your good brothers loss
That does compell me to this course.

V. i. 1–22. *Song . . . Queen.*] *Printed as* II. SONG. *at end of play* (*N4v*) 29. this] *Dodsley*; his *55*

Iolante. Revive not
A sorrow long since dead, and so diminish
The full fruition of those joys, which now
I stand possess'd of: Womanish fear of danger
That may pursue us, I shake off, and with
A masculine spirit.
Severino. 'Tis well said.
Iolante. In you sir
I live; and when, or by the course of nature,
Or violence you must fall, the end of my
Devotions is, that one and the same hour
May make us fit for heaven.
Severino. I join with you
In my votes that way: But how, *Iolante*,
You that have spent your past days slumbring in
The doun of quiet, can endure the hardness
M2v And rough condition of our present being,
Does much disturb me.
Iolante. These woods, *Severino*,
Shall more then seem to me a populous City,
You being present; here are no allurements
To tempt my frailty, nor the conversation
Of such, whose choice behaviour or discourse
May nourish jealous thoughts.
Severino. True, *Iolante*,
Nor shall suspected chastity stand in need here
To be clear'd by miracle.
Iolante. Still on that string?
It yields harsh discord.
Severino. I had forgot my self,
And wish I might no more remember it.
The day wears, sirs, without one prize brought in
As tribute to your Queen. *Claudio*, divide
Our Squadron in small parties, let 'em watch
All passages, that none escape without
The payment of our Customs.
Claudio. Shall we bring in
The persons with the pillage?
Severino. By all means;

58–9. means; / Without reply, about it;] *Gifford*; means, / Without reply about it, *55*.

Without reply, about it; we'll retire *Exeunt* CLAUDIO *and the rest.*
Into my Cave, and there at large discourse
Our fortunes past, and study some apt means
To find our daughter; since she well dispos'd of,
Our happiness were perfect.

Iolante. We must wait
With patience Heavens pleasure.

Severino. 'Tis my purpose. *Exeunt.*

[V. ii] *Enter* LENTULO *and* CAMILLO.

Lentulo. Let the horses graze, they are spent.

M3[r] *Camillo.* Sure I am sleepy,
And nodded as I rode: here was a jaunt
I' th' dark through thick and thin, and all to no purpose:
What a dulness grows upon me.

Lentulo. I can hardly *They sit down.*
Hold ope mine eyes to say so. How did we lose
Adorio?

Camillo. He, *Donato*, and the Wench
That cleaves to him like bird-lime, took the right hand,
But this place is our rendevouz.

Lentulo. No matter,
We'll talk of that anon,—heigh ho. *Sleeps.*

Camillo. He's fast already;
Lentulo; I'll take a nap too. *Sleeps.*

Enter ADORIO, MIRTILLA, DONATO.

Adorio. Was ever man so crost?

Mirtilla. So blest: This is the finest Wild-goose chase.

Adorio. What's that you mutter?

Mirtilla. A short prayer, that you may find
Your wish'd for love, though I am lost for ever.

Donato. Pretty fool. Who have we here?

Adorio. This is *Camillo.*

Mirtilla. This Signior *Lentulo.*

Adorio. Wake 'em.

V. ii. 1. *Camillo.* Sure] *editor*; I am sure *55*; *Cam.* I am sure *Coxeter* 11. *Mirtilla.*] *Dodsley*; 1 *Wom. 55*

Donato. They'll not stir,
Their eye-lids are glu'd, and mine too; by your favour,
I'll follow their example. *Lies down.*
Adorio. Are you not weary?
M3v *Mirtilla.* I know not what the word means, while I travel
To do you service.
Adorio. You expect to reap
The harvest of your flattery; but your hopes
Will be blasted, I assure you.
Mirtilla. So you give leave
To sow it as in me a sign of duty,
Though you deny your beams of gratious favor
To ripen it, with patience I shall suffer.
Adorio. No more; my resolution to finde
Caliste, by what accident lost, I know not,
Binds me not to deny my self what nature
Exacteth from me. To walk alone afoot
(For my Horse is tir'd) were madness, I must sleep;
You could lie down too.
Mirtilla. Willingly; so you please
To use me.
Adorio. Use thee?
Mirtilla. As your pillow Sir,
I dare presume no farther, noble Sir.
Do not too much condemn me; generous feet,
Spurn not a fawning Spaniel.
Adorio. Well! sit down.
Mirtilla. I am ready Sir.
Adorio. So nimble?
Mirtilla. Love is active;
Nor would I be a slow thing: Rest secure Sir,
On my maiden-head, I'll not ravish you.
Adorio. For once,
So far I'll trust you. *Lies down on her Lap.*
Mirtilla All the joys of rest
Dwell on your eye-lids; let no dream disturb
Your soft and gentle slumbers. I cannot sing,
But I'll talk you asleep: And I beseech you
Be not offended, though I glory in
M4r My being thus employ'd; a happiness

That stands for more then ample satisfaction
For all I have, or can endure. He snores,
And does not hear me; would his sense of feeling
Were bound up too: I should—I am all fire.
Such heaps of treasure offer'd as a prey,
Would tempt a modest theef; I can no longer
Forbear. I'll gently touch his Lips, and leave *Kisses him.*
No print of mine. Ah! I have heard of *Nectar*;
But till now never tasted it: These Rubies
Are not clouded by my breath. If once agen
I steal, from such a full Exchequer, trifles *Kisses agen.*
Will not be miss'd; I am entranc'd: our fancy
Some say in sleep works stronger, I will prove
How far my— *Sleeps.*

Enter DURAZZO.

Durazzo. My bones ake,
I am exceeding cold too, I must seek out
A more convenient Truckle-bed. Ha! Do I dream?
No, no, I wake, *Camillo*, *Lentulo*,
Donato this; and as I live, *Adorio*
In a handsom wenches lap, a whoreson; you are
The best accommodated. I will call
My Nephew, and his Mistris to this Pageant:
The object may perhaps do more upon her,
Then all *Caldoro's* rhetorick. With what
Security they sleep! sure *Mercury*
Hath travel'd this way with his charming rod.
Nephew, *Caliste*, Madam.

M4v *Enter* CALDORO *and* CALISTE.

Caldoro. Here Sir, is
Your man return'd with Horses?
Durazzo. No Boy, no;
But here are some you thought not of.
Caliste. *Adorio.*
Durazzo. The Idol that you worshipped.
Caliste. This *Mirtilla*?
I am made a stale.
Durazzo. I knew 'twould take.

Caliste. False man,
But much more treacherous woman; 'tis apparent,
They joyntly did conspire against my weakness,
And credulous simplicity, and have
Prevail'd against it.
Caldoro. I'll not kill 'em sleeping;
But if you please, I'll wake 'em first, and after
Offer them as a fatal sacrifice
To your just anger.
Durazzo. You are a fool, reserve
Your blood for better uses.
Caliste. My fond love
Is chang'd to an extremity of hate,
His very sight is odious.
Durazzo. I have thought of
A pretty punishment for him, and his Comrades,
Then leave him to his harlotry: If she prove not
Torture enough, hold me an Ass. Their horses
Are not far off, I'll cut the Girts and Bridles,
Then turn 'em into the Wood; if they can run
Let 'em follow us as footmen. Wilt thou fight
For what's thine own already?
Caliste. In his Hat
He wears a Jewel, which this faithless Strumpet
As a salary of her Lust, deceiv'd me of,
He shall not keep't to my disgrace, nor will I
M5r Stir till I have it.
Durazzo. I am not good at niming;
And yet that shall not hinder us, by your leave Sir,
'Tis restitution, pray you all bear witness [*Takes the jewel.*]
I do not steal it; here 'tis.
Caliste. Take it not
As a Mistris favor, but a strong assurance
I am your wife. [*Gives it to* CALDORO.]
Caldoro. O Heaven.
Durazzo. Pray i' th' Church.
Let us away, Nephew a word: have you not
Been billing in the brakes? Ha? and so deserv'd

96 SD. *Takes the jewel.*] *editor*; *not in 55* 99 SD. *Gives it to* CALDORO.] *Gifford*; *not in 55*

This unexpected favor?

Caldoro. You are pleasant.

Exeunt DURAZZO, CALDORO, CALISTE.

Adorio. As thou art a Gentleman, kill me not basely, *Starts up;*
Give me leave to draw my Sword. *the rest wake.*

Camillo. Ha? what's the matter?

Lentulo. He talk'd of's Sword.

Donato. I see no enemy near us,
That threatens danger.

Mirtilla. Sure 'twas but a dream.

Adorio. A fearful one. Me thought *Caldoro's* sword
Was at my throat, *Caliste* frowning by,
Commanding him, as he desir'd her favor,
To strike my head off.

Camillo. Meer imagination
Of a disturbed fancy.

Mirtilla. Here's your Hat Sir.

Adorio. But where my Jewel?

Camillo. By all likelihood lost,
This troublesome night.

Donato. I saw it when we came
Unto this place.

Mirtilla. I look't upon't my self,
When you repos'd.

M5v *Adorio.* What is become of it?
Restore it, for thou hast it, do not put me
To the trouble to search you.

Mirtilla. Search me?

Adorio. You have been
Before your Lady gave you entertainment,
A night-walker in the streets.

Mirtilla. How, my good Lord?

Adorio. Traded in picking pockets, when tame gulls
Charm'd with your prostituted flatteries,
Dain'd to embrace you.

Mirtilla. Love give place to anger.
Charge me with theft, and prostituted baseness?
Were you a Judge, nay more, the King; thus urg'd,
To your teeth I would say, 'Tis false.

Adorio. This will not do.

Camillo. Deliver it in private.
Mirtilla. You shall be
In publick hang'd first, and the whole gang of you.
I steal what I presented!
Lentulo. Do not strive.
Adorio. Though thou hast swallow'd it, I'll rip thy entrail,
But I'll recover it.
Mirtilla. Help, help.

Enter CLAUDIO, *and two* BANDITI, (*presenting their Pistols.*)

Adorio. A new plot.
Claudio. Forbear, libidinous Monsters; if you offer
The least resistance, you are dead: if one
But lay his hand upon his sword, shoot all.
Adorio. Let us fight for what we have, and if you can
Win it, enjoy it.
16r *Claudio.* We come not to try
Your valor, but for your money; throw down your sword,
Or I'll begin with you: So if you will
Walk quietly without bonds, you may, if not
We'll force you. Thou shalt have no wrong, [*To* MIRTILLA.]
But justice against these.
1. *Bandit.* We'll teach you Sir
To meddle with wenches in our walks.
2. *Bandit.* It being
Against our Canons.
Camillo. Whether will you lead us?
Claudio. You shall know that hereafter: Guard 'em sure. *Exeunt.*

iii] *Enter* ALPHONSO [*disguised*], MONTECLARO, CAPTAIN.

Alphonso. Are all the passages stopp'd?
Captain. And strongly man'd,
They must use wings, and flie, if they escape us.
Monteclaro. But why, great Sir, you should expose your person
To such apparent danger, when you may

130 SD. *Enter . . . Pistols.*)] *placed as Gifford; after* plot *55* 139 SD. *To* MIRTILLA.] *Gifford; not in 55* 140. you] *Dodsley*; your *55* V. iii. SD. *disguised*] *after Gifford; not in 55*

Have 'em brought bound before you, is beyond
My apprehension.
Alphonso. I am better arm'd
Then you suppose: besides it is confirm'd
By all that have been robb'd, since *Severino*
Commanded these *Banditi*, though it be
Unusual in *Italy*, imitating
The courteous English Theeves, for so they call 'em,
They have not done one murther: I must adde too,
That from a strange relation I have heard
Of *Severino's* Justice, in disposing
M6v The preys brought in, I would be an eye-witness
Of what I take up now but on report:
And therefore 'tis my pleasure that we should
As soon as they encounter us, without
A shew of opposition yield.
Monteclaro. Your will
Is not to be disputed.
Alphonso. You have plac'd
Your ambush so, that if there be occasion
They suddenly may break in?
Captain. My life upon't.
Alphonso. We cannot travail far, but we shall meet
With some of these good fellows; and be sure
You do as I command you.
Monteclaro. Without fear, sir. *Exeunt.*

[V. iv] *Enter* SEVERINO *and* IOLANTE.

Severino. 'Tis true, I did command *Caliste* should not
Without my knowledg and consent, assisted
By your advice, be married: but your
Restraint, as you deliver it, denying
A grown up Maid the modest conversation
Of Men, and warrantable pleasures, relish'd
Of too much rigor, which no doubt hath driven her
To take some desperate course.
Iolante. What then I did,
Was in my care thought best.
Severino. I so conceive it;

But where was your discretion to forbid
Access and fit approaches, when you knew
Her Suiters noble, either of which I would
Have wish'd my son in law? *Adorio*,
However wild, a young man of good parts,
But better fortunes: his Competitor
Caldoro, for his sweetness of behaviour,
Staidness and temperance, holding the first place
Among the Gallants most observ'd in *Naples*;
17r His own revenues of a large extent,
But in the expectation of his Uncles
And Guardians entrata's, by the course
Of nature to descend on him, a Match
For the best Subjects blood, I except none
Of eminence in *Italy*.
Iolante. Your wishes,
Howe'r a while delaid, are not I hope
Impossibilities.
Severino. Though it prove so,
Yet 'tis not good to give a check to Fortune
When she comes smiling to us.— *Cornet within.*
Hark, this Cornet
Assures us of a prize; there sit in state,
'Tis thy first tribute.
Iolante. Would we might enjoy
Our own as Subjects.
Severino. What's got by the sword,
Is better then inheritance: All those Kingdoms
Subdu'd by *Alexander*, were by force extorted,
Though gilded ore with glorious stiles of conquest;
His victories but royal robberies,
And his true definition a Thief;
When circled with huge Navies to the terror
Of such as plough'd the Ocean, as the Pirate
Who from a narrow Creek puts off for prey
In a small Pinace,—from a second place [*Cornet*.]
New spoil brought in,—from a third party, brave! [*Cornet*.]
This shall be registred a day of triumph
Design'd by fate to honor thee.—

V. iv. 40, 41 SD. *Cornet*.] *Gifford*; *not in* 55

M7v *Enter* CLAUDIO, BANDITI, ADORIO, LENTULO, DONATO, CAMILLO, MIRTILLA, (*at one door*;) BANDITI, DURAZZO, CALDORO, CALISTE, (*at another*;) ALPHONSO, MONTECLARO, CAPTAIN, *and* BANDITI.

—Welcome *Claudio*;
Good booty, ha?
Claudio. Their outsides promise so,
But yet they have not made discovery
Of what they stand possest of.
Severino. Welcome all.
Good boys; you have done bravely, if no blood
Be shed in the service.
1. *Bandit*. On our lives no drop sir.
Severino. 'Tis to my wish.
Iolante. My Lord!
Severino. No more, I know 'em.
Iolante. My daughter and her woman too!
Severino. Conceal
Your joys.
Durazzo. Faln in the Devils mouth.
Caliste. My father,
And mother! to what fate am I reserv'd?
Caldoro. Continue masqu'd; or grant that you be known,
From whom can you expect a gentle sentence,
If you despair a Fathers?
Adorio. Now I perceive
Which way I lost my Jewel.
Mirtilla. I rejoice
I am clear'd from theft; you have done me wrong, but I
Unask'd forgive you.
Durazzo. 'Tis some comfort yet
The rivals, men and women, friends and foes, are
Together in one toil.
Severino. You all look pale,
M8r And by your private whisperings and soft murmurs
Express a general fear: pray you shake it off;
For understand you are not faln into
The hands of a *Busiris* or a *Cacus*,
Delighted more in blood then spoil; but given up

43–4. Welcome . . . ha?] *editor; precedes SD in 55*

To the power of an unfortunate Gentleman,
Not born to these low courses, howsoere
My fate, and just displeasure of the King
Design'd me to it: you need not to doubt
A sad captivity here, and much less fear
For profit to be sold for slaves, then ship'd
Into another Country; in a word,
You know the proscrib'd *Severino*, he
Not unacquainted, but familiar with
The most of you: Want in my self I know not,
But for the pay of these my Squires, who eat
Their bread with danger purchas'd, and must be
With others fleeces cloth'd, or live expos'd
To the summers scorching heat and winters cold;
To these before you be compell'd, (a word
I speak with much unwillingness) deliver
Such coin as you are furnish'd with.
Durazzo. A fine method!
This is neither begging, borrowing, nor robbery,
Yet it hath a twang of all of them. But one word Sir.
Severino. Your pleasure?
Durazzo. When we have thrown down our Muck,
What follows?
Severino. Liberty, with a safe convoy,
To any place you chuse.
Durazzo. By this hand you are
A fair fraternity; for once I'll be
The first example to relieve your Covent.
There's a thousand crowns, my Vintage, Harvest, Profits
Arising from my Herds, bound in one Bag,
8v Share it among you.
Severino. You are still the jovial,
And good *Durazzo*.
Durazzo. To the Offering, nay,
No hanging an arse, this is their wedding day.
What you must do spight of your hearts, do freely
For your own sakes.
Camillo. There's mine. *They all throw down their purses.*
Lentulo. Mine.
Donato. All that I have.

Caldoro. This to preserve my Jewel.
Adorio. Which I challenge;
Let me have justice, for my coin I care not.
Monteclaro. I will not weep for mine.
Captain. Would it were more.
Severino. Nay you are priviledg'd; but why old father
Art thou so slow? thou hast one foot in the grave,
And if desire of gold do not increase
With thy expiring lease of life, thou shouldst
Be forwardest.
Alphonso. In what concerns my self,
I do acknowledge it, and I should lie,
(A vice I have detested from my youth)
If I deny'd my present store, since what
I have about me now, weighs down in value
Almost a hundred fold, what ever these
Have laid before you; see I do groan under *Throws down*
The burthen of my treasure; nay 'tis Gold, *three bags.*
And if your hunger of it be not sated
With what already I have shewn unto you,
Here's that shall glut it. In this Casket are
Inestimable Jewels, Diamonds
Of such a piercing lustre, as struck blinde
Th'amazed Lapidary, while he labor'd
N1r To honor his own art in setting 'em. *Opens the Casket.*
Some orient Pearls too, which the Queen of *Spain*
Might wear as Earings, in remembrance of
The day that she was crown'd.
Severino. The spoils I think
Of both the Indies.
Durazzo. The great Sultans poor,
If parallel'd with this *Crœssus.*
Severino. Why dost thou weep?
Alphonso. From a most fit consideration of
My poverty; this though restor'd, will not
Serve my occasions.
Severino. Impossible.
Durazzo. May be he would buy his pasport up to Heaven,
And then 'tis too little, though in the journey

128. 'tis] *editor*; this 55; this is *Dodsley*

It were a good *Viaticum*.
Alphonso. I would make it
A means to help me thither; not to wrong you
With tedious expectation, I'll discover
What my wants are, and yield my reasons for 'em:
I have two sons, twins, the true images
Of what I was at their years; never father
Had fairer, or more promising hopes in his
Posterity: But alas, these sons ambitious
Of glittering honor, and an after-name
Atchiev'd by glorious, and yet pious actions,
(For such were their intentions) put to sea:
They had a well rigg'd Bottom, fully mann'd,
An old experienc'd Master, lusty Sailers,
Stout Land-men, and what's something more then rare,
They did agree, had one design, and that was
In charity to redeem the Christian slaves
Chain'd to the Turkish servitude.
Severino. A brave aim.
1v *Durazzo.* A most heroique enterprise; I languish
To hear how they succeeded.
Alphonso. Prosperously
At first, and to their wishes: divers Gallies
They boarded, and some strong Forts near the shore
They suddenly surpriz'd; a thousand Captives
Redeem'd from th'oar, paid their glad vows and prayers
For their deliverance; their ends acquir'd,
And making homeward in triumphant manner,
(For sure the cause deserv'd it)—
Durazzo. Pray you end here,
The best I fear is told, and that which follows
Must conclude ill.
Alphonso. Your fears are true, and yet
I must with grief relate it; prodigal fame
In every place with her loud trump proclaiming
The greatness of the action, the Pyrates
Of *Tunis* and *Argiers* laid wait for 'em
At their return: To tell you what resistance
They made, and how my poor sons fought, would but
Increase my sorrow, and perhaps grieve you

To hear it passionately describ'd unto you.
In brief they were taken, and for the great loss
The enemy did sustain, their victory
Being with much blood bought, they do endure
The heaviest captivity, wretched men
Did ever suffer. O my sons! my sons!
To me for ever lost, lost, lost for ever.

Severino. Will not these heaps of Gold added to thine,
Suffice for ransome?

Alphonso. For my sons it would,
But they refuse their liberty, if all
That were engaged with them, have not their Irons
With theirs struck off, and set at liberty with them,
Which these heaps cannot purchase.

Severino. Ha? the toughness
N2r Of my heart melts! be comforted old Father,
I have some hidden treasure, and if all,
I and my Squires, these three years have laid up,
Can make the sum up, freely take it.

Durazzo. I'll sell
My self to my shirt, lands, moveables, and thou
Shalt part with thine too Nephew, rather then
Such brave men shall live slaves.

2. *Bandit.* We will not yeeld to't.

3. *Bandit.* Nor loose our parts.

Severino. How's this?

2. *Bandit.* You are fitter far
To be a Churchman, then to have command
Over good-fellows.

Severino. Thus I ever use *Strikes 'em down.*
Such saucy Rascals, second me *Claudio.*
Rebellious? do you grumble? I'll not leave
One rogue of 'em alive.

Alphonso. Hold, give the sign. *He discovers himself.*

All. The King!

Severino. Then I am lost.

Claudio. The Woods are full
Of armed men.

Alphonso. No hope of your escape
Can flatter you.

Severino. Mercy dread Sir.
Alphonso. Thy carriage
In this unlawful course appears so noble,
Especially in this last tryal, which
I put upon you, that I wish the mercy
You kneel in vain for, might fall gently on you.
But when the holy Oyl was pour'd upon
My head, and I anointed King, I swore
Never to pardon murther; I could wink at
Your robberies, though our Laws call 'em death;
But to dispense with *Monteclaro's* blood
Would ill become a King; in him I lost
I2v A worthy subject, and must take from you
A strict accompt of't; 'tis in vain to move,
My doom's irrevocable.
Monteclaro. Not dread Sir,
If *Monteclaro* live.
Alphonso. If? good *Laval.*
Monteclaro. He lives in him Sir, that you thought *Laval.*
Three years have not so altered me, but you may
Remember *Monteclaro.* [*Discovers himself.*]
Durazzo. How?
Iolante. My Brother.
Caliste. Uncle.
Monteclaro. Give me leave, I was
Left dead in the field, but by the Duke *Montpensier*,
Now General at *Millain*, taken up,
And with much care recovered.
Alphonso. Why liv'd you
So long conceal'd?
Monteclaro. Confounded with the wrong
I did my Brother, in provoking him
To fight, I spent the time in *France* that I
Was absent from the Court, making my exile
The punishment impos'd upon my self
For my offence.
Iolante. Now Sir, I dare confess all:
This was the ghest invited to the Banquet,
That drew on your suspition.

209 SD. *Discovers himself.*] *Gifford: not in 55*

Severino. Your intent,
Though it was ill in you, I do forgive,
The rest I'll hear at leisure; Sir, your sentence.
Alphonso. It is a general pardon unto all
Upon my hopes, in your fair lives hereafter
You will deserve it.
Severino, *Claudio etc.* Long live great *Alphonso*!
Durazzo. Your mercy shewn in this, now if you please
Decide these lovers difference.
Alphonso. That is easie.
N3r I'll put it to the womens choice, the men
Consenting to it.
Caliste. Here I fix then, never
To be remov'd.
Caldoro. 'Tis my *nil ultra* Sir.
Mirtilla. O that I had the happiness to say
So much to you, I dare maintain my love
Is equal to my Ladies.
Adorio. But my minde
A pitch above yours. Marry with a servant
Of no descent or fortune?
Severino. You are deceiv'd,
How ere she has been train'd up as a servant,
She is the daughter of a noble Captain,
Who in his voyage to the *Persian* Gulph,
Perish'd by shipwrack, one I dearly lov'd.
He to my care intrusted her, having taken
My word, if he return'd not like himself,
I never should discover what she was,
But it being for her good, I will dispense with it.
So much Sir for her blood, now for her portion.
So dear I hold the memory of my friend,
It shall rank with my daughters.
Adorio. This made good
I will not be perverse.
Durazzo. With a kiss confirm it.
Adorio. I sign all concord here, but must to you Sir
For reparation of my wounded honor,
The justice of the King consenting to it,

230. then] *Dodsley*; them *55*

Denounce a lawful war.
Alphonso. This in our presence?
Adorio. The cause dread Sir commands it, though your Edicts
Call private Combats, Murthers; rather then
Sit down with a disgrace, arising from
A blow, the Bonds of my obedience shook of,
I'll right my self.
N3v *Caldoro.* I do confess the wrong,
Forgetting the occasion, and desire
Remission from you, and upon such terms
As by his sacred Majesty shall be judged
Equal on both parts.
Adorio. I desire no more.
Alphonso. All then are pleas'd, it is the glory of
A King to make, and keep his subjects happy;
For us we do approve the *Roman* Maxim,
To save one Citizen is a greater prize,
Then to have kill'd in War ten Enemies. *Exeunt.*

N5r

EPILOGUE.

I am left to enquire, then to relate
To the still doubtful Author, at what rate
His marchandise are valued. If they prove
Staple Commodities, in your Grace and love,
To this last birth of his Minerva, *he*
Vows, and we do believe him seriously,
Sloth cast of, and all pleasures else declin'd,
He'll search with his best care, until he finde
New ways, and make good in some labor'd Song,
Though he grow old, Apollo *still is yong.*
Cherish his good intentions, and declare
By any sign of favor, that you are
Well pleas'd, and with a general consent,
And he desires no more encouragement.

FINIS

APPENDIX

VERSE REARRANGEMENT

The following lines of verse are undivided in *55*, except where otherwise stated.

I. i

5–6 priviledge / To] *Gifford*
24–5 bear / Your] *Gifford*
25–6 years; / If] *Gifford*
70–1 not, / But] *Gifford*
72–3 Gentleman! / What] *Gifford*
79–80 you; / This] *Gifford*
83–4 sentence! / And] *Gifford*
97–8 sir; / Though] *Gifford*
102–3 you, / And] *Gifford*
120–1 it, / I'le] *Gifford*
134–5 man / Can] *Gifford*
155–6 designs / Are] *Coxeter*
186–7 sir? / To] *Coxeter*
189–90 Lady, / And] *Coxeter*
201–2 sir, / Which] *Coxeter*
202–3 more, / Nor] *Coxeter*
238–9 *Rearranged by Coxeter; 55 reads* In . . . difference; / Some . . . go,
244–5 Madam, / As] *Coxeter*
277–8 rogue: / Why] *Coxeter*
278–9 happy: / Oh] *Coxeter*
282–3 Woman! / Better] *Coxeter*
283–4 generation / Maintain'd] *Coxeter*
284–5 forbear / This] *Coxeter*
308–9 be, / And] *Coxeter*
329–30 grant, / But] *Gifford*
340–1 this, / Is] *Gifford*
341–2 finde / Twenty] *Gifford*

I. ii

5–6 me / To] *Gifford*
10–11 Madam? / What] *Coxeter*
12–13 detraction / Will] *Coxeter*
29–30 do, / I] *Gifford*
30–1 Admirable! / This] *Gifford*
34–5 not / So] *Gifford*
37–8 that; / All] *Coxeter*
42–3 applause, / I] *Coxeter*
43–4 can / Command] *Gifford*
44–5 vassals / To] *Symons*
59–60 over/ With] *Gifford*
90–1 receive / An] *Gifford*
94–5 Mother, / And] *Gifford*
95–6 from't, / Take] *Gifford*
96–7 *Mirtilla*, / How] *Gifford*
120–1 up / My] *Gifford*
131–2 business / To] *Gifford*
132–3 Consideration, / When] *Coxeter*

II. i

25–6 *Alphonso*, / The] *Coxeter*
53–4 form / He] *Coxeter*
56–7 Sir, / Ever] *Coxeter*
66–7 endur'd, / But] *Gifford*

II. ii

2–3 tye; / But] *Coxeter*
45–6 Fetters. / I] *Coxeter*
46–7 imagine / A] *Gifford*

II. iii

19–20 please, / You] *Coxeter*
21–2 sure / 'Tis] *Symons*
34–5 Sir; / It] *Coxeter*
41–2 Sirrah, / And] *Coxeter*
58–9 Sir, / The] *Gifford*
99–100 become / Your] *Coxeter*
101–2 *Mirtilla*! / With] *Coxeter*
112–13 pleas'd / To] *Coxeter*
125–6 well, / And] *Coxeter*
126–7 carry / Some] *Coxeter*
130–1 kiss, / You] *Coxeter*
134–5 kiss? / I] *Coxeter*

II. iv

11–12 not, / Howev'r] *Coxeter*
13–14 indeed / By] *Coxeter*
29–30 that / You] *Coxeter*
31–2 rapines / Live] *Coxeter*
60–1 will, / As] *Gifford*
63–4 lives / At] *Gifford*
75–6 these / Read] *Coxeter*
94–5 not / Have] *Gifford*
116–17 repine / At] *Coxeter*

II. v

5–6 stranger / Newly] *Gifford*
13–14 are. / 'Tis] *Gifford*
35–6 impertinencies, / And] *Coxeter*
42–3 *Iolante*. / I] *Coxeter*
72–3 breath / Would] *Coxeter*
73–4 you; / Now] *Coxeter*
88–9 you / At] *Gifford*
90–1 twelve, / I'll] *Gifford*

III. i

11–12 Viands, / Are] *Coxeter*
22–3 may / And] *Coxeter*
43–4 this? / Stale] *Coxeter*

III. ii

2–3 so, / Or] *Coxeter*
8–9 way / Can] *Gifford*
14–15 miseries / Which] *Gifford*
28–9 necessity / Of] *Coxeter*
54–5 me, / For] *Coxeter*
61–2 night, / And] *Coxeter*

III. iii

7–8 me / For] *Gifford*
19–20 *Cario*, / And] *Gifford*
24–5 do, / We'll] *Coxeter*

III. v

26–7 dream, / And] *Gifford*
31–2 so, / I] *Coxeter*
35–6 Madam, / Think] *Gifford*
44–5 arms, / Your] *Gifford*
68–9 Watch! / I] *Gifford*
76–7 for / A] *McIlwraith*

III. vi

26–7 Ha? / Good] *Coxeter*
43–4 defence? / To] *Coxeter*
48–9 poison Vulturs / And] *Gifford; 55 reads* poison / Vulturs and
63–4 urge / From] *Gifford*
67–8 thoughts / Of] *Coxeter*
108–9 life / Speak] *Coxeter*
111–12 ear, / And] *Coxeter*
115–16 him; / I'll] *Gifford*
116–17 me / For] *Gifford*
117–18 Gentleman, / The] *Gifford*
190–1 for't; / Did] *Coxeter*
201–2 nose, / My] *Gifford*
209–10 he, / And] *Coxeter*
212–13 begin / To] *Gifford*
221–2 devotions, / Affliction] *Coxeter*
222–3 down / Upon] *Coxeter*
231–2 hope / To] *Gifford*
236–7 ever / Canoniz'd] *Gifford*
244–5 profess / I] *Coxeter*
262–3 needless / To] *Gifford*

IV. i

23–4 lives, / Disturb] *Coxeter*
55–6 Lady / Open] *Coxeter*
58–9 know / This] *Coxeter*
107–8 blushes / Confess] *Gifford*
130–1 holidame / Tickling] *Coxeter*
135–6 fire / To] *Coxeter*
145–6 exalted / In] *Coxeter*
158–9 appears / A] *Gifford*

IV. ii

61–2 trouble / For] *Gifford*
65–6 Innocence / Is] *Coxeter*
71–2 life; / Nor] *Gifford*
83–4 left / Her] *Gifford*
94–5 seems / You] *Coxeter*
100–1 fate! / How] *Coxeter*
116–17 'twere / A] *Coxeter*
119–20 yet / How] *Coxeter*
129–30 were / Horsemen] *Gifford*
138–9 servant / That] *Gifford*
144–5 friends / For] *Coxeter*
149–50 please, / I] *Coxeter*
149–151 *Rearranged by Coxeter; 55 reads* So . . . you; / I'll . . . over.

IV. iii

5–6 know / What] *Coxeter*
20–1 may / Forget] *Gifford*
24–5 suffer / A] *Gifford*
31–2 thank'd you for't, / As] *Gifford; 55 reads* thank'd / You for't, as
44–5 along, / You] *Coxeter*

V. i

34–5 sir / I] *Coxeter*
50–1 string? / It] *Coxeter*
57–8 in / The] *Coxeter*
63–4 wait / With] *Coxeter*

V. ii

5–6 lose / *Adorio*] *Gifford*
8–9 matter, / We'll] *Coxeter*
9–10 already; / *Lentulo*] *Coxeter*
30–1 please / To] *Gifford*
37–8 once, / So] *Gifford*
57–8 ake, / I] *Coxeter*
69–70 is / Your] *Gifford*
70–1 no; / But] *Coxeter*
72–3 *Mirtilla*? / I] *Gifford*
79–80 sacrifice / To] *Gifford*
80–1 reserve / Your] *Gifford*
81–2 love / Is] *Gifford*
110–11 imagination / Of] *Coxeter*
112–13 lost, / This] *Coxeter*
113–14 came / Unto] *Gifford*
114–15 self, / When] *Gifford*
141–2 being / Against] *Gifford*

V. iii

19–20 will / Is] *Coxeter*

V. iv

8–9 did, / Was] *Coxeter*
30–1 enjoy / Our] *Coxeter*
50–1 Conceal / Your] *Gifford*
55–6 perceive / Which] *Coxeter*
57 wrong, but I] *Gifford; 55 reads* wrong, / But I
57–8 I / Unask'd] *Gifford*
85–6 Muck, / What] *Coxeter*
86–7 convoy, / To] *Coxeter*
92–3 jovial, / And] *Coxeter*
121–2 think / Of] *Coxeter*
180–1 sell / My] *Coxeter*
185–6 command / Over] *Coxeter*
190–1 full / Of] *Coxeter*
192–3 carriage / In] *Coxeter*
205–6 Sir, / If] *Coxeter*
213–14 you / So] *Coxeter*
230–1 never / To] *Gifford*

A VERY WOMAN

INTRODUCTION

(a) *Authorship and Date*

A Very Woman, or the Prince of Tarent: a Tragi-Comedy was licensed on 6 June 1634: '*A Very Woman*, by Philip Massinger, licensed for the King's Company'.[1] It was not published until 1655. According to the Prologue, the play was a revision of an earlier work:

> *. . . with care*
> *He hath review'd it; and with him we dare*
> *Maintain to any man, that did allow*
> *'Twas good before, it is much better'd now;*
> *Nor is it sure against the Proclamation,*
> *To raise new Piles upon an old Foundation.*

It is clear enough, from evidence of prosody, style, linguistic forms, and the quality of the invention, that some sections of the play as we have it now are not by Massinger but by Fletcher. The consensus of opinion on the division of the play, summarized by McIlwraith in his unpublished thesis (1931) and supported by Cyrus Hoy's later study,[2] is as follows. Massinger: Act I, and Act II as far as Scene iii, line 192 (the beginning of the scene between Pedro and Borachia). Fletcher: the remainder of Act II, the whole of Act III, and the first scene of Act IV. Massinger: Act IV, Scene ii. Fletcher: Act IV, Scene iii. Massinger: Act V. This division gives to Massinger the opening of the plot and its development through to the quarrel of Don John and Martino; the imprisonment and escape of Don John; the description of the sickness of mind of both Martino and Almira. To Fletcher is given the comic scene between Pedro and Borachia; the scene of the slave-market; the intrigue by which Don John, as a Turkish slave, acts as a go-between for Pedro and Leonora, and gets Borachia drunk; the penitence of Martino (III. iii); Leonora's

[1] Adams, *Herbert*, p. 36; from Malone's note.
[2] *Studies in Bibliography*, Virginia, ix (1957), 154–5, 162.

exhortation to Almira (III. iv.). Massinger has the elaborate scene of Doctor Paulo's cure of Martino, and in the last Act he carries on with Almira's passion for the Turkish slave and the eventual recognition of the slave as Don John.

The earlier unrevised play is not extant and there is little evidence to connect it with any known title (see Bentley, iv. 826–8). The only date we can give is 'before 1625', the year of Fletcher's death. It has several times been remarked[1] that the satisfied tone of the Prologue ('it is much better'd now') is inconsistent with the deference of Massinger towards Fletcher, as for example in the prologue to *The Lovers' Progress* ('What's good was Fletcher's, and what's ill, his own.'). A theory which has been offered to explain the tone of *The Very Woman's* prologue is that Massinger was talking about improving a work which was as much his own as Fletcher's in the first place. This suggestion can be supported from a study of the 1655 text. What Massinger seems to have done in 1634 is to take up a play that he and Fletcher had written together and rewrite parts of his own work while leaving Fletcher's contribution much as it was.

The stage-directions in the play are for the most part very curt, indicating no more than exits and entrances and giving no indication of necessary action (e.g. for the fight between Martino and Don John, or for the song in III. i). In marked contrast with the general brevity are Act IV, Scene ii, and Act V (both Massinger's). IV. ii is the scene of Doctor Paulo's cure of Martino and the action is described in great detail. For example, '*A bed drawn forth*, Martino *upon it*, *a book in's hand*.', '*Enter Doctor*, *like a Philosopher: A good*, *an ill Genius presented. Their Song. While it's singing*, *the Doctor goes off*, *and returns in his own shape*.' Examples of the fuller directions in Act V are, '*Enter Don John with a Letter in his hand*', '*Breaks it open*, *and reads*', '*Forces a sword*', '*The Guard take Don John off*.' There is only one similarly explicit direction in the other sections of the play, at II. iii. 23, '*Enter Almira in black*, *carelessly habited*.'

The fuller stage-directions cannot be explained away as being Massinger's as opposed to Fletcher's since the curt directions of Act I are as much his as the extensive ones of Act V. It seems a reasonable hypothesis that those parts of the play with the un-

[1] F. G. Fleay, *Biographical Chronicle of the English Drama*, 1891, i. 227–8; E. H. C. Oliphant, *The Plays of Beaumont and Fletcher*, 1927, p. 253; B. Maxwell, *Studies in Beaumont*, *Fletcher*, *and Massinger*, 1939, pp. 177–93.

informative stage-directions represent a transcript of the original collaborative play, and that Act IV, Scene ii, and Act V represent the manuscript of Massinger's later revision. There is a further inconsistency to be considered. Don Martino Cardenes who is throughout the play 'Martino' in entries and '*Mar.*' in speech-headings, is referred to as 'Martino' in the text except in Act I, where he is always referred to as 'Cardenes'. It may be that Massinger as he set out on his original share was using one form of the name and Fletcher another; 'Martino' became established as the proper form and the stage-directions were altered accordingly. 'Cardenes', anyway, must be a relic of an early version, and it is found in a Massingerian part of the play; it therefore confirms that the play Massinger set himself to revise as *A Very Woman* was partly his own work. On the evidence of the radical alteration in the style of the stage-directions, the main rewriting was of Act IV, Scene ii, and the last Act.

(b) *Source*

The sources of *A Very Woman* have been described by Miss Roma Gill in *Review of English Studies*, N.S. xviii (1967), 136–48. The main source, pointed out by Joseph de Perrott in 1916,[1] is the collection of Spanish tales of chivalry englished as *The Mirror of Knighthood*. Book VIII, from which the play derives, was translated by 'L. A.' and published in 1599. There the story is told of Florisiano who went to Lucania to woo the beautiful princess Pollinarda. He became the friend of her brother Lysander, but Pollinarda chose to wed Agesilaus. Violently jealous of his rival, Florisiano challenged Agesilaus to a duel and killed him. (The play quite alters the occasion of the fight and the character of the participants.) Pollinarda tries to avenge the death of Agesilaus; she wounds Florisiano with his own sword. Florisiano is imprisoned but escapes through the help of the knight in whose custody he was. After adventures at sea he returns to Lucania as a slave in Turkish habit under the name of Iaroe. He serves as Lysander's helper, as the disguised Don John serves Pedro in the play. Pollinarda now falls in love with the 'slave'. She asks him to reveal his true name. He says, 'I cannot conceiue . . . why you are importunate to know the thing that will most of all others greeue you.' She assures him that her affection for him has made her forgive the offence of the first who bore his

[1] *Anglia*, xxxix, 201–8.

name. (This is closely and awkwardly followed in the play: see note to IV. iii. 242–3.) Florisiano despises Pollinarda for the arbitrariness and inconstancy of her affections in forgetting Agesilaus and in falling in love with him when he is a menial slave after she had rejected him in his own guise (see note to V. ii. 10–20). He resolves to keep the secret of his identity until he is convinced that she can be constant in her new affection (see note to V. ii. 20–2). When the King hears of his daughter's strange infatuation for a slave, Florisiano is forced to flee. But eventually the two are united.

Concerning the major alteration of the source, the recovery and repentance of Martino Cardenes, Miss Gill notes the similarity with the cure of Duarte in *The Custom of the Country* (? 1619–20). This part of *The Custom of the Country* was written by Massinger himself so that in the later play he is repeating himself and his dependence on Burton and Ford may be less than Miss Gill suggests, though there can be no doubt that in the therapy which Dr. Paulo uses to banish melancholia Massinger was influenced by *The Anatomy of Melancholy* (1621); Ford's Burtonian play, *The Lover's Melancholy*, may also have influenced him. Miss Gill accepts Gifford's suggestion that for part of the Cuculo–Borachia scenes, Fletcher was indebted to the *Curculio* of Plautus (see note to III. v. 51).

(c) *Text*

A Very Woman was entered in the Stationers' Register by Humphrey Moseley in 1653 and published as the third work in *Three New Playes*, 1655. Details of the entry and publication, and of the physical characteristics of the edition, will be found on pages 103–6, and also in the General Introduction, vol i, pp. xxiii–xxiv. The edition, which is the only early one, will be referred to as *55*; the title-page is reproduced on page 207. *A Very Woman* is separately paginated; the pages are correctly numbered 1–82 but then ($T1^r$) there is a jump to 93 and the paging is continued from there to 103. Each act begins on a new page, and, as with the other plays in the volume, the intermediate scenes are not marked, although each act is headed 'Scæn. 1.'

The copy for *55* was of a different kind from that used for *The Bashful Lover* and *The Guardian*. Although the same compositors seem to be at work, the extended misdivision of verse found in the first two plays is absent. It has already been argued that what the printer had before him was a manuscript representing two periods of composition, separated by ten years or more. From the many errors in the text which appear to arise from misreadings, it would seem that the handwriting in both layers of the play caused difficulty. Massinger's characteristic spellings are not frequent anywhere in the play, but there are a few in IV. ii and Act V (*sowrs*, *peeces*; *course* (coarse), *ere* (e'er), *ghess*). It may be the case that the revised portions were autograph. It is also possible that the copy was composed of two separate transcripts, one of those parts of the play retained from the original collaboration between Fletcher and Massinger, and one of those sections which Massinger rewrote.

A Very Woman has not been republished since 1655 except in the standard collected editions and in Harness's expurgated selection of texts (1830).

The text of the present edition has been prepared from photocopies of the Huntington Library copy, checked against the editor's copy of *Three New Playes*.

(d) *Stage History*

The licence and the title-page of *A Very Woman* tell us that the play was first given by the King's company at Blackfriars. The title-page of 55 is in fact the only evidence of stage-performance of the play at any time. Bentley (iv. 825, 827) noted that Anthony Wood saw performed at Oxford on 11 July 1661, 'in the morning "Tu quoque"; in the afternoone "The Spanish Lady, or The very Woman".'[1] Bentley finds this record 'most puzzling' because '*The Spanish Lady* would be a pointless title for the tragi-comedy as we have it'. He wonders if it was some other play that Wood saw, or if it was the earlier play that Massinger revised. But the title, *The Very Woman*, is not easily explained away, and it would be simpler to suppose that Wood saw Massinger's play, under a new main-title. The performance was one of a series given (with women actors) as the first public performances in Oxford after the Restoration, 'to spite the Presbyterians', Wood says. *A Very Woman* was used slightly in the execrable farce, *Love Lost in the Dark*, 1680 (see the stage-history of *The Guardian*). Langbaine (quoted by Bentley) remarked that the plot of Sir Aston Cokayne's *The Obstinate Lady* (1658) is 'Cousin-German to Massinger's *Very Woman*' (*Account of the English Dramatick Poets*, 1691, p. 69). The play is not in the least like *A*

[1] Andrew Clark, *Life and Times of Antony Wood*, vol. i, 1891, p. 406.

Very Woman, but it does have the important similarity that a rejected lover returns disguised (as a negro), and the woman who has formerly spurned him now falls in love with him. In Cokayne's play, the lover is properly disgusted that he should succeed in his lower role, and he rejects the woman—unlike Don John Antonio. Cokayne may well have thought to alter the uneasy morality of the ending of his friend's play—but whether that is so or not, the plays are so remote from each other that *The Obstinate Lady* cannot be called an alteration or an adaptation. H. S. Arnold noted that J. A. Leisewitz's play, *Julius von Tarent*, written in response to Schroeder's offer to encourage new dramatists in 1775, borrows some ideas and phrases from *A Very Woman*, particularly the scene of Almira's distraction. Arnold suggests that Leisewitz had turned to Massinger expecting some help in Florentine history from *The Great Duke of Florence*.[1]

[1] H. S. Arnold, 'The Reception of Ben Jonson, Beaumont and Fletcher, and Massinger in Eighteenth-century Germany', unpub. Ph.D. thesis, Maryland, 1962.

A
Very Woman,
Or the PRINCE of
TARENT.
A
TRAGI-COMEDY.

As it hath been often acted at the Private-House in *Black-Friars*, by his late MAJESTIES Servants, with great Applause.

Written by

PHILIP MASSENGER, Gent.

LONDON,
Printed for *Humphrey Moseley*, and are to be sold at his shop at the sign of the *Prince's Arms* in St. *Pauls* Church-yard. 1655.

N7r

PROLOGUE.

To such (and some there are, no question here,)
Who happy in their memories do bear
This Subject long since acted, and can say
Truly, we have seen something like this Play,
Our Author with becoming Modesty
(For in this kinde he ne'er was bold) by me,
In his defence, thus answers, By command
He undertook this task, nor could it stand
With his low Fortune to refuse to do
What by his Patron he was call'd unto;
For whose delight and yours, we hope, with care
He hath review'd it; and with him we dare
Maintain to any man, that did allow
'Twas good before, it is much better'd now;
Nor is it sure against the Proclamation,
To raise new Piles upon an old Foundation.
So much to them deliver'd; to the rest,
To whom each scene is fresh, he doth protest,
Should his Muse fail now a fair flight to make,
He cannot fancy what will please, or take.

9. *low*] *Mason*; *love* 55

N7v

[*Dramatis Personæ.*]

Viceroy of *Sicily*
Pedro, his Son
Duke of *Messina*
Don Martino Cardenes, his Son
Don John Antonio, Prince of *Tarent*
Doctor *Paulo*, A Physitian
Cuculo, A Sicilian
[Two Surgeons]
Apothecary
Citizens
Master
Man
Captain
Page
Servants
[An English Slave]
Slaves
Moors
Pyrates
[Sailors]
[Lord]
[Keeper]
Guard.

Almira, The Viceroys Daughter
Leonora, Duke of *Messina's* Neece
Borachia, Wife to *Cuculo*
Two Women.

The Scene SICILY.

1. *Dramatis Personæ.*] *Coxeter*; *not in 55*   5. *Martino*] *Coxeter ; Martinio 55*   9. Two Surgeons] *Gifford ; not in 55*   11. Citizens] *Gifford ;* Citizen *55*   12. Master] *55 ;* Slave-merchant *Gifford*   17. An English Slave] *Gifford ; not in 55*   21. Sailors] *Gifford ; not in 55*   22. Lord] *editor ; not in 55*   23. Keeper] *editor ; not in 55*

N8r

A Very Woman

I. i]

Act. I. *Scœn.* I.

Enter PEDRO *and* LEONORA.

Pedro. MY worthiest Mistress! this day cannot end
But prosperous to *Pedro*, that begins
With this so wish'd encounter.
Leonora. Only, Servant,
To give you thanks in your own Courtly language,
Would argue me more ceremonious
Then heartily affected; and you are
Too well assur'd, or I am miserable,
Our equal loves have kept one rank too long
To stand at distance now.
N8v *Pedro.* You make me happy
In this so wise reproof, which I receive
As a chaste favor from you, and will ever
Hold such a strong command o're my desires,
That though my Blood turn Rebel to my Reason,
I never shall presume to seek ought from you,
But what (your honor safe) you well may grant me,
And Vertue sign the Warrant.
Leonora. Your love to me
So limited, will still preserve your Mistress
Worthy her servant, and in your restraint
Of loose affections, bind me faster to you:
But there will be a time when we may welcome
Those wish'd for pleasures, as Heavens greatest blessings;
When that the Vice-roy your most noble father,
And the Duke my uncle, and to that, my Guardian,
Shall by their free consent confirm them lawful.
Pedro. You ever shall direct, and I obey you:
Is my sister stirring yet?

Leonora. Long since.
Pedro. Some business
With her, join'd to my service to your self,
Hath brought me hither; pray you vouchsafe the favor
T'acquaint her with so much.
Leonora. I am prevented.

Enter ALMIRA *and two* WOMEN.

Almira. Do the rest here; my Cabinet is too hot,
This room is cooler. Brother!
Pedro. 'Morrow sister,
Do I not come unseasonably?
Almira. Why good brother?
O1r *Pedro.* Because you are not yet fully made up,
Nor fit for visitation. There are Ladies
And great ones, that will hardly grant access
On any terms to their own Fathers, as
They are themselves, nor willingly be seen
Before they have ask'd councel of their Doctor,
How the Ceruze will appear, newly laid on,
When they ask blessing.
Almira. Such indeed there are
That would be still young, in despight of time,
That in the wrinkled winter of their age
Would force a seeming *April* of fresh beauty,
As if it were within the power of art
To frame a second nature: But for me,
And for your Mistress, I dare say as much;
The faces, and the teeth you see, we slept with.
Pedro. Which is not frequent, sister, with some Ladies.
Almira. You spie no sign of any night-mask here,
(Tie on my Carkanet) nor does your nosthril
Take in the scent of strong perfumes, to stifle
The sourness of our breaths as we are fasting:
You are in a Ladies chamber, gentle Brother,
And not in your Apothecaries shop.
We use the women, you perceive, that serve us,
Like servants, not like such as do create us:

I. i. 39. Ceruze] *Coxeter*; Cervize *55* 49. night-mask here,] *Coxeter*; night,— / Mask here, *55*

'Faith search our pockets, and if you find there
Comfits of Amber-greece to help our kisses,
Conclude us faulty.
Pedro. You are pleasant, sister.
And I am glad to find you so dispos'd,
You will the better hear me.
Almira. What you please, Sir.
Pedro. I am entreated by the Prince of *Tarent*,
Don *John Antonio*—
O1v *Almira.* Would you would choose
Some other subject.
Pedro. Pray you give me leave,
For his desires are fit for you to hear,
As for me to prefer. This Prince of *Tarent*
(Let it not wrong him, that I call him friend)
Finding your choice of Don *Cardenes* lik'd of
By both your fathers, and his hopes cut off,
Resolves to leave *Palermo*.
Almira. He does well,
That I hear gladly.
Pedro. How this Prince came hither,
How bravely furnish'd, how attended on,
How he hath borne himself here, with what charge
He hath continued; his magnificence
In costly Banquets, curious Masques, rare Presents,
And of all sorts, you cannot but remember.
Almira. Give me my Gloves.
Pedro. Now, for reward of all
His cost, his travel, and his dutious service,
He does intreat that you will please he may
Take his leave of you, and receive the favor
Of kissing of your hands.
Almira. You are his friend,
And shall discharge the part of one to tell him
That he may spare the trouble; I desire not
To see, or hear more of him.
Pedro. Yet grant this,
Which a meer stranger in the way of Courtship
Might challenge from you.
Almira. And obtain it sooner.

Pedro. One reason for this would do well.
Almira. My will
Shall now stand for a thousand; shall I lose
The priviledge of my sex, which is my Will,
To yield a Reason like a man? or you
O2r Deny your Sister that which all true women
Claim as their first prerogative, which Nature
Gave to them for a law, and should I break it,
I were no more a woman?
Pedro. Sure a good one
You cannot be, if you put off that vertue
Which best adorns a good one, Courtesie
And affable behaviour. Do not flatter
Yourself with the opinion that your birth,
Your beauty, or whatever false ground else
You raise your pride upon, will stand against
The censure of just men.
Almira. Why let it fall then,
I still shall be unmov'd.
Leonora. And pray you be you so. [*To* PEDRO.]
Almira. What Jewel's that?
Woman. That which the Prince of *Tarent*—
Almira. Left here, and you receiv'd without my knowledge;
I have use of't now. Does the Page wait without,
My Lord *Cardenes* sent t'enquire my health?
Woman. Yes Madam.
Almira. Give it him, and with it pray him
To return my service to his Lord, and mine.
Pedro. Will you so undervalue one that has
So truly lov'd you, to bestow the pledge
Of his affection (being a Prince) upon
The servant of his Rival?
Leonora. 'Tis not well,
'Faith, weare it Lady: send gold to the Boy,
'Twill please him better.
Almira. Do as I command you, [*Exit* WOMAN.]
I will keep nothing that may put me in mind
Don John Antonio ever lov'd, or was,

102 SD. *To* PEDRO.] *after Mason*; *not in 55* 113. weare it Lady:] *Coxeter*; were it Lady? *55* 114 SD. *Exit* WOMAN.] *after Gifford*; *not in 55*

Being wholly now *Cardenes*.
Pedro. In another
O2v This were meer barbarism, sister, and in you
(For I'll not sooth you) at the best 'tis rudeness.
Almira. Rudeness?
Pedro. Yes rudeness, and what's worse, the want
Of civil manners, nay ingratitude
Unto the many and so fair deservings
Of *Don Antonio*: does this express
Your breeding in the Court, or that you call
The Vice-roy father? A poor peasants daughter
That ne'r had conversation but with beasts
(Or men bred like them) would not so far shame
Her education.
Almira. Pray you leave my chamber;
I know you for a Brother, not a Tutor.
Leonora. You are too violent, Madam.
Almira. Were my Father
Here to command me, (as you take upon you
Almost to play his part) I would refuse it.
Where I love, I profess it; where I hate,
In every circumstance I dare proclaim it:
Of all that wear the shapes of men, I loath
That Prince you plead for; no antipathie
Between things most averse in nature, hold
A stronger enmity then his with mine:
With which rest satisfied; if not, your anger
May wrong your self, not me.
Leonora. My Lord *Cardenes*!
Pedro. Go; in soft terms, if you persist thus,
You will be one—

Enter MARTINO.

Almira. What one? Pray you out with it.
Pedro. Why, one that I shall wish a stranger to me,
That I might curse you: but—
Martino. Whence grows this heat?
O3r *Pedro.* Be yet advis'd, and entertain him fairly,

137. hold] 55; holds *Gifford* 141–2. *rearranged by editor*; Go; . . . terms, / If . . . thus, / You 55; Go; . . . thus. you / Will *Coxeter* 142 SD. *Enter* MARTINO.] *after Gifford; at l. 144 in 55*

For I will send him to you, or no more
Know me a Brother.
Almira. As you please.
Pedro. Good morrow. *Exit.*
Martino. Good morrow, and part thus? you seem mov'd too:
What desperate fool durst raise a tempest here
To sink himself?
Almira. Good sir, have patience;
The cause (though I confess I am not pleas'd)
No way deserves your anger.
Martino. Not mine, Madam?
As if the least offence could point at you,
And I not feel it: As you have vouchsaf'd me
The promise of your heart, conceal it not,
Whomsoever it concerns.
Almira. It is not worth
So serious an enquiry: My kind Brother
Had a desire to learn me some new Courtship
Which I distasted, that was all.
Martino. Your Brother,
In being yours, with more security
He might provoke you; yet if he hath past
A Brothers bounds—
Leonora. What then, my Lord?
Martino. Believe it,
I'll call him to accompt for't.
Leonora. Tell him so.
Almira. No more.
Leonora. Yes, thus much; though my modesty
Be call'd in question for it, in his absence
I will defend him: He hath said nor done
But what *Don Pedro* well might say or do.
Mark me, *Don Pedro*! in which understand
As worthy, and as well as can be hop'd for
O3v Of those that love him best, from *Don Cardenes*—
Martino. This to me Cousin?
Almira. You forget your self.
Leonora. No, nor the cause, (in which you did so Lady)

170. *Cardenes*—] *editor*; ~. *55* 172. (in which] *Coxeter*; in (which *55*

Which is so just, that it needs no concealing
On *Pedro's* part.
Almira. What mean you?
Leonora. I dare speak it,
If you dare hear it, Sir: He did perswade
Almira, your *Almira*, to vouchsafe
Some little conference with the Prince of *Tarent*
Before he left the Court; and that the world
Might take some notice, though he prosper'd not
In his so lov'd design, he was not scorn'd,
He did desire the kissing of her hand,
And then to leave her; this was much!
Martino. 'Twas more
Then should have been urg'd by him, well deni'd
On your part, *Madam*, and I thank you for't.
Antonio had his answer, I your grant:
And why your Brother should prepare for him
An after enterview, or private favor,
I can finde little reason.
Leonora. None at all
Why you should be displeas'd with't.
Martino. His respect
To me, as things now are, should have weigh'd down
His former friendship; 'twas done indiscreetly,
I would be loth to say maliciously,
To build up the demolish'd hopes of him
That was my Rival: What had he to do
(If he view not my happiness in your favor,
With wounded eies) to take upon himself
An office so distasteful?
Leonora. You may ask
As well, what any Gentleman has to do
With civil courtesie.
4r *Almira.* Or you with that,
Which at no part concerns you: Good my Lord
Rest satisfied, that I saw him not, nor will.
And that, nor Father, Brother, nor the world
Can work me unto any thing, but what
You give allowance too; in which assurance,
With this, I leave you.

Leonora. Nay take me along,
You are not angry too?
Almira. Presume on that. *Exeunt.*
Martino. Am I assur'd of her, and shall again
Be tortur'd with suspition to loose her,
Before I have enjoy'd her? the next Sun
Shall see her mine; why should I doubt then? yet
To doubt is safer, then to be secure
But one short day: Great Empires in less time
Have suffer'd change; she's constant, but a woman,
And what a lovers vows, perswasions, tears,
May in a minute work upon such frailty,
There are too many, and too sad examples.
The Prince of *Tarent* gone, all were in safety;
Or not admitted to solicite her,
My fears would quit me; 'tis my fault, if I
Give way to that, and let him ne'er desire
To own what's hard, that dares not guard it.
Who waits there?

Enter SERVANTS *and Page.*

Servant. Would your Lordship aught?
Martino. 'Tis well
You are so neer.

Enter DON JOHN, *and* SERVANT.

John. Take care all things be ready
For my remove.
O4v *Servant.* They are.
Martino. We meet like Friends,
No more like Rivals now: my emulation
Puts on the shape of love and service to you.
John. It is return'd.
Martino. 'Twas rumor'd in the Court
You were to leave the City, and that wan me
To find you out: Your Excellence may wonder
That I that never saw you till this hour,
But that I wish'd you dead, so willingly
Should come to wait upon you to the Ports,

211. secure] *55*; ~. *Gifford* 222. aught] *conj. Coxeter*; might *55*

And there, with hope you never will look back,
Take my last farewell of you.
John. Never look back?
Martino. I said so, neither is it fit you should;
And may I prevail with you as a friend,
You never shall, nor while you live hereafter
Think of the Viceroy's Court, or of *Palermo*,
But as a grave, in which the Prince of *Tarent*
Buried his honor.
John. You speak in a language
I do not understand.
Martino. No? I'll be plainer.
What mad-man, that came hither with that pomp
Don John Antonio did, that exact Courtier
Don John Antonio, with whose brave fame only
Great Princesses have faln in love, and dy'd;
That came with such assurance as young *Paris*
Did to fetch *Helen*, being sent back, contemn'd,
Disgrac'd and scorn'd, his large expence laugh'd at,
His bravery scoff'd, the Lady that he courted
Left quietly in possession of another
(Not to be nam'd that day a Courtier
Where he was mention'd) the scarce known *Cardenes*,
And he to bear her from him! that would ever
Be seen again (having got fairly off)
5r By such as will live ready witnesses
Of his repulse, and scandal?
John. The grief of it,
Believe me, will not kill me. All mans honor
Depends not on the most uncertain favor
Of a fair Mistris.
Martino. Troth, you bear it well.
You should have seen some that were sensible
Of a disgrace, that would have rag'd, and sought
To cure their honor, with some strange revenge:
But you are better temper'd; and they wrong
The *Neapolitans* in their report,
That say they are fiery spirits, uncapable
Of the least injury, dangerous to be talk'd with
After a loss, where nothing can move you,

But, like a Stoick, with a constancy,
Words nor affronts, can shake, you still go on
And smile when men abuse you.
John. If they wrong
Themselves, I can: yet I would have you know,
I dare be angry.
Martino. 'Tis not possible.
A taste of't would do well: And I'd make tryal
What may be done. Come hither Boy. You have seen
This Jewel, as I take it.
John. Yes, 'tis that
I gave *Almira.*
Martino. And in what esteem
She held it, coming from your worthy self,
You may perceive, that freely hath bestowed it
Upon my Page.
John. When I presented it,
I did not indent with her, to what use
She should employ it.
Martino. See the kindness of
O5v A loving soul; who, after this neglect,
Nay gross contempt, will look again upon her,
And not be frighted from it.
John. No indeed Sir,
Nor give way longer: give way, do you mark,
To your loose wit, to run the Wilde-goose chace,
Six syllables further. I will see the Lady,
That Lady, that dotes on you, from whose hate
My love increases, though you stand elected
Her Porter, to deny me.
Martino. Sure you will not.
John. Yes, instantly: Your prosperous success
Hath made you insolent; and for her sake
I have thus long forborne you; and can yet
Forget it, and forgive it, ever provided,
That you end here, and for what is past recalling,
That she make intercession for your pardon,
Which at her suit, I'll grant.
Martino. I am much unwilling

281. *Martino*] *Coxeter*; *not in* 55

To move her for a triffle; bear that too, [*Strikes him.*]
And then she shall speak to you.
John. Men and Angels,
Take witness for me, that I have endur'd
More then a man:— [*They fight.*]
O do not fall so soon,
Stand up; take my hand, so: When I have printed
For every contumelious word, a wound here,
Then sink for ever.
Martino. O! I suffer justly.
1. *Servant*. Murther, murther, murther. *Exit.*
2. *Servant.* Apprehend him.
3. *Servant*. We'll all joyn with you.
John. I do wish you more,
My fury will be lost else, if it meet not
Matter to work on; one life is too little
For so much injury.

6r *Enter* ALMIRA, LEONORA, SERVANT.

Almira. O my *Cardenes*,
Though dead, still my *Cardenes*: Villains, cowards,
What do ye check at? can one arm, and that
A murtherers, so long guard the curs'd Master,
Against so many swords, made sharp with Justice?
1. *Servant*. Sure he will kill us all; he is a devil.
2. *Servant*. He is invulnerable.
Almira. Your base fears
Beget such fancies in you: Give me a sword,
This my weak arm, made strong in my revenge,
Shall force a way to't. [*Wounds him.*]
John. Would it were deeper Madam,
The thrust (which I would not put by, being yours)
Of greater force, to have peirc'd through that heart
Which still retains your figure: Weep still Lady,
For every tear that flows from those griev'd eyes,
Some part of that which maintains life, goes from me;
And so to die, were in a gentle slumber

298 SD. *Strikes him.*] *Coxeter*; *not in 55* 301 SD. *They fight.*] *Coxeter*; *not in 55* 303. every] *Coxeter*; ever *55* 305. *1. Servant*] *Gifford*; *Serv. 55* SD. *Exit.*] *Gifford*; *Exe. Servants. 55* 309 SD. SERVANT] *Gifford*; *Servants 55* 310. Though] *Coxeter*; Thou *55* 318 SD. *Wounds him.*] *after Gifford*; *not in 55*

To pass to Paradise; but you envy me
So quiet a departure from my world,
My world of miseries; therefore take my sword,
And having kill'd me with it, cure the wounds
It gave *Cardenes*.

Enter PEDRO.

Pedro. 'Tis too true: Was ever
Valor so ill employ'd?
John. Why stay you Lady?
Let not soft pity work on your hard nature:
You cannot do a better office to
The dead *Cardenes*, and I willingly
Shall fall a ready sacrifice, to appease him,
Your fair hand offering it.
O6v *Almira.* Thou couldst ask nothing
But this, which I would grant.
Leonora. Flint-hearted Lady!
Pedro. Are you a woman, Sister?
Almira. Thou art not
A Brother, I renounce that title to thee:
Thy hand is in this bloody act; 'twas this
For which that savage homicide was sent hither.
Thou equal Judge of all things, if that blood,
And innocent blood—

. . . .

Almira. Oh *Cardenes*,
How is my soul rent between rage and sorrow,
That it can be, that such an upright Cedar
Should violently be torn up by the roots,
Without an earthquake in that very moment
To swallow them that did it.
John. The hurt's nothing,
But the deep wound is in my conscience, friend,
Which sorrow in death only can recover.
Pedro. Have better hopes.

Enter VICEROY, MESSINA, CAPTAIN, *Guard, and Servants.*

Messina. My son, is this the marriage

336. *Gifford adds SD.: 'Attempts to wound him.'* 342. *See Commentary.*

I came to celebrate? false hopes of man,
I come to find a grave here.
Almira. I have wasted
My stock of Tears, and now just Anger help me
To pay in my Revenge the other part
Of duty which I owe thee. O great Sir,
Not as a Daughter now, but a poor Widow,
Made so before she was a Bride, I flie
To your impartial justice; the offence
Is death, and death in his most horrid form:
Let not then title, or a Princes name
7r (Since a great crime is in a great man greater)
Secure the Offender.
Messina. Give me life for life,
As thou wilt answer it to the great King
Whose Deputy thou art here.
Almira. And speedy Justice.
Messina. Put the damn'd wretch to torture.
Almira. Force him to
Reveal his curs'd Confederates, which spare not,
Although you find a Son among them.
Viceroy. How?
Messina. Why bring you not the Rack forth?
Almira. Wherefore stands
The Murtherer unbound?
Viceroy. Shall I have hearing?
Messina. Excellent Lady, in this you express
Your true love to the dead.
Almira. All love to mankind
From me, ends with him.
Viceroy. Will you hear me yet?
And first to you; you do confess the fact
With which you stand charg'd?
John. I will not make worse
What is already ill, with vain denial.
Viceroy. Then understand, though you are Prince of *Tarent*,
Yet being a Subject to the King of *Spain*,
No priviledge of *Sicily* can free you,

368–9. stands / The] *Coxeter*, *undivided 55* 371–2. mankind / From] *Coxeter*; *undivided 55*

Being convict by a just form of Law,
From the municipal Statutes of that Kingdom,
But as a common man, being found guilty,
Must suffer for it.
John. I prize not my life
So much, as to appeal from any thing
You shall determine of me.
Viceroy. Yet despair not
To have an equal hearing; the exclaims
Of this griev'd Father, nor my Daughters tears
O7v Shall sway me from my self; and where they urge
To have you tortur'd, or led bound to prison,
I must not grant it.
Messina. No?
Viceroy. I cannot sir;
For men of his rank are to be distinguish'd
From other men, before they are condemn'd,
From which (his cause not heard) he yet stands free:
So take him to your charge, and as your life
See he be safe.
Captain. Let me die for him else.
Exeunt PEDRO, JOHN, CAPTAIN *and Guard.*
Messina. The guard of him should have been given to me.
Almira. Or unto me.
Messina. Bribes may corrupt the Captain.
Almira. And our just wreak, by force or cunning practice,
With scorn prevented.
Martino. Oh!
Almira. What groan is that?
Viceroy. There are apparent signs of life yet in him.
Almira. Oh that there were! that I could pour my blood
Into his veins!
Martino. Oh, oh!
Viceroy. Take him up gently.
Messina. Run for Physitians.
Almira. Surgeons.
Messina. All helps else.
Viceroy. This care of his recovery, timely practis'd,
Would have express'd more of a Father in you,

399. There are] *Coxeter*; They'r *55*

Then your impetuous clamors for revenge.
But I shall find fit time to urge that further
Hereafter to you; 'tis not fit for me
To add weight to oppress'd calamitie. *Exeunt.*

08r
. i]
Act. 2. Scæn. 1.

Enter PEDRO, DON JOHN, CAPTAIN.

John. WHY should your love to me, having already
So oft endur'd the test, be put unto
A needless trial? have you not long since
In every circumstance and rite of friendship
Outgone all presidents the Antients boast of,
And will you yet move further?
Pedro. Hitherto
I have done nothing (howsoe'r you value
My weak endeavours) that may justly claim
A title to your friendship, and much less
Laid down the debt, which as a tribute due
To your deservings, not I, but mankind
Stands bound to tender.
John. Do not make an Idol
Of him that should, and without superstition,
To you build up an Altar. O my *Pedro*,
When I am to expire, to call you mine
Assures a future happiness: Give me leave
To argue with you, and the fondness of
Affection struck blind, with justice hear me.
Why should you, being innocent, fling your life
Into the furnace of your fathers anger
For my offence? Or take it granted, (yet
'Tis more then supposition) you prefer
3v My safety 'fore your own, (so prodigally
You waste your favors) wherfore should this Captain,
His blood and sweat rewarded in the favor
Of his great Master, falsifie the trust
Which from true judgment he reposes in him,
For me a stranger?
Pedro. Let him answer that,

He needs no prompter: Speak your thoughts, and freely.
Captain. I ever lov'd to do so, and it shames not
The bluntness of my breeding; from my youth
I was train'd up a Soldier, one of those
That in their natures love the dangers more
Then the rewards of danger. I could add,
My life, when forfeited, the Viceroy pardon'd,
But by his intercession; and therefore
It being lent by him, I were ungrateful
(Which I will never be) if I refus'd
To pay that debt at any time demanded.
Pedro. I hope, friend, this will satisfie you.
John. No, it raises
More doubts within me. Shall I from the school
Of gratitude, in which this Captain reads
The text so plainly, learn to be unthankful?
Or viewing in your actions the Idea
Of perfect Friendship, when it does point to me
How brave a thing it is to be a Friend,
Turn from the object? Had I never lov'd
The fair *Almira* for her outward features,
Nay, were the beauties of her mind suspected,
And her contempt and scorn painted before me,
The being your Sister would anew inflame me
With much more impotence to dote upon her:
No, dear friend, let me in my death confirm
(Though you in all things else have the precedence)
I'll die ten times, ere one of *Pedro's* hairs
Shall suffer in my cause.
P1r *Pedro.* If you so love me,
In love to that part of my soul dwels in you,
(For though two bodies, friends have but one soul)
Loose not both life and me.

Enter a SERVANT.

1. *Servant.* The Prince is dead. *Exit.*
John. If so, shall I leave *Pedro* here to answer
For my escape? As thus I clasp thee, let
The Vice-roys sentence finde me.
Pedro. Flie for Heavens sake,

Consider the necessity; though now
We part *Anthonio*, we may meet again:
But death's division is for ever, friend.

Enter another SERVANT.

2. *Servant*. The rumor spread Sir, of *Martino's* death,
Is check'd, there's hope of his recovery.
John. Why should I flie then? when I may enjoy
With mine own life, my friend.
Pedro. That's still uncertain,
He may have a relapse; for once be rul'd friend.
He's a good debtor that pays when 'tis due;
A prodigal, that before it is requir'd,
Makes tender of it.

Enter three or four SAILORS.

1. *Sailor*. The Bark, Sir, is ready.
2. *Sailor*. The wind sits fair.
3. *Sailor*. Heaven favors your escape.
Whistles within.
Captain. Hark how the Boatswain whistles you aboard.
Will nothing move you?
John. Can I leave my friend?
•1v *Pedro*. I must delay no longer, force him hence.
Captain. I'll run the hazard of my fortunes with you.
John. What violence is this? hear but my Reasons.
Pedro. Poor friendship that is cool'd with Arguments.
Away, away.
Captain. For *Malta*.
Pedro. You shall hear
All our events.
John. I may sail round the world,
But never meet thy like. *Pedro*.
Pedro. *Anthonio*.
John. I breathe my soul back to thee.
Pedro. In exchange
Bear mine along with thee.
Captain. Cheerly my hearts. *Exeunt.*
Pedro. He's gone. May pittying Heaven his Pilot be,
And then I weigh not what becomes of me. *Exit.*

II. i. 77. hence] *Coxeter*; home 55

[II. ii] *Enter* VICEROY, MESSINA, *and Attendants.*

Viceroy. I tell you right Sir.
Messina. Yes, like a rough Surgeon,
Without a feeling in your self, you search
My wounds unto the quick, then predeclare
The tediousness, and danger of the cure,
Never remembring what the Patient suffers.
But you preach this Philosophy to a man
That does pertake of passion, and not
To a dull Stoick.
Viceroy. I confess you have
Just cause to mourn your Son; and yet if reason
Cannot yeeld comfort, let example cure.
I am a Father too, my onely daughter
As dear in my esteem, perhaps as worthy
As your *Martino*, in her love to him
P2r As desperately ill, either's loss equal,
And yet I bear it with a better temper,

Enter PEDRO.

Which if you please to imitate 'twill not wrong
Your pietie, nor your judgment.
Messina. We were fashion'd
In different moulds; I weep with mine own eyes Sir,
Pursue my ends too, pitie to you's a Cordial,
Revenge to me, and that I must, and will have
If my *Martino* die.
Pedro. Your must, and will,
Shall in your full sail'd confidence deceive you. [*Aside.*]
Lord. Here's Doctor *Paulo* Sir.

Enter DOCTOR PAULO, *two* SURGEONS.

Messina. My hand? you rather
Deserve my knee, and it shall bend as to
A second Father, if your saving aids
Restore my son.

II. ii. 3. predeclare] *Mason*; pray declare *55* 16. Which] *Coxeter*; *Pedro.* Which *55* 17–19. *rearranged by Coxeter*; We . . . moulds; / I weep . . . too, / Pitie *55* 22 SD. *Aside.*] *Coxeter*; *not in 55* 23. Here's] *Coxeter*; Hear's *55*

Viceroy. 'Rise thou bright star of knowledge,
The honor of thy art, thou help of nature,
Thou glory of our Academies.
Doctor. If I blush Sir
To hear these attributes ill plac'd on me,
It is excusable. I am no God Sir,
Nor holy Saint that can do miracles,
But a weak sinful man: Yet that I may
In some proportion deserve these favors,
Your excellencies please to grace me with,
I promise all the skill I have acquir'd
In simples, or the careful observation
Of the superior Bodies, with my judgment
2v Deriv'd from long experience, stand ready
To do you service.
Messina. Modestly repli'd.
Viceroy. How is it with your princely Patient?
Messina. Speak,
But speak some comfort Sir.
Doctor. I must speak truth;
His wounds, though many, Heaven so guided yet
Anthonio's sword, it pierc'd no part was mortal.
These Gentlemen who worthily deserve
The names of Surgeons, have done their duties:
The means they practis'd, not ridiculous charms
To stop the blood; no Oyls, nor Balsoms bought
Of cheating Quack-salvers, or Montebanks,
By them appli'd: The rules by *Chiron* taught,
And *Æsculapius*, which drew upon him,
The thunderers envy, they with care pursu'd,
Heav'n prospering their endeavors.
Messina. There is hope then
Of his recovery?
Doctor. But no assurance;
I must not flatter you. That little air
Of comfort that breathes towards us (for I dare not
Rob these t'inrich my self) you ow their care;
For yet I have done nothing.
Messina. Still more modest,

40. your] *Mason*; you 55

I will begin with them, to either give
Three thousand crowns.
Viceroy. I'll double your reward;
See 'em paid presently.
1. *Surgeon.* This magnificence
With equity, cannot be confer'd on us;
'Tis due unto the Doctor.
2. *Surgeon.* True; we were
But his subordinate ministers, and did onely
Follow your grave directions.
P3r *Doctor.* 'Tis your own,
I challenge no part in it.
Viceroy. Brave on both sides.
Doctor. Deserve this, with the honor that will follow,
In your attendance.
2. *Surgeon.* If both sleep at once,
'Tis justice both should die. *Exeunt* SURGEONS.
Messina. For you grave Doctor,
We will not in such petty sums consider
Your high desarts. Our treasury lies open,
Command it as your own.
Viceroy. Choose any Castle,
Nay City, in our Government, and be Lord of't.
Doctor. Of neither Sir, I am not so ambitious;
Nor would I have your Highnesses secure.
We have but faintly yet begun our journey,
A thousand difficulties and dangers must be
Encountred, ere we end it. Though his hurts,
I mean his outward ones, do promise fair,
There is a deeper one, and in his minde,
Must be with care provided for. Melancholy,
And at the height too, near of kin to madness,
Possesses him; his senses are distracted,
Not one, but all; and if I can collect 'em
With all the various ways, invention,
Or industry ever practis'd, I shall write it
My master-piece.
Messina. You more and more engage me.
Viceroy. May we not visit him?

81. too, near] *Gifford*; ∼‸∼ *55*

Doctor. By no means Sir,
As he is now, such courtesies come untimely,
I'll yeeld you reason for't. Should he look on you,
It will renew the memory of that
Which I would have forgotten. Your good prayers
(And those I do presume, shall not be wanting
To my endeavors) are the utmost aids
P3v I yet desire your Excellencies should grant me.
So with my humblest service.
Messina. Go and prosper. *Exit* DOCTOR.
Viceroy. Observe his piety! I have heard, how true
I know not, most Physitians as they grow
Greater in skill, grow less in their Religion;
Attributing so much to natural causes,
That they have little faith in that they cannot
Deliver Reason for: This Doctor steers
Another course; but let this pass; if you please,
Your company to my Daughter.
Messina. I wait on you. *Exeunt.*

iii] *Enter* LEONORA, *and two* WOMEN.

Leonora. Took she no rest to night?
1. *Woman.* Not any Madam,
I am sure she slept not. If she slumbred, strait,
As if some dreadful vision had appear'd,
She started up, her hair unbound, and with
Distracted looks, staring about the Chamber,
She asks aloud; where is *Martino*? where
Have you conceal'd him? sometimes names *Anthonio*,
Trembling in every joynt, her brows contracted:
Her fair face as 'twere chang'd into a curse,
Her hands held up thus, and as if her words
Were too big to finde passage through her mouth,
She groans, then throws her self upon her Bed,
Beating her Brest.
Leonora. 'Tis wondrous strange.
2. *Woman.* Nay more,
She that of late vouchsafed not to be seen,
But so adorn'd, as if she were to rival

Nero's Poppea, or the *Egyptian* Queen,
Now careless of her beauties, when we offer
Our service, she contemns it.
Leonora. Does she not
P4r Sometimes forsake her Chamber?
2. *Woman.* Much about
This hour, then with a strange unsetled gate
She measures twice, or thrice the Gallery,
Silent, and frowning (we dare not speak to her)
And then returns. She's come, pray you now observe her.

Enter ALMIRA *in black, carelessly habited.*

Almira. Why are my eyes fix'd on the ground, and not
Bent upwards? Ha! that which was mortal of
My dear *Martino*, as a debt to nature,
I know this mother Earth hath sepulchred:
But his diviner part, his Soul, o'r which
The tyrant death, nor yet the fatal sword
Of curs'd *Anthonio*, his Instrument,
Had the least power, borne upon Angels wings,
Appointed to that office, mounted far
Above the Firmament.
Leonora. Strange imagination!
Dear Cousin your *Martino* lives.
Almira. I know you,
And that in this you flatter me. He's dead,
As much as could die of him: But look yonder;
Amongst a million of glorious lights
That deck the heavenly Canopy, I have
Discern'd his soul transform'd into a star.
Do you not see it?
Leonora. Lady.
Almira. Look with my eyes.
What splendor circles it! the heavenly Archer
Not far off distant, appears dim with envy,
Viewing himself out-shin'd. Bright Constellation
Dart down thy beams of pity on *Almira*;
And since thou findst such grace where now thou art,
As I did truly love thee on the Earth,
P4v Like a kinde Harbinger, prepare my lodging,

And place me near thee.
Leonora. I much more then fear,
She'll grow into a phrensie.
Almira. How! what's this?
A dismal sound! Come nerer Cousin, lay
Your ear close to the ground, closer I pray you.
Do you howl? are you there *Anthonio*?
Leonora. Where sweet Lady?
Almira. I' th' Vault, in Hell, on the infernal rack,
Where murtherers are tormented: Yirk him soundly,
'Twas *Rhadamanths* sentence; Do your office Furies.
How he rores! what, plead to me to mediate for you?
I am deaf, I cannot hear you.
Leonora. 'Tis but fancy,
Collect your self.
Almira. Leave babling; 'tis rare Musick.
Rhamnusia plays on a pair of tongs
Red hot; and *Proserpine* dances to the consort;
Pluto sits laughing by too. So, enough,
I do begin to pitie him.
Leonora. I wish, Madam,
You would shew it to your self.
2\. *Woman.* Her fit begins
To leave her.
Almira. O my brains! are you there Cousin?
Leonora. Now she speaks temperately. I am ever ready
To do you service: How do you?
Almira. Very much troubled.
I have had the strangest waking dream of Hell
And Heaven, I know not what.
Leonora. My Lord your Father
Is come to visit you. As ye would not grieve him
That is so tender of you, entertain him
With a becoming dutie.

Enter VICEROY, MESSINA, PEDRO, *Attendants.*

Viceroy. Still forlorn?
No comfort my *Almira*?
Messina. In your sorrow,
For my *Martino*, Madam, you have express'd

All possible love and tenderness. Too much of it
Will wrong your self, and him. He may live Lady
(For we are not past hope) with his future service,
In some part to deserve it.
Almira. If Heaven please
To be so gratious to me, I'll serve him
With such obedience, love, and humbleness,
That I will rise up an example for
Good wives to follow: But until I have
Assurance what fate will determine of me,
Thus like a desolate Widow, give me leave
To weep for him; for should he die, I have vow'd
Not to out-live him; and my humble suit is,
One Monument may cover us, and *Anthonio*
(In justice you must grant me that) be offer'd
A Sacrifice to our Ashes.
Viceroy. Prethee put off
These sad thoughts, both shall live (I doubt it not)
A happy pair.

P5v *Enter* CUCULO, *and* BORACHIA.

Cuculo. O Sir, the foulest treason
That ever was discovered.
Viceroy. Speak it, that
We may prevent it.
Cuculo. Nay 'tis past prevention,
Though you allow me wise (in modesty,
I will not say oraculous) I cannot help it.
I am a Statesman, and some say a wise one,
But I could never conjure, nor divine
Of things to come.
Viceroy. Leave fooling; to the point,
What treason?
Cuculo. The false Prince *Don John Anthonio*
Is fled.
Viceroy. It is not possible.
Pedro. Peace, Scriech-owl.
Cuculo. I must speak, and it shall out, sir; the Captain
You trusted with the Fort, is run away too.

II. iii. 90 SD. *Enter* CUCULO . . .] *Coxeter*; *Enter Viceroy, Cuculo* . . . *55*

Almira. O miserable woman, I defie
All comfort, cheated too of my revenge!
As you are my Father sir, and you my Brother,
I will not curse you; but I dare, and will say
You are unjust and treacherous. If there be
A way to death, I'll find it. *Exeunt* ALMIRA, LEONORA, WOMEN.
Viceroy. Follow her,
She'll do some violent act upon herself:
Till she be better temper'd, bind her hands,
And fetch the Doctor to her. Had not you
A hand in this?
Pedro. I sir, I never knew
Such disobedience.
Viceroy. My honor's touch'd in't:
6r Let Gallies be mann'd forth in his pursuit,
Search every Port and Harbor; if I live,
He shall not 'scape thus.
Messina. Fine hypocrisie!
Away dissemblers, 'tis confederacie
Betwixt thy son and self, and the false Captain,
He could not thus have vanish'd else. Ye have murther'd
My Son amongst you, and now murther Justice.
You know it most impossible he should live,
Howe'r the Doctor for your ends dissembled,
And you have shifted hence *Anthonio*.
Viceroy. *Messina*, thou art a craz'd and griev'd old man,
And being in my Court, protected by
The law of hospitality, or I should
Give you a sharper answer: May I perish,
If I knew of his flight.
Messina. Fire then the Castle,
Hang up the Captains wife and children.
Viceroy. Fie sir.
Pedro. My Lord, you are uncharitable; capital treasons
Exact not so much.
Messina. Thanks most noble Signior,
We ever had your good word and your love.
Cuculo. Sir, I dare pass my word, my Lords are clear

107 SD. *Exeunt* . . . WOMEN.] *55*; *Exit*. (l. 107); *Exeunt Leonora, and Waiting Women* (l. 110) *Gifford*

Of any imputation in this case
You seem to load 'em with.
Messina. Impertinent fool;
No, no, the loving faces you put on
Have been but grinning vizors: you have juggled me
Out of my son, and out of justice too.
But *Spain* shall do me right; believe me Viceroy,
There I will force it from thee by the King,
He shall nor eat nor sleep in peace for me
P6v Till I am righted for this treacherie.
Viceroy. Thy worst *Messina*, since no reason can
Qualifie thy intemperance; the corruption
Of my subordinate Ministers cannot wrong
My true integrity; let privy searches
Examine all the Land.
Pedro. Fair fall *Anthonio*.
Exeunt VICEROY, PEDRO, *Attendants.*
Cuculo. This is my wife, my Lord; troth speak your conscience,
Is't not a goodly Dame?
Messina. She is no less Sir,
I will make use of these; may I intreat you
To call my Neece.
Borachia. With speed sir. *Exit* BORACHIA.
Cuculo. You may my Lord
Suspect me as an Agent in these State conveyances.
Let Signior *Cuculo* then be never more,
For all his place, wit, and authority,
Held a most worthy honest Gentleman.

Enter BORACHIA *with* LEONORA.

Messina. I do acquit you Signior. Neece you see
To what extreams I am driven; the cunning Viceroy
And his son *Pedro*, have express'd too plainly
Their cold affections to my son *Martino*;
And therefore I conjure thee *Leonora*,
By all thy hopes from me, which is my Dukedom,
If my son fail; however, all thy fortunes;
Though heretofore some love hath past betwixt
Don Pedro, and thy self, abjure him now.

142. worst] *Coxeter*; worse *55* 157. have] *editor*; having *55*

And as thou keep'st *Almira* company,
In this her desolation, so in hate
To this yong *Pedro* for thy Cousins love,
Be her associate; or assure thy self,
P7r I cast thee like a stranger from my blood.
If I do ever hear, thou seest, or send'st
Token, or receive message, by yon Heaven,
I never more will own thee.

Leonora. O dear Uncle,
You have put a tyrannous yoke upon my heart,
And it will break it. *Exit* LEONORA.

Messina. Gravest Lady; you
May be a great assister in my ends.
I buy your diligence thus: Divide this couple,
Hinder their enterviews; fain 'tis her will
To give him no admittance, if he crave it,
And thy rewards shall be thine own desires.
Whereto good Sir, but adde your friendly aids,
And use me to my uttermost.

Cuculo. My Lord,
If my wife please, I dare not contradict.
Borachia, what do you say?

Borachia. I say, my Lord,
I know my place, and be assur'd I will
Keep fire and toe asunder.

Messina. You in this
Shall much deserve me. *Exit* MESSINA.

Cuculo. We have took upon us
A heavy charge. I hope you'll now forbear
Th'excess of Wine.

Borachia. I will do what I please.
This day the markets kept for slaves, go you
And buy me a fine timber'd one to assist me.
I must be better waited on.

Cuculo. Any thing,
So you'll leave Wine.

Borachia. Still prating?

Cuculo. I am gone Duck. *Exit* CUCULO.

Borachia. Pedro! so hot upon the scent, I'll fit him.

170. yon] *Coxeter*; you 55 191. So] *Coxeter*; *Ped.* So 55

P7v *Enter* PEDRO.

Pedro. *Donna Borachia*, you most happily
Are met to pleasure me.
Borachia. It may be so,
I use to pleasure many. Here lies my way,
I do beseech you Sir, keep on your voyage.
Pedro. Be not so short, sweet Lady, I must with you.
Borachia. With me Sir, I beseech you Sir; why, what Sir
See you in me?
Pedro. Do not mistake me Lady,
Nothing but honesty.
Borachia. Hang honesty;
Trump me not up with honesty. Do you mark Sir,
I have a charge Sir, and a special charge Sir;
And 'tis not honesty can win on me Sir.
Pedro. Prethee conceive me rightly.
Borachia. I conceive ye?
Pedro. But understand.
Borachia. I will not understand sir,
I cannot, nor I do not understand sir.
Pedro. Prethee *Borachia*, let me see my Mistress;
But look upon her, stand you by.
Borachia. How's this?
Shall I stand by? what do you think of me?
Now by the vertue of the place I hold,
You are a Paltry Lord to tempt my trust thus.
I am no *Hellen*, nor no *Heccuba*,
To be deflowred of my loyaltie
With your fair language.
Pedro. Thou mistak'st me still.
Borachia. It may be so; my place will bear me out in't;
P8r And will mistake you still, make you your best on't.
Pedro. A Pox upon thee, let me but behold her.
Borachia. A Plague upon you, you shall never see her.
Pedro. This is a croan in grain! Thou art so testie,
Prethee take breath, and know thy friends.
Borachia. I will not,
I have no friends, nor I will have none this way.
And now I think on't better, why will you see her?

Pedro. Because she loves me dearly, I her equally.
Borachia. She hates you damnably, most wickedly,
(Build that upon my word) most wickedly;
And swears her eies are sick when they behold ye.
How fearfully have I heard her rail upon ye,
And cast, and rail again, and cast again;
Call for hot Waters, and then rail again.
Pedro. How? 'tis not possible.
Borachia. I have heard her swear
(How justly, you best know, and where the cause lies)
That ye are (I shame to tell it) but it must out.
Fie, fie, why, how have you deserv'd it?
Pedro. I am what?
Borachia. The beastliest man; why what a grief must this be,
Sir-reverence of the company, a rank whoremaster:
Ten livery whores, she assur'd me on her credit,
With weeping eies she spake it, and seven Citizens,
Beside all voluntaries that serve under ye,
And of all Countries.
Pedro. This must needs be a lie.
Borachia. Besides ye are so careless of your body,
Which is a foul fault in ye.
Pedro. Leave your fooling,
For this shall be a fable. Happily
My Sisters anger may grow strong against me,
Which thou mistak'st.
P8v *Borachia*. She hates you very well too,
But your Mistress hates you heartily; look upon ye?
Upon my conscience, she would see the divel first,
With eies as big as sawcers. When I but nam'd ye,
She has leapt back thirty foot: If once she smell ye,
For certainly ye are rank, she says extream rank,
And the wind stand with ye too, she is gone for ever.
Pedro. For all this I would see her.
Borachia. That's all one.
Have you new eyes when those are scratch'd out? or a nose
To clap on warm? Have you proof against a Pisspot;
Which if they bid me, I must fling upon you?
Pedro. I shall not see her, then you say?
Borachia. It seems so.

Pedro. Prethee be thus far friend, then good *Borachia*,
To give her but this Letter, and this Ring,
And leave thy pleasant lying, which I pardon;
But leave it in her pocket, there's no harm in't.
I'll take thee up a Petticoat, will that please thee?
Borachia. Take up my Petticoat? I scorn the motion,
I scorn it with my heels; take up my Petticoat?
Pedro. And why thus hot?
Borachia. Sir, you shall finde me hotter
If you take up my Petticoat.
Pedro. I'll give thee a new Petticoat.
Borachia. I scorn the gift: Take up my Petticoat?
Alas my Lord, you are to yong, my Lord;
To yong my Lord to circumcise me that way.
Take up my Petticoat? I am a woman,
A woman of another way, my Lord;
A Gentlewoman: He that takes up my Petticoat,
Shall have enough to do, I warrant him.
Q1r I would fain see the proudest of you all so lusty.
Pedro. Thou art dispos'd still to mistake me.
Borachia. Petticoat.
You show now what you are, but do your worst, Sir.
Pedro. A wild-fire take thee.
Borachia. I ask no favor of ye,
And so I leave ye; and withal I charge ye
In my own name, for sir I would have ye know it,
In this place I present your fathers person:
Upon your life, not dare to follow me;
For if you do— *Exit* BORACHIA.
Pedro. Go, and the Pox go with thee,
If thou hast so much moisture to receive 'em,
For thou wilt have 'em, though a Horse bestow 'em.
I must devise a way, for I must see her,
And very suddenly; and Madam Petticoat,
If all the wit I have, and this can do,
I'll make you break your charge, and your hope too. *Exit.*

Q1v
[III. i]

Act. 3. Scæn. 1.

Enter MASTER, MAN, DON JOHN, CAPTAIN, *with divers* SLAVES.

Master. COME rank your selves, and stand out handsomly.
Now ring the Bell, that they may know my Market.
Stand you two here, you are personable men,
And apt to yeeld good sums, if women cheapen.
Put me that Pig-complexion'd fellow behinde,
He will spoil my sale else, the slave looks like famine:
Sure he was got in a Cheese-press, the whay runs out on's Nose yet.
He will not yeeld above a peck of Oysters,
If I can get a quart of wine in too, ye are gone Sir:
Why sure, thou hadst no father.
Slave. Sure I know not.
Master. No certainly, a *March* Frog kept thy mother;
Thou art but a monster Paddock. Look who comes, Sirrah.
Exit MAN.
And next prepare the Song, and do it lively.
Your tricks too Sirrah; they are ways to catch the buyer,
And if you do 'em well, they'll prove good Dowries.
How now?

Enter MAN.

Man. They come Sir, with their bags full loaden.
Master. Reach me my stool. O! here they come.

Q2r *Enter* DOCTOR, APOTHECARY, CUCULO, *and* CITIZENS.

Cuculo. That's he.
He never fails monethly to sell his slaves here,
He buys 'em presently upon their taking,
And so disperses 'em to every Market.
Master. Begin the song, and chaunt it merrily— [*Song.*]
Well done.
Doctor. Good morrow.
Master. Morrow to you Signiors.
Doctor. We come to look upon your slaves, and buy too,
If we can like the persons, and the prices.

III. i. 11. kept] 55; leapt *Mason* 21 SD. *Song.*] *editor*; *not in* 55; A SONG, *by one of the Slaves Gifford*

Cuculo. They show fine active fellows.
Master. They are no less Sir,
And people of strong labors.
Doctor. That's i' th' proof Sir.
Apothecary. Pray what's the price of this Red-bearded fellow?
If his Gall be good, I have certain uses for him.
Master. My Sorrel slaves are of a lower price,
Because the colours faint. Fifty Chekeens Sir.
Apothecary. What be his vertues?
Master. He will poyson Rats,
Make him but angry, and his eyes kill Spiders;
Let him but fasting, spit upon a Tode,
And presently it bursts, and dies; his dreams kill;
He'll run you in a wheel, and draw up water;
But if his Nose drop in't, 'twill kill an army.
When ye have worn him to the Bones with uses,
Thrust him into an Oven, luted well,
Dry him, and beat him, flesh and bone to powder;
And that kills Scabs, and Aches of all clymates.
Apothecary. Pray at what distance may I talk to him?
Master. Give him but Sage and Butter in a morning,
Q2v And there's no fear: But keep him from all women,
For there his poyson swells most.
Apothecary. I will have him.
Cannot he breed a plague too?
Master. Yes, yes, yes.
Feed him with Frogs, *probatum*. Now to you Sir,
Do you like this slave?
Cuculo. Yes, if I like his price well.
Master. The price is full an hundred, nothing bated.
Sirrah, sell the Moors there; feel, he's high and lusty,
And of a gamesom nature; bold, and secret,
Apt to win favor of the man that owns him,
By diligence, and duty: Look upon him.
Doctor. Do ye hear Sir?
Master. I'll be with you presently.
Mark but his limbs, that slave will cost ye fourscore.
An easie price, turn him about, and view him.
For these two Sir? why they are the finest children,

46. Frogs,] *conj. McIlwraith*; Fogs *55*

Twins on my credit sir. Do you see this Boy, sir,
He will run as far from ye in an hour—
1. *Citizen.* Will he so sir?
Master. Conceive me rightly, if upon an errand,
As any horse you have.
1. *Citizen.* What will this Girl do?
Master. Sure no harm at all sir,
For she sleeps most an end.
1. *Citizen.* An excellent house-wife.
Of what Religion are they?
Master. What you will sir,
So there be meat, and drink in't; they'll do little
That shall offend ye; for their chief desire
Is to do nothing at all sir.
Q3r *Cuculo.* A hundred is too much.
Master. Not a doit bated,
He's a brave slave; his eye shows activeness;
Fire, and the mettle of a man, dwells in him.
Here's one you shall have.
Cuculo. For what?
Master. For nothing,
And thank ye too.
Doctor. What can he do?
Master. Why, any thing that's ill,
And never blush at it: He's so true a theef,
That he will steal from himself, and think he has got by it.
He stole out of his Mothers belly, being an Infant,
And from a lousie Nurse he stole his nature;
From a Dog his look, and from an Ape his nimbleness;
He will look in your face, and pick your pockets,
Rob ye the most wise Rat of a Cheese-paring;
There where a Cat will go in, he will follow,
His body has no backbone. In to my company
He stole, for I never bought him, and will steal in to yours,
And ye stay a little longer. Now if any of ye
Be given to the excellent art of lying,
Behold, before ye here the master-piece;
He will out-lie him that taught him, Monsieur Devil,
Offer to swear he has eaten nothing in a twelve moneth,
When his mouth's full of Meat.

Cuculo. Pray keep him, he's a Jewel,
And here's your money for this fellow.
Master. He's yours sir!
Cuculo. Come follow me. *Exit with* DON JOHN.
Q3v 1. *Citizen*. Twenty Chekeens for these two.
Master. For five and twenty take 'em.
1. *Citizen*. There's your money;
I'll have 'em, if it be to sing in Cages.
Master. Give 'em hard Eggs, you never had such Black-birds.
1. *Citizen*. Is she a Maid, do'st think?
Master. I dare not swear Sir,
She is nine year old, at ten you shall finde few here.
1. *Citizen*. A merry fellow, thou say'st true. Come children.
Exit with the Moors.
Doctor. Here tell your money; if his life but answer
His outward promises, I have bought him cheap Sir.
Master. Too cheap a conscience, he's a pregnant Knave.
Full of fine thoughts, I warrant him.
Doctor. He's but weak timber'd.
Master. 'Tis the better,
He will turn Gentleman a great deal sooner.
Doctor. Very weak Legs.
Master. Strong as the time allows Sir.
Doctor. What's that fellow?
Master. Who this? The finest thing in all the world Sir,
The punctuallest, and the perfitest, an English mettle,
But coyn'd in *France*; your servants servant Sir,
Do you understand that? or your shadows servant.
Will you buy him to carry in a Box! Kiss your hand sirrah;
Let fall your cloak on one shoulder; face to your left hand;
Fether your Hat; slope your Hat; now charge your honor.
What think you of this fellow?
Doctor. Indeed I know not,
I never saw such an Ape before. But hark you,
Q4r Are these things serious in his nature?
Master. Yes, yes;
Part of his Creed: come do some more devices.
Quarrel a little, and take him for your enemy,
Do it in dumb show. Now observe him nearly.

111. now charge your honor.] *55*; now charge.—Your honour, *Gifford*

Doctor. This fellow's mad, stark mad.
Master. Believe they are all so.
I have sold a hundred of 'em.
Doctor. A strange Nation:
What may the women be?
Master. As mad as they;
And as I have heard for truth, a great deal madder;
Yet you may finde some civil things amongst 'em,
But they are not respected. Nay never wonder,
They have a City Sir, I have been in't,
And therefore dare affirm it, where, if you saw
With what a load of vanity 'tis fraughted,
How like an everlasting Morris-dance it looks;
Nothing but Hobby-horse, and Maid-marrian;
You would start indeed.
Doctor. They are handsom men.
Master. Yes: If they would thank their Maker,
And seek no further; but they have new Creators,
God Tailor, and God Mercer; a kinde of Jews Sir,
But faln into Idolatry, for they worship
Nothing with so much service, as the Cow-calfs.
Doctor. What do mean you by Cow-calfs?
Master. Why their women.
Will you see him do any more tricks?
Doctor. 'Tis enough, I thank ye;
But yet I'll buy him, for the rareness of him.
He may make my princely patient mirth, and that done,
I'll claim him in my study, that at void hours
I may run o'r the story of his Country.
Master. His price is forty.
Q4v *Doctor*. Hold, I'll once be foolish,
And buy a lump of levity to laugh at.
Apothecary. Will your worship walk?
Doctor. How now Apothecary,
Have you been buying too?
Apothecary. A little Sir;
A dose or two of mischief.
Doctor. Fare ye well Sir,
As these prove, we shall look the next wind for ye.

135. mean you] *55*; you mean *Coxeter* 139. claim] *55*; chain *Mason*

Master. I shall be with ye Sir.
Doctor. Who bought this fellow?
2. *Citizen*. Not I.
Apothecary. Nor I.
Doctor. Why do's he follow us then?
Master. Did not I tell ye he would steal to ye?
2. *Citizen*. Sirrah.
You mouldy chops, know your crib, I would wish you,
And get from whence you came.
Slave. I came from no place.
Doctor. Wilt thou be my fool, for fools they say, will tell truth.
Slave. Yes, if you will give me leave Sir to abuse you,
For I can do that naturally.
Doctor. And I can beat ye.
Slave. I should be sorry else, Sir.
Master. He looks for that, as duly as his victuals,
And will be extream sick when he is not beaten.
He will be as wanton, when he has a bone broken,
As a Cat in a bowl on the water.
Doctor. You will part with him?
Master. To such a friend as you Sir.
Doctor. And without money?
Master. Not a peny Signior;
And would he were better for ye.
Doctor. Follow me then,
The Knave may teach me something.
Q5r *Slave*. Something, that
You dearly may repent; howe'r you scorn me,
The slave may prove your Master.
Doctor. Farewel once more.
Master. Farewel, and when the wind serves next, expect me.
Exeunt.

[III. ii] *Enter* CUCULO, *and* DON JOHN.

Cuculo. Come Sir, you are mine, Sir, now; you serve a man Sir,
That when you know more, you will finde—
John. I hope so.
Cuculo. What do'st thou hope?
John. To finde ye a kinde master.

Cuculo. Finde you your self a diligent true servant,
And take the precept of the wise before ye,
And then you may hope Sirrah. Understand:
You serve me. What is me? a man of credit.
John. Yes Sir.
Cuculo. Of special credit, special office.
Hear first, and understand again, of special office.
A man that nods upon the thing he meets,
And that thing bows.
John. 'Tis fit it should be so Sir.
Cuculo. It shall do so. A man neer all importance.
Do'st thou digest this truly?
John. I hope I shall Sir.
Cuculo. Besides, thou art to serve a noble Mistress,
Of equal place and trust. Serve usefully,
Serve all with diligence, but her delights,
There make your stop. She is a woman sirrah;
And though a cull'd out vertue, yet a woman.
Thou art not troubled with the strength of blood,
And stirring faculties, for she will show a fair one?
John. As I am a man, I may; but as I am your man,
Your trusty, useful man, those thoughts shall perish.
Q5v *Cuculo*. 'Tis apt, and well distinguish'd. The next precept,
And then observe me, you have all your duty:
Keep as thou wouldst keep thine eye-sight, all Wine from her,
All talk of Wine.
John. Wine is a comfort, Sir.
Cuculo. A Devil, Sir; let her not dream of Wine,
Make her believe there neither is, nor was Wine,
Swear it.
John. Will you have me lye?
Cuculo. To my end, Sir;
For if one drop of Wine but creep into her,
She is the wisest woman in the world straight,
And all the women in the world together
Are but a whisper to her; a thousand Iron-mills
Can be heard no further then a pair of Nut-crackers:
Keep her from Wine, Wine makes her dangerous.
Fall back; my Lord *Don Pedro*!

III. ii. 12. do] *55*; be *Gifford*

Enter PEDRO.

Pedro. Now Mr. Office:
What is the reason that your vigilant greatness,
And your wives wonderful wiseness have lock'd up from me
The way to see my Mistress? whose Dog's dead now,
That you observe these Vigils?
Cuculo. Very well, my Lord;
Belike we observe no law then, nor no order,
Nor feel no power, nor will of him that made 'em,
When State-commands thus slightly are disputed.
Pedro. What State-command? dost thou think any State
Would give thee any thing but Eggs to keep,
Or trust thee with a secret above lousing?
Q6r *Cuculo.* No, no, my Lord, I am not passionate,
You cannot work me that way to betray me.
A point there is in't, that you must not see sir,
A secret and a serious point of State too;
And do not urge it further, do not Lord,
It will not take; you deal with them that wink not:
You try'd my wife, alas you thought she was foolish,
Won with an empty word; you have not found it.
Pedro. I have found a pair of Coxcombs, that I am sure on.
Cuculo. Your Lordship may say three; I am not passionate.
Pedro. How's that?
Cuculo. Your Lordship found a faithful Gentlewoman,
Strong, and inscrutable as the Viceroy's heart,
A woman of another making, Lord:
And lest she might partake with womans weakness,
I have purchas'd her a rib to make her perfect,
A rib that will not shrink, nor break i' th' bending:
This trouble we are put to, to prevent things,
Which your good Lordship holds but necessary.
Pedro. A fellow of a handsom and free promise,
And much methinks I am taken with his countenance.
Do you serve this Yeoman-Porter?
Cuculo. Not a word,
Basta, your Lordship may discourse your freedom;
He is a slave of State sir, so of silence.

67. Yeoman-Porter] *Mason*(?), *Gifford*[1]; Yeoman, Porter *55*, *Gifford*[2]

Pedro. You are very punctual, State-cut; fare ye well,
I shall find time to fit you too, I fear not. *Exit* PEDRO.
Cuculo. And I shall fit you Lord; you would be billing;
You are too hot, sweet Lord, too hot: Go you home,
And there observe these lessons I first taught you,
26v Look to your charge abundantly; be wary,
Trusty and wary: much weight hangs upon me,
Watchful and wary too! this Lord is dangerous,
Take courage and resist; for other uses
Your Mistress will inform ye. Go, be faithful,
And do ye hear? no wine.
John. I shall observe Sir. *Exeunt*.

iii] *Enter* DOCTOR *and* SURGEONS.

Doctor. He must take air.
1. *Surgeon*. Sir, under your correction,
The violence of motion may make
His wounds bleed fresh.
2. *Surgeon*. And he hath lost already
Too much blood, in my judgment.
Doctor. I allow that;
But to choak up his spirits in a dark room,
Is far more dangerous. He comes; no questions.

Enter MARTINO.

Martino. Certain we have no reason, nor that soul
Created of that pureness books perswade us:
We understand not sure, nor feel that sweetness
That men call Vertues chain to link our actions.
Our imperfections form, and flatter us;
A will to rash and rude things, is our reason,
And that we glory in, that makes us guilty.
Why did I wrong this man, unmanly wrong him,
Unmannerly? He gave me no occasion;
In all my heat how noble was his temper!
And when I had forgot both man and manhood,
With what a gentle bravery did he chide me!
And say he had kill'd me, whither had I travell'd?
Kill'd me in all my rage, oh how it shakes me!

70. punctual,] *Coxeter*; ~^ 55

Q7[r] Why didst thou do this, fool? a woman taught me,
The Devil and his Angel woman bid me.
I am a beast, the wildest of all beasts,
And like a beast I make my blood my master.
Farewell, farewell for ever name of Mistress,
Out of my heart I cross thee; love and women
Out of my thoughts.
Doctor. I, now you shew your manhood.
Martino. Doctor believe me, I have bought my knowledge,
And dearly, Doctor; they are dangerous creatures,
They sting at both ends, Doctor; worthless creatures,
And all their loves and favors end in ruines.
Doctor. To man indeed.
Martino. Why now thou tak'st me rightly:
What can they shew, or by what act deserve us
While we have vertue, and pursue her beauties?
Doctor. And yet I have heard of many vertuous women.
Martino. Not many, Doctor, there your reading fails you:
Would there were more, and in their loves less dangers.
Doctor. Love is a noble thing without all doubt sir.
Martino. Yes, and an excellent to cure the itch. *Exit.*
1. *Surgeon.* Strange melancholy!
Doctor. By degrees 'twill lessen,
Provide your things.
2. *Surgeon.* Our care shall not be wanting. *Exeunt.*

[III. iv] *Enter* LEONORA *and* ALMIRA.

Leonora. Good Madam, for your healths sake cleer those clouds up,
That feed upon your beauties like diseases:
Times hand will turn again, and what he ruines
Gently restore, and wipe off all your sorrows.
Q7[v] Believe ye are to blame, much to blame Lady;
You tempt his loving care whose eye has numbred
All our afflictions, and the time to cure 'em:
You rather with this torrent choak his mercies
Then gently slide in to his providence.
Sorrows are well allow'd, and sweeten Nature,

III. iii. 33. by] *conj. Mason*; be? *55* 35. *rearranged by Coxeter*; And . . . heard / Of *55*

Where they express no more then drops on lillies;
But when they fall in storms, they bruise our hopes,
Make us unable (though our comforts meet us)
To hold our heads up: Come, you shall take comfort;
This is a sullen grief becomes condemn'd men,
That feel a weight of sorrow through their souls:
Do but look up: Why so! is not this better
Then hanging down your head still like a Violet,
And dropping out those sweet eyes for a wager?
Pray ye speak a little.
Almira. Pray ye desire no more,
And if ye love me, say no more.
Leonora. How fain
(If I would be as wilful, and partake in't)
Would you destroy your self! how often, Lady,
Ev'n of the same disease have you cur'd me,
And shook me out on't; chid me, tumbled me,
And forc'd my hands thus?
Almira. By these tears no more.
Leonora. You are too prodigal of 'em. Well, I will not,
For though my love bids me transgress your will,
I have a service to your sorrows still. *Exeunt.*

v] *Enter* PEDRO *and* DON JOHN.

John. Indeed my Lord, my place is not so neer;
I wait below stairs, and there sit, and wait
Who comes to seek accesses; nor is it fit Sir
My rudeness should intrude so neer their lodgings.
8r *Pedro.* Thou maist invent a way, 'tis but a tryal;
But carrying up this Letter, and this token,
And giving 'em discreetly to my Mistress,
The Lady *Leonora*; there's my Purse,
Or any thing thou wilt ask me: if thou knew'st me,
And what I may be to thee for this courtesie—
John. Your Lordship speaks so honestly, and freely,
That by my troth I'll venture.
Pedro. I deerly thank thee.
John. And it shall cost me hard; nay, keep your purse Sir:
For though my bodies bought, my minde was never.

Though I am bound, my courtesies are no slaves.
Pedro. Thou shouldst be truly gentle.
John. If I were so,
The state I am in, bids you not believe it.
But to the purpose Sir, Give me your Letter,
And next your counsel, for I serve a crafty Mistress.
Pedro. And she must be remov'd, thou wilt else ne'er do it.
John. I, there's the plague. Think, and I'll think a while too.
Pedro. Her husbands suddenly faln sick.
John. She cares not
If he were dead, indeed it would do better.
Pedro. Would he were hang'd.
John. Then she would run for joy, Sir.
Pedro. Some Lady crying out.
John. She has two already.
Pedro. Her house is a fire.
John. Let the fool, my husband, quench it:
This will be her answer. This may take, it will sure!
Your Lordship must go presently, and send me
Two or three bottles of your best Greek Wine;
The strongest, and sweetest.
Q8v *Pedro*. Instantly;
But will that do?
John. Let me alone to work it; *Exit* PEDRO.
Wine I was charg'd to keep by all means from her,
All secret locks it opens, and all counsels,
That I am sure, and gives men all accesses.
Pray Heaven she be not loving, when she's drunk now;
For drunk she shall be, though my pate pay for it;
She'll turn my stomach then abominably,
She has a most wicked face, and that leud face,
Being a drunken face, what face will there be?
She cannot ravish me. Now if my Master
Should take her so, and know I minister'd,
What will his wisdom do? I hope be drunk too,
And then all's right. Well Lord, to do the service.
Above these Puppit-plays, I keep a life yet.

III. v. 31 SD. *Exit* PEDRO.] *Gifford: after* do? *in* 55 43. the service.] *editor*; the service, 55; thee Service, *Mason*; thee service ^ *Gifford*

Enter SERVANT *with Bottles.*

Here come the executioners: You are welcome,
Give me your load, and tell my Lord, I am at it.
Servant. I will sir, speed you sir. *Exit.*
John. Good speed on all sides.
'Tis monstrous strong Wine: O the yaws that she'll make!
Look to your stern deer Mistress, and steer right,
Here's that will work, as high as the Bay of *Portugal*:
Stay, let me see; I'll try her by the Nose first,
For if she be a right Sowe, sure she'll finde it.

Enter BORACHIA.

She is yonder by her self, the Lady's from her.
Now to begin my sacrifice; she stirs, and vents it.
O how she holds her nose up like a Jennet
I' th' wind of a Grass-mare! She has it full now,
And now she comes. I'll stand aside a while.
R1r *Borachia.* 'Tis wine; I sure 'tis wine! excellent strong wine!
I' th' must I take it: Very wine: this way too.
John. How true she hunts! I'll make the train a little longer.
Borachia. Stronger, and stronger still! still blessed wine!
John. Now she hunts hot.
Borachia. All that I can make for this wine,
This way it went sure.
John. Now she is at a cold scent.
Make out your doubles Mistress. O well hunted,
That's she, that's she.
Borachia. O, if I could but see it!
O what a pretious scent it has! but handle it!
John. Now I'll untappice.
Borachia. What's that? still 'tis stronger.
Why how now sirrah? what's that? answer quickly,
And to the point.
John. 'Tis wine forsooth, good wine,
Excellent Candi-wine.
Borachia. 'Tis well forsooth:
Is this a drink for slaves? Why sawcy sirrah,

44 SD. *Enter . . . Bottles*] *editor*; *after l. 46 in 55*; *after* executioners *in Gifford*
48. monstrous] *McIlwraith*; mon-strong, *55* yaws] *Gifford*; yauns *55*; yawns *Mason* 62. can make] *55*; can *Gifford*

Excellent Candi-wine; draw nearer to me,
Reach me the bottle, Why thou most debauch'd slave—
John. Pray be not angry Mistress, for with all my service
And pains, I purchas'd this for you, I dare not drink it;
For you a present, onely for your pleasure,
To shew in little, what a thanks I owe
The hourly courtesies, your goodness gives me.
Borachia. And I will give thee more; there kiss my hand on't.
John. I thank you deerly for your durty favor,
How ranck it smells! [*Aside.*]
R1v *Borachia.* By thy leave sweet Bottle,
And Sugar-candi-wine, I now come to thee;
Hold your hand under.
John. How does your Worship like it?
Borachia. Under again, again; and now come kiss me,
I'll be a mother to thee, Come, drink to me.
John. I do beseech your pardon.
Borachia. Here's to thee then,
I am easily intreated for thy good,
'Tis naught for thee indeed, 'twill make thee break out;
Thou hast a pure complexion: now for me
'Tis excellent, 'tis excellent for me.
Son slave I have a cold stomach, and the wind—
John. Blows out a cry at your both ends.
Borachia. Kiss again,
Cherish thy Lips, for thou shalt kiss fair Ladies:
Son slave I have them for thee; I'll shew thee all.
John. Heav'n bless mine eyes!
Borachia. Ev'n all the secrets, Son slave,
In my dominion.
John. Oh here come the Ladies,
Now to my business.

Enter ALMIRA *and* LEONORA.

Leonora. This air will much refresh you.
Almira. I must sit down.
Leonora. Do, and take freer thoughts;
The place invites you, and I walk by, like your Sentinel.
Borachia. And thou shalt be my Heir, I'll leave thee all,

73. me the] *Gifford*; in me *55* 81 SD. *Aside.*] *Coxeter*; *not in 55*

Heav'n knows to what 'twill mount to; but abundance:
I'll leave thee two yong Ladies, what think you of that Boy?
R2r Where is the Bottle? Two delicate yong Ladies:
But first you shall commit with me. Do you mark son?
And shew yourself a Gentleman, that's the truth son.
John. Excellent Lady, kissing your fair hand,
And humbly craving pardon for intruding,
This Letter, and this Ring—
Leonora. From whom, I pray you sir?
John. From the most noble, loving Lord, *Don Pedro*,
The servant of your Vertues.
Borachia. And prethee, good son slave, be wise and circumspect,
And take heed of being overtaken with too much drink;
For it is a lamentable sin, and spoils all:
Why 'tis the damnablest thing to be drunk son,
Heav'n cannot endure it. And hark you, one thing
I would have done:
Knock my husband on the head, as soon as may be,
For he is an arrant Puppy, and cannot perform—
Why, where the devil is this foolish Bottle?
Leonora. I much thank you, and this sir for your pains.
John. No, gentle Lady,
That I can do him service, is my merit,
My faith, my full reward.
Leonora. Once more I thank you.
Since I have met so true a friend to goodness,
I dare deliver to your charge, my answer:
Pray you tell him Sir, this night I do invite him
To meet me in the Garden. Means he may finde,
For love, they say, wants no abilities.
John. Nor shall he, Madam, if my help may prosper.
R2v So everlasting Love, and Sweetness, bless ye.
She's at it still, I dare not now appear to her.
Almira. What fellows that?
Leonora. Indeed I know not, Madam,
It seems of some strange Countrey by his habit;
Nor can I shew you by what mystery
He wrought himself into this place, prohibited.
Almira. A handsom man.

107. intruding,] *Coxeter*; ~^ 55

Leonora. But of a minde more handsom.
Almira. Was his business to you?
Leonora. Yes, from a friend
You woot of.
Almira. A very handsom fellow,
And well demean'd.
Leonora. Exceeding well, and speaks well.
Almira. And speaks well too?
Leonora. I passing well, and freely,
And as he promises of a most clear nature,
Brought up sure far above his show.
Almira. It seems so:
I would I had heard him, friend. Comes he again?
Leonora. Indeed I know not if he do.
Almira. 'Tis no matter.
Come let's walk in.
Leonora. I am glad you have found your tongue yet.
[*Exeunt* LEONORA, ALMIRA.]
BORACHIA *sings.*

Enter CUCULO.

Cuculo. My wife is very merry; sure 'twas her voice,
Pray Heav'n there be no drink in't, then I allow it.
John. 'Tis sure my Master, now the game begins;
Here will be spitting of fire a both sides presently,
Send me but safe deliver'd.
Cuculo. O my heart aks!
R3r My head aks too: Mercy o' me she's perish'd!
She has gotten wine! she is gone for ever.
Borachia. Come hither Ladies, carry your bodies swimming;
Do your three duties then, then fall behinde me.
Cuculo. O thou pernitious Raschal! What hast thou done?
John. I done? alas Sir, I have done nothing.
Cuculo. Sirrah,
How came she by this wine?
John. Alas, I know not.
Borachia. Who's that, that talks of wine there?
John. Forsooth, my Master.

137–8. friend / You] *editor*; *undivided 55* 145 SD. *Exeunt . . .* ALMIRA.] *Gifford*; *not in 55* 151. Mercy o' me] *Coxeter*; Mercy, O me *55*

Borachia. Bring him before me, son slave.
Cuculo. I will know it:
This Bottle? how this Bottle?
Borachia. Do not stir it;
For if you do, by this good wine, I'll knock ye,
I'll beat ye damnable, yea, and nay, I'll beat you;
And when I have broke it 'bout your head, do you mark me?
Then will I tie it to your Worship's tail,
And all the dogs i' th' Town shall follow you.
No question, I would avise you, how I came by it.
I will have none of these points handled now.
Cuculo. She'll never be well again, while the world stands.
John. I hope so.
Cuculo. How doest thou Lamb?
Borachia. Well, God-a-mercy,
Bell-wether, how doest thou? Stand out, Son slave,
Sit you here, and before this Worshipful Audience
Propound a doubtful question: See who's drunk now.
Cuculo. Now, now, it works, the devil now dwells in her.
3v *Borachia*. Whether the Heav'n, or the Earth, be neerer the Moon?
Or what's the natural Reason, why a woman longs
To make her husband Cuckold? Bring me your Cousin
The Curate now, that great Philosopher;
He that found out a Pudding had two ends;
That learned Clerk, that notable Gymnosophist,
And let him with his *Jacobs*-Staff discover
What is the third part of Three farthings, three
Half pence, being the half, and I am satisfied.
Cuculo. You see she hath Learning enough, if she could dispose it.
Borachia. Too much for thee, thou Logger-head, thou Bull-head.
Cuculo. Nay good *Borachia*—
Borachia. Thou a sufficient States-man?
A Gentleman of Learning, hang thee Dog-whelp;
Thou shadow of a man of action;
Thou scab o' th' Court, go sleep you drunken Rascal;
Ye debauch'd Puppy, get you home, and sleep sirrah,
And so will I son slave, thou shalt sleep with me.
Cuculo. Prethee look to her tenderly.
Borachia. No words sirrah

169–70. *rearranged by Gifford*; Well . . . thou? / Stand . . . Audience / *55*

Of any wine, or any thing like wine,
Or any thing concerning wine, or by wine,
Or from, or with wine: Come lead me like a Countess.
Cuculo. Thus must we bear, poor men! There is a trick in't,
But when she is well again, I'll trick her for it. *Exeunt.*

R4r
[IV. i]

Act. 4. Scœn. 1.

Enter PEDRO.

Pedro. NOW if this honest fellow do but prosper,
I hope I shall make fair return. I wonder
I hear not from the Prince of *Tarent* yet;
I hope he's landed well, and to his safety,
The winds have stood most gently to his purpose.
My honest friend!

Enter DON JOHN.

John. Your Lordships poorest servant.
Pedro. How hast thou sped?
John. My Lord, as well as wishes;
My way hath reach'd your Mistress, and delivered
Your Letter-love, and Token, who with all joy,
And vertuous constancy, desires to see you,
Commands you this night, by her loving power,
To meet her in the Garden.
Pedro. Thou hast made me,
Redeem'd me, man, again from all my sorrows;
Done above wonder for me. Is it so?
John. I should be now too old to learn to lie sir,
And as I live, I never was good flatterer.
Pedro. I do see some thing in this fellows face still,
R4v That ties my heart fast to him: Let me love thee,
Nay, let me honor thee for this fair service,
And if I ere forget it—
John. Good my Lord,
The onely knowledge of me, is too much bounty.
My service, and my life sir.

IV. i. 3. *Tarent* yet;] *Coxeter* (∼, ∼:); ∼, ∼‸ *55* 9. Letter-love] *55*; Love-letter *Coxeter*

Pedro. I shall think on't;
But how for me to get access?
John. 'Tis easie,
I'll be your guide sir, all my care shall lead you;
My credits better then you think.
Pedro. I thank ye,
And soon I'll wait your promise.
John. With all my duty. *Exeunt.*

ii] *Enter* VICEROY, MESSINA, DOCTOR, *and* CUCULO.

Doctor. All's as I tell you Princes, you shall here
Be witness to his fancies, melancholly,
And strong imagination of his wrongs.
His inhumanity to *Don Anthonio*
Hath rent his minde into so many pieces
Of various imaginations, that
Like the Celestial Bowe, this colour's now
The object, then another, till all vanish.
He says a man might watch to death, or fast,
Or think his spirit out; to all which humors,
I do apply my self, checking the bad,
And cherishing the good. For these, I have
Prepar'd my Instruments, fitting his Chamber
With trap-doors, and descents; sometimes presenting
Good spirits of the air, bad of the earth,
To pull down, or advance his fair intentions.
He's of a noble nature, yet sometimes
5r Thinks that which by confederacie I do,
Is by some skill in Magick. Here he comes.

A bed drawn forth, MARTINO *upon it, a book in's hand.*

Unseen I do beseech you. What do you read Sir?
Martino. A strange position which doth much perplex me:
That every Soul's alike, a musical Instrument,
The Faculties in all men equal Strings,
Well, or ill handled; and thus sweet, or harsh. *Exit* DOCTOR.
How like a Fidler I have plaid on mine then!

IV. ii. 3. his] *Gifford*; the *55* 7. colour's now] *McIlwraith*; colour now *55*; colour now's *Gifford* 20. Unseen] *editor*; Unsent *55* 24. thus] *editor*; those *55*

Declin'd the high pitch of my birth and breeding,
Like the most barbarous Peasant; read my pride
Upon *Anthonio's* meek humility,
Wherein he was far valianter then I.
Meekness, thou wait'st upon couragious spirits,
Enabling sufferance past inflictions:
In patience *Tarent* overcame me more
Then in my wounds. Live then no more to men,
Shut day-light from thine eyes, here cast thee down,
And with a sullen sigh breath forth thy soul.

Enter DOCTOR *like a Frier.*

What art? an Apparition, or a Man?
Doctor. A man, and sent to counsel thee.
Martino. Despair
Has stopt mine ears; thou seem'st a holy Friar?
Doctor. I am, by Doctor *Paulo* sent to tell thee:
Thou art too cruel to thy self in seeking
To lend compassion and aid to others.
My Order bids me comfort thee: I have heard all
Thy various, troubled passions. Hear but my story.
In way of youth I did enjoy one friend,
As good and perfect as Heaven e're made man:
This friend was plighted to a beauteous woman,
(Nature proud of her workmanship) mutual love
R5v Possest 'em both; her heart in his breast lodg'd,
And his in hers.
Martino. No more of love, good father;
It was my surfeit, and I loath it now,
As men in Feavers meat they fell sick on.
Doctor. Howe're 'tis worth your hearing. This betroth'd Lady
(The ties and duties of a friend forgotten)
Spurr'd on by lust, I treacherously pursu'd:
Contemn'd by her, and by my friend reprov'd,
Despis'd by honest men, my conscience sear'd up,
Love I converted into frantick rage;
And by that false guide led, I summon'd him
In this bad cause, his sword 'gainst mine to prove,
If he or I might claim most right in love.
But fortune (that does seld' or never give

Success to right and vertue) made him fall
Under my sword. Blood, blood, a friends dear blood,
A vertuous friends shed by a Villain, me,
In such a monstrous and unequal cause,
Lies on my conscience.

Martino. And durst thou live
After this to be so old? 'tis an illusion
Rais'd up by charms: A man would not have liv'd;
Art quiet in thy bosom?

Doctor. As the sleep
Of Infants.

Martino. My fault did not equal this;
Yet I have emptied my heart of joy,
Only to store sighs up. What were the arts
That made thee live so long in rest?

Doctor. Repentance
Hearty, that cleans'd me; Reason then confirm'd me
I was forgiven, and took me to my Beads. *Exit* DOCTOR.

6r *Martino.* I am i' th' wrong path; tender conscience
Makes me forget mine honor: I have done
No evil like this, yet I pine, whilst he,
A few tears of his true contrition tender'd,
Securely sleeps. Ha, where keeps peace of conscience,
That I may buy her? No where, not in life.
'Tis feign'd that *Jupiter* two Vessels plac'd,
The one with honey fill'd, the other gall,
At th'entry of *Olympus*: Destinie
There brewing these together, suffers not
One man to pass before he drinks this mixture.
Hence is it we have not an hour of life
In which our pleasures relish not some pain,
Our sowrs some sweetness. Love doth taste of both.
Revenge, that thirsty Dropsie of our souls,
Which makes us covet that which hurts us most,
Is not alone sweet, but partakes of tartness.

Messina. Is't not a strange effect?

Viceroy. Past president.

Cuculo. His Brain-pan's perish'd with his wounds: Go to,
I knew 'twould come to this.

68. by charms] *Coxeter*; by my charms *55*

Viceroy. Peace, man of wisdom.
Martino. Pleasure's the hook of evil, ease of care,
And so the general object of the Court:
Yet some delights are lawful. Honor is
Vertue's allow'd ascent: Honor that clasps
All perfect Justice in her arms; that craves
No more respect then what she gives; that does
Nothing but what she'll suffer. This distracts me,
But I have found the right. Had *Don Anthonio*
Done that to me, I did to him, I should have kill'd him;
The injury so foul, and done in publique,
My Footman would not bear it. Then in honor
Wronging him so, I'll right him on my self:
R6v There's honor, justice, and full satisfaction
Equally tender'd; 'tis resolv'd, I'll do't.
They take all weapons from me.
Messina. Bless my son!

Enter DOCTOR (*like a Soldier*) *and the* ENGLISH SLAVE (*like a Courtier.*)

Viceroy. The careful Doctor's come again.
Messina. Rare man!
How shall I pay this debt?
Cuculo. He that is with him,
Is one of the slaves he lately bought, he said
T'accommodate his cure. He's *English* born,
But *French* in his behaviour; a delicate slave.
Viceroy. The slave is very fine.
Cuculo. Your English slaves
Are ever so; I have seen an English slave
Far finer then his master. There's a State-point
Worthy your observation.
Doctor. On thy life
Be perfect in thy lesson. Fewer legs, slave.
Martino. My thoughts are search'd and answer'd; for I did
Desire a Soldier and a Courtier
To yield me satisfaction in some doubts
Not yet concluded of.

110. They] *Coxeter*; *Slave.* They *55* 110 SD. *Enter . . . Courtier.*)] *Gifford*; *after l. 109 in 55*

Doctor. Your Doctor did
Admit us Sir.
English Slave. And we are at your service;
Whate'r it be, command it.
Martino. You appear
A Courtier in the race of Love; how far
In honor are you bound to run?
English Slave. I'll tell you,
You must not spare expence, but wear gay cloaths,
7r And you may be, too, prodigal of oaths
To win a Mistress favor; not afraid
To pass unto her through her Chamber-maid:
You may present her gifts, and of all sorts:
Feast, dance, and revel; they are lawful sports:
The choice of Suiters you must not deny her,
Nor quarrel though you find a Rival by her:
Build on your own deserts, and ever be
A stranger to Loves enemy, Jealousie,
For that draws on—
Martino. No more; this points at me, *Exit* SLAVE.
I ne'r observ'd these rules. Now speak old Soldier,
The height of honor?
Doctor. No man to offend,
Ne'r to reveal the secrets of a friend;
Rather to suffer, then to do a wrong;
To make the heart no stranger to the tongue;
Provok'd, not to betray an Enemy,
Nor eat his meat I choak with flattery;
Blushless to tell wherefore I wear my scars,
Or for my conscience, or my Countries wars;
To aim at just things; if we have wildly run
Into offences, wish 'em all undone.
'Tis poor in grief for a wrong done to die,
Honor to dare to live, and satisfie.
Viceroy. Mark how he winds him.
Messina. Excellent man.
Doctor. Who fights
With passions, and orecomes 'em, is indu'd 154
With the best vertue, passive fortitude. *Exit* DOCTOR.

125–6. service; / Whate'r] *Coxeter*; *undivided* 55

Martino. Thou hast touch'd me Soldier; oh this Honor bears
The right stamp; would all Soldiers did profess
Thy good religion. The discords of my soul
Are tun'd, and make a heavenly harmony: *Musick.*
What sweet peace feel I now! I am ravish'd with it.
R7v *Viceroy*. How still he sits!
Cuculo. Hark, Musique.
Messina. How divinely
This Artist gathers scatter'd sense; with cunning
Composing the fair Jewel of his mind,
Broken in peeces, and nigh lost before.
Viceroy. See *Protean Paulo* in another shape.

Enter DOCTOR, *like a Philosopher*: *A good, an ill Genius presented. Their Song. While it's singing, the* DOCTOR *goes off, and returns in his own shape.*

Doctor. Away, I'll bring him shortly perfect, doubt not.
Messina. Master of thy great Art!
Viceroy. As such we'll hold thee.
Messina. And study honors for him.
Cuculo. I'll be sick
On purpose to take physick of this Doctor. *Exeunt.*
Martino. Doctor, thou hast perfected a Bodies cure
T'amaze the world; and almost cur'd a Mind
Neer phrensie. With delight I now perceive
You for my recreation have invented
The several Objects, which my Melancholy
Sometimes did think you conjur'd, otherwhiles
Imagin'd 'em Chimera's. You have been
My Friar, Soldier, my Philosopher,
My Poet, Architect, my Physitian;
Labor'd for me more then your slaves for you
In their assistance: In your moral Song
Of my good Genius, and my bad, you have won me
A chearful heart, and banish'd discontent;
There being nothing wanting to my wishes,
But once more, were it possible, to behold
Don John Anthonio.
R8r *Doctor*. There shall be Letters sent

165 SD. *Enter . . . shape.*] *editor*; *after l. 164 in 55*

Into all parts of Christendom, to inform him
Of your recovery, which now Sir I doubt not.
Martino. What honors, what rewards can I heap on you?
Doctor. That my endeavours have so well succeeded,
Is a sufficient recompence. Pray you retire Sir,
Not too much air so soon.
Martino. I am obedient. *Exeunt*.

iii] *Enter* ALMIRA *and* LEONORA.

Leonora. How strangely this Fellow runs in her mind!
Almira. Do you hear Cousin?
Leonora. Her sadness clean forsaken!
Almira. A poor slave
Bought for my Governess, say you?
Leonora. I fear so.
Almira. And do you think a *Turk*?
Leonora. His habit shews it,
At least bought for a *Turk*.
Almira. I, that may be so.
Leonora. What if he were one naturally?
Almira. Nay 'tis nothing,
Nothing to the purpose; and yet methinks 'tis strange
Such handsomness of mind and civil outside
Should spring from those rude Countries.
Leonora. If it be no more,
I'll call our Governess, and she can shew you.
Almira. Why, do you think it is?
Leonora. I do not think so.
Almira. Fie! no, no, by no means; and to tell thee truth Wench,
I am truly glad he is here, be what he will;
Let him be still the same he makes a shew of,
For now we shall see something to delight us.
8v *Leonora*. And Heav'n knows, we have need on't.
Almira. Heigh ho! my heart aks.
Prethee call in our Governess. *Exit* LEONORA.
Pox o'this fellow—
Why do I think so much of him? how the devil
Creep'd he in to my head? and yet beshrew me,

IV. iii. 12. Why,] *Gifford*; ~‸ 55

Me thinks I have not seen, I lie, I have seen
A thousand handsomer, a thousand sweeter.
But say this fellow were adorn'd as they are,
Set-off to shew, and glory. What's that to me?
Fie, what a fool am I! what idle fancies
Buz in my brains!

Enter BORACHIA, *and* LEONORA.

Borachia. And how doth my sweet Lady?
Leonora. She wants your company to make her merry.
Borachia. And how does Master Pug, I pray you Madam?
Leonora. Do you mean her little dog?
Borachia. I mean his Worship.
Leonora. Troubled with Fleas a little.
Borachia. Alas poor Chicken!
Leonora. She is here, and drunk, very fine drunk, I take it,
I found her with a Bottle for her Boulster,
Lying along, and making love.
Almira. *Borachia*,
Why, where hast thou been Wench? she looks not well, friend.
Art not with childe?
Borachia. I promise ye, I know not,
I am sure my Bellies full, and that's a shrewd sign:
Besides I am shrewdly troubled with a Tiego
Here in my head, Madam; often with this Tiego,
It takes me very often.
S1[r] *Leonora.* I believe thee.
Almira. You must drink wine.
Borachia. A little would do no harm sure.
Almira. 'Tis a raw humor blows into your head;
Which good, strong wine will temper.
Borachia. I thank your Highness,
I will be rul'd, though much against my nature:
For wine, I ever hated from my Cradle,
Yet for my good—
Leonora. I for your good, by all means.
Almira. *Borachia*, what new fellows that thou hast gotten?
(Now she will sure be free) that handsom stranger?
Borachia. How much wine must I drink, an't please your Ladiship?

28. Pug] *Coxeter*; Bug *55* 35. not with] *Coxeter*; not not with *55*

Almira. She's finely greaz'd. Why two or three round draughts Wench.
Borachia. Fasting?
Almira. At any tıme.
Borachia. I shall hardly do it;
But yet I'll try good Madam.
Leonora. Do, 'twill work well.
Almira. But prethee answer me, what is this fellow?
Borachia. I'll tell you two: But let it go no further.
Leonora. No, no, by no means.
Borachia. May I not drink before bed too?
Leonora. At any hour.
Borachia. And say i' th' night it take me?
Almira. Drink then. But what this man?
Borachia. I'll tell ye Madam,
But pray ye be secret. He's the great Turks son, for certain,
And a fine Christian; my husband bought him for me.
He's circumsing'd.
Leonora. He's circumcis'd, thou wouldst say.
S1v *Almira*. How doest thou know?
Borachia. I had an eye upon him;
But ev'n as sweet a Turk, an't like your Ladiship,
And speaks ye as pure Pagan—I'll assure ye,
My husband had a notable peni-worth of him.
And found me out the Turks own son, his own son
By father and mother, Madam.
Leonora. She's mad drunk.
Almira. Prethee *Borachia* call him, I would see him,
And tell thee how I like him.
Borachia. As fine a Turk, Madam,
For that which appertains to a true Turk—
Almira. Prethee call him.
Borachia. He waits here at the stairs; son slave come hither.

Enter DON JOHN.

Pray ye give me leave a little to instruct him,
He's raw yet in the way of entertainment.
Son slave, where's the other bottle?
John. In the bed-straw,

64. out] *Mason*; but 55

I hid it there.
Borachia. Go up and make your honors.
Madam, the Tiego takes me now, now Madam,
I must needs be unmannerly.
Almira. Pray ye be so.
Leonora. You know your cure.
Borachia. I' th' bed-straw?
John. There you'll finde it.
Exit BORACHIA.
Almira. Come hither sir: How long have you serv'd here?
John. A poor time, Madam, yet, to shew my service.
Almira. I see thou art diligent.
S2r *John.* I would be, Madam,
'Tis all the portion left me, that and truth.
Almira. Thou art but yong?
John. Had Fortune meant me so,
Excellent Lady, Time had not much wronged me.
Almira. Wilt thou serve me?
John. In all my prayers, Madam,
Else such a misery as mine but blasts ye.
Almira. Beshrew my heart he speaks well, wondrous honestly.
Aside.
John. Madam, your loving Lord stays for ye.
Leonora. I thank ye.
Your pardon for an hour deer friend.
Almira. Your pleasure.
Leonora. I deerly thank ye sir.
John. My humblest service.
Exit LEONORA.
She views me narrowly, yet sure she knows me not:
I dare not trust the time yet, nor I must not.
Almira. Ye are not as your habit shews?
John. No Madam,
His hand, that for my sins lies heavy on me,
I hope will keep me from being a slave to the devil.
Almira. A brave cleer minde he has, and nobly season'd.
What Country are ye of?
John. A Biscan, Lady.
Almira. No doubt, a Gentleman.

89 SD. *Exit* LEONORA.] *editor*; *opposite* sir *in 55*

John. My father thought so.
Almira. I, and I warrant thee a right fair woman
Thy mother was; he blushes, that confirms it.
Upon my soul, I have not seen such sweetness.
I prethee blush again.
John. 'Tis a weakness, Madam,
S2ᵛ I am easily this way woo'd to.
Almira. I thank ye;
Of all that ere I saw, thou art the perfittest. *Aside.*
Now you must tell me sir, for now I long for't—
John. What would she have?
Almira. The story of your fortune;
The hard, and cruel fortune brought you hither.
John. That makes me stagger; yet I hope I am hid still; *Aside.*
That I came hither, Madam, was the fairest.
Almira. But how this misery ye bear, fell on ye?
John. Infandum regina jubes renovare dolorem.
Almira. Come, I will have it; I command ye tell it,
For such a speaker I would hear for ever.
John. Sure, Madam, 'twil but make you sad and heavy,
Because I know your goodness full of pity,
And 'tis so poor a subject too, and to your ears,
That are acquainted with things, sweet and easie,
So harsh a harmony.
Almira. I prethee speak it.
John. I ever knew Obedience the best Sacrifice,
Honor of Ladies, then first passing over
Some few years of my youth, that are impertinent,
Let me begin the sadness of my story,
Where I began to loose my self, to love first.
Almira. 'Tis well, go forward. Some rare peece I look for.
John. Not far from where my Father lives, a Lady,
A neighbor by, blest with as great a beauty,
As nature durst bestow without undoing,
Dwelt, and most happily, as I thought then,
And blest the house a thousand times she dwelt in.
S3ʳ This beauty in the blossom of my youth,
When my first fire knew no adulterate Incense,
Nor I no way to flatter, but my fondness,

102. to] *Mason*; too 55

In all the bravery, my friends could shew me,
In all the faith my innocence could give me,
In the best language my true Tongue could tell me,
And all the broken sighs my sick heart lend me,
I su'd, and serv'd. Long did I love this Lady,
Long was my travel, long my trade to win her,
With all the duty of my Soul, I serv'd her.
Almira. How feelingly he speaks! and she lov'd you too;
It must be so.
John. I would it had deer Lady,
This story had been needless, and this place
I think unknown to me.
Almira. Were your bloods equal?
John. Yes, and I thought our hearts too.
Almira. Then she must love.
John. She did, but never me, she could not love me,
She would not love, she hated, more she scorn'd me,
And in so poor, and base a way abus'd me;
For all my services, for all my bounties,
So bold neglects flung on me.
Almira. An ill woman!
Be-like you found some Rival in your love then?
John. How perfectly she points me to my story. *Aside.*
Madam, I did, and one whose pride, and anger,
(Ill manners, and worse man) she doted on;
Doted to my undoing, and my ruine;
S3v And but for honor to your sacred beauty,
And reverence to the noble Sex, though she fall,
As she must fall, that durst be so unnoble,
I should say something unbeseeming me.
What out of love, and worthy love, I gave her
(Shame to her most unworthy minde) to fools,
To girls, and fidlers, to her boys she flung,
And in disdain of me.
Almira. Pray ye take me with ye.
Of what complexion was she?
John. But that I dare not
Commit so great a sacriledge 'gainst vertue,

152. (Ill . . . man)] *editor*; ‸~ . . . ~‸ *55* man] *55*; Mien *Coxeter*

She look'd not much unlike—though far, far short.
Some thing I see appears, your pardon, Madam,
Her eyes would smile so, but her eyes would cousin,
And so she would look sad, but yours is pity,
A noble *Chorus* to my wretched story,
Hers was disdain and cruelty.
Almira. Pray Heaven
Mine be no worse: he has told me a strange story, *Aside.*
And said 'twould make me sad! he is no lier.
But where begins this poor state? I will have all,
For it concerns me truly.
John. Last to blot me
From all remembrance, what I have been to her,
And how, how honestly, how nobly serv'd her,
'Twas thought she set her gallant to dispatch me.
'Tis true, he quarrell'd, without place, or reason.
We fought, I kill'd him, Heav'ns strong hand was with me;
For which I lost my Countrey, Friends, acquaintance,
And put my self to Sea, where a Pirate took me,
Forcing this habit of a Turk upon me,
And sold me here.
$S4^{r}$ *Almira.* Stop there a while, but stay still.
In this mans story, how I look! how monstrous!
How poor and naked now I shew! what *Don John*
In all the vertue of his life, but aim'd at,
This thing hath conquer'd with a tale, and carried.
Forgive me thou that guid'st me! Never Conscience
Touch'd me till now, nor true love: Let me keep it.

Enter PEDRO *and* LEONORA.

Leonora. She is there, speak to her, you will finde her altered.
Pedro. Sister, I am glad to see you, but far gladder,
To see you entertain your health so well.
Almira. I am glad to see you too sir, and shall be gladder
Shortly to see you all.
Pedro. Now she speaks heartily,
What do ye want?

164. unlike—] *Gifford*; unlikely *55*; unlike you *Coxeter*; unlike ye *McIlwraith* 184. naked now I shew!] *Mason*; naked? now I shew‸ *55* 188 SD. *Enter* ... LEONORA] *Coxeter*; *after line 189 in 55*

Almira. Onely an hour of privateness,
I have a few thoughts.
Pedro. Take your full contentment,
We'll walk aside again; but first to you friend,
Or I shall much forget my self. My best friend,
Command me ever, ever, you have won it.
John. Your Lordship overflows me.
Leonora. 'Tis but due sir. *Exeunt.*
Almira. He's there still. Come sir, to your last part now,
Which onely is your name, and I dismiss you.
Why, whether go ye?
John. Give me leave, good Madam,
Or I must be so seeming rude to take it.
Almira. You shall not go, I swear, you shall not go:
I ask ye nothing but your name, ye have one,
S4v And why should that thus fright you?
John. Gentle Madam,
I cannot speak; pray pardon me, a sickness
That takes me often, ties my tongue: Go from me,
My fit's infectious, Lady.
Almira. Were it death
In all his horrors, I must ask, and know it.
Your sickness is unwillingness. Hard heart,
To let a Lady of my youth and place
Beg thus long for a trifle.
John. Worthiest Lady,
Be wise and let me go; you'll bless me for't,
Beg not that poison from me that will kill ye.
Almira. I only beg your name sir.
John. That will choak you,
I do beseech you pardon me.
Almira. I will not.
John. You'll curse me when you hear it.
Almira. Rather kiss thee,
Why shouldst thou think so?
John. Why, I bear that name,
And most unluckily, as now it happens,
(Though I be innocent of all occasion)
That since my coming hither people tell me
You hate beyond forgiveness. Now heaven knows,

So much respect, (although I am a stranger)
Duty, and humble zeal I bear your sweetness,
That for the world I would not grieve your goodness:
I'll change my name, dear Madam.
Almira. People lye,
And wrong thy name; thy name may save all others,
And make that holy to me, that I hated:
Prethee what is't?
John. *Don John Anthonio.*
What will this woman do? what thousand changes [*Aside.*]
S5r Run through her heart and hands? no fixt thought in her;
She loves for certain now, but now I dare not,
Heav'n guide me right.
Almira. I am not angry, Sir,
With you, nor with your name; I love it rather,
And shall respect ye, ye deserve. For this time
I licence you to go; be not far from me,
I shall call for you often.
John. I shall wait, Madam. *Exit* JOHN.

Enter CUCULO.

Almira. Now what's the news with you?
Cuculo. My Lord your father
Sent me to tell your Honor, Prince *Martino*
Is well recover'd, and in strength.
Almira. Why let him.
The stories and the names so well agreeing, *Aside.*
And both so noble Gentlemen.
Cuculo. And more, an't please you.
Almira. It doth not please me neither more nor less on't.
Cuculo. They'll come to visit you.
Almira. They shall break through the dores then.
Exit ALMIRA.

Cuculo. Here's a new trick of State; this shews foul weather;
But let her make it when she please, I'll gain by it. *Exit.*

227–8. *rearranged by Coxeter*; People . . . others, 55 231 SD. *Aside.*] *Coxeter*; *not in* 55

S5v
[V. i]

Act. 5. Scæn. 1.

Enter SEA-PIRATE, *one* SLAVE, *and* SAILORS.

Pirate. SOLD for a slave, saist thou?
Slave. 'Twas not so well:
Though I am bad enough, I personated
Such base behavior, barbarism of manners,
With other pranks, that might deter the buyer;
That the market yeelded not one man that would
Vouchsafe to own me.
Pirate. What was thy end in't?
Slave. To be giv'n away for nothing, as I was
To the Vice-roys Doctor; with him I have continued
In such contempt, a slave unto his slaves;
His horse, and dog of more esteem; and from
That villainous carriage of my self, as if
I had been a lump of flesh, without a soul,
I drew such scorn upon me, that I pass'd,
And pried in every place without observance.
For which, if you desire to be made men,
And by one undertaking, and that easie,
Ye are bound to Sacrifice unto my suffrings,
The seed I sow'd, and from which you shall reap
A plentiful harvest.
Pirate. To the point, I like not
These castles built in the air.
Slave. I'll make 'em real,
And you the Neptunes of the Sea, you shall
No more be Sea-rats.
S6r *Pirate.* Art not mad?
Slave. Ye have seen
The star of *Sicilie*, the fair *Almira*,
The Vice-roys daughter, and the beauteous Ward
Of the Duke of *Messina*?
Pirate. Madam *Leonora*.
Slave. What will you say, if both these Princesses
This very night, for I will not delay you,
Be put in your possession?

V. i. 14. pried] *Coxeter* (pry'd); pride *55*

Pirate. Now I dare swear
Thou hast Magots in thy brains, thou wouldst not else
Talk of impossibilities.
Slave. Be still
Incredulous.
Pirate. Why canst thou think we are able
To force the Court?
Slave. Are we able to force two women,
And a poor Turkish slave? Where lies your Pinnace?
Pirate. In a Creek not half a league hence.
Slave. Can you fetch Ladders
To mount a Garden wall?
1. *Sailor.* They shall be ready.
Slave. No more words then, but follow me, and if
I do not make this good, let my throat pay for't.
Pirate. What heaps of Gold, these beauties would bring to us
From the great Turk, if it were possible
That this could be effected.
Slave. If it be not
I know the price on't.
Pirate. And be sure to pay it. *Exeunt.*

ii] *Enter* DON JOHN *with a Letter in his hand.*

John. Her fair hand threw this from the window to me,
And as I took it up, she said, Peruse it,
S6v And entertain a fortune offer'd to thee.
What may the inside speak?— *Breaks it open, and reads.*
For satisfaction
Of the contempt I shew'd *Don John Anthonio*,
Whose name thou bear'st, and in that dearer to me,
I do profess I love thee. (How! 'tis so,)
I love thee, this night wait me i' th' Garden,
There thou shalt know more,
subscrib'd Thy *Almira*—
Can it be possible such levitie
Should wait on her perfections? when I was
My self, set off with all the grace of greatness,

V. ii. 5. Of] *Mason*; If 55 12. with all] *Coxeter*; withal 55

Pomp, bravery, circumstance, she hated me,
And did profess it openly; yet now
Being a slave, a thing she should in reason
Disdain to look upon, in this base shape,
And since I wore it, never did her service,
To dote thus fondly? And yet I should glory
In her revolt from constancy, not accuse it,
Since it makes for me. But ere I go further,
Or make discovery of my self, I'll put her
To th'utmost tryal, i' th' Garden: Well,
There I shall learn more. Women! Giddy women,
In her the blemish of your sex, you prove;
There is no reason for your hate or love. *Exit.*

[V. iii] *Enter* ALMIRA, LEONORA, *and two* WOMEN.

Leonora. At this unseasonable time to be thus brave,
No visitants expected? you amaze me.
Almira. Are these Jewels set forth to the best advantage
To take the eye?
1. *Woman.* With our best care.
2. *Woman.* We never
Better discharg'd our duties.
S7r *Almira.* In my sorrows,
A Princess name (I could perceive it) strook
A kinde of reverence in him, and my beauty
As then neglected, forc'd him to look on me
With some sparks of affection; but now
When I would fan them to a glorious flame,
I cannot be too curious. I wonder
He stays so long.
Leonora. These are strange fancies.
Almira. Go
Intreat, I do forget my self, command
My Governess' Gentleman, her Slave, I should say,
To wait me instantly; and yet already *Exit* WOMAN.
He's here. His figure graven on my heart,
Never to be raz'd out.

V. iii. 5. discharg'd] *Coxeter*; discharge *55*

Enter SLAVE, PIRATE, *and* SAILORS.

Slave. There is the prize,
Is it so rich, that you dare not seise upon it?
Here I begin.
Almira. Help! Villain!
Pirate. You are mine.
Sailor. Though somewhat course, you'll serve after a storm,
To bid fair wether welcome.
Leonora. Ravisher,
Defend me Heaven.
Almira. No aid neer?
Woman. Help!
Slave. Dispatch.
No glove, nor handkercher to stop their mouths?
Their cries will reach the guard, and then we are lost.

S7v *Enter* DON JOHN *and* WOMAN.

John. What shrieks are these? from whence? O blessed Saints!
What sacrilege to beauty? Do I talk,
When 'tis almost too late to do. Take that. *Forces a sword.*
Slave. All set upon him.
Pirate. Kill him.
John. You shall buy
My life at a dear rate, you Rogues.

Enter PEDRO, CUCULO, BORACHIA, *and Guard.*

Cuculo. Down with 'em.
Pedro. Unheard of treason!
Borachia. Make in Loggerhead;
My son Slave fights like a dragon: Take my bottle,
Drink courage out on't.
John. Madam, you are free.
Pedro. Take comfort, dearest Mistress.
Cuculo. O you Micher,
Have you a hand in this?
Slave. My aims were high,
Fortune's my enemy: To dy's the worst,
And that I look for.
Pirate. Vengeance on your plots.

23. glove] *Coxeter*; glory *55*

Pedro. The rack at better leisure shall force from 'em
A full discovery: Away with 'em.
Cuculo. Load 'em with irons.
Borachia. Let 'em have no wine
To comfort their cold hearts.
The Guard take the PIRATE *and the rest.*
Pedro. Thou man of men.
Leonora. A second *Hercules*.
Almira. An Angel thus disguis'd.
Pedro. What thanks?
S8r *Leonora*. What service?
Borachia. He shall serve me by your leave, no service else.
John. I have done nothing but my duty, Madam;
And if the little you have seen exceed it,
The thank due for it pay my watchful Master,
And this my sober Mistress.
Borachia. He speaks truth, Madam,
I am very sober.
Pedro. Far beyond thy hopes
Expect reward.
Almira. We'll straight to Court, and there
It is resolv'd what I will say and do.
I am faint, support me.
Pedro. This strange accident
Will be heard with astonishment. Come friend,
You have made your self a fortune, and deserve it. *Exeunt.*

[V. iv] *Enter* VICEROY, MESSINA, DOCTOR.

Messina. Perfectly cur'd?
Doctor. As such I will present him,
The thanks be given to Heaven.
Messina. Thrice reverend man,
What thanks but will come short of thy desert?
Or bounty, though all we possess were given thee,
Can pay thy merit? I will have thy Statue
Set up in Brass.
Viceroy. Thy name made the sweet subject
Of our best Poems; thy unequall'd Cures

40. hearts] *Coxeter*; heart *55* 46. thank] *55*; thanks *Coxeter*

Recorded to posterity.
Doctor. Such false glories
(Though the desire of fame be the last weakness
Wise men put off) are not the marks I shoot at:
But if I have done any thing that may challenge
S8v Your favors (mighty Princes) my request is,
That for the good of such as shall succeed me,
A Colledge for Physitians may be
With care and cost erected, in which no man
May be admitted to a Fellowship,
But such as by their vigilant studies shall
Deserve a place there; this magnificence,
Posterity shall thank you for.
Viceroy. Rest assur'd
In this, or any boon you please to ask,
You shall have no repulse.
Doctor. My humblest service
Shall ne'r be wanting. Now if you so please,
I'll fetch my Princely Patient, and present him.
Messina. Do, and imagine in what I may serve you,
And by my honor with a willing hand
I will subscribe to't. *Exit* DOCTOR.

Enter PEDRO, ALMIRA, LEONORA, DON JOHN, CUCULO, BORACHIA [, *and Guard*].

Cuculo. Make way there!
Viceroy. My daughter!
How's this? a Slave crown'd with a Civick garland!
The mysterie of this?
Pedro. It will deserve
Your hearing and attention. Such a truth
Needs not rhetorical flourishes, and therefore
With all the brevity and plainness that
I can, I will deliver it. If the old *Romans*,
When of most power and wisdom, did decree
A Wreath like this to any common Soldier
That sav'd a Citizens life, the bravery
And valor of this man may justly challenge
Triumphant Laurel. This last night a crew

V. iv. 26 SD. *Exit* DOCTOR.] *Coxeter*; *after l. 23 in 55* *and Guard*] *Gifford*; *not in 55*

T1r Of Pirates brake in Signior *Cuculo's* house,
With violent rudeness, ceasing on my sister,
And my fair Mistress, both were in their power,
And ready to be forc'd hence; when this man
Unarm'd, came to their rescue, but his courage
Soon furnish'd him with weapons: In a word,
The lives and liberties of these sweet Ladies,
You ow him, for the Rovers are in hold,
And ready when you please, for punishment.
Viceroy. As an induction of more to come,
Receive this favor.
Messina. With my self, my son
Shall pay his real thanks. He comes, observe now
Their amorous meeting.

Enter DOCTOR, *and* MARTINO.

Martino. I am glad you are well Lady.
Almira. I grieve not your recovery.
Viceroy. So coldly?
Messina. Why fall you off?
Martino. To shun captivity sir;
I was too long a slave, I'll now be free.
Almira. 'Tis my desire you should. Sir my affection
To him was but a trifle, which I play'd with
I' th' childhood of my love; which now grown elder,
I cannot like of.
Viceroy. Strange inconstancy!
Martino. 'Tis judgement sir in me, or a true debt
Tender'd to Justice rather. My first life
Loaden with all the follies of a man,
Or what could take addition from a woman,
Was by my head-strong passions (which o'errul'd
My understanding) forfeited to death:
T1v But this new being, this my second life,
Begun in serious contemplation of
What best becomes a perfect man, shall never
Sink under such weak frailties.
Messina. Most unlook'd for.
Doctor. It does transcend all wonders.

45. ow him, for] *55*; owe him for; *Mason*

Martino. 'Tis a blessing
I owe your wisdom, which I'll not abuse:
But if you envy your own gift, and will
Make me that wretched creature which I was,
You then again shall see me passionate,
A lover of poor trifles, confident
In mans deceiving strength, or falser fortune,
Jealous, revengeful, in unjust things daring,
Injurious, quarrelsom, stor'd with all diseases
The beastly part of man infects his soul with;
And to remember what's the worst, once more
To love a woman, but till that time never. *Exit.*
Viceroy. Stand you affected so to men, *Almira*?
Almira. No Sir; if so, I could not well discharge
What I stand bound to pay you, and to nature.
Though Prince *Martino* does profess a hate
To womankind, 'twere a poor world for women
Were there no other choice, or all should follow
The example of this new *Hippolitus*:
There are men, Sir, that can love, and have lov'd truly;
Nor am I desperate but I may deserve
One that both can and will so.
Viceroy. My allowance
Shall rank with your good liking, still provided
Your choice be worthy.
Almira. In it I have us'd
The judgment of my mind, and that made clearer
With calling oft to heaven it might be so.
I have not sought a living comfort from
T2r The reverend ashes of old Ancestors;
Nor given my self to the meer name and titles
Of such a man, that being himself nothing,
Derives his substance from his Grandsires tomb:
For wealth, it is beneath my birth to think on't,
Since that must wait upon me, being your daughter.
No Sir, the man I love, though he wants all
The setting forth of fortune, gloss, and greatness,
Has in himself such true and real goodness,
His parts so far above his low condition,
That he will prove an ornament, not a blemish,

Both to your name and family.
Pedro. What strange creature
Hath she found out?
Leonora. I dare not ghess.
Almira. To hold you
No longer in suspence, this matchless man
That sav'd my life and honor, is my husband,
Whom I will serve with duty.
Borachia. My son Slave!
Viceroy. Have you your wits?
Borachia. I'll not part with him so.
Cuculo. This I foresaw too.
Viceroy. Do not jest thy self
Into the danger of a Fathers anger.
Almira. Jest, Sir? by all my hope of comfort in him
I am most serious. Good Sir look upon him,
But let it be with my eyes, and the care
You should owe to your daughters life and safety,
Of which without him she's uncapable,
And you'll approve him worthy.
Viceroy. O thou shame
Of women! thy sad Fathers curse, and scandal:
With what an impious violence thou tak'st from him
His few short hours of breathing!
T2v *Doctor.* Do not add, Sir,
Weight to your sorrow in th'ill bearing of it.
Viceroy. From whom, degenerate Monster, flow these low
And base affections in thee? what strange philters
Hast thou receiv'd? what Witch with damned spels
Depriv'd thee of thy reason? Look on me,
(Since thou art lost unto thy self) and learn
From what I suffer for thee, what strange tortures
Thou do'st prepare thy self.
Messina. Good Sir, take comfort;
The councel you bestow'd on me, make use of.
Doctor. This Villain, (for such practises in that Nation
Are very frequent) it may be hath forc'd
By cunning potions and by sorcerous charms
This phrensie in her.
Viceroy. Sever 'em.

Almira. I grow to him.
Viceroy. Carry the Slave to torture, and wrest from him
By the most cruel means, a free confession
Of his impostures.
Almira. I will follow him,
And with him take the Rack.
Borachia. No, hear me speak,
I can speak wisely: Hurt not my son slave,
But rack or hang my husband, and I care not;
For I'll be bound body to body with him:
He's very honest, that's his fault.
Viceroy. Take hence
This drunken beast.
Borachia. Drunk! am I drunk? Bear witness.
Cuculo. She is indeed distemper'd.
Viceroy. Hang 'em both,
If ere more they come near the Court.
T3[r] *Cuculo.* Good sir,
You can recover dead men; can you cure
A living drunkenness?
Doctor. 'Tis the harder task:
Go home with her, I'll send you something that
Shall once again bring her to better temper,
Or make her sleep for ever.
Cuculo. Which you please, sir.
Exeunt CUCULO, BORACHIA.
Viceroy. Why linger you? rack him first, and after break him
Upon the wheel.
Pedro. Sir, this is more then justice.
John. Is't death in *Sicily*, to be lov'd
Of a fair Lady?
Leonora. Though he be a slave,
Remember yet he is a man.
Viceroy. I am deaf
To all perswasions: Drag him hence.
The Guard take DON JOHN *off.*
Almira. Do Tyrant,
No more a Father; feast thy cruelty
Upon thy Daughter: but Hell's plagues fall on me,

154. be lov'd] *55*; be belov'd *Gifford*

If I inflict not on my self whatever
He can endure for me.
Viceroy. Will none restrain her?
Almira. Death hath a thousand dores to let out life,
I shall find one. If *Portia*'s burning coals,
The Knife of *Lucrece*, *Cleopatra*'s Aspicks,
Famine, deep waters have the power to free me
From a loath'd life, I'll not an hour outlive him.
Pedro. Sister.
Leonora. Dear Cousin.
Exeunt ALMIRA, PEDRO, LEONORA.
Viceroy. Let her perish.
Doctor. Hear me;
Th'effects of violent love are desperate:
And therefore in the execution of
T3^{v} The Slave be not too sudden. I was present
When he was bought, and at that time my self
Made purchase of another. He that sold 'em
Said that they were companions of one Country.
Something may rise from this to ease your sorrows:
By circumstance I'll learn what's his condition,
I' th' mean time use all fair and gentle means
To pacifie the Lady.
Viceroy. I'll endeavour
As far as grief and anger will give leave,
To do as you direct me.
Messina. I'll assist you. *Exeunt*.

[V. v] *Enter* PEDRO *and* KEEPER.

Pedro. Hath he been visited already?
Keeper. Yes sir,
Like one of better fortune; and t'increase
My wonder of it, such as repair to him,
In their behavior rather appear
Servants, then friends to comfort him.
Pedro. Go fetch him. *Exit* KEEPER.
I am bound in gratitude to do more then wish
The life and safety of a man that hath
So well deserv'd me.

Enter KEEPER, DON JOHN, *Servant.*

Keeper. Here he is, my Lord.
Pedro. Who's here? thou art no Conjurer to raise
A spirit in the best shape man ere appear'd in.
My friend, the Prince of *Tarent*! doubts forsake me,
I must and will embrace him.
John. *Pedro* holds
One that loves life for nothing, but to live
To do him service.
T4r *Pedro.* You are he most certain,
Heaven ever make me thankful for this bounty:
Run to the Viceroy, let him know this rarity. *Exit* KEEPER.
But how you came here thus? yet since I have you,
Is't not enough I bless the prosperous means
That brought you hither?
John. Dear friend, you shall know all;
And though in thankfulness I should begin
Where you deliver'd me—
Pedro. Pray you pass that over,
That's not worth the relation.
John. You confirm
True friends love to do courtesies, not to hear 'em.
But I'll obey you. In our tedious passage
Towards *Malta*, I may call it so, for hardly
We had lost the ken of *Sicily*, but we were
Becalm'd, and hull'd so up and down twelve hours,
When to our more misfortune we descri'd
Eight well mann'd Gallies making amain for us,
Of which th'Arch Turkish Pyrate cruel *Dragut*
Was Admiral. I'll not speak what I did
In our defence; but never man did more
Then the brave Captain that you sent forth with me.
All would not do; Courage opprest with number,
We were boarded, pillag'd to the skin, and after
Twice sold for slaves; by the Pyrate first, and after
By a *Maltese* to Signior *Cuculo*:
Which I repent not, since there 'twas my fortune
To be to you my best friend some ways useful.
I thought to cheer you up with this short story,

But you grow sad on't.
Pedro. Have I not just cause,
When I consider I could be so stupid
As not to see a friend through all disguises;
Or he so far to question my true love,
To keep himself conceal'd?
T4v *John.* 'Twas fit to do so,
And not to grieve you with the knowledge of
What then I was; where now I appear to you,
Your sister loving me, and *Martino* safe,
Like to my self and birth.
Pedro. May you live long so.
How dost thou honest friend? your trustiest servant.
Give me thy hand. I now can ghess by whom
You are thus furnish'd.
John. Troth he met with me
As I was sent to prison, and there brought me
Such things as I had use of.
Pedro. Let's to Court,
My father never saw a man so welcome,
As you'll be to him.
John. May it prove so friend. *Exeunt.*

[V. vi] *Enter* VICEROY, MESSINA, MARTINO, DOCTOR, CAPTAIN, ALMIRA, LEONORA, *Waiting Women*, *Attendants.*

Viceroy. The slave chang'd to the Prince of *Tarent*, says he?
Captain. Yes sir, and I the Captain of the Fort,
Worthy of your displeasure, and th'effect of't,
For my deceiving of that trust your Excellency
Repos'd in me.
Doctor. Yet since all hath faln out
Beyond your hopes, let me become a suiter,
And a prevailing one, to get his pardon.
Almira. O dearest *Leonora*, with what forehead
Dare I look on him now? Too powerful love,
The best strength of thy unconfined Empire
Lies in weak womens hearts. Thou art fain'd blinde,
And yet we borrow our best sight from thee.
Could it be else, the person still the same,

Affection over me such power should have,
T5r To make me scorn a Prince, and love a slave?
Martino. But art thou sure 'tis he?
Captain. Most certain sir.
Martino. Is he in health, strong, vigorous, and as able
As when he left me dead?
Captain. Your own eyes sir
Shall make good my report.
Martino. I am glad of it,
And take you comfort in it sir, there's hope,
Fair hope left for me, to repair mine honor.
Messina. What's that?
Martino. I will do something that shall speak me
Messina's son.
Messina. I like not this. One word sir.
Viceroy. We'll prevent it.
Nay, look up my *Almira*, now I approve
Thy happy choice. I have forgot my anger,
I freely do forgive thee.
Almira. May I finde
Such easiness in the wrong'd Prince of *Tarent*,
I then were happy.
Leonora. Rest assur'd you shall.

Enter DON JOHN, PEDRO, *Servant*.

Viceroy. We all with open arms hast to embrace you.
Messina. Welcome, most welcome.
Martino. Stay.
Messina. 'Twas this I fear'd.
Martino. Sir, 'tis best known to you, on what strict terms
The reputation of mens fame, and honors
Depend in this so punctual age, in which,
A word that may receive a harsh construction,
Is answer'd, and defended by the sword.
T5v And you that know so much, will I presume,
Be sensibly tender of anothers credit,
As you would guard your own.
John. I were unjust else.
Martino. I have received from your hands, wounds, and deep ones,

V. vi. 23. this. One] *after Gifford*; this one *55*

My honor in the general report
Tainted and soil'd, for which I will demand
This satisfaction, That you would forgive
My contumelious words, and blow, my rash
And unadvised wildness first threw on you.
Thus I would teach the world a better way,
For the recovery of a wounded honor,
Then with a savage fury, not true courage,
Still to run headlong on.
John. Can this be serious?
Martino. I'll adde this, He that does wrong, not alone
Draws, but makes sharp his enemies sword against
His own life, and his honor. I have paid for't,
And wish that they, who dare most, would learn from me,
Not to maintain a wrong, but to repent it.
Doctor. Why this is like your self.
Martino. For farther proof,
Here sir, with all my interest, I give up
This Lady to you.
Viceroy. Which I make more strong,
With my free grant.
Almira. I bring mine own consent,
Which will not weaken it.
All. All joy confirm it.
John. Your unexpected courtesies amaze me,
Which I will study with all love and service
To appear worthy of.
Doctor. Pray you understand Sir,
T6r There are a pair of Suiters more, that gladly
Would hear from you as much, as the pleas'd Viceroy
Hath said unto the Prince of *Tarent.*
Messina. Take her,
Her dowry shall be answerable to
Her birth, and your desert.
Pedro. You make both happy.
John. One onely suit remains, That you would please
To take again into your Highness favor
This honest Captain: Let him have your grace.
What's due to his much merit, shall from me
Meet liberal rewards.

Viceroy. Have your desire.
John. Now may all here that love, as they are friends
To our good fortunes, find like prosperous ends. *Exeunt.*

6v

EPILOGUE.

Custom, and that a Law we must obey,
I' th' way of Epilogue, bids me something say.
Howe'r to little purpose, since we know,
If you are pleas'd, unbeg'd, you will bestow
A gentle censure: On the other side,
If that this Play deserve to be decri'd
In your opinions, all that I can say,
Will never turn the stream the other way.
Your gratious smiles, will render us secure.
Your frowns without despair, we must endure.

FINIS

THE BASHFUL LOVER

INTRODUCTION

(a) *Date*

The Epilogue of *The Bashful Lover* refers to Massinger as '*A strange old Fellow*' (l. 9), and this indication that the play was written late in his career is borne out by Malone's note of Herbert's licence: '*The Bashful Lover*, by Philip Massinger, licensed for the King's Company'.[1] The licence is dated 9 May 1636; the dramatist was then 53, an elderly man by the standards of the time.

One of the very few topical allusions in the play establishes that *The Bashful Lover* was written after 1634. At IV. iii. 16–24, Uberti remarks:

> I have read
> Some piece of story, yet ne'r found but that
> The General that gave way to cruelty,
> The profanation of things sacred, rapes
> Of virgins, butchery of infants, and
> The massacre in cold blood of reverend age,
> Against the discipline and law of Arms,
> Did feel the hand of heaven lie heavy on him,
> When most secure: We have had a late example . . .

What is said here does not refer to anything in the plot of the play itself, but Gifford pointed out in his 1813 edition of Massinger that the passage constitutes a clear allusion to the assassination of Albertus Wallenstein, Duke of Friedland, on 25 February 1634. News of the death of the great Imperial general reached England by mid March.[2]

Although he behaved no more savagely than many other leaders in a barbaric war, Wallenstein was associated in the popular mind

[1] Adams, *Herbert*, p. 37.

[2] *C.S.P. Venetian* (*1632–1636*), p. 206. A pamphlet entitled *The Relation of the Death of that Great Generalissimo* (*of His Imperial Maiestie*) *the Duke of Micklenburg, Fridland, Sagan and Great Glogaw*, was entered in the Stationers' Register on 22 Mar. 1634, and several accounts of Wallenstein's death were printed in *The History of the present Warres of Germany. A Sixt Part* [*The Swedish Intelligencer*], 1634, pp. 134–60.

with atrocities committed against the German Protestants,[1] and his sudden death caused a sensation. Gifford was able to illustrate his reputation for war crimes from Alexander Gill's Latin poem 'In cædem Alberti Wallenstenii, ducis Fridlandiæ. 1634', prefaced to Glapthorne's play *The Tragedy of Albertus Wallenstein*, which may have been performed not long before the composition of *The Bashful Lover*, in 1634 or 1635.[2]

It is fairly certain, then, that Massinger's play was written not long before the licensing date of May, 1636.

(b) *Sources*

The plot of *The Bashful Lover* consists of two interlaced narratives. The first is basically the story, familiar in courtly literature, of a woman's difficult choice between the claims of rival lovers; in Gonzaga's words, 'you may at leisure prove / Whose plea will prosper in the Court of Love' (IV. iii. 176–7). There are three princely suitors—the martial Lorenzo, the humble servant Galeazzo, and the noble friend Uberti—and each of them demonstrates his prowess as a warrior and his generous and noble nature in matters of love. At the close of the play, Matilda must decide between the rivals, who compete in acts of renunciation; and before she can be united with her chosen lover, the obstacle of Galeazzo's apparent low birth must be overcome by the familiar discovery that he is a prince in disguise.

The second narrative is a variation on the even commoner story of the woman who disguises herself as a boy, to follow and serve her lover—compounded with the motif of a father's discovery of his long-lost daughter.

In short, as Alfred Harbage points out, 'in all ways the play is a compendium of ultra-romantic themes'; nor is the establishment of a literary source or sources made easier by the fact that (in Harbage's words) 'so close is the resemblance among all the romances and all the plays [of this kind] that it is dangerous to assert that any particular romance is the source of any particular play'.[3]

[1] In 1633, for instance, the Venetian ambassador received a report that 'the mark of Brandenburg . . . has been all but totally devastated by Volestain', *C.S.P. Venetian* (*1632–1636*), p. 175; see also C. V. Wedgwood, *The Thirty Years War*, 1938, pp. 255–7, and F. Watson's biography of Wallenstein, *Soldier Under Saturn*, 1938.

[2] See Bentley, iv. 477–9.

[3] *Cavalier Drama*, New York and London, 1936, pp. 161 and 30.

However, there is one prose narrative which, if it was not Massinger's immediate source, at least provides an analogue to the story of Matilda and her suitors. This is the tale of Queen Erona, in Sidney's *Arcadia* (1590), Book two, chapter thirteen.[1]

The story runs as follows. The King of Lycia had a beautiful daughter, Erona, who fell in love with Antiphilus, 'a yong man but of mean parentage, in her fathers court.'[2] Her father tried to force her to marry Tiridates, the King of Armenia, but her resistance finally broke his heart and he died, leaving Erona Queen of Lycia. Tiridates now waged war against her, 'only for her person; towards whom (for her ruine) Love had kindled his cruel hart.' Although 'his fair sister *Artaxia* (who would accompany him in the army) sought all meanes to appease his fury', Tiridates besieged Erona 'in her best citie', and had brought her 'to the point ether of wofull consent, or a ruinous deniall', when two 'excellent yong Princes, *Pyrocles* and *Musidorus*, the one Prince of *Macedon*, the other of *Thessalia*', came to her assistance. They fiercely attacked Tiridates in his camp, but were repulsed by Plangus, son of the King of Iberia, his cavalry commander, 'especially ayded by the two mightie men, *Euardes* and *Barzanes*'. Tiridates then proposed a combat to decide the issue of the war between his three champions and Antiphilus, Pyrocles, and Musidorus. This was agreed to; Euardes and Barzanes were slain, but Antiphilus was captured by Plangus. Tiridates now threatened to decapitate his prisoner unless Erona yielded to him, and 'Love in her passions . . . whispered to both sides arguments of quarrell'. However, Pyrocles and Musidorus made a bold sortie, rescued Antiphilus, and killed Tiridates. Erona married her lover, and the two princes left, 'being called away by an other adventure'.

Allowing for obvious differences such as the death of Erona's father and of Tiridates, here is in outline the main plot of *The Bashful Lover*, with Erona corresponding to Matilda, Tiridates to Lorenzo, Antiphilus to Galeazzo, and Pyrocles and Musidorus to Uberti and Farneze. In Plangus, Euardes, and Barzanes may be found the originals of Alonzo, Pisano, and Martino, Lorenzo's commanders. The capture of Antiphilus parallels that of Galeazzo, and it places Erona in a dilemma like the one facing Matilda. In the good

[1] The twelfth edition of this enormously popular romance was printed in 1633.

[2] Quotations are taken from A. Feuillerat's edition of *The Countess of Pembroke's Arcadia (1590)*, 1912, pp. 232–6.

offices of Tiridates's sister, Artaxia, Massinger might have found the idea for the episode in which Maria (disguised as Ascanio) saves Alonzo from Galeazzo's fury.

The Bashful Lover is given an Italian Renaissance setting, and for this purpose the dramatist took names and titles from the chapters on the Dukedoms of Milan and Florence in André Favyn's *Le Théâtre d'honneur et de chevalerie*, published at Paris in 1620 and translated into English by 'I. W.' in 1623 (Book three, chapter eleven, and Book eight, chapter seven). Massinger worked with his usual freedom; in his original, 'Beatrix' is the name of a Duchess, 'Gonzaga' is a ducal family name, and 'Gothrio' was probably suggested by repeated references to the 'Gothes'. Massinger also found in Favyn the accession with which his play closes,

> *John*, called *Galeas*, third of the name, and first Duke of *Millaine*, dying in September, One thousand foure hundred and two; his elder Sonne *John Maria*, called the Cruell, succeeded him.

though, for obvious reasons, he replaced the name 'John Maria' with that of Galeazzo, another Duke of Milan. Lorenzo of Florence's successful attack on the city of Mantua is the dramatist's own invention.

Favyn's history of Milan further provided the narrative base for the secondary plot.

> By his Wife *Blanch Maria*, Bastard daughter to *Phillip*, he [Galeas Maria] left sixe Sonnes and two daughters. The Sonnes were named *Galeas*, *Iohn*, *Phillip*, *Ascanio*, *Cardinall*, *Lodowicke Sforza*, and *Octauius*, all Sirnamed *Maria* . . . *Iohn Maria*, the sixt Duke of *Millaine*, succeeded in the said Dukedome, being onely aged nine yeares; remaining in the Tutelage of his Mother, and of his Vnckles *Lodowicke*, *Ascanio* and *Octavian*. The State affairs were ordered and managed by one named *Cico de Calabria*, a man trained vp in the House of *Frances Sforza*. But such was his nature, as being vnable to endure so many Companions, and winning the fauour of *Bonna* of *Sauoye* [wife of Galeas Maria]: *Lodowicke* and *Ascanio* (by this meanes) were banished from the State of *Millaine*, the two other yonger Bretheren put to death, and the plots and deuises of all such preuented, as could make any head against him.
>
> (pp. 475–6)

To the fall and banishment of his Octavio, and to Alonzo's courtship of Maria (Favyn's Cico and Bonna), Massinger added a conventional woman-in-disguise motif,[1] rounding off the action with

[1] Harbage, op. cit., p. 32, notes that this theme is 'endlessly repeated' in plays of this

a father's discovery of his long-lost daughter. In keeping with the courtly tone of his play, the dramatist further changed Favyn's account of the eventual fall and brutal death of Cico de Calabria into Alonzo's repentance and marriage to his devoted lover.

Koeppel pointed out that the opening scene of *The Bashful Lover* resembles an episode in the first act of Fletcher's *The Mad Lover*, in which Memnon first sees the beautiful Calis. In both plays the lover offers silent adoration, and asks only to look on the lady, while waiting-women jest at his behaviour.[1] Koeppel may also be right in finding traces of Caliban (*The Tempest*, II. ii) and Geta (*The Prophetess*, I. iii) in Gothrio, but these plays can have supplied little more than occasional lines. The 'Hungry Knave' is a familiar type in the Beaumont and Fletcher plays,[2] and the dramatist who created Justice Greedy and Belgarde was certainly capable of inventing a thirsty thief.

(c) *Text*

The Bashful Lover was entered in the Stationers' Register by Humphrey Moseley in 1653, and published by him in 1655 as the first play in the volume *Three New Playes.* The registration and publication are described in the introduction to the whole volume (pp. 103–6),[3] where some characteristics of the text, shared by *The Guardian*, are also discussed. The edition will be referred to as *55*; the title-page is reproduced on page 299.[4] The running titles show that one skeleton was used to print both inner and outer formes. There is a general consistency in spelling habits, speech headings, and style of composition.[5] The three patterns in the use of roman

period, and R. S. Forsyth, *The Relations of Shirley's Plays to the Elizabethan Drama*, New York, 1914, pp. 94–6, provides a long list of titles. James Howell, *Epistolæ Ho-Elianæ* (1645), ed. J. Jacobs, 1890, i. 317, and ii. 654, reports contemporary instances from real life.

[1] Koeppel, *Quellen Studien*, pp. 146–8. *The Mad Lover* (1616) was a highly popular play, given a command performance in 1630; see Bentley, iii. 373–6.

[2] Baldwin Maxwell has studied this line of characters, in *Studies in Beaumont, Fletcher, and Massinger*, New York, 1939, 74–83.

[3] See also the General Introduction, vol. i, pp. xxiii–xxiv, xlv.

[4] This edition of the play is named in booksellers' lists and catalogues in 1656, 1661, 1663, and 1671. See Greg, *Bibliography*, iii. 1179, 1331, 1341; iv. 1655.

[5] *I'll* is invariable; there is a consistent preference for *-al*, *-el*, *-ick*, *-or*, and *-y* endings. Only two speech headings show much variation: *Ascanio* is generally abbreviated as *Asc.*, but becomes *Asca.* on $B3^v$, $B6^r$, and $D4^r$; *Gonzaga* is generally abbreviated as *Gon.*, but becomes *Gonza.* and *Gonz.* on five pages each respectively. Square brackets are used throughout for directions other than exits and entrances, and, with two exceptions, speakers' names are not supplied after a single entry.

and italic type for entries discussed on pp. 104–5 of the introduction to the whole volume appear in the text of *The Bashful Lover*, but one type ('Enter *Name*') is plainly dominant, being invariable in the first three-quarters of sheet B, the inner forme of C, half of sheets D and E, and throughout G. Only one press-correction has been found in the copies collated, and a minimum of editorial emendation (other than relineation) is required.

It is argued in the introduction to *Three New Playes* that the copy for *The Bashful Lover* was a transcript prepared by a scribe who also prepared *The Guardian*. The successive intervention of scribe and compositor has resulted in the almost complete absence of spellings and spelling habits characteristic of Massinger.

There are traces of confused lineation or alteration in the original manuscript, and in six passages a whole line is printed as two half-lines.[1] That the scribal transcript was made from an authorial manuscript which was not annotated for the stage is indicated in several ways. A number of exits are omitted, there are no directions for music or flourishes, and groups are designated vaguely as '*Captains, Soldiers*', '*Attendants*', and '*Waiting-women*'. Properties and entrances are generally noted, but there is nothing beyond the range of an experienced dramatist. A stage annotator is unlikely to have been responsible for Latinate directions such as '*Exeunt. manet Gal.*' or '*Ex. cum suis.*', and there are many long descriptive directions, characteristic of an author who seems to have visualized in considerable detail the stage performance of the work on which he was engaged.[2] For instance, '*Galeaz. bowing, offers to go off*'; he '*Walks sadly*'; Uberti enters '*like a soldier, and shuffles in among 'em*'; Lorenzo is visualized with attendants '*imployed about him as from his chamber*'; he is to stand, '*His foot on the Doctors breast*'.

The present text of *The Bashful Lover* has been prepared from the Bodleian Library copy, Malone 237.

The play was printed in the standard collected editions of Massinger, but has otherwise atttracted little interest. For the droll *Love Lost in the Dark*, which included material from *The Bashful Lover*, and for Thomas Hull's alteration, *The Disinterested Lover*, see the following section on theatrical history. Excerpts from

[1] II. v. 50 and 94, II. viii. 69, III. i. 5, III. iii. 46, IV. ii. 108. It is not possible to explain all of these cases as a device to indicate a strong dramatic pause.

[2] Instances of comparable stage directions in the text of *The Guardian* and *A Very Woman* are discussed on pp. 111 and 202–3.

the play were printed in *The British Muse*, edited by T. Hayward, 1738, and in *The Beauties of Massinger*, printed for John Porter in 1817. A. K. McIlwraith prepared the only modern critical edition of *The Bashful Lover* for his unpublished Oxford thesis (1931).

(d) *Stage History*

The Bashful Lover was licensed for performance by the King's men on 9 May 1636 (see p. 291), but only three days later an outbreak of plague led to the closing of the London theatres until 2 October 1637.[1] It is quite possible, then, that the play was not given its first performance until the autumn of 1637. The title-page of the 1655 text offers the information that *The Bashful Lover* was 'often Acted at the Private-House in *Black-Friers*, by His late MAIESTIES Servants, with great Applause'. That the play was a profitable one is further suggested by the fact that on 7 August 1641, the company secured an order from the Lord Chamberlain protecting sixty of their plays against unauthorized printing; among them were 'The Citty madam' and 'The bashfull Louer'.[2]

After the Restoration, to limit the keen competition between the King's and the Duke's companies for plays which had been in the repertoires of the pre-war companies, Killigrew, the manager of the King's Majesty's Servants at the New Theatre, was given exclusive rights to 108 plays, including 'The Bashfull Lover'.[3] No record of any performance has survived.

Early in 1681, a droll called *Love Lost in the Dark; or, The Drunken Couple* was printed with two other farces under the general title of *The Muse of New-Market: or, Mirth and Drollery*, published by Browne, Major, and Vade, and dated 1680. The anonymous author of *Love Lost in the Dark*[4] has simply cobbled together a play text from a copy of *Three New Playes*; most of his material came from *The Guardian*, but there are also lines from *The Bashful Lover* and *A Very Woman*, and the episode in which Gothrio robs Pisano (*The Bashful Lover*, III. ii) is incorporated. A passage in the epilogue to *The Merry Milkmaid of Islington* suggests that all three

[1] See Bentley, ii. 661–5.

[2] The list is printed with a brief discussion in 'Plays of the King's Men in 1641', E. K. Chambers, *Malone Society Collections*, vol. i, Parts 3 and 4, 1911, pp. 364–9.

[3] The list, dated 12 Jan. 1669, is printed in Nicoll, *History of English Drama*, i, 1955, pp. 353–4.

[4] The prologue to the first droll, *The Merry Milkmaid of Islington*, describes him as '*a Country Muse / Vntaught such Tricks the Wits of* London *vse*'. For a fuller account of *The Muse of New-Market* see J. G. McManaway, *Studies*, pp. 23–5.

drolls were given as a single entertainment in the presence of Charles and his court, probably at the time of the Newmarket races, in the autumn of 1680.

On 30 May 1798, an alteration of Massinger's play, titled *The Disinterested Lover*, was produced at Covent Garden, for the benefit of the author, Thomas Hull, and for Mrs. Litchfield and Waddy.[1] Receipts totalled £261 but the play was not repeated. The cast consisted of Johnston (Hortensio), Holman (Lorenzo), Toms (Uberti), Hull (Octavio), Murray (Gonzaga), Whitfield (Alonzo), Clarke (Bellario), Davenport (Manfroy), Powell (an ambassador), Claremont (Alberto), Thompson (Bernado), Mrs. Litchfield (Ascanio), Mrs. Platt (Beatrice), Miss Leserve (a gentlewoman), and Mrs. Pope (Matilda).[2] An advertisement in *The Morning Chronicle* for 30 May indicates that a prologue written by Taylor was spoken by Holman (it was later printed in his *Poems*, i. 60), and that the play was accompanied by songs by Incledon and 'The Highland Reels and other entertainments'. Hull's text was never published, but the manuscript, with its licence dated 19 May 1798, has survived among the Larpent collection now in the Huntington Library (Larpent 1215). Hull's is a fairly close version of Massinger's play. The changes mostly involve compression of the original (II. vi and vii are removed, and other scenes are abbreviated); there is no significant alteration to the plot. The names of Farneze and two other characters are changed, there is some verbal 'sophistication' of Massinger's lines, and any coarseness is pruned. The part of Gothrio is largely cut away as part of this bowdlerization. By and large, *The Disinterested Lover* is the original tragi-comedy touched up and tightened a little.

No modern performance of *The Bashful Lover* is known.

[1] Genest, vii. 370.

[2] *The London Stage 1660–1800*, Part 5, ed. C. B. Hogan, Carbondale, Illinois, 1968, pp. 2076–7. W. C. Oulton, *A History of the Theatres of London*, 1818, ii. 36, says that Johnston replaced Pope, who had fallen ill, and read the part of Hortensio.

THE BASHFUL LOVER.

A

TRAGI-COMEDY.

As it hath been often Acted at the Private-House in *Black-Friers*, by His late MAIESTIES Servants, with great Applause.

WRITTEN
By *PHILIP MASSENGER*, Gent.

LONDON,

Printed for *Humphrey Moseley*, and are to be sold at his Shop at the Sign of the *Prince's Arms* in St. *Pauls* Church-yard. 1655.

A2r

PROLOGUE.

This from our Author, far from all offence,
To abler writers, or the Audience
Met here to judge his Poem. He by me
Presents his service, with such modesty
As well becomes his weakness. 'Tis no crime
He hopes, as we do in this curious time,
To be a little diffident, when we are
To please so many with one Bill of Fare.
Let others, building on their merit, say
Y'are in the wrong, if you move not that way
Which they prescribe you, as you were bound to learn
Their maximes, but uncapable to discern
'Twixt truth and falshood. Ours had rather be
Censur'd by some, for too much obsequy,
Then tax'd of self-opinion: If he hear
That his endeavors thriv'd, and did appear
Worthy your view (though made so by your grace,
With some desert) he in another place
Will thankfully report, one Leaf of Bays
Truly confer'd upon this work, will raise
More pleasure in him, you the givers free,
Then Garland ravisht from the Virgin-Tree.

22. *Garland*] 55; *Garlands Coxeter*

A2v

Dramatis Personæ.

Gonzaga, Duke of *Mantua*
Lorenzo, Duke of *Tuscany*
Uberti, Prince of *Parma*
Farneze, Cousin to *Gonzaga*
Alonzo, Cousin to *Lorenzo*
Manfroy, a Lord of *Mantua*
Octavio, General once to *Gonzaga*, now exil'd
Gothrio, his Servant
Galeazzo, a Nobleman disguised [as *Hortensio*]
Julio, his Man
Pisano, a *Tuscan* Lord
Martino, a Captain
Two Captains more
Ambassadors
Soldiers
[Attendants]
[Guard]
[Doctor]
[Gentleman]
[Page]

Matilda, Daughter to *Gonzaga*
Beatrice, her waiting Gentlewoman
[*Maria*, Daughter to *Octavio*, disguised as a Page, *Ascanio*]
Two Women

10. as *Hortensio*] *Gifford*; *not in 55* 13. *Martino*] *Gifford*; *Martinio 55* 17–21. Attendants . . . Page] *Gifford*; *not in 55* 24. *Maria* . . . *Ascanio*] *Gifford*; *not in 55*

B1r

The Bashful Lover

[I. i]

Act. 1. Scæn. 1.

Enter GALEAZZO *and* JULIO.

Julio. I DARE not cross you sir, but I would gladly
(Provided you allow it) render you
My personal attendance.
Galeazzo. You shall better
Discharge the duty of an honest servant,
In following my instructions which you have
Receiv'd already, then in questioning
What my intents are, or upon what motives
My stay's resolv'd in *Mantua*: Believe me,
B1v That servant overdoes, that's too officious;
And in presuming to direct your master,
You argue him of weakness, and your self
Of arrogance and impertinence.
Julio. I have done sir;
But what my ends are—
Galeazzo. Honest ones, I know it:
I have my bills of exchange, and all provisions
Entrusted to you; you have shewn your self
Just and discreet, what would you more? and yet
To satisfie in some part your curious care,
Hear this, and leave me: I desire to be
Obscur'd; and as I have demean'd my self
These six moneths past in *Mantua*, I'll continue
Unnoted and unknown, and at the best
Appear no more then a Gentleman, and a stranger,
That travails for his pleasure.
Julio. With your pardon,
This hardly will hold weight, though I should swear it,
With your noble friends and brother.

Galeazzo. You may tell 'em,
Since you will be my Tutor, there's a rumor
(Almost cry'd up into a certainty)
Of wars with *Florence*, and that I am determin'd
To see the service: Whatere I went forth,
(Heaven prospering my intents) I would come home
A Soldier, and a good one.
Julio. Should you get
A Captains place, nay Colonels, 'twould add little
To what you are; few of your rank will follow
That dangerous profession.
Galeazzo. 'Tis the noblest,
And Monarchs honor'd in it: but no more
On my displeasure.
Julio. Saints and Angels guard you. *Exit.*
Galeazzo. A war indeed is threatned, nay expected
From *Florence*; but it is 'gainst me already
Proclaim'd in *Mantua*: I find it here,
B2r No forein, but intestine war: I have
Defied my self, in giving up my reason
A slave to passion, and am led captive
Before the battel's fought; I fainted when
I only saw mine enemy, and yielded
Before that I was charg'd: And though defeated,
I dare not sue for mercy; like *Ixion*
I look on *Juno*, feel my heart turn cinders
With an invisible fire: And yet should she
Daign to appear cloth'd in a various cloud,
The majesty of the substance is so sacred,
I durst not clasp the shadow: I behold her
With adoration, feast my eye, while all
My other senses starve; and oft frequenting
The place which she makes happy with her presence,
I never yet had power with tongue or pen
To move her to compassion, or make known
What 'tis I languish for; yet I must gaze still,
Though it increase my flame. However I
Much more then fear I am observ'd and censur'd
For bold intrusion. *Walks sadly.*

Enter BEATRICE *and* ASCANIO.

Beatrice. Know you, boy, that Gentleman?
Ascanio. Who, Monsieur *Melancholy*? hath not your Honor
Marked him before?
Beatrice. I have seen him often wait
About the Princess lodgings, but ne'r ghess'd
What his designs were.
Ascanio. No? what a sigh he breath'd now!
Many such will blow up the roof; on my small credit
There's gunpowder in 'em.
Beatrice. How Crack! gunpowder?
He's flesh and blood, and devils only carry
B2v Such roaring stuff about 'em: you cannot prove
He is or Spirit or Conjurer.
Ascanio. That I grant;
But he's a Lover, and that's as bad; their sighs
Are like petards, and blow all up.
Beatrice. A Lover!
I have been in love my self, but never found yet
That it could work such strange effects.
Ascanio. True, Madam,
In women it cannot; for when they miss th'enjoying
Of their full wishes, all their sighs and heigh-hoes
At the worst breed timpanies, and these are cur'd too
With a kiss or two of their Saint, when he appears
Between a pair of sheets: but with us men
The case is otherwise.
Beatrice. You will be breech'd, boy,
For your physical maxims: But how are you assur'd
He is a Lover?
Ascanio. Who, I? I know with whom too,
But that is to be whisper'd. *Whispers.*
Beatrice. How? the Princess!
Th'unparallel'd *Matilda*! Some proof of it;
I'll pay for my intelligence. *Gives him gold.*
Ascanio. Let me kiss
Your Honors hand; 'twas ever fair, but now
Beyond comparison.
Beatrice. I ghess the reason;
A giving hand is still fair to the receiver.

Ascanio. Your Ladiship's in the right: but to the purpose,
He is my Client, and pays his fees as duly
As ever Usurer did in a bad cause
To his man of law; and yet I get, and take 'em
Both easily and honestly: All the service
I do him, is to give him notice when
And where the Princess will appear; and that
I hope's no treason. If you miss him when
B3r She goes to the Vesper or the Mattins, hang me;
Or when she takes the air, be sure to find him
Near her coach, at her going forth, or coming back:
But if she walk, he's ravisht; I have seen him smel out
Her footing like a Limc-hound, and he knows it
From all the rest of her train.
Beatrice. Yet I ne'r saw him
Present her a petition.
Ascanio. Nor e'r shall:
He only sees her, sighs, and sacrifices
A tear or two; then vanishes.
Beatrice. 'Tis most strange:
What a sad aspect he wears! but I'll make use of't.
The Princess is much troubled with the threats
That come from *Florence*; I will bring her to him,
The novelty may afford her sport, and help
To purge deep melancholy. Boy, can you stay
Your Client here for the third part of an hour?
I have some ends in't.
Ascanio. Stay him, Madam? fear not:
The present receipt of a round sum of crowns,
And that will draw most Gallants from their prayers,
Cannot drag him from me.
Beatrice. See you do. [*Exit.*]
Ascanio. Ne'r doubt me,
I'll put him out of his dream. Good morrow Signior.
Galeazzo. My little friend, good morrow: Hath the Princess
Slept well to night?
Ascanio. I hear not from her women
One murmur to the contrary.

I. i. 100. he knows] *McIlwraith*; knows *55*; nose *Mason* 111. Madam?] *Coxeter*; ~; *55* 114 SD. *Exit.*] *Coxeter*; *not in 55*

Galeazzo. Heaven be prais'd for't:
Does she go to Church this morning?
Ascanio. Troth I know not;
I keep no key of her devotion, Signior.
Galeazzo. Goes she abroad? pray tell me.
Ascanio. 'Tis thought rather
She is resolv'd to keep her chamber.
Galeazzo. Ay me!
B3v *Ascanio.* Why do you sigh? If that you have a business
To be dispatch'd in Court, shew ready mony,
You shall find those that will prefer it for you.
Galeazzo. Business! can any man have business, but
To see her, then admire her, and pray for her,
She being compos'd of goodness? For my self,
I find it a degree of happiness
But to be near her; and I think I pay
A strict religious vow, when I behold her,
And that's all my ambition.
Ascanio. I believe you:
Yet she being absent, you may spend some hours
With profit and delight too. After dinner
The Duke gives audience to a rough Ambassador,
Whom yet I never saw, nor heard his title,
Imploy'd from *Florence*: I'll help you to a place
Where you shall see and hear all.
Galeazzo. 'Tis not worth
My observation.
Ascanio. What think you of
An excellent Comedy to be presented
For his entertainment? He that penn'd it, is
The Poet of the time; and all the Ladies
(I mean the amorous and learned ones)
Except the Princess, will be there to grace it.
Galeazzo. What's that to me? without her all is nothing,
The light that shines in Court, Cimerian darkness:
I will to bed agen, and there contemplate
On her perfections.

Enter MATILDA, BEATRICE, *and two* WOMEN.

Ascanio. Stay sir! see the Princess,
Beyond our hopes.

Galeazzo. Take that. As *Moors* salute
B4r The rising Sun with joyful superstition,
I could fall down and worship.—O my heart! *Aside.*
Like *Phœbe* breaking through an envious cloud,
Or something which no simile can express,
She shews to me; a reverend fear, but blended
With wonder and amazement, does possess me;
Now glut thy self, my famish'd eye.

Beatrice. That's he,
An't please your Excellence.

1 *Woman.* Observe his posture,
But with a quarter-look.

2 *Woman.* Your eye fix'd on him,
Will breed astonishment.

Matilda. A comely Gentleman!
I would not question your relation, Lady,
Yet faintly can believe it: How he eyes me!
Will he not speak?

Beatrice. Your Excellence hath depriv'd him
Of speech and motion.

Matilda. 'Tis most strange.

Ascanio. These fits
Are usual with him.

Matilda. Is it not, *Ascanio*,
A personated folly? or he a statue?
If it be, it is a master-piece; for man
I cannot think him.

Beatrice. For your sport vouchsafe him
A little conference.

Matilda. In compassion rather:
For should he love me as you say (though hopeless)
It should not be return'd with scorn; that were
An inhumanity, which my birth nor honor
Could priviledge, were they greater.

GALEAZZO *bowing, offers to go off.*

Now I perceive
He has life and motion in him; to whom, Lady,
Pays he that duty?

Beatrice. Sans doubt to your self.

172 SD. GALEAZZO . . . *off.*] *editor*; *SD. follows* duty (l. 174) *55*

Matilda. And whither goes he now?
Ascanio. To his private lodging,
B4v But to what end I know not; this is all
I ever noted in him.
Matilda. Call him back:
In pitty I stand bound to counsel him,
Howe'r I am denied, though I were willing
To ease his sufferings.
Ascanio. Signior, the Princess
Commands you to attend her.
Galeazzo. How? the Princess!
Am I betraid?
Ascanio. What a lump of flesh is this!
You are betraid, sir, to a better fortune
Then you durst ever hope for: What a *Tantalus*
Do you make your self? the flying fruit stays for you,
And the water that you long'd for, rising up
Above your lip, do you refuse to taste it?
Move faster, sluggish Camel, or I will thrust
This goad in your breech: Had I such a promising beard,
I should need the reins, not spurs.
Matilda. You may come nearer;
Why do you shake, sir? If I flatter not
My self, there's no deformity about me,
Nor any part so monstrous to beget
An ague in you.
Galeazzo. It proceeds not, Madam,
From guilt, but reverence.
Matilda. I believe you sir;
Have you a suit to me?
Galeazzo. Your Excellence
Is wondrous fair.
Matilda. I thank your good opinion.
Galeazzo. And I beseech you that I may have licence
To kneel to you.
Matilda. A suit I cannot cross.
Galeazzo. I humbly thank your Excellence.
Matilda. But what,
As you are prostrate on your knee before me,
Is your petition?

B5[r] *Galeazzo.* I have none, great Princess.
Matilda. Do you kneel for nothing?
Galeazzo. Yes, I have a suit;
But such a one, as if denied, will kill me.
Matilda. Take comfort; it must be of some strange nature,
Unfitting you to ask, or me to grant,
If I refuse it.
Galeazzo. It is, Madam,—
Matilda. Out with't.
Galeazzo. That I may not offend you, this is all,
When I presume to look on you.
Ascanio. A flat Eunuch!
To look on her? I should desire my self
To move a little further.
Matilda. Only that?
Galeazzo. And I beseech you, Madam, to believe
I never did yet with a wanton eye
Or cherish one lascivious wish beyond it.
Beatrice. You'll never make good Courtier, or be
In grace with Ladies.
1 *Woman.* Or us Waiting-women,
If that be your *Nil ultra*.
2 *Woman.* He's no Gentleman,
On my virginity it is apparent:
My Tailor has more boldness, nay my shoo-maker
Will fumble a little further, he could not have
The length of my foot else.
Matilda. Only to look on me?
Ends your ambition there?
Galeazzo. It does, great Lady,
And that confin'd too, and at fitting distance:
The Fly that plays too neer the flame, burns in it.
As I behold the sun, the stars, the Temples,
I look upon you, and wish 'twere no sin,
Should I adore you.
B5[v] *Matilda.* Come, there's somthing more in't;
And since that you will make a Goddess of me,
As such a one, I'll tell you, I desire not
The meanest Altar rais'd up to mine honor
To be pull'd down; I can accept from you

(Be your condition nere so far beneath me)
One grain of incense with devotion offer'd,
Beyond all perfumes or Sabean spices
By one that proudly thinks he merits in it:
I know you love me.

Galeazzo. Next to heaven, Madam,
And with as pure a zeal. That we behold
With th'eyes of contemplation, but can
Arrive no nearer to it in this life;
But when that is divorc'd, my soul shall serve yours,
And witness my affection.

Matilda. Pray you rise,
But wait my further pleasure.

Enter FARNEZE *and* UBERTI.

Farneze. I'll present you,
And give you proof I am your friend, a true one;
And in my pleading for you, teach the age
That cals erroniously Friendship but a name,
It is a substance. Madam, I am bold
To trench so far upon your privacie,
As to desire my friend (let not that wrong him,
For he's a worthy one) may have the honor
To kiss your hand.

Matilda. His own worth challengeth
A greater favor.

Farneze. Your acknowledgment
Confirms it, Madam: If you look on him
As he's built up a man, without addition
Of fortunes liberal favors, wealth or titles,
He doth deserve no usual entertainment.
B6r But as he is a Prince, and for your service
Hath left fair *Parma* (that acknowledges
No other Lord) and uncompell'd exposes
His person to the dangers of the war,
Ready to break in storms upon our heads;
In noble thankfulness you may vouchsafe him
Neerer respect, and such grace as may nourish,

259. the war] *Gifford*; war *55*

Not kill his amorous hopes.
Matilda. Cozen, you know
I am not the disposer of my self,
The Duke my father challengeth that power:
Yet thus much I dare promise; Prince *Uberti*
Shall find the seed of service that he sows
Fals not on barren ground.
Uberti. For this high favor
I am your creature, and profess I owe you
Whatever I call mine. *They walk.*
Galeazzo. This great Lord is
A Suitor to the Princess.
Ascanio. True, he is so.
Galeazzo. Fame gives him out too for a brave Comander.
Ascanio. And in it does him but deserved right;
The Duke hath made him General of his horse
On that assurance.
Galeazzo. And the Lord *Farneze*
Pleads for him, as it seems.
Ascanio. 'Tis too apparent:
And this consider'd, give me leave to ask
What hope have you sir?
Galeazzo. I may still look on her,
Howe'r he wear the garland.
Ascanio. A thin diet,
And will not feed you fat, sir.
Uberti. I rejoice,
Rare Princess, that you are not to be won
By Carpet-courtship, but the sword: with this
Steel-pen I'll write on *Florence* helm, how much
I can, and dare do for you.
B6v *Matilda.* 'Tis not question'd,
Some private business of mine own dispos'd of,
I'll meet you in the presence.
Uberti. Ever your servant.
Exeunt UBERTI, FARNEZE.
Matilda. Now sir to you: You have observ'd, I doubt not,
(For Lovers are sharp sighted) to what purpose
This Prince sollicites me; and yet I am not
So taken with his worth, but that I can

Vouchsafe you further parle. The first command
That I'll impose upon you, is to hear
And follow my good councel: I am not
Offended that you love me; persist in it,
But love me vertuously, such love may spur you
To noble undertakings, which atchiev'd,
Will raise you into name, preferment, honor:
For all which, though you ne'r enjoy my person,
(For that's impossible) you are indebted
To your high aims. Visit me when you please,
I do allow it, nor will blush to own you,
(So you confine your self to what you promise)
As my vertuous servant.
Beatrice. Farewel sir, you have
An unexpected Cordial.
Ascanio. May it work well.
Exeunt. Manet GALEAZZO.
Galeazzo. Your love, yes, so she said, may spur you to
Brave undertakings: Adding this, You may
Visit me when you please. Is this allowed me,
And any act within the power of man
Impossible to be effected? no,
I will break through all oppositions that
May stop me in my full carier to honor;
And borrowing strength to do, from her high favor,
Add somthing to *Alcides* greatest labor. *Exit.*

B7r
[I. ii] *Enter* GONZAGA, UBERTI, FARNEZE, MANFROY, *Attendants.*

Gonzaga. This is your place, and were it in our power,
You should have greater honor, Prince of *Parma*:
The rest know theirs; let some attend with care
On the Ambassador, and let my Daughter
Be present at his audience. Reach a chair,
We'll do all fit respects; and pray you put on
Your milder looks; you are in a place where frowns
Are no prevailing agents.

I. ii. *Scene division Coxeter; undivided 55*

Enter (*at one door*) ALONZO *and Attendants*: MATILDA, BEATRICE, ASCANIO, GALEAZZO, *and Waiting-women* (*at the other.*)

Ascanio. I have seen
More then a wolf, a Gorgon! *Swouns.*
Gonzaga. What's the matter?
Matilda. A Page of mine is faln into a swoun,
Look to him carefully. [*Exeunt* ASCANIO, *Waiting-women.*]
Gonzaga. Now when you please,
The cause that brought you hither?
Alonzo. The protraction
Of my dispatch forgotten, from *Lorenzo*
The Tuscan Duke, thus much to you *Gonzaga*
The Duke of *Mantua*: By me his nephew
He does salute you fairly, and intreats
(A word not suitable to his power and greatness)
You would consent to tender that, which he
Unwillingly must force, if contradicted.
Ambition, in a private man a vice,
Is in a Prince the vertue—
B7v *Gonzaga.* To the purpose;
These ambages are impertinent.
Alonzo. He demands
The fair *Matilda* (for I dare not take
From her perfections) in a noble way;
And in creating her the consort of
His royal bed, to raise her to a height
Her flattering hopes could not aspire, where she
With wonder shall be gaz'd upon, and live
The envy of her sex.
Gonzaga. Suppose this granted.
Uberti. Or if denied, what follows?
Alonzo. Present war,
With all extremities the Conqueror can
Inflict upon the vanquish'd.
Uberti. Grant me licence
To answer this defiance: What intelligence
Holds your proud Master with the will of Heaven,

11 SD. *Exeunt . . . Waiting-women.*] *after Gifford*; *not in 55* 21. the vertue—] *editor*; the vertue. *55*; a vertue. *Coxeter* 25. consort] *Coxeter*; comfort *55*

That ere th'uncertain Dye of War be thrown,
He dares assure himself the victory?
Are his unjust invading Arms of fire?
Or those we put on in defence of right,
Like chaff to be consum'd in the encounter?
I look on your dimensions, and find not
Mine own of lesser size; the blood that fills
My veins, as hot as yours; my sword as sharp,
My nerves of equal strength, my heart as good,
And confident we have the better cause,
Why should we fear the trial?
Farneze. You presume
You are superior in numbers; we
Lay hold upon the surest anchor, vertue;
Which when the tempest of the war roars loudest,
Must prove a strong protection.
Gonzaga. Two main reasons
(Seconding those you have already heard)
Gives us encouragement: The duty that
B8r I owe my mother Country, and the love
Descending to my daughter. For the first,
Should I betray her liberty, I deserv'd
To have my name with infamy raz'd from
The catalogue of good Princes: And I should
Unnaturally forget I am a father,
If like a Tartar, or for fear or profit,
I should consign her as a bondwoman
To be dispos'd of at anothers pleasure,
Her own consent or favor never su'd for,
And mine by force exacted. No, *Alonzo*,
She is my only child, my heir; and if
A fathers eyes deceive me not, the hand
Of prodigal nature hath given so much to her,
As in the former ages Kings would rise up
In her defence, and make her cause their quarrel:
Nor can she, if that any spark remain
To kindle a desire to be possest
Of such a beauty, in our time want swords
To guard it safe from violence.

67. make] *Coxeter*; makes *55*

Galeazzo. I must speak, [*Aside.*]
Or I shall burst; now to be silent, were
A kind of blasphemy. If such purity,
Such innocence, an abstract of perfection,
The soul of beauty, vertue, in a word,
A Temple of things sacred, should groan under
The burthen of oppression, we might
Accuse the Saints, and tax the Powers above us
Of negligence or injustice.—Pardon, sir,
A strangers boldness, and in your mercy call it
True zeal, not rudeness: In a cause like this,
The Husbandman would change his ploughing-irons
To weapons of defence, and leave the earth
Untill'd, although a general dearth should follow:
The Student would forswear his book; the Lawyer
Put off his thriving gown, and without pay
B8v Conclude this case is to be fought, not pleaded:
The women will turn *Amazons*, as their sex
In her were wrong'd; and boys write down their names
I' th' muster-book for soldiers.
Gonzaga. Take my hand;
Whatev'r you are, I thank you: how are you call'd?
Galeazzo. Hortensio, a Millanoise.
Gonzaga. I wish
Mantua had many such. My Lord Ambassador,
Some privacie if you please: *Manfroy*, you may
Partake it, and advise us. *They go aside.*
Uberti. Do you know, friend,
What this man is, or of what country?
Farneze. Neither.
Uberti. I'll question him my self; what are you sir?
Galeazzo. A Gentleman.
Uberti. But if there be gradation
In Gentry, as the Heralds say, you have
Been overbold in the presence of your betters.
Galeazzo. My betters, sir?
Uberti. Your betters! as I take it,
You are no Prince.
Galeazzo. 'Tis fortunes gift you were born one:

71 SD. *Aside.*] *Coxeter*; *not in 55* 87. case] *55*; cause *Coxeter*

I have not heard that glorious title crowns you
As a reward of vertue; it may be
The first of your house deserv'd it, yet his merits
You can but faintly call your own.
Matilda. Well answer'd.
Uberti. You come up to me.
Galeazzo. I would not turn my back
If you were the Duke of *Florence*, though you charg'd me
I' th' head of your troops.
Uberti. Tell me in gentler language,
(Your passionate speech induces me to think so)
Do you love the Princess?
C1r *Galeazzo.* Were you mine enemy,
Your foot upon my breast, sword at my throat,
Even then I would profess it. The ascent
To th'height of honor, is by arts or arms:
And if such an unequall'd prize might fall
On him that did deserve best in defence
Of this rare Princess, in the day of battail
I should lead you a way would make your Greatness
Sweat drops of blood to follow.
Uberti. Can your Excellence
Hear this without rebuke from one unknown?
Is he a Rival for a Prince?
Matilda. My Lord,
You take that liberty I never gave you:
In justice you should give encouragement
To him or any man that freely offers
His life to do me service, not deter him;
I give no suffrage to it. Grant he loves me,
As he professes, how are you wrong'd in it?
Would you have all men hate me but your self?
No more of this I pray you: If this Gentleman
Fight for my freedom, in a fit proportion
To his desert and quality, I can
And will reward him, yet give you no cause
Of jealousie or envy.
Galeazzo. Heavenly Lady!
Gonzaga. No peace, but on such poor and base conditions?

106. You] *Coxeter*; Yon *55* 109. your] *Coxeter*; our *55*

We will not buy it at that rate. Return
This answer to your Master: Though we wish'd
To hold fair quarter with him, on such terms
As honor would give way to, we are not
So thunder-struck with the loud voice of war,
As to acknowledg him our Lord before
His sword hath made us Vassals: we long since
Have had intelligence of the unjust gripe
He purpos'd to lay on us; neither are we
C1v So unprovided as you think, my Lord.
He shall not need to seek us, we will meet him
And prove the fortune of a day, perhaps
Sooner then he expects.

Alonzo. And find repentance
When 'tis too late. Farewell. *Exit with* FARNEZE.

Gonzaga. No, my *Matilda*,
We must not part so: Beasts and birds of prey
To their last gasp defend their brood; and *Florence*
Over thy fathers breast shall march up to thee,
Before he force affection: The arms
That thou must put on for us and thy self,
Are prayers and pure devotion, which will
Be heard, *Matilda. Manfroy*, to your trust
We do give up the City, and my daughter;
On both keep a strong guard: No tears, they are ominous.
O my *Octavio*, my try'd *Octavio*
In all my dangers! now I want thy service,
In passion recompenc'd with banishment.
Error of Princes, who hate vertue when
She's present with us, and in vain admire her
When she is absent! 'Tis too late to think on't:
The wish'd for time is come, Princely *Uberti*,
To shew your valour; Friends being to do, not talk.
All rhetorick is fruitless, only this,
Fate cannot rob you of deserv'd applause,
Whether you win or lose in such a cause. *Exeunt.*

C2r

[II. i] *Act. 2. Scæn. 1.*

Enter MATILDA, BEATRICE, *and two* WOMEN.

Matilda. NO matter for the Ring I ask'd you for:
The Boy not to be found?
Beatrice. Nor heard of, Madam.
1 *Woman.* He hath been sought and searcht for, house by house,
Nay, every nook of the City, but to no purpose.
2 *Woman.* And how he should escape hence, the Lord *Manfroy*
Being so vigilant ore the guards, appears
A thing impossible.
Matilda. I never saw him
Since he swouned in the presence, when my Father
Gave audience to the Ambassador: but I feel
A sad miss of him; on any slight occasion
He would find out such pretty arguments
To make me sport, and with such witty sweetness
Deliver his opinion, that I must
Ingeniously confess his harmless mirth,
When I was most opprest with care, wrought more
In the removing of it, then musick on me.
Beatrice. An't please your Excellence, I have observ'd him
Waggishly witty; yet sometimes on the sudden
He would be very pensive, and then talk
So feelingly of love, as if he had
Tasted the bitter sweets of't.
1 *Woman.* He would tell too
A pretty tale of a sister that had been
C2v Deceiv'd by her Sweetheart; and then weeping swear
He wonder'd how men could be false.
2 *Woman.* And that
When he was a Knight, he would be the Ladies Champion,
And travel ore the world to kill such Lovers
As durst play false with their Mistresses.
Matilda. I am sure
I want his company.

Enter MANFROY (*with a Letter.*)

Manfroy. There are Letters, Madam,

II. i. 1. *Matilda.*] *Coxeter*; *not in* 55 28. *Manfroy.*] *Coxeter*; *not in* 55

In post come from the Duke; but I am charg'd
By the careful bringer, not to open them
But in your presence.
Matilda. Heaven preserve my Father!
Good news, an't be thy will!
Manfroy. Patience must arm you
Against what's ill.
Matilda. I'll hear 'em in my Cabinet. *Exeunt.*

[II. ii] *Enter* GALEAZZO *and* ASCANIO (*with a Ring.*)

Galeazzo. Why have you left the safety of the City
And service of the Princess, to partake
The dangers of the Camp? and at a time too
When the Armies are in view, and every minute
The dreadful charge expected.
Ascanio. You appear
So far beyond your self, as you are now
Arm'd like a soldier, (though I grant your presence
Was ever gracious) that I grow enamour'd
Of the profession, in the horror of it
There is a kind of majesty.
Galeazzo. But too heavy
To sit on thy soft shoulders, Youth; retire
C3r To the Dukes tent that's guarded.
Ascanio. Sir, I come
To serve you: Knights adventurers are allow'd
Their Pages; and I bring a will that shall
Supply my want of power.
Galeazzo. To serve me, boy!
I wish (believe it) that 'twere in my nerves
To do thee any service; and thou shalt
If I survive the fortune of this day,
Be satisfied I am serious.
Ascanio. I am not
To be put off so, sir: since you do neglect
My offer'd duty, I must use the power
I bring along with me, that may command you:
You have seen this Ring.

II. ii. *Scene division Coxeter; undivided 55*

Galeazzo. Made rich by being worne
Upon the Princess finger.
Ascanio. 'Tis a favour
To you, by me sent from her: view it better;
But why coy to receive it?
Galeazzo. I am unworthy
Of such a blessing, I have done nothing yet
That may deserve it; no Commanders blood
Of th'adverse party hath yet dy'd my sword
Drawn out in her defence. I must not take it.
This were a triumph for me when I had
Made *Florence* Duke my prisoner, and compell'd him
To kneel for mercy at her feet.
Ascanio. 'Twas sent, sir,
To put you in mind whose cause it is you fight for;
And as I am her creature, to revenge
A wrong to me done.
Galeazzo. By what man?
Ascanio. *Alonzo.*
Galeazzo. Th'Ambassador?
Ascanio. The same.
C3v *Galeazzo.* Let it suffice,
I know him by his armor and his horse;
And if we meet—I am cut off, the Alarum
Commands me hence: sweet Youth, fall off.
Ascanio. I must not;
You are too noble to receive a wound
Upon your back; and following close behind you,
I am secure, though I could wish my bosom
Were your defence.
Galeazzo. Thy kindness will undo thee. *Exeunt.*

iii] *Enter* LORENZO, ALONZO, PISANO, MARTINO.

Lorenzo. We'll charge the main Battalia, fall you
Upon the Van, preserve your Troops intire
To force the Rear: he dies that breaks his ranks,
Till all be ours and sure.
Pisano. 'Tis so proclaim'd. *Exeunt.*

II. iii. *Scene division Coxeter; undivided 55*

[II. iv] *Enter* GALEAZZO, ASCANIO, *and* ALONZO.

Galeazzo. 'Tis he, *Ascanio*: Stand!
Alonzo. I never shunn'd
A single opposition; but tell me
Why in the battel, of all men, thou hast
Made choice of me?
Galeazzo. Look on this Youth; his cause
Sits on my sword.
Alonzo. I know him not.
Galeazzo. I'll help
Your memory. *Fight*.
Ascanio. What have I done? I am doubtful
To whom to wish the victory; for still
My resolution wavering, I so love
The enemy that wrong'd me, that I cannot
Without repentance wish success to him
That seeks to do me right.—Alas he's faln. ALONZO *falls*.
As you are gentle, hold sir! or if I want
C4r Power to perswade so far, I conjure you
By her lov'd name I am sent from.
Galeazzo. 'Tis a charm
Too strong to be resisted: He is yours.
Yet why should you make suit to save that life
Which you so late desir'd should be cut off
For injuries receiv'd, begets my wonder.
Ascanio. Alas, we foolish spleenful boys would have
We know not what: I have some private reasons,
But now not to be told.
Galeazzo. Shall I take him prisoner?
Ascanio. By no means, sir; I will not save his life
To rob him of his honor: when you give,
Give not by halves. One short word, and I follow.
Exit GALEAZZO.
My Lord *Alonzo*, if you have receiv'd
A benefit, and would know to whom you owe it,
Remember what your entertainment was
At old *Octavio's* house, one you call'd friend,

II. iv. *Scene division McIlwraith; undivided 55 Gifford*
16. should you] *55*; you should

And how you did return it. *Exit.*
Alonzo. I remember
I did not well; but it is now no time
To think upon't; my wounded honor calls
For reparation, I must quench my fury
For this disgrace in blood, and some shall smart for't. *Exit.*

I. v] *Enter* UBERTI, FARNEZE (*wounded.*)

Farneze. O Prince *Uberti*, valour cannot save us;
The body of our Army's pierc'd and broken,
The wings are routed, and our scattered Troops
Not to be rallied up.
Uberti. 'Tis yet some comfort,
The enemy must say we were not wanting
In courage or direction; and we may
Accuse the powers above as partial, when
C4v A good cause, well defended too, must suffer
For want of fortune.
Farneze. All is lost; the Duke
Too far engag'd, I fear, to be brought off:
Three times I did attempt his rescue, but
With odds was beaten back: Only the stranger
(I speak it to my shame) still follow'd him,
Cutting his way; but 'tis beyond my hopes
That either should return.
Uberti. That noble stranger,
Whom I in my proud vanity of greatness
As one unknown contemn'd, when I was thrown
Out of my saddle by the great Dukes lance,
Hors'd me again in spight of all that made
Resistance; and then whisper'd in mine ear,
Fight bravely Prince *Uberti*, there's no way else
To the fair *Matilda's* favour.
Farneze. 'Twas done nobly.
Uberti. In you, my bosom friend, I had call'd it noble:
But such a courtesie from a Rival, merits
The highest attribute.

II. v. *Scene division Coxeter*; *undivided* 55   7. as] *Gifford*; us 55

Enter GALEAZZO *and* GONZAGA.

Farneze. Stand on your guard,
We are pursu'd.
Uberti. Preserv'd! wonder on wonder.
Farneze. The Duke in safety?
Gonzaga. Pay your thanks, *Farneze*,
To this brave man, if I may call him so,
Whose acts were more then humane: if thou art
My better Angel, from my infancie
Design'd to guard me, like thy self appear,
For sure thou art more then mortal.
C5r *Galeazzo.* No, great sir,
A weak and sinful man, though I have done you
Some prosperous service, that hath found your favour.
I am lost to my self; but lose not you
The offer'd opportunity to delude
The hot pursuing enemy: these woods
Nor the dark vail of night cannot conceal you,
If you dwell long here: You may rise again,
But I am faln for ever.
Farneze. Rather borne up
To the supreme sphere of honor.
Uberti. I confess
My life your gift.
Gonzaga. My liberty: You have snatch'd
The wreath of conquest from the Victors head,
And do alone in scorn of *Lorenzo's* fortune
Though we are slav'd, by true heroick valour
Deserve a triumph.
Uberti. From whence then proceeds
This poor dejection?
Galeazzo. In one suit I'll tell you,
Which I beseech you grant:—I lov'd your daughter,
But how? as beggers in their wounded fancie
Hope to be Monarchs: I long languish'd for her,
But did receive no Cordial, but what
Despair my rough Physitian prescrib'd me.

33. man,] *55*; ~; *Coxeter* 34. favour.] *editor*; ~, *55* 42. My liberty] *55*; I my ~ *Coxeter* You] *55*; *Uberti.* You *Gifford* 46. *Uberti.*] *55*; *omitted Coxeter*; *Gonzaga. Gifford*

At length her goodness and compassion found it:
And whereas I expected, and with reason,
The distance and disparity consider'd
Between her birth and mine, she would contemn me,
The Princess gave me comfort.
Gonzaga. In what measure?
C5v *Galeazzo.* She did admit me for her Knight and servant,
And spurr'd me to do something in this battel
Fought for her liberty, that might not blemish
So fair a favour.
Gonzaga. This you have perform'd
To th'height of admiration.
Uberti. I subscribe to't,
That am your Rival.
Galeazzo. You are charitable:
But how short of my hopes, nay the assurance
Of those atchievements which my love and youth
Already held accomplish'd, this days fortune
Must sadly answer. What I did, she gave me
The strength to do; her piety preserv'd
Her Father; and her gratitude for the dangers
You threw your self into for her defence,
Protected you by me her instrument:
But when I came to strike in mine own cause,
And to do somthing so remarkable,
That should at my return command her thanks
And gracious entertainment, then alas
I fainted like a coward; I made a vow too
(And it is registred) ne'r to presume
To come into her presence, if I brought not
Her fears and dangers bound in fetters to her,
Which now's impossible.—Hark, the enemy
Makes his approaches: save your selves, this only
Deliver to her Sweetness; I have done
My poor endeavours, and pray her not repent
Her goodness to me. May you live to serve her,
This loss recover'd, with a happier fate,
And make use of this sword: Arms I abjure,
And conversation of men; I'll seek out
Some unfrequented cave, and die Loves martyr. *Exit.*

Gonzaga. Follow him.
Uberti. 'Tis in vain; his nimble feet
Have born him from my sight.
C6r *Gonzaga*. I suffer for him.
Farneze. We share in it, but must not sir forget
Your means of safety.
Uberti. In the war I have serv'd you,
And to the death will follow you.
Gonzaga. 'Tis not fit,
We must divide our selves. If I retain yet
A Soveraigns power ore thee, or friends with you,
Do, and dispute not; by my example change
Your habits: As I thus put off my purple,
Ambition dies; this garment of a shepherd
Left here by chance will serve; in lieu of it
I leave this to the owner. Raise new forces,
And meet me at S. *Leo's* Fort; my daughter,
As I commanded *Manfroy*, there will meet us.
The City cannot hold out, we must part,
Farewell, thy hand—
Farneze. You still shall have my heart. *Exeunt*.

[II. vi] *Enter* LORENZO, ALONZO, PISANO, MARTINO, *Captains*, *Soldiers*.

Lorenzo. The day is ours, though it cost dear; yet 'tis not
Enough to get a victory, if we lose
The true use of it. We have hitherto
Held back your forward swords, and in our fear
Of ambushes, deferr'd the wish'd reward
Due to your bloody toil: But now give freedom;
Nay, licence to your fury and revenge;
Now glut your selves with prey, let not the night
Nor these thick woods give sanctuary to
The fear-struck Hares our Enemies: fire these trees,
And force the wretches to forsake their holes,
And offer their scorch'd bodies to your swords,

94. our selves. If] *Mason*; our selves. / My daughter, if *55*; our selves. My daughter— / If *Gifford* yet] *55*; not *Coxeter* II. vi. *Scene division Coxeter*; *undivided 55*

C6v Or burn 'em as a sacrifice to your angers.
Who brings *Gonzaga's* head, or takes him prisoner,
(Which I incline to rather, that he may
Be sensible of those tortures, which I vow
T'inflict upon him, for denial of
His daughter to our bed) shall have a Blank
With our hand and signet made authentical,
In which he may write down himself, what wealth
Or honors he desires.
Alonzo. The great Dukes will
Shall be obeyed.
Pisano. Put it in execution.
Martino. Begirt the wood, and fire it.
Soldiers. Follow, follow. *Exeunt.*

vii] *Enter* FARNEZE (*with a Florentine soldiers coat.*)

Farneze. Uberti, Prince *Uberti*! O my friend
Dearer then life! I have lost thee. Cruel fortune,
Unsatisfied with our sufferings! We no sooner
Were parted from the Duke, and even then ready
To make a mutual farewel, when a troop
Of the enemies horse fell on us: we were forc'd
To take the woods again, but in our flight
Their hot pursuit divided us: we had been happy
If we had died together; to survive him
To me is worse then death, and therefore should not
Embrace the means of my escape, though offer'd.
When nature gave us life, she gave a burthen,
But at our pleasure not to be cast off,
Though weary of it; and my reason prompts me,
This habit of a *Florentine* which I took
From a dying soldier, may keep me unknown
Till opportunity mark me out a way
For flight, and with security.

C7r *Enter* UBERTI.

Uberti. Was there ever
Such a night of horror?

II. vii. *Scene division Coxeter*; *undivided 55* 1. *Farneze. Uberti*] *Coxeter*; *Uberti 55*
18. *Uberti.*] *Coxeter*; *not in 55*

Farneze. My friends voice! I now
In part forgive thee, fortune.
Uberti. The wood flames,
The bloody sword devours all that it meets,
And death in several shapes rides here in triumph.
I am like a Stag clos'd in a toil; my life
As soon as found, the cruel Huntsmans prey:
Why fliest thou then what is inevitable?
Better to fall with manly wounds before
Thy cruel Enemy, then survive thine honor:
And yet to charge him, and die unreveng'd,
Meer desperation.
Farneze. Heroick spirit!
Uberti. Mine own life I contemn, and would not save it
But for the future service of the Duke
And safety of his daughter; having means,
If I escape, to raise a second Army,
And what is nearest to me, to enjoy
My friend *Farneze*.
Farneze. I am still his care.
Uberti. What shall I do? If I call loud, the foe
That hath begirt the wood, will hear the sound.
Shall I return by the same path? I cannot,
The darkness of the night conceals it from me:
Something I must resolve.
Farneze. Let friendship rouze
Thy sleeping soul, *Farneze*: wilt thou suffer
Thy friend, a Prince, nay one that may set free
Thy captiv'd Country, perish, when 'tis in
Thy power with this disguise to save his life?
Thou hast liv'd too long, therefore resolve to die;
C7v Thou hast seen thy Country ruin'd, and thy Master
Compell'd to shameful flight, the fields and woods
Straw'd ore with carkasses of thy fellow-soldiers:
The miseries thou art faln in, and before
Thy eyes the horror of this place, and thousand
Calamities to come; and after all these
Can any hope remain? shake off delays,
Dost thou doubt yet? To save a Citizen,
The conquering *Roman* in a General

Esteem'd the highest honor; can it be then
Inglorious to preserve a Prince? thy friend?
Uberti, Prince *Uberti*, use this means
Of thy escape; conceal'd in this thou maist
Pass through the enemies guards: the time denies
Longer discourse; thou hast a noble end,
Live therefore mindful of thy dying friend. *Exit.*

Uberti. Farneze, stay thy hasty steps: *Farneze*!
Thy friend *Uberti* cals thee: 'tis in vain,
He's gone to death an Innocent, and makes life
The benefit he confers on me, my guilt.
Thou art too covetous of anothers safety,
Too prodigal, and careless of thine own:
'Tis a deceit in friendship to enjoin me
To put this garment on, and live, that he
May have alone the honor to die nobly.
O cruel piety, in our equal danger
To rob thy self of that thou givest thy friend!
It must not be, I will restore his gift
And die before him. How? where shall I find him?
Thou art orecome in friendship; yield *Uberti*
To the extremity of the time, and live:
A heavy ransom, but it must be paid.
I will put on this habit: pittying Heaven
As it loves goodness, may protect my friend,
And give me means to satisfie the debt
I stand engag'd for; if not, pale despair
8r I dare thy worst, thou canst but bid me die,
And so much I'll force from an enemie. *Exit.*

ii] *Enter* ALONZO, PISANO, FARNEZE (*bound*), *Soldiers* (*with torches*), FARNEZE'S *sword in one of the Soldiers hands.*

Alonzo. I know him, he's a man of ransom.
Pisano. True,
But if he live 'tis to be paid to me.
Alonzo. I forc'd him to the woods.
Pisano. But my art found him,

II. viii. *Scene division Coxeter*; *undivided 55*

Nor will I brook a partner in the prey
My fortune gave me.
Alonzo. Render him, or expect
The point of this.
Pisano. Wer't lightning, I would meet it
Rather then be outbrav'd.
Alonzo. I thus decide
The difference.
Pisano. My sword shall plead my title. *They fight.*

Enter LORENZO, MARTINO, *two Captains.*

Lorenzo. Ha! where learn'd you this discipline? my Commanders
Oppos'd 'gainst one another? what blind fury
Brings forth this brawl? *Alonzo* and *Pisano*
At bloody difference! hold, or I tilt
At both as enemies. Now speak, how grew
This strange division?
Pisano. Against all right,
By force *Alonzo* strives to reap the harvest
Sown by my labour.
Alonzo. Sir, this is my prisoner,
The purchase of my sword, which proud *Pisano*
That hath no interest in him, would take from me.
Pisano. Did not the presence of the Duke forbid me,
I would say—
C8v *Alonzo.* What?
Pisano. 'Tis false.
Lorenzo. Before my face!
Keep 'em asunder. And was this the cause
Of such a mortal quarrel? this the base
To raise your fury on? the tyes of blood,
Of fellowship in arms, respect, obedience
To me your Prince and General, no more
Prevailing on you? this a price for which
You would betray our victory, or wound
Your reputation with mutinies?
Forgetful of your selves, allegiance, honor?
This is a course to throw us headlong down
From that proud height of empire, upon which

14. right,] *Gifford*; ~; *55*

We were securely seated: shall division
Oreturn what concord built? If you desire
To bath your swords in blood, the enemy
Still flies before you: Would you have spoil? the Country
Lies open to you. O unheard of madness!
What greater mischief could *Gonzaga* wish us,
Then you pluck on our heads? no, my brave Leaders,
Let unity dwell in our tents, and discord
Be banish'd to our enemies.
Alonzo. Take the prisoner,
I do give up my title.
Pisano. I desire
Your friendship, and will buy it: He is yours. *They embrace.*
Alonzo. No man's a faithful Judg in his own cause;
Let the Duke determine of him, we are friends sir.
Lorenzo. Shew it in emulation to oretake
The flying foe; this cursed wretch dispos'd of,
With our whole strength we'll follow.
Exeunt ALONZO *and* PISANO, *embracing.*
Farneze. Death at length
Will set a period to calamity.
D1r I see it in this Tyrants frowns haste to me.
Lorenzo. Thou machine of this mischief, look to feel

Enter UBERTI *like a soldier, and shuffles in among 'em.*

Whate're the wrath of an incensed Prince
Can pour upon thee: With thy blood I'll quench
(But drawn forth slowly) the invisible flames
Of discord,—by thy charms first fetch'd from Hell,
Then forc'd into the breasts of my Commanders.
—Bring forth the tortures.
Uberti. Hear, victorious Duke,
The story of my miserable fortune,
Of which this Villain (by your sacred tongue
Condemn'd to die) was the immediate cause:
And if my humble suit have justice in it,
Vouchsafe to grant it.
Lorenzo. Soldier be brief; our anger
Can brook no long delay.
Uberti. I am the last

Of three sons, by one father got, and train'd up
With his best care for service in your wars:
My father dyed under his fatal hand,
And two of my poor brothers. Now I hear,
Or fancie wounded by my grief, deludes me,
Their pale and mangled ghosts, crying for vengeance
On perjury and murther. Thus the case stood.—
My father (on whose face he durst not look
In equal mart) by his fraud circumvented,
Became his Captive: we his sons lamenting
Our old sires hard condition, freely offer'd
Our utmost for his ransom. That refus'd,
The subtile Tyrant for his cruel ends,
(Conceiving that our piety might insnare us)
D1v Propos'd my Fathers head to be redeem'd,
If two of us would yield our selves his slaves.
We (upon any terms resolv'd to save him,
Though with the loss of life which he gave to us)
With an undaunted constancie drew lots
(For each of us contented to be one)
Who should preserve our Father. I was exempted,
But to my more affliction; my brothers
Delivered up, the perjur'd Homicide
Laughing in scorn, and by his hoary locks
Pulling my wretched Father on his knees,
Said, Thus receive the Father you have ransom'd;
And instantly struck off his head.
Lorenzo. Most barbarous!
Farneze. I never saw this man.
Lorenzo. One murmur more,
I'll have thy tongue pull'd out. Proceed.
Uberti. Conceive, sir,
How thunder-struck we stood, being made spectators
Of such an unexpected tragedy:
Yet this was a beginning, not an end
To his intended cruelty; for pursuing
Such a revenge, as no Hircanian tigress
Rob'd of her whelps durst aim at, in a moment,

82. contented] *55*; contended *Coxeter* 88. Said, Thus receive] *Gifford*; Said thus, Receive *55* 97. moment,] *Gifford*; ~^ *55*

Treading upon my Fathers trunk, he cut off
My pious Brothers heads, and threw 'em at me.
Oh what a spectacle was this! what mountain
Of sorrow overwhelm'd me! My poor heartstrings
As tenter'd by his tyrannie, crack'd; my knees
Beating 'gainst one another, groans and tears
Blended together followed; not one passion
Calamity ever yet express'd, forgotten.
Now mighty sir, (bathing your feet with tears)
Your suppliants suit is, that he may have leave
With any cruelty revenge can fancie,
To sacrifice this Monster, to appease
2r My Fathers ghost and Brothers.
Lorenzo. Thou hast obtain'd it;
Choose any torture; let the memory
Of what thy Father and thy Brothers suffer'd
Make thee ingenious in it, such a one
As *Phalaris* would wish to be call'd his.
Martino, guarded with your soldiers, see
The execution done; but bring his head
On forfeiture of your own, to us: Our presence
Long since was elswhere look'd for. *Exit cum suis.*
Martino. Soldier to work;
Take any way thou wilt for thy revenge,
Provided that he die: his body's thine,
But I must have his head.
Uberti. I have already
Concluded of the manner: O just heaven,
The instrument I wish'd for offer'd me!
Martino. Why art thou rapp'd thus?
Uberti. In this soldiers hand
I see the murtherers own sword, I know it,
Yes, this is it by which my Father and
My brothers were beheaded: Noble Captain
Command it to my hand. Stand forth and tremble;
This weapon of late drunk with innocent blood
Shall now carouse thine own. Pray, if thou canst;
For though the world shall not redeem thy body,
I would not kill thy soul.
Farneze. Canst thou believe

There is a heaven, or hell, or soul? thou hast none,
In death to rob me of my fame, my honor,
With such a forged lye! tell me thou hangman,
Where did I ever see thy face? or when
Murder'd thy sire or brothers? look on me
And make it good: thou dar'st not.
Uberti. Yes I will *Unbinds his arms.*
In one short whisper, and that told thou art dead.
D2v I am *Uberti*; take thy sword, fight bravely,
We'll live or die together.
Martino. We are betraid.
MARTINO *struck down, the soldiers run away.*
Farneze. And have I leave once more, brave Prince, to ease
My head on thy true bosom?
Uberti. I glory more
To be thy friend, then in the name of Prince
Or any higher title.
Farneze. My preserver!
Uberti. The life you gave to me, I but return;
And pardon, dearest friend, the bitter language
Necessity made me use.
Farneze. O sir, I am
Outdone in all; but comforted, that none
But you can wear the laurel.
Uberti. Here's no place
Or time to argue this; let us flie hence.
Farneze. I follow. *Exeunt.*
Martino. A thousand Furies keep you company!
I was at the gate of heaven but now I feel
My wounds not mortal; I was but astonish'd,
And coming to my self, I find I am
Reserv'd for the gallows: there's no looking on
Th'enraged Duke, excuses will not serve,
I must do something that may get my pardon;
If not, I know the worst, a halter ends all. *Exit.*

153. of heaven] *McIlwraith*; of —— *55*; of hell *Gifford*

D3r

[. i] *Act. 3. Scæn. 1.*

Enter OCTAVIO, (*a Book in's hand.*)

Octavio. 'TIS true, by proof I find it, humane reason
Views with such dim eyes what is good or ill,
That if the great Disposer of our being
Should offer to our choice all worldly blessings,
We know not what to take.—When I was young,
Ambition of Court-preferment fir'd me;
And as there were no happiness beyond it,
I labour'd for't and got it; no man stood
In greater favour with his Prince, I had
Honors and offices, wealth flow'd in to me,
And for my service both in peace and war
The general voice gave out I did deserve 'em.
But oh vain confidence in subordinate greatness!
When I was most secure, it was not in
The power of fortune to remove me from
The flat I firmly stood on: in a moment
My vertues were made crimes, and popular favor
(To new-rais'd men still fatal) bred suspition
That I was dangerous: which no sooner entred
Gonzaga's breast, but straight my ruine follow'd;
My offices were took from me, my state seis'd on;
And had I not prevented it by flight,
The jealousie of the Duke had been remov'd
With the forfeiture of my head.
Within Galeazzo. Or shew compassion,
Or I will force it.
D3v *Octavio.* Ha! is not poverty safe?
I thought proud war that aim'd at kingdoms ruines,
The sack of palaces and cities, scorn'd
To look on a poor cottage.

Enter GALEAZZO (*with* ASCANIO *in's arms*), GOTHRIO *following.*

Gothrio. What would you have?
The devil sleeps in my pocket, I have no cross
To drive him from it. Be you or thief, or soldier,

III. i. 5. know] *Coxeter*; knew *55*

Or such a begger as will not be denied,
My scrip, my tar-box, hook and coat will prove
But a thin purchase; if you turn my inside outwards,
You'll find it true. [GALEAZZO] *searches his scrip.*

Galeazzo. Not any food?

Gothrio. Alas sir,
I am no glutton, but an under-shepherd,
The very picture of famine; judg by my cheeks else:
I have my pittance by ounces, and starve my self
When I pay a pensioner I have, an antient mouse,
A crum a meal. [GALEAZZO] *takes the bottle.*

Galeazzo. No drop left? Drunkard, hast thou
Swill'd up all?

Gothrio. How? Drunkard, sir!
I am a poor man, you mistake me sir:
Drunkard's a title for the rich, my betters;
A calling in repute: some sell their lands for't,
And rore, Wines better then mony. Our poor beveridg
Of buttermilk or whey allaid with water,
Ne'r raise our thoughts so high. Drunk! I had never
The credit to be so yet.

Galeazzo. *Ascanio*,
Look up dear youth: *Ascanio*, did thy sweetness
Command the greedy enemy to forbear
To prey upon it? and I thank my fortune
D4r For suffering me to live, that in some part
I might return thy courtesies. And now
To heighten my afflictions, must I be
Inforc'd, no pittying Angel near to help us,
Heaven deaf to my complaints too, to behold thee
Die in my arms for hunger? no means left
To lengthen life a little? I will open
A vein, and pour my blood, not yet corrupted
With any sinful act, but pure as he is,
Into his famish'd mouth.

Octavio. Young man forbear
Thy savage pitty; I have better means

34 SD. GALEAZZO] *editor*; *not in 55*; *SD follows* food? *Coxeter* 37. self] *Coxeter*; ~; *55* 38. pensioner I have,] *Coxeter*; pensioner, I have *55*
39 SD. GALEAZZO] *editor*; *not in 55*; *SD follows* left? *Coxeter*

To call back flying life. *They apply themselves to* ASCANIO.
Gothrio. You may believe him,
It is his sucking-bottle, and confirms
An old man's twice a child; his nurses milk
Was ne'r so chargeable, should you put in too
For sope and candles. Though he sell his flock for't,
The baby must have this dug: he swears 'tis ill
For my complexion, but wondrous comfortable
For an old man that would never die.
Octavio. Hope well sir,
A temperate heat begins to thaw his numness,
The blood too by degrees takes fresh possession
On his pale cheeks, his pulse beats high; stand off,
Give him more air, he stirs. GOTHRIO *steals the bottle.*
Gothrio. And have I got thee,
Thou bottle of immortality?
Ascanio. Where am I?
What cruel hand hath forc'd back wretched life?
Is rest in death denied me?
Gothrio. O sweet liquor!
Were here enough to make me drunk, I might
Write my self Gentleman, and never buy
A coat of the Heralds.
Octavio. How now slave?
D4v *Gothrio.* I was fainting,
A clownlike qualm seis'd on me, but I am
Recover'd, thanks to your bottle, and begin
To feel new stirrings, gallant thoughts; one draught more
Will make me a perfect Signior.
Octavio. A tough cudgel
Will take this gentle itch off: Home to my cottage,
See all things handsom.
Gothrio. Good sir, let me have
The bottle along to smell to: O rare perfume! *Exit.*
Galeazzo. Speak once more, dear *Ascanio*! How he eyes you,
Then turns away his face! Look up sweet youth,
The object cannot hurt you; this good man
Next heaven is your preserver.
Ascanio. Would I had perish'd

65. chargeable,] *Gifford*; ~: *55* 66. candles.] *after Gifford*; ~, *55*

Without relief, rather then live to break
His good old heart with sorrow. O my shame!
My shame, my never dying shame!
Octavio. I have been
Acquainted with this voice, and know the face too:
'Tis she, 'tis too apparent; O my daughter!
I mourn'd long for thy loss; but thus to find thee,
Is more to be lamented.
Galeazzo. How? your daughter!
Octavio. My only child: I murmur'd against heaven
Because I had no more; but now I find
This one too many. Is *Alonzo* glutted ASCANIO *weeps.*
With thy embraces?
Galeazzo. At his name a shower
Of tears fals from her eyes: she faints agen.
Grave sir, overrule your passion, and defer
The story of your fortune: On my life
She is a worthy one, her innocence
Might be abus'd, but mischiefs self wants power
To make her guilty. Shew your self a Father
D5r In her recovery; then as a Judge,
When she hath strength to speak in her own cause,
You may determine of her.
Octavio. I much thank you
For your wise counsel: you direct me sir
As one indebted more to years, and I
As a pupil will obey you. Not far hence
I have a homely dwelling; if you please there
To make some short repose, your entertainment
Though course, shall relish of a gratitude,
And that's all I can pay you. Look up Girl,
Thou art in thy Fathers arms.
Galeazzo. She's weak and faint still:
O spare your age! I am young and strong, and this way
To serve her is a pleasure, not a burthen:
Pray you lead the way.
Octavio. The Saints reward your goodness. *Exeunt.*

104. your] *55*; her *Gifford*

III. ii] *Enter* MANFROY, *and* MATILDA (*disguis'd.*)

Matilda. No hope of safety left?
Manfroy. We are descry'd.
Matilda. I thought, that cover'd in this poor disguise
I might have pass'd unknown.
Manfroy. A diamond,
Though set in horn, is still a diamond,
And sparkles as in purest gold. We are follow'd:
Out of the troops that scour'd the plains, I saw
Two gallant horsmen break forth, (who by their
Brave furniture and habiliments for the war
Seem'd to command the rest) spurring hard towards us;
See with what winged speed they climb the hill
Like Falcons on the stretch to seise the prey;
Now they dismount, and on their hands and knees
Orecome the deep ascent that guards us from them.
Your beauty hath betraid you; for it can
No more be night when bright *Apollo* shines
In our Meridian, then that be conceal'd.
D5v *Matilda.* It is my curse, not blessing; fatal to
My Country, Father, and my self: why did you
Forsake the City?
Manfroy. 'Twas the Dukes command,
No time to argue that; we must descend:
If undiscover'd your soft feet (unus'd
To such rough travail) can but carry you
Half a league hence, I know a cave which will
Yield us protection.
Matilda. I wish I could lend you
Part of my speed; for me, I can outstrip
Daphne or *Atalanta*.
Manfroy. Some good Angel
Defend us, and strike blind our hot pursuers. *Exeunt.*

Enter ALONZO *and* PISANO.

Alonzo. She cannot be far off; how gloriously
She shew'd to us in the valley!

III. ii. *Scene division Coxeter*; *undivided* 55

13. deep] 55; steep *Coxeter* them] *Coxeter*; him 55

Pisano. In my thought
Like to a blazing Comet.
Alonzo. Brighter far:
Her beams of beauty made the hill all fire;
From whence remov'd, 'tis cover'd with thick clouds.
But we lose time; I'll take that way.
Pisano. I this. *Exeunt.*

[III. iii] *Enter* GALEAZZO.

Galeazzo. 'Tis a degree of comfort in my sorrow,
I have done one good work in reconciling
Maria, long hid in *Ascanio's* habit,
To griev'd *Octavio*: what a sympathie
I found in their affections! she with tears
Making a free confession of her weakness
In yielding up her honor to *Alonzo*,
D6r Upon his vows to marry her: *Octavio*
Prepar'd to credit her excuses, nay
T'extenuate her guilt; she the Delinquent,
And Judge, as 'twere, agreeing. But to me
The most forlorn of men, no beam of comfort
Daigns to appear; nor can I in my fancie
Fashion a means to get it. To my Country
I am lost for ever, and 'twere impudence
To think of a return; yet this I could
Endure with patience: But to be divorc'd
From all my joy on earth, the happiness
To look upon the excellence of nature,
That is perfection in herself, and needs not
Addition or epithite, rare *Matilda*,
Would make a Saint blaspheme. Here *Galeazo*
In this obscure abode 'tis fit thou shouldst
Consume thy youth, and grow old in lamenting
Thy star-crost fortune, in this shepherds habit;
This hook thy best defence, since thou couldst use
(When thou didst fight in such a Princess cause)
Thy sword no better. *Lies down.*

III. iii. *Scene division Coxeter*; *undivided 55* 1. *Galeazzo.*] *Coxeter*; *not in 55*
21. epithite, rare] *55*; epithite rare, *conj. Gifford*

Enter ALONZO, PISANO, MATILDA.

Matilda. Are you men, or monsters?
Whither will you drag me? can the open ear
Of heaven be deaf, when an unspotted Maid
Cries out for succor!
Pisano. 'Tis in vain; cast lots
Who shall enjoy her first.
Alonzo. Flames rage within me,
And such a spring of Nectar neer to quench 'em!
My appetite shall be cloy'd first: here I stand
Thy friend, or enemy; let me have precedence,
I write a friends name in my heart; deny it,
As an enemy I defie thee.
D6v *Pisano.* Friend or foe
In this alike I value, I disdain
To yield priority; draw thy sword.
Alonzo. To sheath it
In thy ambitious heart.
Matilda. O curb this fury!
And hear a wretched Maid first speak!
Galeazzo. I am marble.
Matilda. Where shall I seek out words, or how restrain
My Enemies rage, or Lovers? oh the latter
Is far more odious: did not your lust
Provoke you, for that is its proper name,
My chastity were safe; and yet I tremble more
To think what dire effects lust may bring forth,
Then what as enemies you can inflict,
And less I fear it. Be friends to your selves,
And enemies to me: Better I fall
A sacrifice to your attonement, then
Or one, or both should perish. I am the cause
Of your division; remove it, Lords,
And concord will spring up: poison this face
That hath bewitch'd you; this grove cannot want
Aspicks or Toads, creatures though justly call'd
For their deformity the scorn of nature,
More happy then my self with this false beauty
(The seed and fruit of mischief) you admire so.

I thus embrace your knees, and yours, a suppliant;
If Tigres did not nurse you, or you suck
The milk of a fierce Lioness, shew compassion
Unto your selves in being reconcil'd,
And pitty to poor me, my honor safe,
In taking loath'd life from me.
Pisano. What shall we do?
Or end our difference in killing her,
Or fight it out?
D7r *Alonzo.* To the last gasp. I feel
The moist tears on my cheeks, and blush to find
A Virgins plaints can move so.
Pisano. To prevent
Her flight while we contend, let's bind her fast
To this Cipress-tree.
Alonzo. Agreed.
Matilda. It does presage
My funeral rites.
Galeazzo. I shall turn Atheist,
If heaven see and suffer this: why did I
Abandon my good sword? with unarm'd hands
I cannot rescue her. Some Angel pluck me
From the apostasie I am falling to,
And by a miracle lend me a weapon
To underprop falling honor.
Pisano. She is fast,
Resume your arms.
Alonzo. Honor, revenge, the Maid too
Lie at the stake.
Pisano. Which thus I draw— *They fight,*
Alonzo. All's mine, PISANO *fals.*
But bought with some blood of mine own: *Pisano*,
Thou wert a noble Enemy; wear that laurel
In death to comfort thee; for the reward,
'Tis mine now without Rival.
GALEAZZO *snatches up* PISANO'S *sword.*
Galeazzo. Thou art deceiv'd;
Men will grow up like to the Dragons teeth
From *Cadmus* helm sown in the field of *Mars*,
To guard pure Chastity from lust and rape.

Libidinous monster, Satyre, Fawn, or what
Does better speak thee slave to appetite
And sensual baseness; if thy profane hand
But touch this virgin-temple, thou art dead.
Matilda. I see the aid of Heaven, though slow, is sure.
Alonzo. A rustick swain dare to retard my pleasure?
D7v *Galeazzo.* No swain, *Alonzo*, but her knight and servant
To whom the world should owe and pay obedience;
One that thou hast encountred, and shrunk under
His arm, that spar'd thy life in the late battel
At th'intercession of the Princess page;
Look on me better.
Matilda. 'Tis my vertuous Lover,
Under his guard 'twere sin to doubt my safety.
Alonzo. I know thee, and with courage will redeem
What fortune then took from me. *Fight.* ALONZO *fals.*
Galeazzo. Rather keep
Thy Compeer company in death—lie by him
A prey for Crows and Vulturs; these fair arms *He unbinds*
Unfit for bonds, should have been chains to make MATILDA.
A Bridegroom happy, though a Prince, and proud
Of such captivity: whatsoe'r you are,
I glory in the service I have done you;
But I intreat you pay your vows and prayers
For preservation of your life and honor,
To the most vertuous Princess, chaste *Matilda*:
I am her creature, and what good I do
You truly may call hers; what's ill, mine own.
Matilda. You never did do ill, my vertuous servant,
Nor is it in the power of poor *Matilda*
To cancel such an obligation as
With humble willingness she must subscribe to.
Galeazzo. The Princess? ha!
Matilda. Give me a fitter name,
Your manumissed Bondwoman, but even now
In the possession of lust, from which
Your more then brave heroick valor bought me;
And can I then for freedom unexpected
But kneel to you my Patron?

89. thee] *55*; ~, *Gifford*

Galeazzo. Kneel to me!
For heav'ns sake rise; I kiss the ground you tread on,
D8r My eyes fix'd on the earth; for I confess
I am a thing not worthy to look on you,
Till you have sign'd my pardon.
Matilda. Do you interpret
The much good you have done me, an offence?
Galeazzo. The not performing your injunctions to me,
Is more then capital. Your allowance of
My love and service to you, with admission
To each place you made paradise with your presence,
Should have inabled me to bring home Conquest,
Then, as a sacrifice to offer it
At the altar of your favor. Had my love
Answer'd your bounty or my hopes, an Army
Had been as dust before me; whereas I
Like a coward turn'd my back, and durst not stand
The fury of the Enemy.
Matilda. Had you done nothing
In the battel, this last act deserves more
Then I, the Duke my father joining with me,
Can ever recompence. But take your pleasure,
Suppose you have offended in not grasping
Your boundless hopes; I thus seal on your lips
A full remission.
Galeazzo. Let mine touch your foot,
Your hand's too high a favour.
Matilda. Will you force me
To ravish a kiss from you?
Galeazzo. I am intranc'd.
Matilda. So much Desert, and Bashfulness, should not march
In the same file. Take comfort, when you have brought me
To some place of security, you shall find
You have a seat here, a heart that hath
Already studied, and vow'd to be thankful.
Galeazzo. Heaven make me so! oh I am overwhelm'd
With an excess of joy! Be not too prodigal,
D8v Divinest Lady, of your grace and bounties
At once, if you are pleas'd I shall enjoy 'em,

151. seat] *55*; servant *conj. McIlwraith* a heart] *55*; in a heart *Gifford*

Not taste 'em and expire.
Matilda. I'll be more sparing. *Exeunt.*

Enter OCTAVIO, GOTHRIO, *and* MARIA.

Octavio. What noise of clashing swords, like armor fashion'd
Upon an anvile, pierc'd mine ears? the eccho
Redoubling the loud sound through all the vallies,
This way the wind assures me that it came.
Gothrio. Then with your pardon I'll take this.
Octavio. Why sirra?
Gothrio. Because, sir, I will trust my heels before
All winds that blow in the sky. We are wiser far
Then our Grandsires were, and in this I'll prove it;
They said, Haste to the beginning of a Feast,
(There I am with 'em) but to the end of a Fray,
That is apocryphal, 'tis more canonical
Not to come there at all; after a storm
There are still some drops behind.
Ascanio. Pure fear hath made
The Fool a Philosopher.
Octavio. See *Maria*, see!
I did not erre; here lie two brave men weltring
In their own gore.
Ascanio. A pittiful object.
Gothrio. I am in a swoun to look on't.
Octavio. They are stiff already.
Gothrio. But are you sure they are dead?
Octavio. Too sure, I fear.
Gothrio. But are they stark dead?
Octavio. Leave prating.
Gothrio. Then I am valiant, and dare come nearer to 'em,
This fellow without a sword shall be my Patient.
E1r *Octavio.* Whate'r they are, humanity commands us
To do our best endeavour: Run *Maria*
To the neighbour Spring for water; you will find there
A wooden dish, the beggers plate, to bring it. *Exit* MARIA.
Why dost not, dull drone, bend his body, and feel
If any life remain?
Gothrio. By your leave he shall die first,
And then I'll be his Surgeon.

Octavio. Tear ope his doublet,
And prove if his wounds be mortal.
Gothrio. Fear not me sir;
Here's a large wound, how it is swoln and impostum'd! *His pocket.*
This must be cunningly drawn out; should it break,
Puls out his purse.
'Twould strangle him: what a deal of foul matter's here!
His little pocket.
This hath been long a gathering: Here's a gash too
On the rime of his belly, it may have matter in it.
He was a cholerique man sure: what comes from him *Gold.*
Is yellow as gold: How? troubled with the Stone too!
A Diamond-Ring.
I'll cut you for this.
Pisano. Oh, oh! *Starts up and quakes.*
Gothrio. He roars before I touch him.
Pisano. Robb'd of my life?
Gothrio. No sir, nor of your mony
Nor jewel, I keep 'em for you;—if I had been [*Aside.*]
A perfect Mountebank, he had not liv'd
To call for his fees again.
Octavio. Give me leave, there's hope
Of his recovery.
Gothrio. I had rather bury him quick
Then part with my purchase; let his ghost walk, I care not.

E1v *Enter* MARIA (*with a dish of water.*)

Octavio. Well done *Maria*, lend thy helping hand;
He hath a deep wound in his head, wash off
The clotted blood: He comes to himself.
Alonzo. My lust!
The fruit that grows upon the tree of lust!
With horror now I taste it.
Octavio. Do you not know him?
Ascanio. Too soon, *Alonzo*! oh me! though disloyal,
Still dear to thy *Maria*.
Gothrio. So they know not [*Aside.*]
My Patient, all's cock-sure: I do not like

191. rime] *Coxeter*; reme 55 196 SD. *Aside.*] *editor*; *not in* 55 207 SD. *Aside.*] *Gifford*[2]; *not in* 55

The Romanish restitution.
Octavio. Rise and leave him,
Applaud heavens justice.
Ascanio. 'Twill become me better
T'implore its saving mercy.
Octavio. Hast thou no gall?
No feeling of thy wrongs?
Ascanio. Turtles have none;
Nor can there be such poison in her breast
That truly loves, and lawfully.
Octavio. True, if that love
Be plac'd on a worthy subject. What he is,
In thy disgrace is publish'd; Heaven hath mark'd him
For punishment, and 'twere rebellious madness
In thee t'attempt to alter it: Revenge,
A soveraign balm for injuries, is more proper
To thy rob'd honor. Join with me, and thou
Shalt be thy self the Goddess of revenge,
This wretch the vassal of thy wrath: I'll make him
While yet he lives, partake those torments which
For perjur'd Lovers are prepar'd in hell,
Before his curs'd ghost enter it. This oil
Extracted and sublim'd from all the simples
The earth when swoln with venom e'r brought forth,
E2r Pour'd in his wounds, shall force such anguish as
The Furies whips but imitate; and when
Extremity of pain shall hasten death,
Here is another that shall keep in life,
And make him feel a perpetuity
Of lingring tortures.
Gothrio. Knock 'em both on the head, I say,
And it be but for their skins; they are embroider'd,
And will sell well i' th' market.
Ascanio. Ill-look'd Devil,
Tie up thy bloody tongue. O sir! I was slow
In beating down those propositions which
You urge for my revenge; my reasons being
So many, and so forcible, that make
Against yours, that until I had collected
My scatter'd powers, I waver'd in my choice

Which I should first deliver. Fate hath brought
My Enemy (I can faintly call him so)
Prostrate before my feet: shall I abuse
The bounty of my fate, by trampling on him?
He alone ruin'd me, nor can any hand
But his rebuild my late demolish'd honor.
If you deny me means of reparation
To satisfie your spleen, you are more cruel
Then ever yet *Alonzo* was; you stamp
The name of Strumpet on my forehead, which
Neavens mercy would take off; you fan the fire
Ev'n ready to go out; forgetting that
'Tis truly noble, having power to punish,
Nay King-like, to forbear it. I would purchase
My husband by such benefits, as should make him
Confess himself my equal, and disclaim
Superiority.

Octavio. My blessing on thee!
What I urg'd, was a trial; and my grant
To thy desires shall now appear, if art
Or long experience can do him service,
Nor shall my charity to this be wanting,
E2v Howe'r unknown. Help me *Maria*; You sir,
Do your best to raise him.—So.

Gothrio. He's wondrous heavy;
But the Porter's paid, there's the comfort.

Octavio. 'Tis but a trance,
And 'twill forsake both.

Ascanio. If he live, I fear not
He will redeem all, and in thankfulness
Confirm he ows you for a second life,
And pays the debt in making me his wife. *Exeunt.*

[IV. i]

Act. 4. Scæn. 1.

Enter LORENZO, CAPTAINS.

Lorenzo. MANTUA is ours; place a strong garrison in it
To keep it so; and as a due reward
To your brave service, be our Governor in it.

1 *Captain.* I humbly thank your Excellence. *Exit.*
Lorenzo. *Gonzaga*
Is yet out of our gripe; but his strong Fort
St. *Leo*, which he holds impregnable
By the aids of art, as nature, shall not long
Retard our absolute conquest. The escape
Of fair *Matilda*, my supposed Mistress,
(For whose desir'd possession 'twas given out
I made this war) I value not; alas
Cupid's too feeble-ey'd to hit my heart,
Or could he see, his arrows are too blunt
To pierce it; his imagin'd torch is quench'd
With a more glorious fire of my ambition
T'enlarge my Empire: soft and silken amours,
With Carpet-Courtship, which weak Princes stile
The happy issue of a flourishing peace,
3r My toughness scorns: Were there an abstract made
Of all the eminent and canoniz'd Beauties
By truth recorded, or by Poets feign'd,
I could unmov'd behold it, as a Picture
Commend the workmanship, and think no more on't;
I have more noble ends. Have you not heard yet
Of *Alonzo*, or *Pisano*?
2 *Captain.* My Lord, of neither.
Lorenzo. Two turbulent spirits unfit for discipline,
Much less command in war; if they were lost,
I shall not pine with mourning.

Enter MARTINO, MATILDA, GALEAZZO, *and Guard.*

Martino. Bring 'em forward;—
This will make my peace, though I had kill'd his father, [*Aside.*]
Besides the reward that follows.
Lorenzo. Ha! *Martino*?
Where is *Farneze's* head? dost thou stare? and where
The soldier that desir'd the torture of him?
Martino. An't please your Excellence—
Lorenzo. It doth not please us;
Are our commands obey'd?
Martino. *Farneze's* head, sir,

IV. i. 29 SD. *Aside.*] *editor*; *not in* 55

Is a thing not worth your thought, the soldiers less sir:
I have brought your Highness such a head, a head
So well set on too, a fine head.
Lorenzo. Take that *Strikes him.*
For thy impertinence: what head, ye Rascal?
Martino. My Lord, if they that bring such presents to you
Are thus rewarded, there are few will strive
To be near your Graces pleasures: but I know
You will repent your choler. Here's the head,
And now I draw the curtain, it hath a face too,
And such a face.
Lorenzo. Ha!
E3v *Martino.* View her all o're, my Lord;
My company on't, she's sound of wind and limb,
And will do her labour tightly, a *Bona Roba*:
And for her face, as I said, there are five hundred
City-dub'd Madams in the Dukedom, that would part with
Their Jointures to have such another: Hold up your head, Maid.
Lorenzo. Of what age is the day?
Martino. Sir, since Sun-rising
About two hours.
Lorenzo. Thou lyest; the Sun of Beauty
In modest blushes on her cheeks, but now
Appear'd to me, and in her tears breaks forth
As through a shower in *April*, every drop
An orient pearl, which as it fals, congeal'd,
Were Ear-rings for the Catholick King,
Worn on his birth-day.
Martino. Here's a sudden change.
Lorenzo. Incensed *Cupid*, whom even now I scorn'd,
Hath took his stand, and by reflexion shines
(As if he had two bodies, or indeed
A brother-twin, whom sight cannot distinguish)
In her fair eyes; see how they head their arrows
With her bright beams, now frown, as if my heart
Rebellious to their edicts, were unworthy,
Should I rip up my bosom, to receive
A wound from such divine artillery.
Martino. I am made for ever. [*Aside.*]

56. King,] *55*; King, to be *conj. Gifford* 67 SD. *Aside.*] *Coxeter*; *not in 55*

Matilda. We are lost,
Dear servant.
Galeazzo. Vertue's but a word;
Fortune rules all.
Matilda. We are her Tennis-balls.
Lorenzo. Allow her fair, her symetrie and features
So well proportion'd, as the heavenly object
With admiration would strike *Ovid* dumb,
Nay force him to forget his faculty
In verse, and celebrate her praise in prose.
E4r What's this to me? I that have pass'd my youth
Unscorch'd with wanton fires, my sole delight
In glittering arms, my conquering sword my mistress;
Neighing of barbed horse, the cries and groans
Of vanquish'd foes suing for life, my musick:
And shall I in the Autumn of my age,
Now when I wear the livery of time
Upon my head and beard, suffer my self
To be transform'd, and like a puling Lover
With arms thus folded up, eccho *Ay me's*!
And write my self a Bondman to my Vassal?
It must not, nay it shall not be: Remove
The object, and the effect dies. Nearer, *Martino*.
Martino. I shall have a Regiment, Colonel *Martino*, [*Aside.*]
I cannot go less.
Lorenzo. What thing is this thou hast brought me?
Martino. What thing? Heaven bless me, are you a *Florentine*?
Nay, the Great Duke of *Florentines*, and having had her
So long in your power, do you now ask what she is?
Take her aside and learn; I have brought you that
I look to be dearly paid for.
Lorenzo. I am a Soldier;
And use of women will, *Martino*, rob
My nerves of strength.
Martino. All armor, and no smock?
Abominable! A little of the one with the other
Is excellent: I ne'r knew General yet,
Nor Prince that did deserve to be a Worthy,
But he desir'd to have his sweat wash'd off

88 SD. *Aside.*] *Coxeter*; *not in* 55

By a juicie Bedfellow.
Lorenzo. But say she be unwilling
To do that office?
Martino. Wrastle with her, I will wager
Ten to one on your Graces side.
Lorenzo. Slave, hast thou brought me
E4v Temptation in a Beauty not to be
With prayers resisted; and in place of councel
To master my affections, and to guard
My honor now besieg'd by lust, with the arms
Of sober temperance, mark me out a way
To be a ravisher? Would thou hadst shewn me
Some monster, though in a more ugly form
Then *Nile* or *Africk* ever bred. The Basilisk
(Whose envious eye yet never brook'd a neighbour)
Kills but the body; Her more potent eye
Buries alive mine honor. Shall I yield thus?
And all brave thoughts of victory and triumphs,
The spoils of Nations, the loud applauses
Of happy subjects made so by my conquests;
And what's the crown of all, a glorious name
Insculp'd on Pyramids to posterity,
Be drench'd in *Lethe*, and no object take me
But a weak Woman, rich in colours only,
Too delicate a touch, and some rare features
Which age or sudden sickness will take from her,
And where's then the reward of all my service?
Love-soothing passions, nay idolatry
I must pay to her. Hence, and with thee take
This second, but more dangerous *Pandora*,
Whose fatal box, if open'd, will pour on me
All mischiefs that mankind is subject to.
To the desarts with this *Circe*, this *Calipso*,
This fair Inchantress; let her spels and charms
Work upon beasts and thee, then whom wise nature
Ne'r made a viler creature.
Matilda. Happy exile!
Galeazzo. Some spark of hope remains yet.
Martino. Come, you are mine now;

122. a touch] *55*; to touch *Coxeter*

I will remove her where your Highness shall not
Or see or hear more of her: what a sum
Will she yield for the Turks *Serraglio*!
E5r *Lorenzo.* Stay, I feel
A sudden alteration.
Martino. Here are fine whimsies.
Lorenzo. Why should I part with her? can any foulness
Inhabit such a clean and gorgeous palace?
The fish, the fowl, the beasts may safer leave
The elements they were nourish'd in, and live,
Then I endure her absence; yet her presence
Is a torment to me: Why do I call it so?
My sire enjoy'd a woman, I had not been else;
He was a compleat Prince, and shall I blush
To follow his example? Oh but my choice,
Though she gave suffrage to it, is beneath me:
But even now in my proud thoughts I scorn'd
A Princess, fair *Matilda*; and is't decreed
For punishment, I straight must dote on one
What, or from whence I know not? Grant she be
Obscure, without a Coat or family,
Those I can give; and yet if she were noble,
My fondness were more pardonable. *Martino*,
Dost thou know thy prisoner?
Martino. Do I know my self?
I kept that for the Lenvoy; 'tis the daughter
Of your enemy, Duke *Gonzaga*.
Lorenzo. Fair *Matilda*!
I now call to my memory her picture,
And find this is the substance; but her Painter
Did her much wrong, I see it.
Martino. I am sure
I tugg'd hard for her, here are wounds can witness,
Before I could call her mine.
Lorenzo. No matter how:
Make thine own ransom, I will pay it for her.
Martino. I knew it would come at last.
Matilda. We are lost again.
Galeazzo. Variety of afflictions!
E5v *Lorenzo.* That his knee

That never yet bow'd to mortality, *Kneels.*
Kisses the earth, happy to bear your weight,
I know begets your wonder. Hear the reason,
And cast it off. Your beauty does command it.
Till now I never saw you; fame hath been
Too sparing in report of your perfections,
Which now with admiration I gaze on.
Be not afraid, fair Virgin; had you been
Imploy'd to mediate your Fathers cause,
My drum had been unbrac'd, my trumpet hung up,
Nor had the terror of the war e're frighted
His peaceful confines; your demands had been
As soon as spoke, agreed to. But you'll answer,
And may with reason; Words make no satisfaction
For what's in fact committed. Yet take comfort,
Something my pious love commands me do,
Which may call down your pardon.

Matilda. This expression
Of reverence to your person, better suits *Takes him up, and kneels.*
With my low fortune. That you daign to love me,
My weakness would perswade me to believe
(Though conscious of mine own unworthiness)
You being as the liberal eye of heaven
Which may shine where it pleases. Let your beams
Of favour warm and comfort me, not consume me;
For should your love grow to excess, I dare not
Deliver what I fear.

Lorenzo. Dry your fair eyes;
I apprehend your doubts, and could be angry
If humble love could warrant it, you should
Nourish such base thoughts of me: Heaven bear witness,
And if I break my vow, dart thunder at me,
You are and shall be in my tent as free
E6r From fear of violence, as a cloyster'd Nun
Kneeling before the Altar. What I purpose
Is yet an Embrion; but grown into form,
I'll give you power to be the sweet disposer
Of blessings unexpected; that your Father,
Your Country, people, children yet unborn too,
In holy hymns on Festivals shall sing

The triumph of your beauty. On your hand
Once more I swear it: O imperious Love!
Look down, and as I truly do repent,
Prosper the good ends of thy Penitent. *Exeunt.*

V. ii] *Enter* OCTAVIO *and* MARIA.

Octavio. You must not be too sudden, my *Maria*,
In being known: I am in this Friars habit
As yet conceal'd; though his recovery
Be almost certain, I must work him to
Repentance by degrees. When I would have you
Appear in your true shape of sorrow to
Move his compassion, I will stamp thus, then
You know to act your part.
Ascanio. I shall be careful.
Octavio. If I can cure the ulcers of his mind,
As I despair not of his bodies wounds,
Felicity crowns my labour. *Gothrio*!

Enter GOTHRIO.

Gothrio. Here sir.
Octavio. Desire my Patients to leave their chamber,
And take fresh air here: how have they slept?
Gothrio. Very well sir,
I would we were so rid of 'em.
Octavio. Why?
Gothrio. I fear
One hath the art of memory, and will
Remember his gold and jewels: could you not minister
A potion of forgetfulness? what would Gallants
E6v That are in debt, give me for such a receipt
To pour in their Creditors drink?
Octavio. You shall restore all,
Believ't you shall: will you please to walk?
Gothrio. Will you please to put off
Your holy habit, and spic'd conscience? One
I think infects the other. *Exit.*
Octavio. I have observ'd

IV. ii. *Scene division Coxeter; undivided 55*

Compunction in *Alonzo*; he speaks little,
But full of retir'd thoughts: The other is
Jocund and merry, no doubt, because he hath
The less accompt to make here.

Enter ALONZO.

Alonzo. Reverend sir,
I come to wait your pleasure; but my friend
(Your creature I should say, being so my self)
Willing to take farther repose, intreats
Your patience a few minutes.
Octavio. At his pleasure;
Pray you sit down, you are faint still.
Alonzo. Growing to strength,
I thank your goodness: but my mind is troubled,
Very much troubled, sir; and I desire,
Your pious habit giving me assurance
Of your skill and power that way, that you would please
To be my Minds physitian.
Octavio. Sir, to that
My order binds me; if you please to unload
The burthen of your conscience, I will minister
Such heavenly cordials as I can, and set you
In a path that leads to comfort.
Alonzo. I will open
My bosoms secrets to you; that I am
A man of blood, being brought up in the wars,
E7r And cruel executions, my profession
Admits not to be question'd: but in that
Being a subject, and bound to obey
Whate'r my Prince commanded, I have left
Some shadow of excuse: with other crimes
As pride, lust, gluttony, it must be told
I am besmear'd all over.
Octavio. On repentance
Mercy will wash it off.
Alonzo. O sir, I grant
These sins are deadly ones; yet their frequencie
With wicked men, make them less dreadful to us:
But I am conscious of one crime, with which

All ills I have committed from my youth
Put in the scale weigh nothing: such a crime,
So odious to heaven and man, and to
My sear'd up conscience so full of horror,
As penance cannot expiate.
Octavio. Despair not,
'Tis impious in man to prescribe limits
To the divine compassion; out with it.
Alonzo. Hear then, good man; and when that I have given you
The character of it, and confess'd my self
The wretch that acted it, you must repent
The charity you have extended towards me.
Not long before these wars began, I had
Acquaintance ('tis not fit I stile it Friendship,
That being a vertue, and not to be blended
With vitious breach of faith) with the Lord *Octavio*,
The Minion of his Prince and Court, set off
With all the pomp and circumstance of greatness:
To this then happy man I offer'd service,
And with insinuation wrought my self
Into his knowledg, grew familiar with him,
Ever a welcom guest. This noble Gentleman
Was bless'd with one fair daughter, (so he thought
E7v And boldly might believe so, for she was
In all things excellent without a Rival)
Till I (her Fathers mass of wealth before
My greedy eyes, but hoodwink'd to mine honor)
With far more subtle arts then perjur'd *Paris*
E're practis'd on poor credulous *Oenone*,
Besieg'd her Virgin-fort, in a word took it,
No vows or imprecation forgotten
With speed to marry her.
Octavio. Perhaps she gave you
Just cause to break those vows.
Alonzo. She cause! alas
Her innocence knew no guilt, but too much favor
To me unworthy of it: 'twas my baseness,
My foul ingratitude, what shall I say more?
The good *Octavio* no sooner fell
In the displeasure of his Prince, his state

Confiscated, and he forc'd to leave the Court,
And she expos'd to want; but all my oaths
And protestation of service to her,
Like seeming flames rais'd by inchantment, vanish'd;
This, this sits heavy here.

Octavio. He speaks as if [*Aside.*]
He were acquainted with my plot:—You have reason
To feel compunction, for 'twas most inhumane
So to betray a Maid.

Alonzo. Most barbarous.

Octavio. But does your sorrow for the fact beget
An aptness in you to make satisfaction
For the wrong you did her?

Alonzo. Gracious heaven! an aptness!
It is my only study; since I tasted
Of your compassion, these eyes ne'r were clos'd,
But fearful dreams cut off my little sleep,
And being awake, in my imagination,
Her apparition haunted me.

E8r *Octavio.* 'Twas meer fancie. *He stamps.*

Alonzo. 'Twas more, grave sir, nay 'tis;

Enter MARIA.

now it appears.

Octavio. Where?

Alonzo. Do you not see there the gliding shadow
Of a fair Virgin? that is she, and wears
The very garments that adorn'd her when
She yielded to my Crocodile tears: A cloud
Of fears and diffidence then so chac'd away
Her purer white and red, as it foretold
That I should be disloyal. Blessed shadow!
For 'twere a sin, far, far exceeding all
I have committed, to hope only that
Thou art a substance: look on my true sorrow,
Nay, souls contrition; hear again those vows
My perjury cancell'd, stamp'd in brass, and never
To be worn out.

95 SD. *Aside.*] *editor*; *not in* 55

Enter GOTHRIO.

Ascanio. I can endure no more;
Action, not oaths must make me reparation:
I am *Maria.*
Alonzo. Can this be?
Octavio. It is,
And I *Octavio.*
Alonzo. Wonder on wonder!
How shall I look on you? or with what forehead
Desire your pardon?
Ascanio. You truly shall deserve it
In being constant.
Octavio. If you fall not off,
But look on her in poverty with those eyes
As when she was my heir in expectation
You thought her beautiful.
Alonzo. She's in herself
Both *Indies* to me.
Gothrio. Stay, she shall not come
A begger to you, my sweet young Mistress! no,
She shall not want a dower. Here's white and red
Will ask a jointure; but how you should make her one,
E8v Being a Captain, would beget some doubt,
If you should deal with a Lawyer.
Alonzo. I have seen this purse.
Gothrio. How the world's given, I dare not say to lying,
Because you are a Soldier; you may say as well
This gold is mark'd too: you being to receive it,
Should ne'r ask how I got it. I'll run for a Priest
To dispatch the matter; you shall not want a Ring,
I have one for the purpose. Now sir, I think I am honest. *Exit.*
Alonzo. This Ring was *Pisano's.*
Octavio. I'll dissolve this riddle
At better leisure: the wound given to my daughter,
Which in your honor you are bound to cure,
Exacts our present care.
Alonzo. I am all yours sir. *Exeunt.*

[IV. iii] *Enter* GONZAGA, UBERTI, MANFROY.

Gonzaga. Thou hast told too much to give assurance that
Her honor was too far engag'd to be
By humane help redeem'd: If thou hadst given
Thy sad narration this full period,
She's dead; I had been happy.
Uberti. Sir, these tears
Do well become a father; and my eyes
Would keep you company as a forlorn Lover,
But that the burning fire of my revenge
Dries up those drops of sorrow. We once more,
Our broken forces rallied up, and with
Full numbers strengthen'd, stand prepar'd to endure
A second trial; nor let it dismay us
That we are once again to affront the fury
Of a victorious Army; their abuse
F1r Of Conquest hath disarm'd themselves, and call'd down
The powers above to aid us. I have read
Some piece of story, yet ne'r found but that
The General that gave way to cruelty,
The profanation of things sacred, rapes
Of virgins, butchery of infants, and
The massacre in cold blood of reverend age,
Against the discipline and law of Arms,
Did feel the hand of heaven lie heavy on him,
When most secure: We have had a late example,
And let us not despair but that in *Lorenzo*
It will be seconded.
Gonzaga. You argue well,
And 'twere a sin in me to contradict you:
Yet we must not neglect the means that's lent us
To be the Ministers of Justice.
Uberti. No, sir:
One day given to refresh our wearied Troops
Tir'd with a tedious march, we'll be no longer
Coop'd up, but charge the Enemy in his trenches,
And force him to a battel. *Shouts within.*
Gonzaga. Ha! how's this?

IV. iii. *Scene division Coxeter*; *undivided 55*

In such a general time of mourning, shouts
And acclamations of joy?
(*Within they cry* Long live the Princess! long live *Matilda*!)
Uberti. *Matilda*!
The Princess name, *Matilda*, oft re-eccho'd.

Enter FARNEZE.

Gonzaga. What speaks thy haste?
Farneze. More joy and happiness
Then weak words can deliver, or strong faith
Almost give credit to: The Princess lives,
I saw her, kist her hand.
Gonzaga. By whom deliver'd?
1v *Farneze.* That is not to be stall'd by my report,
This only must be told: As I rode forth
With some choise troops to make discovery
Where the Enemy lay, and how intrench'd, a Leader
Of th'adverse party, but unarm'd, and in
His hand an Olive-branch, encounter'd me;
He shew'd the great Dukes seal that gave him power
To parly with me: his desires were, that
Assurance for his safety might be granted
To his royal Master, who came as a friend
(And not as an enemy) to offer to you
Conditions of peace. I yielded to it.
This being return'd, the Dukes *Pretorium* open'd;
When suddenly in a triumphant Chariot
Drawn by such soldiers of his own as were
For insolence after victory condemn'd
Unto this slavish office, the fair Princess
Appear'd, a wreath of Laurel on her head,
Her robes majestical, their richness far
Above all value, as the present age
Contended that a womans pomp should dim
The glittering triumphs of the Roman *Cæsars*.
I am cut off; no Canons throat now thunders,
Nor Fife nor Drum beat up a charge; choise Musique
Ushers the parent of security,
Long absent Peace.

42. stall'd] *55*; 'stall'd *Coxeter*; stal'd *Gifford*

Manfroy. I know not what to think on't.
Uberti. May it poise the expectation!

Enter Soldiers (unarm'd, with olive-branches), Captains; LORENZO, GALEAZZO, MARTINO, MATILDA *(a wreath of laurel on her head, in her chariot drawn through them.)*

Gonzaga. Thus to meet you
Great Duke of *Tuscany*, throws amazement on me:
F2r But to behold my daughter, long since mourn'd for,
And lost even to my hopes, thus honour'd by you,
With an excess of comfort overwhelms me:
And yet I cannot truly call my self
Happy in this solemnity, till your Highness
Vouchsafe to make me understand the motives
That in this peaceful way hath brought you to us.
Lorenzo. I must crave licence first; for know, *Gonzaga*,
I am subject to anothers will, and can
Nor speak nor do without permission from her:
My curled forehead, of late terrible
To those that did acknowledge me their Lord,

While LORENZO *speaks,* UBERTI *and the rest present themselves to* MATILDA.

Is now as smooth as rivers when no wind stirs:
My frowns or smiles, that kill'd or sav'd, have lost
Their potent awe, and sweetness: I am transform'd
(But do not scorn the Metamorphosis)
From that fierce thing men held me; I am captiv'd,
And by the unresistable force of beauty
Led hither as a prisoner. Is't your pleasure that
I shall deliver those injunctions which
Your absolute command impos'd upon me,
Or daign your self to speak 'em?
Matilda. Sir, I am
Your property, you may use me as you please;
But what is in your power and breast to do,
No Orator can dilate so well.
Lorenzo. I obey you.
That I came hither as an enemy
With hostile arms, to the utter ruine of

75. motives] *55*; motive *Coxeter*

Your Country, what I have done, makes apparent:
That fortune seconded my will, the late
Defeature will make good: That I resolv'd
To force the scepter from your hand, and make
Your Dukedom tributary, my surprizal
Of *Mantua* your Metropolis can well witness:
F2v And that I cannot fear the change of fate,
My Army flesh'd in blood, spoil, glory, conquest
Stand ready to maintain: Yet I must tell you
By whom I am subdu'd, and what's the ransom
I am commanded to lay down.
Gonzaga. My Lord,
You humble your self too much, 'tis fitter
You should propose, and we consent.
Lorenzo. Forbear,
The articles are here subscrib'd and sign'd
By my obedient hand: All prisoners
Without a ransom set at liberty,
Mantua to be deliver'd up; the Rampires
Ruin'd in the assault, to be repair'd;
The loss the husbandman receiv'd, his crop
Burnt up by wanton licence of the soldier
To be made good; with whatsoever else
You could impose on me, if you had been
The Conqueror, I your Captive.
Gonzaga. Such a change
Wants an example: I must owe this favour
To the clemencie of the old Heroique valour,
That spar'd when it had power to kill; a vertue
Buried long since, but rais'd out of the grave
By you to grace this latter age.
Lorenzo. Mistake not
The cause that did produce this good effect,
If as such you receive it: 'twas her beauty
Wrought first on my rough nature; but the vertues
Of her fair soul, dilated in her converse,
That did confirm it.
Matilda. Mighty sir, no more;
You honor her too much, that is not worthy
To be your servant.

Lorenzo. I have done, and now
Would gladly understand that you allow of
The articles propounded.
F3r *Gonzaga.* Do not wrong
Your benefits with such a doubt; they are
So great and high, and with such reverence
To be receiv'd, that if I should profess
I hold my Dukedom from you as your vassal,
Or offer'd up my daughter as you please
To be dispos'd of, in the point of honor
And a becoming gratitude, 'twould not cancel
The bond I stand engag'd for: but accept
Of that which I can pay; my all is yours sir,
Nor is there any here (though I must grant
Some have deserv'd much from me) for so far
I dare presume, but will surrender up
Their interest to that your Highness shall
Daign to pretend a title.
Uberti. I subscribe not
To this condition.
Farneze. The services
This Prince hath done your Grace in your most danger,
Are not to be so slighted.
Galeazzo. 'Tis far from me
To urge my merits, yet I must maintain
Howe'r my power is less, my love is more,
Nor will the gracious Princess scorn to acknowledge
I have been her humble servant.
Lorenzo. Smooth your brows,
I'll not incroach upon your right, for that were
Once more to force affection (a crime
With which should I the second time be tainted,
I did deserve no favour) neither will I
Make use of what is offer'd by the Duke,
Howe'r I thank his goodness: I'll lay by
My power; and though I should not brook a Rival,
(What we are, well consider'd) I'll descend
To be a third Competitor; he that can
With love and service best deserve the garland,
F3v With your consent let him wear it; I despair not

The trial of my fortune.
Gonzaga. Bravely offer'd,
And like your self, great Prince.
Uberti. I must profess
I am so taken with it, that I know not
Which way to express my service.
Galeazzo. Did I not build
Upon the Princess grace, I could sit down,
And hold it no dishonor.
Matilda. How I feel
My soul divided! all have deserv'd so well,
I know not where to fix my choice.
Gonzaga. You have
Time to consider: will you please to take
Possession of the Fort? then having tasted
The fruits of peace, you may at leisure prove
Whose plea will prosper in the Court of Love. *Exeunt.*

F4r
. i]

Act. 5. Scæn. 1.

Enter ALONZO, OCTAVIO, PISANO, MARIA (*with a purse*), GOTHRIO.

Alonzo. YOU need not doubt sir, were not peace proclaim'd
And celebrated with a general joy,
The high displeasure of the *Mantuan* Duke,
Rais'd on just grounds, not jealous suppositions.
The saving of our lives (which next to heaven
To you alone is proper) would force mercy
For an offence though capital.
Pisano. When the Conqueror
Uses Intreaties, they are arm'd Commands
The vanquish'd must not check at.
Ascanio. My piety pay the forfeit,
If danger come but near you. I have heard
My gracious Mistress often mention you,
(When I serv'd her as a Page) and feelingly
Relate how much the Duke her sire repented
His hasty doom of banishment, in his rage

Pronounc'd against you.
Octavio. In a private difference,
I grant that Innocence is a wall of brass,
And scorns the hottest battery: but when
The cause depends between the Prince and Subject,
'Tis an unequal competition; Justice
Must lay her ballance by, and use her sword
For his ends that protects it. I was banish'd,
And till revoked from exile, to tread on
My Soveraigns territories with forbidden feet,
F4v The severe letter of the Law calls death,
Which I am subject to in coming so neer
His Court and person. But my onely Child
Being provided for, her honor salv'd too,
I thank your noble change, I shall endure
Whate'r can fall with patience.
Alonzo. You have us'd
That medicine too long; prepare your self
For honor in your age, and rest secure of't.
Ascanio. Of what is your wisdom musing?
Gothrio. I am gazing on
This gorgeous House, our Cote's a dishclout to it;
It has no sign, what do you call't?
Ascanio. The Court;
I have liv'd in't a Page.
Gothrio. Page! very pretty:
May I not be a Page? I am old enough,
Well timber'd too, and I have a beard to carry it:
Pray you let me be your Page, I can swear already
Upon your pantable.
Ascanio. What?
Gothrio. That I'll be true
Unto your smock.
Ascanio. How, Rascal?
Octavio. Hence, and pimp
To your Rams and Ews; such foul pollution is
To be whipt from Court: I have now no more use of you,
Return to your trough.
Gothrio. Must I feed on husks,
Before I have plaid the prodigal?

Octavio. No, I'll reward
Your service; live in your own element
Like an honest man; all that is mine in the cottage
I freely give you.
Gothrio. Your Bottles too, that I carry
For your own tooth?
Octavio. Full as they are.
F5r *Ascanio.* And gold,
That will replenish 'em.
Gothrio. I am made for ever,
This was done in the nick.
Octavio. Why in the nick?
Gothrio. O sir,
'Twas well for me that you did reward my service
Before you enter'd the Court; for 'tis reported
There is a drink of Forgetfulness, which once tasted,
Few masters think of their servants, who grown old,
Are turn'd off like lame hounds and hunting-horses,
To starve on the Commons. [*Exit.*]
Alonzo. Bitter Knave! there's craft
I'the clouted shoo. Captain!

Enter MARTINO.

Martino. I am glad to kiss
Your valiant hand, and yours: but pray you take notice
My title's chang'd, I am a Colonel.
Pisano. A Colonel! where's your Regiment?
Martino. Not rais'd yet;
All the old ones are cashier'd, and we are now
To have a new Militia. All is peace here,
Yet I hold my title still, as many do
That never saw an Enemy.
Alonzo. You are pleasant,
And it becomes you. Is the Duke stirring?
Martino. Long since,
Four hours at least, but yet not ready.
Pisano. How?
Martino. Even so; you make a wonder of't, but leave it:
Alas, he is not now (sir) in the Camp,

V. i. 56 SD. *Exit.*] *Gifford*; *not in* 55

To be up and arm'd upon the least alarum;
There's something else to be thought on. Here he comes,
With his Officers, new rigg'd.

F5v *Enter* LORENZO, DOCTOR, *Gentleman*, *Page* (*imployed about him as from his chamber*.)

Alonzo. A looking-glass!
Upon my head he saw not his own face
These seven years past, but by reflexion
From a bright armor.
Martino. Be silent, and observe.
Lorenzo. So, have you done yet?
Is your building perfect?
Doctor. If your Highness please,
Here is a water.
Lorenzo. To what use? my Barber
Hath wash'd my face already.
Doctor. But this water
Hath a strange vertue in't, beyond his art;
It is a sacred Relique, part of that
Most powerful Juice, with which *Medea* made
Old *Æson* young.
Lorenzo. A fable; but suppose
I should give credit to it, will it work
The same effect on me?
Doctor. I'll undertake
This will restore the honour'd hair that grows
Upon your Highness head and chin, a little
Inclining unto gray.
Lorenzo. Inclining! Doctor.
Doctor. Pardon me, mighty sir, I went too far,
Not gray at all; I dare not flatter you,
'Tis something chang'd, but this apply'd will help it
To the first amber-colour, every hair
As fresh as when, your manhood in the prime,
Your Grace arriv'd at thirty.
Lorenzo. Very well.
Doctor. Then here's a pretious oil (to which the maker
F6r Hath not yet given a name) will soon fill up

81. with which] *Gifford*; which with *55*

These dimples in your face and front. I grant
They are terrible to your enemies, and set off
Your frowns with majesty: but you may please
To know (as sure you do) a smooth aspect,
Softness and sweetness, in the Court of Love,
Though dumb, are the prevailing Orators.
Lorenzo. Will he new create me?
Doctor. If you daign to taste too
Of this Confection.
Lorenzo. I am in health,
And need no physick.
Doctor. Physick sir! an Empress
(If that an Empress lungs, sir, may be tainted
With putrifaction) would taste of it
That night on which she were to print a kiss
Upon the lips of her long absent Lord,
Returning home with conquest.
Lorenzo. It is predominant
Over a stinking breath, is it not Doctor?
Doctor. Clothe the infirmity with sweeter language,
'Tis a preservative that way.
Lorenzo. You are then
Admitted to the Cabinets of great Ladies,
And have the government of the borrowed beauties,
Of such as write neer forty?
Doctor. True, my good Lord
And my attempts have prosper'd.
Lorenzo. Did you never
Minister to the Princess?
Doctor. Sir, not yet;
She's in the April of her youth, and needs not
The aids of art, my gracious Lord: but in
The Autumn of her age I may be useful,
And sworn her Highness Doctor, and your Grace
Partake of the delight.
Lorenzo. Slave! Witch! Impostor! *Kicks him.*
F6v Mountebank! Cheater! Traitor to great Nature
In thy presumption to repair what she
In her immutable decrees design'd
For some few years to grow up, and then wither;

Or is't not crime enough thus to betray
The secrets of the weaker sex, thy patients,
But thou must make the honor of this age
And envy of the time to come, *Matilda*,
(Whose sacred name I bow to) guilty of
A future sin in thy ill-boding thoughts,
Which for a perpetuity of youth
And pleasure she disdains to act, such is
Her purity and innocence? *His foot on the* DOCTORS *breast.*
Alonzo. Long since
I look'd for this Lenvoy.
Martino. Would I were well off!
He's dangerous in these humours.
Octavio. Stand conceal'd.
Doctor. O sir, have mercy! in my thought I never
Offended you.
Lorenzo. Me? most of all, thou monster:
What a Mock-man property in thy intent
Wouldst thou have made me? a meer Pathick to
Thy devilish art, had I given suffrage to it.
Are my gray hairs, the ornament of age,
And held a blessing by the wisest men,
And for such warranted by holy Writ,
To be conceal'd, as if they were my shame?
Or plaister up these furrows in my face,
As if I were a painted Bawd or Whore?
By such base means if that I could ascend
To the height of all my hopes, their full fruition
Would not wipe off the scandal. No, thou wretch,
Thy cozening Water and adulterate Oil
I thus pour in thine eyes, and tread to dust
Thy loth'd Confection, with thy trumperies:
Vanish for ever.
F7r *Martino.* You have your fee, as I take it,
Dear Domine Doctor! I'll be no sharer with you. *Exit* DOCTOR.
Lorenzo. I'll court her like my self; these rich adornments
And Jewels, worn by me an absolute Prince,
My Order too, of which I am the Soveraign,
Can meet no ill construction: yet 'tis far
From my imagination to believe

She can be taken with sublimed clay,
The Silk-worms spoils, or rich Embroderies;
Nor must I borrow helps from power or greatness,
But as a loyal Lover plead my cause,
If I can feelingly express my ardor,
And make her sensible of the much I suffer
In hopes and fears, and she vouchsafe to take
Compassion on me,—Ha! compassion?
The word sticks in my throat: what's here that tels me
I do descend too low? rebellious spirit,
I conjure thee to leave me: there is now
No contradiction or declining left,
I must and will go on.

Martino. The tempest's laid;
You may present your selves.

Alonzo. My gracious Lord!

Pisano. Your humble Vassal.

Lorenzo. Ha! both living?

Alonzo. Sir,
We owe our lives to this good Lord, and make it
Our humble suit—

Lorenzo. Plead for your selves: we stand
Yet unresolv'd whether your knees or prayers
Can save the forfeiture of your own heads:
Though we have put our armor off, your pardon
For leaving the Camp without our licence
Is not yet sign'd. At some more fit time wait us.

Exeunt LORENZO *and Attendants.*

Alonzo. How's this?

F7v *Martino.* 'Tis well it is no worse; I met with
A rougher entertainment, yet I had
Good cards to shew: He's parcel mad, you'll find him
Every hour in a several mood, this foolish Love
Is such a shuttlecock; but all will be well
When a better fit comes on him, never doubt it. *Exeunt.*

[V. ii] *Enter* GONZAGA, UBERTI, FARNEZE, MANFROY.

Gonzaga. How do you find her?

182. the] 55; of the *Gifford* V. ii. *Scene division Coxeter; undivided 55*

Uberti. Thankful for my service,
And yet she gives me little hope; my Rival
Is too great for me.
Gonzaga. The great Duke you mean.
Uberti. Who else? the *Millanois* (although he be
A compleat Gentleman) I am sure despairs
More then my self.
Farneze. A high estate, with women,
Takes place of all desert.
Uberti. I must stand my fortune.

Enter LORENZO *and Attendants.*

Manfroy. The Duke of *Florence*! sir.
Gonzaga. Your Highness presence
Answers my wish. Your private ear:—I have us'd
My best perswasion with a Fathers power
To work my daughter to your ends; yet she
Like a small Bark on a tempestuous sea
Toss'd here and there by opposite winds, resolves not
At which port to put in, this Prince's merits,
Your grace and favor; nor is she unmindful
Of the brave acts (under your pardon sir
I needs must call them so) *Hortensio*
Hath done to gain her good opinion of him:
All these together tumbling in her fancie,
F8r Do much distract her; I have spies upon her,
And am assur'd this instant hour she gives
Hortensio private audience; I will bring you
Where we will see and hear all.
Lorenzo. You oblige me.
Uberti. I do not like this whispering.
Gonzaga. Fear no foul play. *Exeunt.*

[V. iii] *Enter* GALEAZZO, [BEATRICE,] *and two* WAITING-WOMEN.

1 *Woman.* The Princess, sir, long since expected you;
And would I beg a thanks, I could tell you that
I have often mov'd her for you.
Galeazzo. I am your servant.

V. iii. *Scene division Coxeter*; *undivided 55* SD. BEATRICE,] *Coxeter*; *not in 55*

Enter MATILDA.

Beatrice. She's come; there are others I must place to hear [*Aside.*]
The conference. *Exit.*
1 *Woman.* Is't your Excellencies pleasure
That we attend you?
Matilda. No, wait me in the gallery.
1 *Woman.* Would each of us, Wench, had a Sweetheart too!
To pass away the time.
2 *Woman.* There I join with you.
Exeunt WAITING-WOMEN.
Matilda. I fear this is the last time we shall meet.
Galeazzo. Heaven forbid!

Enter (*above*) BEATRICE, LORENZO, GONZAGA, UBERTI, FARNEZE.

Matilda. O my *Hortensio*!
In me behold the misery of Greatness,
F8ᵛ And that which you call Beauty: had I been
Of a more low condition, I might
Have call'd my will and faculties mine own,
Not seeing that which was to be belov'd
With others eyes: But now, ay me, most wretched
And miserable Princess! in my fortune
To be too much engag'd for service done me,
It being impossible to make satisfaction
To my so many Creditors, (all deserving)
I can keep touch with none.
Lorenzo. A sad *Exordium.*
Matilda. You lov'd me long, and without hope; (alas,
I die to think on't!) *Parma's* Prince invited
With a too partial report of what
I was, and might be to him, left his Country
To fight in my defence. Your brave atchievements
I'the war, and what you did for me, unspoken,
(Because I would not force the sweetness of
Your modesty to a blush) are written here.
And that there might be nothing wanting to
Sum up my numerous engagements (never
In my hopes to be cancell'd) the great Duke
Our mortal enemy, when my Fathers Country

4 SD. *Aside.*] *Gifford* ; *not in* 55

Lay open to his fury, and the spoil
Of the victorious Army, and I brought
Into his power, hath shewn himself so noble,
So full of honor, temperance, and all vertues
That can set off a Prince, that though I cannot
Render him that respect I would, I am bound
In thankfulness to admire him.

Galeazzo. 'Tis acknowledg'd,
And on your part to be return'd.

Matilda. How can I
Without the brand of foul ingratitude
To you, and Prince *Uberti*?

Galeazzo. Hear me, Madam,
G1r And what your servant shall with zeal deliver,
As a Dedalean clew may guide you out of
This labyrinth of distraction. He that loves
His Mistress truly, should prefer her honor
And peace of mind, above the glutting of
His ravenous appetite: He should affect her,
But with a fit restraint, and not take from her
To give himself: He should make it the heigth
Of his ambition, if it lie in
His stretch'd out nerves to effect it, though she flie in
An eminent place, to add strength to her wings,
And mount her higher, though he fall himself
Into the bottomless Abyss; or else
The services he offers are not real,
But counterfeit.

Matilda. What can *Hortensio*
Infer from this?

Galeazzo. That I stand bound in duty
(Though in the act I take my last farewell
Of comfort in this life) to sit down willingly,
And move my suit no further. I confess,
While you were in danger, and Heavens mercy made me
Its instrument to preserve you, (which your goodness
Priz'd far above the merit) I was bold
To feed my starv'd affection with false hopes
I might be worthy of you: For know, Madam,

49. affect] *Coxeter*; affect from *55* 50. take from] *Coxeter*; take *55*

How mean soever I appear'd in *Mantua*,
I had in expectation a fortune,
Though not possess'd of't, that encourag'd me
With confidence to prefer my suit, and not
To fear the Prince *Uberti* as my Rival.
Gonzaga. I ever thought him more then what he seem'd.
Lorenzo. Pray you forbear.
Galeazzo. But when the Duke of *Florence*
Put in his plea, in my consideration
Weighing well what he is, as you must grant him,
G1v A *Mars* of men in Arms; and those put off,
The great example for a Kingly Courtier
To imitate: Annex to these his wealth,
Of such a large extent, as other Monarchs
Call him the King of Coin; and what's above all,
His lawful love, with all the happiness
This life can fancie, from him flowing to you;
The true affection which I have ever borne you,
Does not alone command me to desist,
But as a faithful Councellor to advise you
To meet and welcom that felicity
Which hastes to crown your vertues.
Lorenzo. We must break off this parley.
Something I have to say. *Exeunt above.*
Matilda. In tears I thank
Your care of my advancement, but I dare not
Follow your councel: Shall such piety
Pass unrewarded? such a pure affection,
For any ends of mine, be undervalu'd?
Avert it Heaven! I will be thy *Matilda*,
Or cease to be; No other heat but what
Glows from thy purest flames, shal warm this bosom;
Nor *Florence*, nor all Monarchs of the earth
Shall keep thee from me.

Enter LORENZO, GONZAGA, UBERTI, FARNEZE, *two* WAITING-WOMEN.

Galeazzo. I fear, gracious Lady,
Our conference hath been oreheard.

88. *Lorenzo.*] *Coxeter*; *Mat.* 55   98 SD. FARNEZE,] *editor*; *Farneze*, *Manfroy*, 55

Matilda. The better:
Your part is acted; give me leave at distance
To zanie it, sir, on my knees thus prostrate
Before your feet.
Lorenzo. This must not be, I shall
Both wrong my self and you in suffering it.
G2r *Matilda.* I will grow here, and weeping thus turn marble,
Unless you hear and grant the first petition
A virgin, and a Princess ever tendred:
Nor doth the suit concern poor me alone,
It hath a strong reference to you
And to your honor; and if you deny it,
Both ways you suffer. Remember, sir, you were not
Born only for your self; Heavens liberal hand
Design'd you to command a potent Nation,
Gave you heroick valour, which you have
Abus'd in making unjust war upon
A neighbour Prince, a Christian; while the *Turk*,
Whose scourge and terror you should be, securely
Wastes the *Italian* Confines: 'tis in you
To force him to pull in his horned Crescents,
And 'tis expected from you.
Lorenzo. I have been
In a dream, and now begin to wake.
Matilda. And will you
Forbear to reap the harvest of such glories,
Now ripe and at full growth, for the embraces
Of a slight woman? or exchange your triumphs
For chamber-pleasures? melt your able nerves
(That should with your victorious sword make way
Through the Armies of your Enemies) in loose
And wanton dalliance? Be your self, great sir,
The thunderbolt of war, and scorn to sever
Two hearts long since united: your example
May teach the Prince *Uberti* to subscribe
To that which you allow of.
Lorenzo. The same tongue
That charm'd my sword out of my hand, and threw
A frozen numness on my active spirit,

108. strong] *55*; stronger *Coxeter*

Hath dis-enchanted me. Rise, fairest Princess!
And that it may appear I do receive
G2v Your councel as inspir'd from heaven, I will
Obey and follow it: I am your debtor,
And must confess you have lent my weakned reason
New strengths once more to hold a full command
Over my passions. Here to the world
I freely do profess that I disclaim
All interest in you, and give up my title
Such as it is, to you sir; and as far
As I have power, thus join your hands.
Gonzaga. To yours
I add my full consent.
Uberti. I am lost, *Farneze.*
Farneze. Far neerer to the port then you suppose:
In me our laws speak, and forbid this contract.
Matilda. Ay me! new stops!
Galeazzo. Shall we be ever cross'd thus?
Farneze. There is an Act upon record, confirm'd
By your wise predecessors, that no Heir
Of *Mantua* (as questionless the Princess
Is the undoubted one) must be join'd in marriage,
But where the match may strengthen the estate
And safety of the Dukedom. Now this Gentleman,
However I must stile him honorable,
And of a high desert, having no power
To make this good in his alliance, stands
Excluded by our laws: whereas this Prince
Of equal merit, brings to *Mantua*
The power and Principality of *Parma*:
And therefore since the great Duke hath let fall
His plea, there lives no Prince that justlier can
Challenge the Princess favor.
Lorenzo. Is this true, sir?
Gonzaga. I cannot contradict it.

Enter MANFROY.

Manfroy. There's an Ambassador
G3r From *Milain*, that desires a present audience;

146. Far neerer] *McIlwraith*; neerer *55*; Much nearer *Coxeter*

His business is of highest consequence,
As he affirms: I know him for a man
Of the best rank and quality.
Galeazzo. From *Milain*?
Gonzaga. Admit him.

Enter AMBASSADOR, *and* JULIO *with a Letter, which he presents on his knee to* GALEAZZO.

—How? so low!
Ambassador. I am sorry, sir,
To be the bringer of this heavy news:
But since it must be known—
Galeazzo. Peace rest with him,
I shall find fitter time to mourn his loss.
My faithful servant too, *Julio*!
Julio. I am orejoy'd
To see your Highness safe.
Galeazzo. Pray you peruse this,
And there you'll find that the objection
The Lord *Farneze* made, is fully answer'd.
Gonzaga. The great *John Galeas* dead?
Lorenzo. And this his brother,
The absolute Lord of *Milain*.
Matilda. I am reviv'd.
Uberti. There's no contending against destiny,
I wish both happiness.

Enter ALONZO, MARIA, OCTAVIO, PISANO, MARTINO.

Lorenzo. Married, *Alonzo*?
I will salute your Lady, she's a fair one,
And seal your pardon on her lips.
Gonzaga. *Octavio*,
Welcom even to my heart! Rise, I should kneel
To thee for mercy.
Octavio. The poor remainder of
My age shall truly serve you.
Matilda. You resemble
A Page I had, *Ascanio*.
Ascanio. I am
Your Highness servant still.

G3v *Lorenzo.* All stand amaz'd
At this unlook'd for meeting: But defer
Your several stories. Fortune here hath shewn
Her various power; but Vertue in the end
Is crown'd with laurel: Love hath done his parts too;
And mutual friendship after bloody jars,
Will cure the wounds received in our wars. *Exeunt omnes.*

FINIS.

G4r

EPILOGUE.

Pray you Gentlemen keep your seats; something I would
Deliver to gain favour, if I could,
To us, and the still doubtful Author. He,
When I desir'd an Epilogue, answer'd me,
'Twas to no purpose: He must stand his fate,
Since all intreaties now would come too late;
You being long since resolv'd what you would say
Of him, or us, as ye rise, or of the Play.
A strange old Fellow! yet this sullen mood
Would quickly leave him, might it be understood
You part not hence displeas'd. I am design'd
To give him certain notice: If you find
Things worth your liking, shew it. Hope and Fear,
Though different passions, have the self-same ear.

APPENDIX

VERSE REARRANGEMENT

The following lines of verse are undivided in *55*, except where otherwise stated.

I. i	12–13	sir; / But] *Coxeter*
	34–6	*rearranged by Coxeter; 55 reads* That . . . profession / 'Tis . . . it: / But . . . displeasure. / Saints . . . you.
	69–72	*rearranged by Coxeter; 55 reads* He . . . Conjurer / That . . . sighs / Are . . . up: / A . . . yet
	82–4	*rearranged by Gifford; 55 reads* But . . . whisper'd. / How ? . . . *Matilda* ! / Some . . . intelligence. / Let . . . kiss
	101–3	*rearranged by Coxeter; 55 reads* From . . . train. / Yet . . . petition, / Nor . . . sacrifices
	119–20	not; / I] *Coxeter*
	138–9	worth / My] *Coxeter*
	156–60	*rearranged by Coxeter; 55 reads* Now . . . eye. / That's . . . Excellence. / Observe . . . posture, / But . . . look. / Your . . . astonishment. / A . . . Lady,
	163–4	fits / Are] *Mason*
	167–8	him / A] *Coxeter*
	177–8	back: / In] *Coxeter*
	180–2	*rearranged by Coxeter; 55 reads* To . . . sufferings. / Signior . . . her. / How ? . . . betraid ? / What . . . this ?
	194–7	*rearranged by Coxeter; 55 reads* An . . . you. / It . . . reverence. / I . . . me ? / Your . . . fair. / I . . . opinion.
	209–10	Eunuch ! / To] *Coxeter*
	216–18	*rearranged by Coxeter; 55 reads* In . . . Ladies. / Or . . . *ultra.* / He's . . . apparent:
	221–2	me ? / Ends] *Coxeter*
	241–2	rise, / But] *Coxeter*
	250–1	challengeth / A] *Coxeter*

	263–4	know / I] *Coxeter*
	275–6	*Farneze* / Pleads] *Coxeter*
	279–81	*rearranged by Coxeter; 55 reads* Howe'r . . . garland. / A . . . sir. / I . . . won
I. ii	11–12	please, / The] *Coxeter*
	21–2	purpose; / These] *Coxeter*
	30–1	war, / With] *Coxeter*
	45–6	presume / You] *Coxeter*
	49–50	reasons / (Seconding] *Coxeter*
	71–2	speak, / Or] *Coxeter*
	92–3	wish / *Mantua* had] *Gifford;* wish *Mantua* had *55*; wish *Mantua* / had *Coxeter*
	101–2	it, / You] *Coxeter*
	121–2	Lord, / You] *Coxeter*
	147–8	repentance / When] *Coxeter*
II. i	21–2	too / A] *Coxeter*
	24–5	that / When] *Coxeter*
	27–8	sure / I] *Coxeter*
	32–3	you / Against] *Coxeter*
II. ii	5–6	appear / So] *Coxeter*
	10–11	heavy / To] *Coxeter*
	15–16	boy! / I] *Coxeter*
	23–4	worne / Upon] *Coxeter*
	37–8	suffice, / I] *Coxeter*
	40–1	not; / You] *Coxeter*
II. iv	5–6	help / Your] *Coxeter*
	29–30	remember / I] *Coxeter*
II. v	25–6	guard, / We] *Coxeter*
	41–2	confess / My] *Coxeter*
	46–7	proceeds / This] *Coxeter*
	50	Monarchs: I] *Coxeter;* Monarchs: / I *55*
	61–3	*rearranged by Coxeter; 55 reads* So . . . favour / This . . . admiration. / I . . . Rival. / You . . . charitable:
	94	selves. If] *after Coxeter;* selves. / My *55*
II. vi	21–2	will / Shall] *Coxeter*
II. vii	18–19	ever / Such] *Coxeter*
II. viii	1–2	True, / But] *Coxeter*
	5–6	expect / The] *Coxeter*
	7–8	decide / The] *Coxeter*
	40–2	*rearranged by Coxeter; 55 reads* Be . . . enemies / Take . . . title. / I . . . yours.
	61–2	anger / Can] *Gifford*
	69	murther. Thus] *Coxeter;* murther. / Thus *55*

	110–11	it; / Choose] *Coxeter*
	118–19	work; / Take] *Coxeter*
III. i	5	take.—When] *Coxeter;* take.— / When *55*
	24–5	compassion, / Or] *Coxeter*
	33–4	*rearranged by Gifford; 55 reads* But . . . inside / Outwards, . . . true. / Not . . . food? / Alas sir,
	39–40	*rearranged by editor; 55 reads* A . . . meal. / No . . . left? / Drunkard . . . all? / How? . . . sir:
	47–8	*Ascanio*, / Look] *Coxeter*
	73–4	thee, / Thou] *Coxeter*
III. ii	3–4	diamond, / Though] *Coxeter*
III. iii	31–2	lots / Who] *Coxeter*
	39–40	it / In] *Coxeter*
	46	safe; and] *Coxeter;* safe; / And *55*
	71–2	presage / My] *Coxeter*
	78–9	fast, / Resume] *Coxeter*
	98–9	page; / Look] *Coxeter*
	145–7	*rearranged by Coxeter; 55 reads* A . . . remission. / Let . . . favour. / Will . . . you? / I intranc'd.
	170–1	made / The] *Coxeter*
	184–5	first, / And] *Gifford*
	198–9	hope / Of] *Gifford*
	209–13	*rearranged by Coxeter; 55 reads* Rise . . . justice. / 'Twill . . . better / T'implore . . . mercy. / Hast . . . wrongs? / Turtles . . . breast
III. iv	232–3	perpetuity / Of] *Coxeter*
	257–8	disclaim / Superiority] *Coxeter*
	265–6	trance, / And] *Coxeter*
IV. i	4–5	*Gonzaga* / Is] *Coxeter*
	33–4	us; / Are] *Coxeter*
	50–1	Sun-rising / About] *Coxeter*
	67–9	*rearranged by editor; 55 reads* I . . . ever: / We . . . servants. / Vertue's . . . all. / We . . . Tennis-balls.
	94–5	Soldier; / And] *Coxeter*
	101–2	unwilling / To] *Coxeter*
	158–9	*Matilda*! / I] *Coxeter*
	166–7	knee / That] *Coxeter*
IV. ii	15–16	fear / One] *McIlwraith*
	30–1	pleasure; / Pray] *Coxeter*
	49–50	repentance / Mercy] *Coxeter*
	84–5	you / Just] *Coxeter*
	108	'tis; now] *Coxeter;* 'tis, / Now *55*
	122–3	is, / And] *Coxeter*

	129–30	herself / Both] *Coxeter*
	142–5	*rearranged by Gifford; 55 reads* This . . . *Pisano's.* / I'll . . . leisure: / The . . . honor / You . . . care. / I . . . sir.
IV. iii	29–30	sir: / One] *Coxeter*
	35–6	*rearranged by Gifford; 55 reads* And . . . joy? / Long . . . *Matilda*! / *Matilda*! . . . name, / *Matilda*, . . . re-eccho'd,
	66–7	security, / Long] *Coxeter*
	94–5	you. / That] *Coxeter*
	107–8	Lord, / You] *Coxeter*
	119–20	change / Wants] *Coxeter*
	147–8	not / To] *Coxeter*
	166–7	offer'd, / And] *Coxeter*
V. i	29–30	us'd / That] *Coxeter*
	34–5	Court; / I] *Coxeter*
	39–40	true / Unto] *Coxeter*
	43–4	husks, / Before] *Coxeter*
	47–51	*rearranged by Coxeter; 55 reads* I . . . you. / Your . . . tooth? / Full . . . are. / And . . . 'em. / I . . . nick. / Why . . . nick? / O . . . service.
	56–7	craft / I'the] *Gifford*
	70–1	on. Here he comes, / With] *Gifford;* on. / Here he comes, with *55*
	76–7	please, / Here] *Coxeter*
	103–4	health, / And] *McIlwraith*
	112–13	then / Admitted] *Coxeter*
	115–17	*rearranged by Coxeter; 55 reads* Of . . . forty? / True, . . . prosper'd. / Did . . . Princess? / Sir . . . yet;
	121–2	Grace / Partake of] *Coxeter;* Grace partake / Of *55*
	135–6	since / I] *Coxeter*
	174–5	laid; / You] *Coxeter*
	176–7	Sir, / We] *Coxeter*
V. ii	5–6	despairs / More] *Coxeter*
V. iii	5–6	pleasure / That] *Coxeter*
	36–7	so noble, / So] *Coxeter;* so / Noble, so *55*
	37–41	*rearranged by Gifford; 55 reads* Noble . . . temperance, / And . . . Prince, / That . . . respect / I . . . him. / 'Tis . . . return'd. / How . . . I,
	58–9	*Hortensio* / Infer] *Coxeter*
	119–21	*rearranged by Coxeter; 55 reads* And . . . you. / I . . . wake. / And . . . glories,
	144–5	yours / I] *Coxeter*

169–70 sir, / To] *Coxeter*
173–4 orejoy'd / To] *Coxeter*
180–1 *Alonzo*? / I] *Coxeter*
182–3 *Octavio*, / Welcom] *Coxeter*
185–7 *rearranged by Gifford; 55 reads* My . . . you. / You . . . *Ascanio*. / I . . . still:

THE POEMS

THE COPY OF A LETTER

INTRODUCTION

(a) *Date*

The precise date of composition of this poem is unknown. Since William Herbert, Earl of Pembroke, to whom it is addressed, became Lord Chamberlain on 23 December 1615,[1] the lines must have been written (or at least titled) in or after 1615. Lines 41–4 suggest that Massinger had not yet published anything under his own name, nor achieved a public reputation, so the poem must antedate 1623, the year in which *The Duke of Milan* was published as Massinger's work.

With less certainty the limits of the date of composition may be further narrowed. In 1622 Massinger's name first appeared on the title-page of a printed play, *The Virgin Martyr*, linked with that of Thomas Dekker. Earlier still, in 1620 John Taylor the Water Poet ranked Massinger with Jonson, Chapman, Marston, Middleton, Rowley, Fletcher, and Heywood under the heading 'Phylosophers, Hystorians, Chronographers, Poets ancient and moderne, the best sort mentioned'.[2]

Taylor's lines at least confirm that by this time Massinger had achieved some kind of fame, therefore *The Copy of a Letter* may be dated *c.* 1615–20, with 1623 as the latest possible date of composition.

(b) *Text*

Two seventeenth-century texts of *The Copy of a Letter* are known to scholars. The first is a manuscript of the poem found in the library of Trinity College, Dublin (MS. G.2.21). This is a folio paper

[1] G. E. Cokayne, *The Complete Peerage*, 1910–59, x. 413.

[2] *The Praise of Hemp-seed* (*Works*, 1630, Gggl^{r}); first noted in D. S. Lawless, *Philip Massinger and his Associates*, Muncie, Indiana, 1967, p. 26.

manuscript of 289 leaves, written in several hands of the first half of the seventeenth century.[1] Grosart, who first called attention to the poem in 1899, was informed that the manuscript had been in the library for a century; Cruickshank suggested that it might have originally formed part of Archbishop Ussher's library, which passed to Trinity College in 1661.

The manuscript consists of two collections of poems. Folios 1–292 contain poems by Donne and others, which Gardner believes were gathered some time after 1625. On folios 293–565 there is another, miscellaneous, collection. Grierson noted that these poems contained many references to the Duke of Buckingham, but none to the Long Parliament or to later events, and concluded that they were assembled before 1640.

The Copy of a Letter is among the second group, on pages 554–7, written in a fine Italian hand. At the top of page 555, a second hand has written the fourth verse of Donne's *Sweetest love, I do not go*, and there is a partially clipped marginal note in a third hand, '[T]his verse is / [t]he 5th in y^{e} / [1]61 page'. (Page 161 contains the poem, lacking the fourth verse.)

In 1956, G. E. Bentley recorded the existence of another text, in an octavo miscellany of 126 pages, *Poems consisting of Epistles & Epigrams, Satyrs, Epitaphs and Elegies, Songs and Sonnets. With variety of other drolling Verses upon several Subjects*, printed at London in 1658 for Henry Brome.[2] The main author is John Eliot, otherwise unknown (he signs his name to one poem on page 34 and his initials to several others). In an address to the reader, the anonymous editor explains that 'These Poems were given me neer sixteen years since by a Friend of the Authors, with a desire they might be printed, but I conceived the Age then too squeemish to endure the freedom which the Authour useth; and therefore I hitherto smother'd them' (A2^{r}). The British Museum possesses a duplicate copy with a variant title-page, *Poems or Epigrams, Satyrs, Elegies, Songs and Sonnets, Upon several Persons and Occasions*, also

[1] For accounts of the manuscript see *The Appendix to the Eighth Report of the Historical Manuscripts Commission*, 1881, Part 1, p. 584; T. K. Abbot, *Catalogue of the Manuscripts in the Library of Trinity College, Dublin*, 1900, p. 877; H. J. C. Grierson, *The Poems of John Donne*, 1912, ii, pp. xcii–xciv and cix–cx; and Donne's *The Divine Poems*, ed. Helen Gardner, 1952, pp. lxvi–lxviii.

[2] Bentley, iv. 756. Gifford also knew of this text (he quotes a few lines from it in his edition of Jonson's *Works*, 1816, i, p. clxxi), but he attributed it to Eliot, and made no mention of it in his editions of Massinger.

printed at London in 1658 by Henry Brome (238.b.47). In both copies Massinger's poem appears on pages 108–11, with a short title and without attribution.

A second edition of the miscellany was printed for Henry Brome at London in 1661.[1] There is a fresh title-page, *Choyce Poems, being Songs, Sonnets, Satyrs and Elegies. By the Wits of both Universities*, and seven preliminary leaves of new verse. Massinger's poem again appears on pages 108–11; the text is identical with that in the earlier edition.

Among substantive differences, the printed text supplies only two superior readings (ll. 20, 72) where the Dublin scribe has made simple errors, seven indifferent readings (ll. 4, 17, 22, 27, 39, 52, 61), and five inferior readings (ll. 34, 35, 63, 67, 70). The error 'beautie' for the Dublin reading 'Bounty' (l. 35) is particularly striking since it destroys the immediate line of argument; 'theirs' for 'These' probably represents a common misreading of the Massinger spelling 'theis'. The Dublin text is also demonstrably closer to its original in its accidentals, showing a preference for doubled terminal consonants and noun forms with a final 'e' mute, few apostrophes or elisions, no italics, and light punctuation. In 42 cases the manuscript retains a Massinger spelling, while the printed text does so in only 12; Massinger's strong preference for 'soe, doe' forms is largely ignored in the London text, but observed in the Dublin one.

For this edition, a microfilm of the Dublin manuscript (siglum *MS*) has been used as the copy-text, checked against a transcript from the original made by A. K. McIlwraith, and collated with the three British Museum copies (E. 2134. (3); 238.b.47; 238.b.35) of the London text (siglum *Eliot*).

The Dublin text of *The Copy of a Letter* was published by A. B. Grosart, 'Literary-Finds in Trinity College, Dublin, and Elsewhere', *Englische Studien*, xxvi (1899), 4–6 (siglum *Grosart*), and reprinted by P. Simpson, 'Two Poems of Philip Massinger', *The Athenaeum*, 4115 (8 Sept. 1906), 273 (siglum *Simpson*); also by A. H. Cruickshank, *Philip Massinger*, 1920. A. K. McIlwraith prepared a text for his Oxford thesis (1931), and D. S. Lawless reproduced the Dublin text in *The Poems of Philip Massinger*, Muncie, Indiana, 1968. The London text of the poem has never been reprinted.

[1] Number 131 in *A Bibliography of English Poetical Miscellanies, 1521–1750*, A. E. Case, 1935.

554 # The Copie of a Letter written vpon occasion to the Earle of Pembrooke Lo: Chamberlaine.

My Lord
Soe subiect to the worser fame
Are euen the best that clayme a Poets name,
Especially poore they that serue the stage
Though worthily in this Verse-halting Age,
And that dread curse soe heauie yet doth lie
Wch the wrong'd Fates falne out wth Mercurie
Pronounc'd foreuer to attend vpon
All such as onely dreame of Helicon,
That durst I sweare cheated by selfe opinion
I were Apolloes or the Muses Mynion
Reason would yet assure me, t'is decreed
Such as are Poets borne, are borne to need.
If the most worthy then, whose pay's but praise
Or a few spriggs from the now withering bayes
Grone vnderneath their wants what hope haue I
(Scarce yet allowed one of the Company)
555 Of better fortune, That wth their good parts
Euen want the wayes, the bold and thriuing arts
By wch they grow remarkeable and are priz'd;
Since sure I could not liue a thing despiz'd
Durst I professe t'were in my power to giue
A patron that should euer make him liue
Or tell great Lords that the maine Reason why
They hold A Poets prayses flatterie
Is their owne guilt, that since they left to doe
Things worthy praise euen praise is odious too!
Some few there are that by this boldnes thriue
Wch yet I dare not follow; others striue

Title. The . . . Chamberlaine] *MS*; *To the Lord Chamberlain Eliot* 2. euen] *MS*; ev'n *Eliot* 4. Verse-halting] *MS*; verse hating *Eliot* 17. fortune] *MS*; fortunes *Eliot* 18. Euen] *MS*; Ev'n *Eliot* 20. liue] *Eliot*; line *MS* 22. euer make him liue] *MS*; make him ever live *Eliot* 26. euen] *MS*; ev'n *Eliot* 27. that] *MS*; who *Eliot*

In some high mynded Ladies grace to stand,
Euer prouided that her liberall hand
Pay for the Vertues they bestow vpon her
And soe long shees the miracle and the honor
Of her whole Sex, and has forsooth more worth
Then was in any Sparta e're brought forth;
But when the Bounty failes a change is neare
And shee's not then what once shee did appeare,
For the new Giuer (shee dead) must inherit
What was by purchase gott and not by merit.
Lett them write well that doe this and in grace,
I would not for a pension or A place
p. 556 Part soe wth myne owne Candor; lett me rather
Liue poorely on those toyes I would not father,
Not knowne beyond A Player or A Man
That does pursue the course that I haue ran,
Ere soe grow famous: yet wth any paine
Or honest industry could I obteyne
A noble Fauorer, I might write and doe
Like others of more name and gett one too
Or els my Genius is false. I know
That Iohnson much of what he has does owe
To you and to your familie, and is neuer
Slow to professe it, nor had Fletcher euer
Such Reputation, and credit wonne
But by his honord Patron, Huntington;
Vnimitable Spencer ne're had been
Soe famous for his matchlesse Fairie Queene
Had he not found a Sydney to preferr
His plaine way in his Shepheards Calender,
Nay Virgills selfe (or Martiall does lye)
Could hardly frame a poore Gnatts Elegie
Before Mecænas cherisht him; and then
He streight conceiu'd Aeneas and the men
That found out Italie. These are Presidents
I cite wth reuerence: my lowe intents

32. soe long] *MS*; so, long, *Grosart* 34. e're] *MS*; ere *Eliot* 35. Bounty] *MS*; beautie *Eliot* 39. them] *MS*; such *Eliot* 44. ran] *MS*; run *Grosart* 52. it] *MS*; that *Eliot* 57. Spencer *deleted before* Sydney *in MS* 61. and] *MS*; but *Eliot* 63. These] *MS*; theirs *Eliot*

Looke not soe high, yet some worke I might frame
557 That should nor wrong my duty nor your Name,
Were but your Lo:pp pleas'd to cast an eye
Of fauour on my trodd downe pouertie.
How euer I confesse myselfe to be
Euer most bound for your best charitie
To others that feed on it, and will pay
My prayers wth theirs that as yu doe yu may
Liue long, belou'd and honor'd: doubtles then
Soe cleere a life will find a worthier Penn.
For me I rest assur'd besides the glory
T'wold make a Poet but to write your story.

Phill: Messinger.

66. nor wrong] *MS*; not wrong *Grosart* 67. Lo: pp] *MS*; *Honour Eliot* 70. for] *MS*; to *Eliot* 72. that] *Eliot*; thas *MS*; thus *Simpson* 73. honor'd:] *Eliot*; ∼‸ *MS* then] *MS*; ∼. *Grosart* Subscription *missing in Eliot*

A NEW YEAR'S GIFT

INTRODUCTION

(a) *Date*

The main clue to the date of this poem lies in what is known of Massinger's connection with the dedicatee, the Countess of Chesterfield. Katherine, daughter of Francis, Lord Hastings, and granddaughter of the fourth Earl of Huntingdon, was born in or before 1595. In 1605 she married Philip Stanhope, who was knighted in the same year, raised to the peerage as Baron Stanhope in 1616, and created Earl of Chesterfield in 1628. She died on 28 August 1636.[1]

On the evidence of the title alone, the poem must have been written in 1628 or later, but since there are two passages in the body of the text (ll. 17–18 and 31–3) which seem to indicate that Massinger was addressing her for the first time and had not yet written publicly in her honour, the likelihood is that this poem was written before 1623, when *The Duke of Milan* was published with a dedication to Lady Stanhope.

On the other hand, it was probably written after *The Copy of a Letter* (?1615–20) since the title and the text (ll. 1–2 and 15–16) acknowledge Lady Stanhope's patronage, whilst the other poem deplores the lack of a patron (ll. 45–9), and its scathing comments on those who strive 'In some high mynded Ladies grace to stand' could only have seemed ridiculous if Massinger had already found such patronage himself.

As A. K. McIlwraith observed,[2] 1621 or 1622 seems a likely date of composition, but a later date is not impossible.

(b) *Text*

Only one seventeenth-century copy of *A New Year's Gift* has been found. It is in the same manuscript in the library of Trinity College,

[1] The available biographical material is gathered by D. S. Lawless, *The Poems of Philip Massinger*, Muncie, Indiana, 1968, pp. 12–13; see also the General Introduction, vol. i, p. xxiii.

[2] *The Cambridge Bibliography of English Literature*, i. 631.

Dublin, which contains *The Copy of a Letter*, and was discovered with the other poem by A. B. Grosart in 1898.[1] In this manuscript the text of *A New Year's Gift* immediately follows that of *The Copy of a Letter*, and is written by the same hand. It occupies pages 557–9.

The present text is based on a microfilm of the original, checked against A. K. McIlwraith's direct transcript of the poem.

The Dublin text (siglum *MS*) was first printed by A. B. Grosart, 'Literary-Finds in Trinity College, Dublin, and Elsewhere', *Englische Studien*, xxvi (1899), 6–7. It was reprinted by P. Simpson, 'Two Poems of Philip Massinger', *The Athenaeum*, 4115 (8 Sept. 1906), p. 273; T. W. Baldwin, in his edition of *The Duke of Milan*, Lancaster, Pennsylvania, 1918; A. H. Cruickshank, *Philip Massinger*, 1920; and D. S. Lawless, *The Poems of Philip Massinger*, Muncie, Indiana, 1968. A. K. McIlwraith edited the text for his Oxford thesis (1931).

1 For a full account of the manuscript, see the Introduction to *The Copy of a Letter*, pp. 386–7.

557

A Newyeares Guift presented to my Lady and M:rs the then Lady Katherine Stanhop now Countesse of Chesterfeild.

By Phill: Messinger.

Madame
Before I ow'd to you the name
Of Seruant, to your birth, your worth your fame
I was soe, and t'was fitt since all stand bound
To honour Vertue in meane persons found,
Much more in you, that as borne great, are good
Wch is more then to come of noble blood
Or be A Hastings; it being too well knowne
558 An Empresse cannot challenge as her owne
Her Grandsires glories; And too many staine
Wth their bad Actions the noble straine

From whence they come, But as in you to be
A branch to add fresh honor to the tree
By vertue planted, and adorne it new
Is graunted vnto none or Very few.
To speake you further would appeare in me
Presumption or a seruants flattery
But there may be a tyme when I shall dare
To tell the world and boldly what y^{u} are
Nor sleight it Madame, since what some in me
Esteeme a blemish, is a guift as free
As their best fortunes. this tooke from the graue
Penelopies chastitie, and to it gaue
Still liuing Honors; this made Aiax strong
Vlisses wise: such power lies in a Song
W^{ch} Phæbus smiles on wch can find noe Vrne
While the Sea his course, or starrs obserue their turne.
Yet t'is not in the power of tinckling Rime
That takes rash iudgments and deceiues the tyme
Wth Mountebanke showes: a worke that shold indure
Must haue a Genius in it, strong, as pure.
But you beginne to smile, as wondring why
I should write thus much to y^{u} now since I
Haue heretofore been silent: may y^{u} please
p. 559 To know the cause, it is noe new disease
Growne in my iudgment, nor am I of those
That thinke good wishes cannot thriue in prose
Aswell as Verse: but that this Newyeares day
All in their loues and duties, what they may
Present vnto you; though perhaps some burne
Wth expectation of a glad returne
Of what they Venture for. But such I leaue
To their deceiptfull guiftes giuen to deceiue;
What I giue I am rich in, and can spare,
Nor part for hope wth ought deserues my care.
He that hath little and giues nought att all
To them that haue is truly liberall.

11. come,] *MS*; ~. *Grosart*   14. few.] *McIlwraith*; ~‸ *MS*   28. deceiues] *conj. Grosart*; deceiue *MS*

TO SIR FRANCIS FOLJAMBE

INTRODUCTION

(a) *Date*

This poem was almost certainly written in 1623, soon after the publication of *The Duke of Milan* (in a copy of which the manuscript was found), and before Massinger's next published work, *The Bondman*, became available for presentation, early in 1624.[1]

(b) *Text*

A unique manuscript of the poem, in Massinger's hand and with his signature, is prefixed to a presentation copy of the first edition of *The Duke of Milan*, now in the Victoria and Albert Museum, London (Dyce 6323). This quarto was loaned to Gifford by Octavius Gilchrist while Gifford's second edition of Massinger's plays (1813) was being prepared for the press. Gilchrist himself had been given the copy by Thomas Blore, who had found it while seeking material for a history of Derbyshire among the papers of Philip Gell of Hopton, whose widow Blore had married. The quarto, with its accompanying manuscript poem, subsequently appeared in the sale of Gilchrist's books in 1824, passing in turn to Heber and to Dyce.[2]

The present edition is based on a microfilm of the Dyce manuscript checked against the original, and against a transcript made by A. K. McIlwraith. Another transcript, made by Dawson Turner (British Museum, Add. MS. 28.655, fols. 194^{v}–195^{r}) and referred to as *Turner*, has also been consulted.

The poem was included in the second and third editions of Gifford's Massinger, and in the editions of Coleridge and Cunningham. There are facsimiles in *The Handbook of the Dyce and Forster Collections*, 1880, in R. Garnett and E. Gosse, *English Literature*, ii, 1903, and in W. W. Greg's *English Literary Autographs*,

[1] *The Bondman* was entered in the Stationers' Register on 12 Mar. 1624.

[2] Gifford², i, pp. i–iii; Greg, *Collected Papers*, p. 110.

1925. A. K. McIlwraith prepared a text of the poem for his Oxford thesis (1931), and more recently the poem was included in D. S. Lawless's monograph, *The Poems of Philip Massinger*, Muncie, Indiana, 1968.

To my Honorable ffreinde S^r^ ffrancis ffoliambe knight and Baronet.

S^r^. wth my service I præsent this booke
  a trifle I confesse, but pray yow looke
vpon the sender, not his guift, wth your
  accustomde favor, and then 't will indure
your serch the better. somethinge there may bee
  you'l finde in the pervsall fit for mee
to gieve to one I honor, and may pleade
  in your defence, though yow descende to reade
a Pamplet of this nature. may it prove
  in your free iudgement, though not worth your^r^ love
yet fit to finde a pardon, and I'll say
  vpon your warrant that it is a play.

ever at your comãndment

Philip Massinger

2. confesse] *MS*; confess't *Turner*

LONDON'S LAMENTABLE ESTATE

INTRODUCTION

(a) *Date*

There was a serious outbreak of plague at London in 1603, when Massinger was still in residence at Oxford,[1] but there is little doubt that the occasion of this poem was the more terrible outbreak in 1625. The St. John's manuscript of the poem explicitly mentions 'the visitation 1625' in its title, and the Bodleian manuscript containing the poem carries a dedication dated 23 October 1626, on folio 78^{r} immediately after the text of *London's Lamentable Estate*. The limits for the date of composition are accordingly from about September 1625 (by which time the fury of the plague was spent) to October 1626, with the probability that Massinger wrote the poem in late 1625.

(b) *Text*

Two seventeenth-century texts of *London's Lamentable Estate* are known. The first is in MS. Rawl. poet. 61, now in the Bodleian Library. This is a quarto paper manuscript, in the hand of Ralph Crane, containing a dedication to John Piers dated 23 October 1626. Its provenance has not been established, but it is not surprising that lines by Massinger should appear in the compilation. Crane was scrivener to the King's men, the company with which the dramatist was associated from about 1616, and prepared a theatrical manuscript of Fletcher and Massinger's *Sir John van Olden Barnavelt* (1619). Among the authors represented in the Bodleian manuscript is William Bagnall, who was Massinger's fellow plaintiff in a Chancery suit of 1624, and probably wrote the commendatory verses signed 'W. B.' in *The Duke of Milan* and *The Bondman*.[2]

[1] See F. P. Wilson, *The Plague in Shakespeare's London*, 1927, chapter 3.

[2] Bagnall appears on fol. 6^{r} as the author of an 'Induction' to *Certain Selected Psalms of David*, by Francis Davison and others. See also the note to *The Duke of Milan*, Verse, 3.

Attention was first called to the existence of this text in an article on Crane published in 1926 by F. P. Wilson.[1] *London's Lamentable Estate* is found among a collection of religious poems, hymns, paraphrases and meditations by Francis Davison, William Austin, Crane, and others. It covers eleven unnumbered pages, folios 71^r–76^r.

Crane's work is elaborate in its use of an Italian hand to denote italics, but there is no ground for questioning its substantial accuracy, though the calligraphic embellishments and some of the spellings are probably his rather than the author's.

A second manuscript copy of the poem exists in MS. S.23 at St. John's College, Cambridge. A quarto paper manuscript of the mid seventeenth century, it contains poems by Shakespeare, Jonson, Carew, Herrick, Francis Beaumont, Corbett, King, Randolph, and Townshend. Its provenance has not been established. Massinger's poem occupies folios 26^r–30^r; it is titled 'A trewe discription of the lamentable / estate of the Cittie of London / in the visitation 1625.' and is attributed to 'P Messinger'. The title and signature were first recorded by M. R. James in his catalogue of the manuscripts of the college in 1913,[2] but they escaped the notice of writers on Massinger until B. M. Wagner again directed attention to the manuscript in 1933.[3]

The St. John's scribe wrote in a clear, extremely regular and pleasantly ornamented hand and, unlike Crane, capitalized lines of verse and indented alternate lines. As Wagner noted, this text is substantially less correct than Crane's. There are some twenty-three unimportant differences (for instance, Crane usually elides to preserve the metre, where the St. John's scribe supplies the unelided form of a word), but in ten readings the Bodleian text is the superior one (ll. 6, 23, 30, 32, 59, 119, 162, 178, 179, 190). Both scribes have their individual spelling habits, but of those spellings which can be checked against a known Massinger spelling, in thirty-seven cases Crane's manuscript preserves authorial spellings, where the St. John's manuscript preserves them in twenty-seven cases.

For the present edition, the Bodleian text has been used as a

[1] 'Ralph Crane, Scrivener to the King's Players', *The Library*, 4th Series, vii (1926), 194–215. See also T. H. Hill, *Spelling Analysis and Ralph Crane*, unpublished doctoral thesis, Victoria University, Wellington, 1960.

[2] *A Descriptive Catalogue of the Manuscripts of St. John's College Cambridge*, 1913, p. 352.

[3] *TLS*, 28 Sept. 1933, 651.

copy-text (siglum *B*), collated with photostats of the St. John's College manuscript (siglum *J*), and checked against transcripts of both texts made by A. K. McIlwraith.

The Bodleian text was edited by McIlwraith for his Oxford thesis (1931); it has since been published by H. W. Garrod, *Genius Loci and Other Essays*, 1950, and by D. S. Lawless, *The Poems of Philip Massinger*, Muncie, Indiana, 1968. The St. John's text has not been published.

71r

Londons
Lamentable *Estate*, in any great *Visitation*

O London; Where are now those powerfull Charmes
which weake Men (though oft warned by their Harmes)
could not resist? Inforcing them to fill
thy *Streetes* with *Clients* (Subiects to thy Will)
and lawles *Riots*? Where is now that *Pride*,
Pomp, *Brauerie*, *Circumstance*, that did deride
all *Citties* els, as base? Where that *Command*
that, from each fruitfull Corner of the *Land*,
call'd, (in full *Plentie*) every *Raritie*?
(as the whole *Isle* paid *Tribute* vnto thee.)
The *Isle* (said I?) Alas that was noe Scope
or lymit, to suffice thy narrowest Hope:
From all parts of the *World*, thou hadst Supplie
of what was wanting to thy *Luxurie*:
France, *Spaine*, and her *Canaries* sent thee *Wine*:
slav'd *Cyprus*, *Sucketts*: Stately *Florence*, fine,
71v and well-wrought *Silkes* (ripp'd from the labouring wombe

Title. *Londons . . . Visitation*] *B*; *A trewe discription of the lamentable / estate of the Cittie of London / in the visitation 1625*. *J*

4. Subiects] *B*; subiect *J* 4–5. Will) / . . . *Riots*?] *editor*; Will, / . . . *Riots*?) *B*; will / . . . riots, *J* 6. *Circumstance*, that] *B*; that *J* 17. labouring] *B*; labring *J*

of the poore *Worme*, that should haue byn her *Tombe*):
Barbary, *Sugers*: *Zant*, *Oile*: *Tapistrie*
t'adorne thy prowd *Walls*, *Brabant* made for *Thee*:
Nor were the *Indies* slowe to feed thy *Sence*
with *Cassia*, *Mirrhe* (farr-fetch'd with deere expence):
The *Sea*, her *Pearle*: and many a boystrous knock
compelld the sparckling *Diomond*, from the *Rock*,
to deck thy *Daughters*: In a word th'adst All
that could in compasse of thy wishes fall:
But theis great *Guiftes* (abus'd) first bredd in *Thee*
a stupid *Sloth*, and dull *Securitie*
the *Parent* of *Destruction*. grym *War*
from whose rough hand long since thou hadst no Scar,
The *Kingdomes* walls, the *Nauy* kep'd farr-off,
so what brought *dread* to others, was thy Scoff.
Famine, the second *Scourge* of *God*, by *Thee*
was slighted: as the *Chambers Threasurie*
out of the Surplusage of her cram'd-Store,
could warrant full Supply from any *Shore*.
72r Against the *third*, *Sicknes*, Thou didst provide
Colledges of *Phisitians*: Beside
their Aydes, *Chirurgions*, *Empericques*, *Montebancks*,
some *Ladjes* too, turn'd *Doctors*, cur'de for thancks:
So that no new *Infection* could grow,
but mett a *Remedie* (at least in showe.)
But *He*, before whose Breath, heauens *Fabricqꝫ* flies
(awak'd at length, with thy *Impieties*)
out of the *Store-house* of his *Veng'ance*, tooke
the *Plague*; and charg'd it, with a dreadfull Looke
to make Such know, that serv'd not him, for Love,
with trembling Feare, there was a *Power aboue*.
The great Charge given, like Lightning strayt descends
the Saile-Wing'd-*Monster*. *Agents* to her Ends
were sent before, which might prepare the way
Where She resolu'd to make her fatall Stay;
Vnseasond-*Weather*: *Heate* in *Winter*: *Cold*

22. farr-fetch'd] *B*; far fetched *J* 23. her] *B*; for *J* 25. th'adst] *B*; thow hadst *J* 30. hand] *B*; head *J* 32. brought] *B*; bred *J* 39. their] *J*; the *B* Aydes] *B*; ayders *J* *Empericques*] *B*; Empriqus *J* 44. awak'd] *B*; awaked *J* 47. not him] *B*; him not *J*

in *Iulie*; the rent Clowdes, in Thunder scold,
and yet not purge the *Aire*: Vnhollsom *Showers*
72v drawne-vp in foggy *Mists*: Tempestuous howers:
The *Sun*, with fainting Beames, scarce yeilding Light,
While *Natures-self*, runs back ward at the sight.
The *Plague*, (thus guarded) at the first sitts downe,
strongly intrench'd before the Careles *Towne*:
And, as in *War*, the *Generall* doth not vse
his vtmost *Forces*, till the *Foe* refuse
Sommons of *Mercie*; but, with light *Assaultes*,
Scalados, *Skirmishes*, and deepe-digg'd *Vaultes*
to blowe-vp all *Defences*, gives a touch
how sure his Hopes are, if provoak'd too much:
But theis, scorn'd, and contempn'd *he* mounts on high
the roring *Cannon*, to make *Batterie*,
and force a bloody *Entrance*; Then, too late
all *Composition* comes: Soe, swolne with *hate*,
this *hell-bred-Furie*, of her *Prey* secure,
knowing the *Cittie* was her owne, and sure:
In *Lanes*, and *obscure Alleys* makes Assay,
if yet the *Deathes* of some few *Wretches*, may
draw-on *Repentance*: But when *She* did see
73r the *Liuing*, to disclaime her *Liuorie*,
the dreadfull *Markes*; giving them other names,
(as *Spotts*, and *Purples*) which, to their owne shames,
some *Doctors* did maintaine: *She* then lets flie
her Breath at large; Which, like *Artillerie*
loaden with *Murdring Shott*, peirc'd every *Streete*,
and laid th' *opposers* dead, at her prowd Feete.
Then (all too late) they doe confesse *Shee's* there:
but to avoyd her, none know how, or where:
All *Antidotes* forgot, the generall strife
was to fly first, and save a wretched life.
The *Rich* begin the game: and happy they
esteeme themselues, that can make any way
for *Shelter*, in the *Cuntrie*: The nyce *Dame*
that stop'd her nose, not long since, at the name

58. back ward] *B*; backwards *J* 59. sitts] *B*; settes *J* 61. vse] *B*; lose *J* 66. provoak'd] *B*; prouoked *J* 79. lets flie] *B*; letfly *J* 82. th' *opposers*] *B*; the opposers *J*

of a plaine *Farme-house*, now is glad to be
a *Cottage-Tenant*, and learnes *housewifrie*:
The *Merchants* leave their *Ware-houses*, and range;
their Meetings now forgot, on the *Exchange*.
73v ffatt *Trades-men* too beleeue that it may be
that *Cosonage* is a *Sin*, and *Perjurie*,
in venting their *Commodities*, a *Crime*,
not an authoriz'd *Fashion* of the *Time*:
Some *Aldermen*, 'tis thought too, while they Live
(frighted with others sodaine deathes) will give
to *Charitable-vses*; and not leave
to their vnmindfull *heires*, power to deceaue
the *Poore* of that they did intend should be
full *Satisfaction* for their *Vsurie*.
Your *Lawyers* too, that swore there was no *hell*
but in a long *Vacation*, could well
put off the *Tearme* now, and would gladly pay
treble-*Fees* back, that they at home might stay:
Nor doe (their *haruest* in) Litigious *Clownes*
long to see *Westminster*, to tender Crownes
at every Barr; but quietly desire
to eate their Labours Fruit, by their owne Fire:
Your *Lords* too, that could rellish no delight
74r but *Dice*, and *Drinck*, and loosenes of the Night
(and therefore lou'd the *Cittie*) now begin
to know their *Tenants* faces, and would wyn
their good opinion, if it might be
without the charge of *Hospitalitie*.
Nor *King*, nor *Court* secure; (though now it prove
a running-One, and every day Remove,)
Contagion followes still: There is no *Guard*
of Stall-fedd-*yeomen*; Nor the vigilant *Ward*
of the *great Porters* (though their Courage were
like to their Giant Stature) that can beare
this dreadfull *Shock*: Nor *Pensioners* so stowt
that for one howre, dare say they'll keep it out:
No Place can promise *Safetie*: Not to be

101. *vses*] *B*; vses *altered from* houses *J* 105–8, 109–12 *transposed J* 112. Fruit, by] *B*; fruites at *J* 119. secure] *B*; securd *J* 121. followes still] *B*; still followes *J* 126. howre] *B*; hower *J*

hid in deepe Caves, a certaine Sanctuarie,
the *Earth* being growne Infectious as the *Aire*,
Yet, if to *London*, thou but back repaire,
the Suffrings of the *Cuntrie* are but slight,
74v compard with what *She* groanes for, at the height.
Ô widdowed *Towne*, late Married to *Delight*,
but now left desolate, in the Bed of Night:
No beame of *Comfort* gayning an Accesse
to cheere thy Spirits, or make thy *Sorrowes* lesse:
Solitude dwells about *Thee*: Thy lowd *Bells*
(vsd oft in *Triumphes*) now sound dolefull knells:
Yeilding noe other *Musick*, to the eare
that is inforc'd vnwillingly to heare
greiv'd *Soules* departing hence; and yet to dye
(since to that end we were borne) deserves not why
We should lament, or with continued Teares
strive to deferr, what neither Cares nor Feares
could ere prevent: The Load, to which we bowe
is not to dye, but the strange manner how.
Each Man owes one life, which although he paie
the *Debt's* not fully satisfide: for that daie
he layes it downe, his neere *Frends* over-fond,
in Death, to serve him, seale to the same Bond.
75r To be belou'd is fatall; Let me Haue
the *hate* of dying Men, who'm for the *Graue*
this bloodles *Furie* markes-out; since to be
thought only worthie of a *Legacie*
is a Disease: but he may well dispaire
of long life, that's *Executor*, or *heire*
to the *deceas'd*, since ev'n the *Clothes* they weare,
and hold most pretious, still about them beare
deadly *Contagion*: *Iewels*, *Gold*, and *Plate*
touch'd only, hasten on the *Ownors* Fate:
The dying *Father*, that with his last Breath
would blesse his *Son*, gives (in his *Blessing*) *death*;
Which is the reason, that the *Son* denies
(though present) to cloase vp his *Fathers* Eies.
Nay, such as should give *Phisique* to the *Soule*

131. Suffrings] *B*; sufferings *J* 157. *deceas'd*] *B*; deceased *J* 162. in] *B*; him *J*

departing hence, pale Feare doth so controule,
that those last pious Duties are forborne,
and wretches, groaning for their *Sins*, forlorne.
The Crying Infant, that would fayne take rest,
75v for *Milke*, sucks *Poison*, from his *Mothers* brest:
Nay, often in the *Viands*, that we eate
to nourish life, wee meete with *death*: so greate
and generall is the Danger. But the Feare
that waytes vpon't, workes Wonders every where:
It hath taught some *Religion*, that neu'r knew
what the Word meant: the false way and the trew
duely examin'd, with the Reasons why
wee choose in this Faith, or in that to dye:
Strumpetts feele *Stings* with in 'em: old *Bawdes* scent
hells plagues (this fraile life pa'sd) and would repent:
Nay, there are *Gamsters*, after losse, some say
that (Leaving *Dampne-Mees*) practise how to pray:
Your *Atheist* too, but looking on *heau'ns Rod*
acknowledges (with Horror) ther's a *God*
that populous *Citties* can depopulate
without the *Sword*, or *Famine*. May thy *Fate*
Humble *Thee* (*London*) and but cast an eie
on the small *Remnant* of thy numerous-*Frie*,
76r Whom nor the *Walls*, nor *Suburbs* could containe,
but still incroaching on the Neighbouring-plaine
enlarg'd thy Vastnes, as they strove to drowne
the name of *Midlesex*; making It one *Towne*,
And thou must grant those Multitudes are dead
in this late *Visitation*; or so fledd
that if thou wert devided, there would be
a want, in all thou hast, to people *Thee*.
Make the true *Vse* of this: and not applie
to naturall *Causes*, thy *Calamitie*;
but piously confesse, the *Plague* was sent
from the high *Tribunall*, as a *Punishment*
for thy so many *Sins*: but cheifest, due
to that abhominable *Lust*, which drue

178. in that] *B*; that *J* 179. feele] *B*; fell *J* 182. *Dampne-Mees*] *B*; damemees *J* 183. *heau'ns*] *B*; heauens *J* 189. the] *B*; thy *J* 190. incroaching] *B*; incresing *J* 201. cheifest] *B*; cheefely *J*

Consuming Fire on *Sodom*. May this be
Insculp'd in Brasse, to all *Posteritie*:
and zealously beleeu'd; Not writt in *Sand*;
So may th'Almightie stay his vengefull hand.

Finis *Ph. M*:

204. in] *B*; on *J* 206. *th'Almightie*] *B*; the almightie *J* 207. Finis] *B*; *not in J* Subscription. *Ph. M*:] *B*; *P Messinger. J*

THE VIRGIN'S CHARACTER

INTRODUCTION

(a) *Date*

Massinger's poem is addressed to 'Kneuets first daughter' (l. 36), and McIlwraith has argued convincingly that this is Dorothy Knyvett, later Countess of Buchan, the eldest of three daughters of Sir Philip Knyvett, who is named as one of the dedicatees of the 1629 quarto of *The Roman Actor*.[1] She was born in 1611 at New Buckenham, Norfolk, and married James Erskine, sixth Earl of Buchan, some time after 20 August 1628, the date of his first wife's death. The date of her own death is uncertain; the latest possible date is 1647.

Since this poem speaks of her as a 'virgin' and 'maide', but implies that she is ready for marriage,[2] if not already being courted (ll. 133–8), McIlwraith's view that the poem was written between 1625 and 1630 may be accepted until a more precise dating is possible.

(b) *Text*

Three seventeenth-century copies of *The Virgin's Character* have been found in a group of related manuscripts: British Museum MS. Harleian 6918, Bodleian MS. Eng. Poet. c. 50, and Harvard MS. Eng. 626F (Huntington MS. HM 172—from which a number of leaves have been removed—and British Museum MS. Harleian 6917 belong to the same group).[3]

[1] '*The Virgins Character*: A New Poem by Philip Massinger', *RES*, iv (1928), 64–8. D. S. Lawless has assembled the available biographical information in *The Poems of Philip Massinger*, Muncie, Indiana, 1968, pp. 20–1. For Sir Philip Knyvett, see the commentary on *The Roman Actor*, Dedication, 2–3.

[2] The minimum legal age for marriage for girls was twelve years, but there is some discrepancy between the literary and the sociological evidence as to the normal age for marriage. Peter Laslett, *The World We Have Lost*, 1965, pp. 81–106, suggests that the average age of a bride was 24, but that a gentlewoman tended to marry a little earlier than others, normally between the age of 20 and 22. Cf. the note to *The Renegado*, I. i. 2.

[3] See L. C. Martin, *The Poems of Richard Crashaw*, 1957, pp. lxxvi–lxxviii for an account of the Harleian manuscript; Margaret Crum, 'An Unpublished Fragment of

MS. Harleian 6918 is a quarto paper manuscript commonplace book of 102 leaves, which was purchased from Lord Somers' library. The name of Peter Calfe, the author of several poems at the end of the manuscript, appears on folio 1^r, and McIlwraith, Crum, and the present editor are agreed that with the possible exception of folios 94, 101^v–102^r, the collection is in Calfe's hand. (However, L. C. Martin, *The Poems of Richard Crashaw*, 1957, p. lxxvi, disagrees.) *The Virgin's Character* occupies folios 52^r–54^r. The rhyme scheme implies a stanzaic arrangement, but stanzas are not distinguished, nor are capitals used to commence each line. Punctuation is light and no abbreviations are used. The *Catalogue of the Harleian Manuscripts*, 1808, iii. 448, doubtfully attributed the poem to 'Peter Massinger'; it was A. K. McIlwraith who first drew attention to its significance, in the article cited earlier.

Bodleian MS. Eng. Poet. c. 50 is a folio paper manuscript containing some 250 poems, copied out by five hands of the first half of the seventeenth century. This manuscript first came to light in 1780, when it was anonymously given to Bishop Percy. Massinger's poem is found on folios 106^v–108^v, among a group of nearly 150 poems copied out by the fourth hand, and covering folios 47–125. In this text, as in the Harvard one, the poem is divided into stanzas, though it is possible that the scribe's original was not so divided, since the first line of the second stanza on folio 107^r was first written immediately following on the last line of the preceding stanza, then erased and rewritten as part of a separate stanza. The Bodleian copyist capitalizes initial letters very irregularly; he uses many abbreviations and practically no punctuation. On the second page of his text he adopts the practice of insetting lines 2–4 of each stanza, but occasional lapses to the format of his first page suggest that he was working rather hastily from an original much like the Harleian one.

Harvard MS. Eng. 626F (formerly Phillipps MS. 13, 187) consists of 81 leaves, with a preliminary leaf of thinner paper and a final blank leaf. The fly paper is inscribed 'Anthony St John / Ann: St John / 1640 Bletso'. The manuscript is written throughout in a bold

Verse by Herrick', *RES*, xi (1960), 186–9, for an account of the Bodleian manuscript; and C. L. Day, 'New Poems by Randolph', *RES*, viii (1932), 29–36, for an account of the Harvard manuscript. The Harleian manuscript is also briefly discussed in 'Some Unpublished Poems of James Shirley', R. G. Howarth, *RES*, ix (1933), 24–9; *The Poems of John Cleveland*, ed. B. Morris and E. Withington, 1967, pp. liii–liv; and *The Poems of Henry King*, ed. M. Crum, 1965, p. 57.

Italian hand of the middle of the seventeenth century; probably, as Day suggests, it is Anthony St. John's, who may well have transcribed this collection while at university *c.* 1638.[1] *The Virgin's Character* occupies folios 60^{r}–62^{v}; B. M. Wagner first drew attention to it in 1933.[2] This is the most sophisticated of the three texts: stanzas are separated, with the final couplet uniformly set out to the left, initial letters are capitalized and capitals are freely used in the body of the text, no abbreviations are employed, and there is a consistent spelling '–'d' where the pronunciation requires it, for the '–d' or '–ed' of the Harleian manuscript. It suggests the work of a careful anthologist, anxious to give his manuscript as attractive an appearance as possible.

It is probable that the Harleian, the Bodleian, and the Harvard texts belong to a group of manuscripts which drew material from a common source, an original series of rather more than 100 poems, including one or more poems each by Jonson, Fletcher, and Massinger.[3] At least one characteristic of all three texts, doubled final consonants, especially 't', must derive from the copy-text itself, and this suggests that in the case of the Massinger poem at least the copy-text was a scribal transcript rather than a holograph, since such duplications are not a feature of Massinger's hand.[4]

Of the three texts, the Bodleian is plainly the least reliable. It supplies inferior readings at lines 20, 31, 33, 39, 59, 60, 72, 87, 89, 101, 108, 113, 115, 132 and 133; 'ffrench Ida's greene' for 'fresh Idas greene' (l. 89) is particularly striking. There is less to choose between the Harleian and Harvard texts. Harvard preserves better readings where the Harleian scribe has made a slip of the pen (l. 86, 'maque' for 'masque'), or of the eye (l. 33, 'of whom' for 'on whom', the 'of' being caught up from the beginning of the next line); but it has one substantial error of its own at line 64. The Harleian version is a slightly more primitive text, probably closer to Massinger's manuscript, and it is therefore taken as the copy-text, though corrections are adopted from the Harvard text when Harleian's errors are certain and explicable.

[1] Born in 1618, son of the fourth Baron Bletso and first Earl of Bolingbroke, St. John was admitted to Christ's College, Cambridge on 4 May 1636. After graduation, he married Ann Kensham in 1639, and died at Bletso in 1673; see Day's article cited above.

[2] *TLS*, 28 Sept. 1933, 651.

[3] See Margaret Crum's article cited previously.

[4] Instances from the Bodleian manuscript are 'att, Sunne, Starrs, doubtt, preferre'; from the Harleian, 'sett, Courtshipp, farre, putt'.

The present text is based on the Harleian manuscript (siglum *BM*), collated with the Bodleian manuscript (siglum *B*), and with a microfilm of the Harvard text (siglum *H*) McIlwraith's transcripts of each of these manuscripts have also been consulted. One conjectural reading, communicated by Professor Philip Edwards, is included in the textual apparatus at line 111. In the apparatus only substantive variants and agreements are recorded; no attempt has been made to list the many differences in accidentals between the three texts.

The Harleian text of *The Virgin's Character* was printed by A. K. McIlwraith in '*The Virgins Character*: A New Poem by Philip Massinger', *RES*, iv (1928), 64–8, and edited for his Oxford thesis (1931). In *The Poems of Philip Massinger*, Muncie, Indiana, 1968, D. S. Lawless reprinted the Harleian text; neither the Harvard nor the Bodleian text has been published.

52r

The Virgins Character:

Such as doe Trophies striue to raise
to others worth for after dayes,
should in themselues some touches haue
of what they would keepe from the graue,
Since they can neuer truely Iudge of light
who are depriued the power, and use of sight;
yet tis allowd men may admire
that heigth they neuer can aspire,
and things deformd at distance loue
those rare parts which in faire ones moue;
The Sunne, the Starres, the Temples soe are seene,
and soe A Beggar may affect a Queene:
Let none thinke then I ouerdare
presuming to write what you are,
or what you doe deserue to bee
in my free thought held flattery,
Since Enuy dare not say you can inherite
one blessing that's Superiour to your meritt;

1. doe] *BM*, *B*; due *H* 6. depriued] *BM*; depriu'd *B*, *H* 17. dare] *BM*, *B*; dares *H*

for those perfections good, as great
which make a spotlesse maide compleate
52v As high discent, a heauenly minde
in natures master peece confined,
soe meete in you, that it begets some doubt
which of the three with most grace sett you out;
Yet whilst I write, deare muse, forbeare
all words not suiting a Chast Eare,
it being fitt that I should bee
when shee's the subiect, in thought free;
that shee who but to goodnes hath noe will,
and liues euen ignorance it selfe in ill;
And yet that noe Contention bee
among the virgins which is shee,
on whom with Iudgement, I conferre
of vertues selfe this Character;
I doe professe I offer at thy shrine
Kneuets first daughter what is only thine;
If beauty then soe perfect made
in limbe, and feature, noe dimme shade
darkning the splendour, may call on
mens loue with admiration,
make women Iudges, and they will consent
in all they wish for, thou art Excellent;
And yet to sett thy praises forth
I neede not borrow others worth,
as Thetis foote, or Venus hand,
or that maiesticall command
which graced olimpique Iuno at the feast
when Ioue borne Hercules was first her ghest:
53r But these old flourishes layd by,
a stocke left by Antiquitie
to helpe Invention when tis weake
or teach a muse borne Dumbe to speake;
Ile only fancy what a maide should bee
in all things good, and great and thou art shee:

20. make] *BM*, *H*; makes *B* 30. euen] *BM*, *B*; ev'n *H* 31. noe Contention] *BM*, *H*; contention *B* 33. on] *H*; of *BM*, *B* 36. Kneuets] *BM*; Knivett's *H*; Kinuets *B* 39. darkning] *BM*, *H*; darkinge *B* 54. good, and great] *BM*, *H*; great & good *B*

Ile haue her then of noble bloud,
and faire too must be understood;
And yet that forme which tempts the eye
soe mixt with Saint like modesty,
that she at once might make old nestor younge,
yet from loose accents charme a favourites tongue;
Then to this forme a voice soe cleare
as should enchaunt all such as heare
her well weighed words, which stay too long
by her pronounc'd to grace a song
sett soe exactly, as Art then did trye
to Ioyne with nature to make harmony;
And that her chast thoughts may bee knowne
in forraigne parts as in her owne
they should french dressings sometimes weare
as she were borne, and bredd up there,
not as their Garbe shee lightly did affect
but spake it as the English Dialect;
With her choice language her faire hand
bee euer skillfull to commaund
each string and stopp, that may consent
in her to grace the Instrument;
soe Lesbian Sappho could loues sharpe wounds ease
and not alone her selfe, but others please:
53v In entertainement let her bee
from Courtshipp, and Rusticity
equally distant, not to flye,
nor ouer fond of company,
soe wheresoeuer she shall place her Sceane
her actions still obserue the golden meane:
Or if invited to the court
at some Grand masque, or Royall sport,
there if tooke forth her skill to proue
she should with such proportion moue
as all should sweare, thus on fresh Idas greene
the Graces were ledd by the paphian Queene:

59. at once] *BM*, *H*; once *B* 60. accents] *BM*, *H*; Actions *B* 64. grace] *BM*, *B*; growe *H* 72. spake] *BM*, *H*; speake *B* 78. alone her selfe] *BM*, *H*; her selfe alone *B* 84. still] *H*; shall *BM*; will *B* 87. tooke] *BM*, *H*; too *B* 89. fresh] *BM*, *H*; ffrench *B*

These her exteriour parts thus showne,
what she within is would be knowne,
and there to right her would require
A muse thrice purged with phæbus fire,
and yet with his best aydes twere hard to finde
words worthy to expresse her heauenly minde;
yet as I may, though I shall wrong
such softnesse in my rougher songe,
I will goe on, and yet her store
makes my imagination poore,
all her soules faculties being soe diuine,
and purer farre then I can fancy mine:
That heauenly minde is now my Theame,
which nere thought ill once in a dreame,
nor wak'd ere cherishd one intent
white Innocence could ere repent;
Vertue, and that in action, being still
the ready obiects of her power, and will;
54r And as she nere did Iniury
soe apt to doe a Courtesy
as she esteemes that day quite past
in which none of her bounties taste;
one gracious looke from her, or kinde salute
being a guift that needes noe attribute;
But now admire! these parts that take
most virgins, and selfe louers make
could nere teach her to lay aside
humility to putt on pride;
yet still she so preserues her dignity
that such as serue her thinke themselues most free;
And to crowne all, Religion
the Rocke she strongly builds upon,
against all change a sure defence,
and Rampire to her Innocence
keepes her so firme in her race well begunne
that to the end with glory she must runne:

101. soules] *BM*, *H*; Soule *B* 104. nere thought ill once] *BM*; neuer thought ill *H*, *B* 105. wak'd *H*; nake'd *BM*; nak'd *B* 108. power, and will] *BM*, *H*; will B 111. past] *MSS*; waste *conj. Edwards* 112. bounties] *BM*, *H*; beauties *B* 113. looke from her,] *BM*, *H*; looke, *B* 115. admire!] *BM*, *H*; ~‸ *B*

Duty made up of reuerend feare,
and loue to her that did her beare,
with pious care to be knowne his
whose liuing picture sure shee is
soe winns on both, that as they Ioy in her
their Ioy before her owne shee doth preferre:
Thrice blessed maide, but more blest hee
that is markd out by destinye
T'embrace thee with a lawfull flame,
and soe to Change thy virgin name;
well may Kings enuy him, and hee professe
In her hee's circled with true happinesse.

P: M:

132. before her] *BM*, *H*; her *B* doth] *BM*, *B*; does *H* 133. blest] *BM*, *H*; blest is *B* 135. T'embrace] *BM*, *H*; To embrace *B* lawfull] *BM*, *H*; louinge *B* 136. virgin] *BM*, *H*; virgins *B* 139. P: M:] *BM*; Finis. P: M: *H*; P. M. ffinis *B*

TO JAMES SHIRLEY

INTRODUCTION

(a) *Date and Occasion*

The date of composition of the poem is certainly 1630; it must have been written immediately before the publication early in that year of Shirley's *The Grateful Servant*,[1] which (as one of ten such poems) it commends.

The reason for such a crowd of supporters seems to have been a literary quarrel occasioned by the fact that while Shirley's play had enjoyed considerable success at the Cockpit in late 1629,[2] a rival play at the Blackfriars theatre, Davenant's *The Just Italian*, had failed dismally. Davenant's friend Thomas Carew took advantage of the publication of *The Just Italian* early in 1630 to defend Davenant and slander the work of the dramatists and actors associated with the Cockpit, whereupon Shirley's friends and associates (including Massinger) hastened to reply in the commendations attached to the quarto of *The Grateful Servant*.[3]

Massinger deals obliquely with two of the main issues in the quarrel, the moral character and literary style of the rival writers. With his lines may be compared John Fox's tribute to Shirley:

> . . . thou dost not swell with mighty rimes
> Audacious metaphors, like verse like times
> (*The Grateful Servant*, ²A1ʳ)

[1] The entry in the Stationers' Register is dated 26 Feb. 1630; Arber, iv. 195.

[2] The play was licensed on 3 Nov.; Adams, *Herbert*, p. 33.

[3] *The Just Italian* was entered in the Stationers' Register on 10 Jan. 1630, and almost certainly appeared before Shirley's play was published. Bentley prints Carew's attack (i. 224–5), and relevant portions of the poems by Shirley's champions (v. 1115–18). There are detailed studies of the quarrel by Michel Grivelet, 'Th'Untun'd Kennell: Note sur Thomas Heywood et le Théâtre sous Charles Iᵉʳ', *Études Anglaises*, vii (1954), 101–6, and by Georges Bas, 'James Shirley et "Th' Untun'd Kennell": Une petite guerre des théâtres vers 1630', *Études Anglaises*, xvi (1963), 11–22. See also Paul Delany, 'Attacks on Carew in William Habington's Poems', *Seventeenth Century News*, xxvi (1968), 36, though Delany does not associate Habington's attacks on the poet with this theatrical quarrel.

or William Habington's lines, written for Shirley's *The Wedding* (published in late 1629):

Blemish'd with the staine
Of impure life, some by Atheisticke rimes,
And witty surfeits, force these ruder times
To fond amazement; but thy faire defence
Rests in cleare Arte, and secure Innocence.

(A4^{v})

(b) *Text*

To James Shirley was first printed in the first quarto of *The Grateful Servant* (1630), the second of Shirley's plays to appear in print. Those who seconded the dramatist were so numerous that signature A, left by the printer for preliminaries, had to be duplicated.[1] Massinger's poem appears on ^{2}A4^{r}.

The light pointing and the spelling of the printed text raise no doubts that the compositor worked from anything other than Massinger's autograph, and the reading 'which' for 'with' (l. 2) is a common misreading of Massinger's abbreviation 'wth'.

A second quarto of Shirley's play appeared within Massinger's lifetime, in 1637, with the poem printed on a2^{v}. The first edition had been printed by Bernard Alsop and Thomas Fawcett for John Grove; the second edition was printed by John Okes for William Leake. Heavier but not excessive punctuation is introduced, 'v' replaces medial 'u', and there is a slight increase in capitalization. The new text emends one plain misreading (l. 2) and a turned letter (l. 15), but it introduces two substantive errors (ll. 1 and 6). One further substantive alteration might be authorial (l. 23), but since the balance of the alterations take the text further away from Massinger's known scribal habits, the changes made in the 1637 text are probably the ordinary work of a printing-house corrector.

The commendatory poems were omitted from a third edition of *The Grateful Servant*, published no earlier than 1662.[2]

The present text has been set up from a Bodleian copy of the 1630 quarto (4° S.34. Arts), collated with a British Museum copy and a microcard of the Huntington Library copy, and with three copies of the 1637 quarto. The first and second editions of *The Grateful Servant* will be referred to from now on as *30* and *37*.

The poem was included in each of the standard collected editions

[1] In some copies this second signature A is missing; Greg, *Bibliography*, ii. 579–80.
[2] See Greg, *Bibliography*, ii. 580, and Bentley, v. 1115.

of Massinger, and in *The Dramatic Works and Poems of Shirley*, edited by Dyce and Gifford, 1833. A. K. McIlwraith prepared a text for his Oxford thesis (1931), and more recently the poem was edited by D. S. Lawless, in his monograph *The Poems of Philip Massinger*, Muncie, Indiana, 1968.

To my Iudicious and learned friend the Author upon his ingenious poem the Gratefull seruant.

Though I well know, that my obscurer name
  Listed with theirs, who heere aduance thy fame
Cannot adde to it, giue me leaue to be
  Among the rest a modest votarie
At the altar of thy muse. I dare not raise
  Giant *Hyperboles* vnto thy praise,
Or hope it can find credit in this age
  Though I should sweare in each triumphant page
Of this thy worke, thers no line but of weight
  And poesie it selfe shewne at the height:
Such common places friend will not agree
  With thy owne vote and my integrity.
Ile steere a midde way, haue cleare truth my guide
  And vrge a praise which cannot be denyde.
Here are no forc'd expressions, no rack'd phraze
  No Babell compositions to amaze
The tortur'd reader, no beleeu'd defence
  To strengthen the bold atheists insolence,
No obscene sillable, that may compell
  A blush from a chast maide, but all so well
Exprest and orderd, as wise men must say
  It is a gratefull Poem, a good play:
And such as read ingenuously shall find,
  Few haue out strip'd thee, many halt behind.

Philip Massenger.

1. obscurer] *30*; obscure *37* 2. with] *37*; which *30* 6. *Hyperboles*] *30*; *Hyperbolize 37* 15. expressions] *37*; expressious *30* 23. read] *Gifford*; ~, *30* ingenuously] *30*; ingniously *37*[1]; ingeniously *37*[2]

SERO, SED SERIO

INTRODUCTION

(a) *Date*

The date of composition is established by the occasion of the elegy. Charles, Lord Herbert, the fifteen-year-old son of the fourth Earl of Pembroke and Montgomery, married Mary, daughter of the Duke of Buckingham, in January 1634. The following year, while travelling in France and Italy with his brother Philip, he paid a visit to Sir Robert Dudley, a boyhood friend of his father, now living in exile in Florence. After a short stay with Dudley's second daughter Maddalena and her husband, Don Spinetta Malaspina, Marchese d'Olivola, at the castle of Olivola on the slopes of the Carrara mountains, Charles returned to Florence, where he contracted smallpox and died in January 1636,[1] to which year the poem must belong.

(b) *Text*

Only one seventeenth-century copy of this poem is known, found in MS. Royal 18A. xx, in the British Museum. This is an octavo paper manuscript, consisting of eight leaves, bound up with three other manuscripts. Folios 2–5 are numbered 1–4 in modern pencil; the remainder is left blank. The text is written by an unknown scribe in a mid seventeenth-century secretary hand, with a careful use of italic forms to distinguish certain words. However, the signature is in Massinger's own hand.

Although the provenance of the manuscript is uncertain, the poem has long been known, and was included in all the collected editions of Massinger's works.

There are many Massinger spellings in the text, but the scribe has imposed his own spelling on such words as 'so, credit, greefe,

[1] *The Poems of Philip Massinger*, D. S. Lawless, Muncie, Indiana, 1968, p. 26; *The Son of Leicester. The Story of Sir Robert Dudley*, A. G. Lee, 1964, pp. 208–9. News of the death reached London by 5 Mar. 1636.

Stoicke'. This, together with the light punctuation of the lines and the presence of several Massinger abbreviations, suggests that this is a careful fair copy, made from the author's original. The anticipation error at line 14 supports such a view; the alteration at line 38 may be due to a correction in the original or to the author himself. That the text is authoritative may be assumed from the presence of the poet's signature (though the error at line 41 was left standing).

The present text is set up from the British Museum manuscript (siglum *MS*); a transcript of the original made by A. K. McIlwraith has also been consulted. Marginal references are to the modern pencil foliation.

Serio, sed Serio was included in the standard collected editions of Massinger. It was edited by A. K. McIlwraith for his Oxford thesis (1931), and more recently by D. S. Lawless, in *The Poems of Philip Massinger*, Muncie, Indiana, 1968.

1^{v}

Sero, sed Serio.

To the right ho:^{ble} my most singular good
Lord and Patron
Philip
Earle of Pembrooke and
Montgomerye, Lord Chamberlaine
of his Ma:^{ties} Houshould &c.

Vppon
The deplorable and vntimely death
of his late truely noble Sonne
Charles
Lord Herbert &c.

T'was ffate, nott want of dutie did mee wronge,
  Or w:th the rest my *Hymeneall songe*
Had beene presented, when the knott was ti'de
  That made the *Bridegroome* and ye virgin *Bride*

A happie paire. I cursd my absence then
That hindred itt, and bitt my Star-crost pen
Too busie in Stage-blanks, and trifeling Rime
When such a Cause calld, and soe apt a time
To pay a generall debt, mine being more
Then they could owe, who since or heretofore
Haue labourd w:th exalted Lines to raise
Brave *Piles*, or rather *Pyramids* of praise
To *Pembroake*, and his ffamilie, and dare I
Being silent then, aime att an *Elegie*
Or hope my weake *Muse* can bring forth one *Verse*
Deserveing to waite on the *Sable Herse*
Of yo:^{r} late hopefull *Charles*? his obsequies
Exact the mourning of all *Hearts* and *Eyes*
2^{r} That knew him; Or lov'd vertue: hee that would
Write what hee was to all posteritie, should
Haue ample Creditt in himselfe to borrowe
(Nay make his owne) the saddest accents *Sorrowe*
Ever exprest, and a more movinge *Quill*
Then *Spencer* vs'd, when hee gave *Astrophill*
A liveing Epicedium. For poore *Mee*
By Truthe I vowe, itt is no fflatterie
I from my Soule wishe (if itt might remove
Greefes Burthen, w:^{ch} too feelinglie you proove)
Though I have beene ambitious of *ffame*
As *Poets* are, and would preserve a *Name*,
That my Toyes burnt, I had liu'd vnknowne to men
And ne're had writt, nor ne're to write againe.
2^{v} *Vaine wishe*, and to bee scorn'd! can my foule drosse
With such pure Gold bee valu'd? or the Losse
Of Thousand Lives like mine meritt to bee
The same age thought on, when his *Destinye*
Is only mention'd? No, *My Lord*, his ffate
Is to bee prised att a higher rate;
Nor are the groanes of common men to bee
Blended w:th those, w:^{ch} the Nobilitie
Vent howerly for him. That great *Ladyes* mourne
His suddaine death, and Lords *vie* att his *vrne*

14. silent] *in MS* then *is deleted before* silent 36. *Destinye*] *altered in MS from* Destine 38. prised] *written over* val . . d [valu'd]

Dropps of Compassion; that true Sorrowe fed
W:th showers of Teares still bathe ye widdowed Bed
Of his deare *Spouse*; That our great *King* & *Queene*
(To grace yo:^{r} *Greefe*) disdaind not to be seene
3^{r} Yo:^{r} Royall Comforters: These well become
The losse of such a *Hope*, and on his *Tombe*
Deserve to liue; But since no more could bee
Presented to sett of his *Tragedie*,
And w:th a generall sadnes, why should you
(Pardon my boldnes) pay more then is due,
Bee the debt ne're soe great? No Stoicke can
As you were a loveing Father, and a Man
Forbid a moderate sorrowe, but to take
Too much of it, for *His* or yo:^{r} owne sake
If wee may trust Divines, will rather bee
Censur'd repineing then true *Pietie*.
3^{v} I still presume too farre, and more then feare
My dutie may offend, pressing too neere
Yo:^{r} private passions. I thus Conclude
If now you shewe yo:^{r} passive *ffortitude*
In bearing this affliction, and prove,
You take itt as a Triall of *Heaven's* love,
And ffavo:^{r} to you, you ere longe shall see
Yo:^{r} second *Care* retorn'd from Italie
To blesse his native England, each rare part
That in his *Brother* liv'd and ioy'd yo:^{r} heart
4^{r} Transferd to him, and to the world make knowne
Hee takes possession of what's now his owne.

Yo:^{r} Hono:^{rs}
most humble
and faithfull Servant
Philip Massinger.

43. Compassion;] *Coxeter*; ~, *MS* 44. bathe] *MS*; bathes *Gifford*^{2} 52. is] *MS*; his *Coxeter*

TO HIS SON, UPON HIS MINERVA

INTRODUCTION

(a) *Date*

It is difficult to determine the date of composition of Massinger's poem or of the poem which it commends, *The Innovation of Penelope and Ulysses, A Mock-Poem*, by James Smith.[1] The downward limit is set by Massinger's death in 1640, and a late date is suggested by the fact that here he writes as an older man of established reputation—though lines 1–2 need not be taken too seriously, since the poems prefixed to Smith's work are all part of an elaborate literary joke (Smith includes two of his own poems written in praise of himself). If the James Atkins who signed one of the commendatory poems was the Scottish divine who studied at Oxford from 1637 to 1638 and later became Bishop of Moray and Galloway, Massinger's poem may have been written in the late 1630s.

It is unlikely that Smith wrote his mock poem before he was twenty or so (in 1625), and among other contemporary allusions of indeterminate date there is one passage in the poem which indicates a date in the 1630s. This is a reference to contemporary fashion:

> She don'd new cloaths, and sent the old ones packing,
> And had her shoes rub'd over with Lamp blacking,
> Her new rebato, and a falling band,
> And Rings with severall poesies on her hand.
> A stomacher upon her breast so bare,
> For Strips and Gorgets was not then the weare.
>
> (L7^{v}–8^{r})

The fashion which Smith mentions[2] is also mocked by Richard

[1] Smith was born in 1605, and after matriculating from Christ Church, Oxford in 1623, went to Lincoln College. On graduating from the University he took holy orders, proceeding B.D. in 1633 and holding benefices in Lincolnshire (1634) and Devonshire (1639). He died in 1667. Some of his verses appeared in print at least as early as 1640, in the miscellany *Wit's Recreations. Selected from the finest Fancies of Modern Muses*; see D. S. Lawless, *The Poems of Philip Massinger*, Muncie, Indiana, 1968, pp. 28–30.

[2] On the dating of this fashion see C. W. and P. Cunnington, *Handbook of English Costume in the Seventeenth Century*, 1955, p. 101.

Corbett in a poem called 'To the Ladies of the New Dress that wear their Gorgets and Rails down to their Waists'. In *The Poems of Richard Corbett*, ed. J. A. W. Bennett and H. R. Trevor-Roper, 1955, pp. 159–60, evidence is given that this poem was in circulation by 1633 and was probably written in 1632.

In the absence of other strong evidence, then, the probability is that Massinger wrote his commendation of Smith's poem in the mid 1630s.

(b) *Text*

The earliest known text of this poem appeared in a poetic miscellany, *Wit Restored in several select Poems not formerly published*, printed in 1658 for R. Pollard, N. Brooks, and T. Dring.[1] Massinger's lines appear among other commendatory poems on signature L1 v (page 142) of the octavo volume.

The slender evidence of the text and of its subscription is sufficient to show that the compositor has imposed his own spelling habits (for instance, 'choyse, do, merit, heareing'); on the other hand, there is no reason to doubt that he worked from Massinger's autograph, or that the text is a reliable one. No press corrections have been found among copies of the original edition.

The present text is based on a British Museum copy of *Wit Restored* (C.40.a.1), collated with a Bodleian copy of the miscellany and checked against a transcript made by A. K. McIlwraith. Italic type in the original is replaced by roman in this edition, and roman by italic.

To his Son, upon his Minerva was included in the standard collected editions of Massinger, and as part of the original poetic miscellany the poem was reprinted by T. Park and E. Dubois in *Facetiae. Musarum Deliciae: or, The Muses' Recreation . . . Wit Restored . . . Wit's Recreations . . . with a thousand outlandish proverbs*, 1817.[2] J. C. Hotten reprinted this collection in 1874. The poem was published separately by A. B. Grosart, 'Literary-Finds in Trinity College, Dublin, and Elsewhere', *Englische Studien*, xxvi (1899), 7, and by D. S. Lawless, *The Poems of Philip Massinger*, Muncie, Indiana, 1968. A. K. McIlwraith prepared a text of the poem for his Oxford thesis (1931).

[1] Wing 1719; a full bibliographical description is given in *A Bibliography of English Poetical Miscellanies, 1521–1750*, A. E. Case, 1935, number 120.

[2] Issued as two separate limited editions, one edited by Park, the other by Park and Dubois, both dated 1817.

To his Sonne, upon his Minerva.

Thou art my son, in that my choyse is spoke;
Thine with thy fathers muse strikes equall stroke.
It shewd more art in *Virgil* to relate,
And make it worth th'heareing, his Gnats fate;
Then to conceive what those great mindes must be
That sought and found out fruitfull Italie.
And such as read and do not apprehend
And with applause the purpose and the end
Of this neat Poem, in themselves confesse
A dull stupiditie and barrennesse.
Methinks I do behold in this rare birth
A temple built up to facetious mirth,
Pleasd *Phœbus* smiling on it; doubt not then,
But that the suffrage of juditious men
Will honour this Thalia; and for those
That praise Sir Bevis, or whats worse in prose,
Let them dwell still in ignorance. To write
In a new strain, and from it raise delight
As thou in this hast done, doth not by chance
But merit, crowne thee with the laurell branch.

Phillip Massenger.